MARINER'S
WEATHER
HANDBOOK

First Edition

*A Guide To
Forecasting & Tactics*

Steve **&** Linda
DASHEW

B E O W U L F

Also by Steve and Linda Dashew:

Circumnavigator's Handbook
Bluewater Handbook
Offshore Cruising Encyclopedia–First Edition
Offshore Cruising Encyclopedia–Second Edition
In Search of the Perfect Yacht
Dashew Offshore Video
Defensive Seamanship (available spring 1999)

Library of Congress Catalog Card Number 98-093808
Dashew, Steve and Linda, 1941-
    Mariner's Weather Handbook

First Printing, December 1998

Beowulf, Inc.
6140 East Finisterra Drive
Tucson, Arizona 85750 USA
www.SetSail.com

ISBN 09658028-2-5

DEDICATION

Voyaging around the world, it soon becomes evident one can call upon a number of unofficial sources of weather data.

These are retired or amateur land-based forecasters, with access to the Internet, facsimile charts from governments, and sometimes various computer models.

They broadcast weather data to sailors within their radio range on both SSB and Ham frequencies, answer questions, and try to keep us all in fair winds and smooth seas.

Forecasters like Arnold Gibbons in the South Pacific and Herb Hilgenberg in the Atlantic (along with many others) work long hours without pay and often without thanks from those they serve so selflessly.

We, along with thousands of other sailors, have benefited from their services at various times all over the world. It is to these selfless men and women that we dedicate *Mariner's Weather Handbook*.

TABLE OF CONTENTS

TABLE OF CONTENTS

INTRODUCTION

Nearly everyone who sails much has a clear image in mind of such weather phenomena as warm and cold fronts and highs and lows and roughly what to expect as they arch majestically across the daily weather maps in newspapers and the TV screen. It all seems easy to understand and forecasts are, at least somewhat more often than not, correct. But it's the times that forecasts are not correct which most concern us when we're at sea.

There are so many variables which all together must be accounted for in order to arrive at an accurate weather forecast that we may as well forget about reaching that ideal in our lifetimes. One scientist pointed out years ago that a butterfly flapping its wings over a parking lot on a hot day in Dallas may be the cause of a thunderstorm in Boston three days later. It was meteorologists who led the way to the new science named, appropriately, CHAOS.

But take heart!

In Steve and Linda Dashew's *Mariner's Weather Handbook*, we are given an expanded, three-dimensional view of the atmosphere in which we live. They describe a swirling, boiling cauldron of rising, deciding, veering, backing, colliding and diverging air currents of uneven temperatures and moisture contents. With this expanded vision and with some of the more recently available tools—such as the Internet, high seas radio, weather fax, satellite photos, and others—the voyager can come closer than ever before in relating macro scale forecasts to his/her own particular patch of ocean, and making decisions on whether to begin evasive actions, and which ones.

Their book is well-named a handbook. Just once through will suggest a new way of looking at weather. Repeated return visits as puzzling or threatening weather is observed will confirm and amplify its value.

Knowles L. Pittman, Circumnavigator and Publisher of *One Design Yachtsman*

PREFACE

Weather effects everything we do—especially when it comes to boats. It has an impact on the speed, comfort and safety of our passages, and on the security of our anchorages.

It is the final consideration of how a varnish job will turn out, and if our vessel will be protected in her slip or mooring when we're away.

In the context of preparing oneself to voyage—regardless of whether it's for a weekend or a circumnavigation—there's nothing more important to the enjoyment and success of your time on the sea than a *thorough* understanding of weather forecasting and tactics.

In many respects, the basics of weather forecasting have been understood for several centuries. Certainly the professional seamen of the eighteenth century knew when a blow was coming, and for the most part, how to find the center of a low pressure system.They also knew how to use high pressure systems to keep the breeze aft of the beam for their trading voyages.

We are happy to report to you that for most of the cruising your authors have done, these time-proven methods have kept us out of harm's way.

Fast forward to the latter part of the twentieth century. We have supercomputers, satellites, remote sensing buoys in mid-ocean, and a huge infrastructure of professional forecasters and scientists studying weather. And we have high seas radios, satellite receivers and weather faxes with which to reliably garner this data.

In many situations the weather infrastructure does a marvelous job of predicting and forecasting what is going to happen. However, there are so many variables in the entire weather-making process that the professionals are not always on target—and this is where the traditional, onboard methods of weather forecasting come into play.

Which brings us to the reason for this book.

HAVING A FEEL FOR THE WEATHER

Having a feel for what the weather may do a few days hence, a day from now, or a few hours from now can mean the difference between a comfortable passage or night at anchor, and a flat-out battle with the forces of nature.

The matter of half a day's time—departing a little sooner or later—can be the difference between life or death.

As little as fifty miles of difference in position can mean a modest gale to be dealt with, or hurricane-force winds.

Unfortunately, we can't totally rely on the forecasters to tell us when to leave on a passage, or whether to stay at anchor. We cannot expect them to advise us to move 50 or 75 miles to the west to avoid the worst of a storm when they may not be sure of a storm track.

UNDERSTANDING THE BASICS

Happily, there's an answer for much of this—understanding the basics of what makes weather do what it does, and then having a feel for a set of simple forecasting tools.

Because you are on the spot, the data available to you by looking outside and checking the barometer can be used to make a reasonably accurate forecast most of the time.

With this knowledge in hand, along with a well-found vessel and crew, you are going to have faster, safer, and more comfortable passages.

You will do a better job of avoiding bad weather, and when it cannot be avoided, of mitigating the range of difficulties coming your way.

Towards this goal our *Mariner's Weather Handbook* takes two tracks. The first is to recite the basics of what makes weather work the way it does.

Then after discussing these basic topics, we will spend quite a lot of time on tactics. You'll learn how to use the passage of fronts and their associated lows

There are two levels of interest which we have in the weather. One is the forecast of the most likely weather scenario— perhaps the right place to position yourself for an approaching low or the correct distance from the center of a high to have the best winds and shortest course.

The other area has to do with assessing risk factors. We want to know what the possibilities are for a major weather event to arise, so that we can take evasive action early.

to your advantage—whether you're headed up or downwind.

We spend a considerable amount of time on tropical cyclones—the most devastating of all storms. Hopefully, much of the discussion on this topic will remain academic.

PROXIMITY—A KEY INGREDIENT

You may be thinking, "If the professionals have such a hard time, how are we ever going to get it right?".

The answer lies in your proximity to the events as they are unfolding. The professionals are sitting in offices thousands of miles away. They work with images from space, sophisticated computer models, and sometimes real-time data from ships or reporting buoys in your area.

When they have real-time data, if their forecast is broadcast in a timely manner, and if you can receive it clearly, you have all you need.

But often the professionals lack the information you have at your fingertips—wind speed, wind direction, cloud type, barometric pressure, and the *trends* in all of this data.

With just this locally available information you will be pleasantly surprised at what a good job you can do in foretelling the weather.

Our endeavor in this book is to make you as self-sufficient in weather analysis and tactical decision-making as possible.

You may be interested in knowing that in the last 200,000 miles (plus) of cruising, we have seen less than 48 hours of weather—two blows—that might be considered dangerous. Since most of this sailing was done without benefit of a weather fax or even SSB receiver you can see the odds are very much in your favor.

Today, with a weather fax and the techniques in this book, we would probably have avoided both of those blows.

So, while we dwell throughout the book on the riskier outcomes of various scenarios, we do this to teach evasive action so that you are not caught out.

In this regard there are two areas of the book to which we'd like you to pay particular attention. The first is the use of the 500mb (upper level) fax charts. These are by far the most valuable forecasting tool at our disposal. We cannot emphasize too strongly the importance of understanding these charts, and having a reliable means to receive them.

If you get a handle on the use of 500mb data this will do more to promote your safety, comfort, and mental well-being than anything else you can possibly do in the way of preparation.

The second area of which we'd like you to be mindful deals with tropical storms. There are always warning signals well in advance of these blows, so there is no reason to be caught unawares. We recommend that you study this area carefully even if you are sailing in the tropics in what is normally out of the hurricane season—these storms can occur at almost any time of the year. While out-of-season storms are rare in most parts of the world, it is still worth keeping a weather eye peeled.

USING THIS BOOK

Mariner's Weather Handbook is loosely organized into four sections. Initially you will find the basics of what creates the weather, and how low pressure systems and their fronts interact. You will find an emphasis towards onboard forecasting first, based on your current conditions. We then cover what is available in outside weather data, starting with an overview of the forecasting process, as well as a discussion of the various ways of acquiring this data. A major part of this discussion centers around the use of 500mb charts—long the secret weapon of government forecasters and race-winning weather routers.

From here we travel to warmer climates with a discussion of tropical meteorology. The focus is on tropical storms, their forecast, and avoidance.

We then return to discuss tropical storms transitioning to the higher latitudes, and compare extratropical and tropical storm structure.

The last section of the book covers a series of topics ranging from land breezes, to fog, to using the Internet for practice and real-world analysis.

You will find extensive discussions of the tactics to be used in both fair and foul weather. And, while heavy weather avoidance is certainly a major part of this book, we hope you will find that by getting up to speed on forecasting, your fair weather passages will be faster and more comfortable than before.

You may want to read some of the sections more than once, as the need arises.

We also suggest you avail yourself of other books (there's a bibliography at the back) and strongly urge you to find a course in weather forecasting. These exist in many junior colleges and universities as well as within the sailing and commercial shipping industry — no book is a substitute for the formal training you can get in the academic environment.

And then practice. Look at the sky, check the barometric pressure, pick up fax charts from the Internet when you're land-bound, and practice making forecasts. Pit your skill against the professionals. You will be pleasantly surprised at how easily you become proficient.

While weather can be serious business, the vast majority of the time conditions will be benign — but forecasting and tactics are still important. Once you get a feel for the weather patterns, and understand *tactically* how to use these varying patterns, your passages are going to be faster, more comfortable, and a lot more fun.

BACKGROUND DATA

Linda and I have been sailing together a long time now, and throughout, weather has played a big part in our enjoyment (or occasional lack thereof).

When we first dated it was aboard small racing catamarans. While boat speed and handling was always important, the key ingredient to winning or losing was short-term weather trends—the deciding factor at the trophy presentations on Sunday evening was if we were in or out of phase with the wind shift running and going to weather.

We decided to go cruising in 1975, and by 1976 had acquired a lovely 50-foot (15.3m) ketch. *Intermezzo* took us most of the way around the world, and in spite of sailing without benefit of high seas

Intermezzo, our first keel boat after years of racing dinghies and catamarans.

This photo was taken in Cocos Keeling atoll, during our circumnavigation, after a very windy passage across the Indian Ocean.

radio (we did have ham) or weather fax, we were able to avoid most bad weather. Occasionally we made a tactical error, but these typically resulted in discomfort and added days to a passage.

By the early 1980s we were involved in the yacht design and construction business, and continued to make many passages.

Intermezzo ll was a new design concept, a 62-foot (19-meter) yacht with a long waterline and modest beam. We quickly put 20,000 miles under her keel, still without benefit of weather fax. The extra boat speed made weather tactics a lot easier as we had more options on where to position ourselves.

By the latter part of the 1980s we had launched our next generation cruiser, *Sundeer*. This 67-foot (20.5-meter) yacht was not only very quick, but she was equipped with a weather fax and a recording

Intermezzo II, *one of our early Deerfoot Series designs, shown here power-reaching in the Gulf Stream of Fort Lauderdale. She took us over 20,000 miles in just a couple of years.*

barometer. This was a huge step up in our tactical arsenal, and while the forecasts were sometimes less than satisfactory in terms of their relevance to the real world, there was enough data scattered amongst the faxes to make weather routing easier by an order of magnitude.

Not only were our passages much faster, but a lot more comfortable too.

Our latest creation is *Beowulf*, a 78-foot (24-meter) high-performance cruising ketch. *Beowulf* is capable of moving at an easy 280 to 300 miles a day, and this brings with it the ability to pick and choose

Sundeer was the first vessel aboard which we voyaged with the aid of a weather fax and recording barometer. What a difference this small investment made in passage times and wear and tear on the boat and her crew!

amongst different optimal positions relative to the weather systems.

The speed, however, also puts more of a premium on our ability to forecast what is going to happen with the wind. Being right can mean a 20 to 30 percent or more reduction in passage time.

Fortunately the professional forecasters and their computer models have gotten a lot better in the last decade, so it is actually getting a bit easier to know

Beowulf is our latest design and the subject of several of the weather stories in this text.

This photo was taken during sea trials in New Zealand, shortly before departing for Raivavai in the Austral Islands of French Polynesia.

Linda Dashew at the helm.

where to go. We still find ourselves, however, frequently using the barometer, sky, wind and sea state to confirm the professional forecasters.

OUR APPROACH AT SEA

A word is probably in order on our own approach to this subject when we are at sea.

First, we make every effort to get as much outside data as possible. We treat this information as suspect until confirmed by firsthand observations. At the same time, we are updating our own analysis of what we think is about to happen, and what's the best way to deal with the unfolding scenario.

There are usually several tactical approaches to every situation. We like to have more than one option, so that if the weather does not go as we or the outside experts project, we have a fallback position.

With weather, as with everything else to do with the sea, there are conservative and there are risky courses of action you can take when dealing with the elements.

We feel it is always better to take the most conservative approach. This may result in a few extra miles sailed, or a delayed departure, but in the end the passages are usually over more quickly and we are a lot more comfortable while we're at sea.

Steve Dashew at the controls of his unlimited aerobatic glider. Ocean weather mechanics and soaring weather have much in common.

Before you get on with the text, a final word about the risks inherent in weather forecasting is in order.

Weather is the ultimate variable. There are an almost infinite number of possibilities that can happen at any given time. As such, no book can possibly have all the answers within it—not even the most sophisticated computer models can do that.

You always need to be alert to special situations which do not fit the normal rules—or what we say in this text. You may find situations where the weather is unfolding in an entirely unusual manner—or in a way which is totally different from what we've covered herein. When that happens, you need to re-adjust your thinking and look for different possibilities.

We wish you fair winds and smooth seas.

Steve & Linda

Steve and Linda Dashew

ACKNOWLEDGMENTS

In the process of putting this book together a large number of people have been extremely helpful.

We wish to acknowledge the invaluable assistance of Dave Feit, Chief of Operations at the National Weather Service's Marine Prediction Center, along with Senior Marine Forecasters Joe Sienkiewicz and Lee Chesneau. These busy gentlemen answered innumerable questions, dug through their archives for many weather fax charts, and had numerous excellent suggestions for improving this book. Joe and Lee were particularly helpful in assisting us with the explanation of 500mb weather data, and in allowing us to excerpt from a technical article they had written. James Partain, Chief Scientist at the MPC brought us up to speed in a number of areas and helped to clarify numerous points.

At the NOAA Environmental Modeling Center Dr. Jordan Alpert assisted us with Vis 5D modeling and Hank Tolman brought us up to date on the latest thinking on the ocean current/wave interaction process.

Nancy Iverson at NOAA/NESDIS helped us find various satellite images and in the use of the Dvorak technique materials.

Carla Wallace at the NOAA Center in Asheville, North Carolina dug through her archives for various slides.

At the National Hurricane Tropical Prediction Center, Christopher Burr, Chief of Operations, was kind enough to answer numerous questions during a very busy summer hurricane season as well as digging out visual materials to illustrate certain points and taking time to review the manuscript. Likewise, Hurricane Forecaster Miles Lawrence answered many of our questions.

On the other side of the globe, Bob MacDavitt of the New Zealand Met Service helped ferret out information on the infamous Queen's Birthday Storm and was kind enough to review that portion of the manuscript as well as the section on our passage from Auckland to Raivavai. In both instances he had valuable comments to make.

Ian Hunter of the South African Weather Bureau, David Turner and Peter Boemo at the Australian National Meteorological Operations Centre, and Ian MacGregor in the U.K. Met. Office all were kind enough to dig up materials for us and/or answer questions.

Steve Davis did his usual first-class job in turning our hard to interpret sketches into the finished art you see in this book—and sometimes re-doing those drawings a time or two until everyone was satisfied.

This project would not have been possible without the technical assistance of Doug Lochner at HLI Systems in Ojai, California. Doug not only supplies us with all of our computer systems and helps us to sort out any problems which arise, but he is also responsible for the overall page design as well as our website design.

Mike Hammond at Kinkos went beyond the call of duty in helping us print out drafts for edit on his Docutech printer.

Dr. Nilton Renno at the University of Arizona was kind enough to comment on our section dealing with thunderstorm activity. Also at the U. of A., Dr. Louis Faran helped us with Vis5D and with digging up data on various hurricanes.

Jim Corenman provided us valuable insights into the Queen's Birthday Storm. Ralph Naranjo, Technical Editor of *Cruising World Magazine*, Professor at the United States Naval Academy, circumnavigator and good friend going back many years had his usual thoughtful comments and suggestions to make.

We also wish to thank race winning navigator Stan Honey for reviewing the manuscript and making suggestions in many areas.

In doing a book like this it is easy to lose sight of the objective—clear, simple transmission of information. We get so close to what we are writing that we sometimes miss the target. To keep us headed in the right direction a number of sailors have reviewed the manuscript, and offered numerous valuable suggestions for improving the end product. Amongst these are Skip Schroeder and Melinda Bessko, Knowles Pittman, Dave Wyman, Oscar Linde, Chuck Hawley, Kent Williams, Keith Lamarr, Rudi Wiedeman, Martin Alkin, Richard Findlay, and Warwick Tompkins.

Judge Anthony Mohr gave us his usual sage advice.

On the production end we would like to thank Sarah Dashew for taking time out from her music career to help with proofreading and editorial comment. Elyse Dashew worked her usual magic with editing, layout, scanning, and the host of other chores necessary to get a book like this into print. Thanks to Nim Marsh for doing the copy edit.

Finally, we want to thank Emma Beveridge and her dad Todd for their patience while Mom was hard at work.

WEATHER REPORTS

One of the most valuable ways we can increase our knowledge of weather is by sharing examples from the real world offshore.

If you experience a weather scenario you feel would be of interest drop us a line, or better yet, e-mail us the data (you can send your e-mail to us at weather@SetSail.com). This applies to storms as well as nicer weather patterns.

We'd like to know how the barometer behaved, wind conditions (direction, speed, and gustiness), cloud cover, sea state, and how the current analyses and forecasts from the weather bureau in question turned out.

Photos of yourself, vessel, clouds and seas, and copies of fax charts always help flesh out the story.

We'll be posting these on our website (set-sail.com) and using some of them in a series of workbooks which are to follow.

STAY IN TOUCH

We love to hear from our readers. If you find something you don't understand or want to see more of, let us know. We'll try to attend to your desires in future editions. Again, the best way to do this is by e-mail, or by writing us (Dashew, 6140 E. Finisterra Drive, Tucson, Arizona, 85750 USA).

REGISTER YOUR BOOK

If you purchased your book directly from Beowulf we'll have your name and address in our computer. If the book was a gift, or purchased from a book or marine store, send us an e-mail at register@Set-Sail.com or write us at the address above with your name, regular mail and e-mail address. This way we'll be able to notify you when the new workbooks come out.

VISIT US ON THE INTERNET

Stay up to date on your weather by visiting us at http://www.SetSail.com. You'll find weather updates, interesting storm scenarios, and excellent links to weather sites around the world.

Weather is such a diverse and complex phenomenon that it is impossible to cover it in one book—even a fat one like this.

So, we will be issuing a series of work-books on offshore weather over the next few years. These will include lots of surface and upper-level synoptic charts along with satellite images of cloud formations. Our intent is to lay before you typical and atypical weather scenarios from around the world.

You will have a chance to review these and make your own forecasts—then compare your results to what really happened.

WHAT CREATES THE WEATHER?

Some very simple principles are behind what creates our weather. The first is heat from the sun. As the sun strikes the earth, energy is absorbed by the atmosphere, land, and the oceans.

INSOLATION

The part of the earth that is directly aligned with the sun, the equator on June 21 and September 21, for example, receives the most heat. The poles, being at a very flat angle, receive the least heat. As the year progresses and the earth rotates around the sun, it tilts on its axis. This tilt changes the area of maximum heat absorbtion from the Northern Hemisphere to the Southern and back again—hence our seasons.

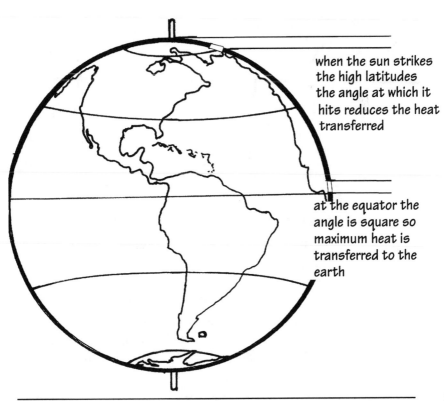

when the sun strikes the high latitudes the angle at which it hits reduces the heat transferred

at the equator the angle is square so maximum heat is transferred to the earth

As the earth travels around the sun it maintains a fixed tilt on its axis. As the earth circles the sun, during one part of the year the Northern half of the globe is angled towards the sun and during another part of the year the Southern half is tilted towards the sun. These are the summer seasons (and winter is when the earth is tilted away from the sun).

In this drawing, the Northern Hemisphere is in summer, and the Southern, which is tilted away from the sun, is in winter.

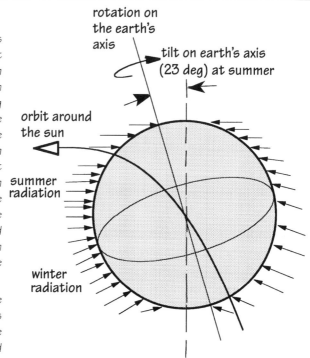

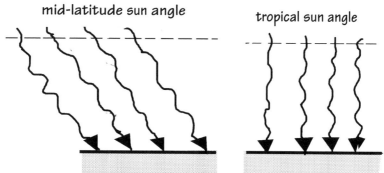

EFFECT ON THE ATMOSPHERE

When a gas (in this case the atmosphere) is heated, it expands. This expansion lowers the pressure of the gas. The density (weight) is also reduced.

When a gas cools it contracts and becomes more dense, and the pressure increases.

Air that has been heated is lighter and rises up, leaving behind an area of lowered pressure. Air that has been cooled falls, becomes more dense, and increases the pressure.

Another interesting factor is that air masses of different densities and humidity levels do not mix well.

GLOBAL WEATHER PATTERNS

In a global context, it is easy to see how these factors create our weather.

As we've already mentioned, there's a substantial difference between the sun energy received by the tropical areas and that received by the polar regions.

The result of this is that the tropical areas have warm, low-density, rising air. A the same time, the polar regions have cooler, heavier, sinking air.

The rising and sinking air systems set up a flow between them which forms the basis of our global weather patterns. Low pressure in the tropics (specifically the doldrum belts) rise up and flow toward the North and South Poles. The polar air masses sink and flow toward the tropics.

Warm, low-density air rises along the equator and then flows towards the poles where it sinks to the surface, and then flows back toward the equator.

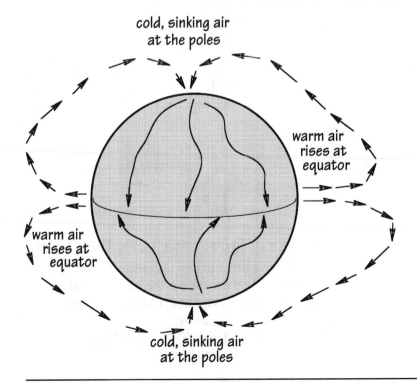

cold, sinking air
at the poles

warm air
rises at
equator

warm air
rises at
equator

cold, sinking air
at the poles

SEASONAL VARIATIONS

You are probably aware that the earth tilts on its axis during the year. In the wintertime, we are tilted away from the sun, and during the summer, tilted toward the sun.

This change in angle relative to the sun's radiation affects the amount of heat energy received, which in turn affects the weather patterns.

Gales are typically more robust as the seasons change in spring and fall.

One of the results of this change in heating is the "equinoctal" gale season.

You will find that gales are typically more robust as the seasons change in spring and fall. At these times of the year, there is a greater temperature differential between high latitudes and the tropics. And, when the respective air masses from these areas clash, the results are more vigorous than what you find in the middle of winter or summer.

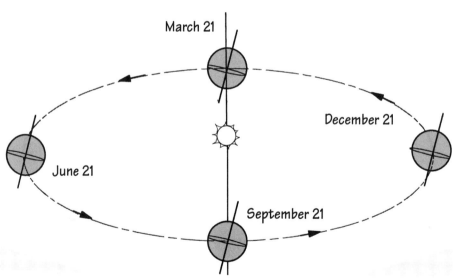

EFFECTS OF DIFFERENCES IN PRESSURE

If you have a low tire and pull into a filling station to pump it up, you are taking the high pressure from the station's compressor and allowing it to flow into the low pressure of your tire.

The same thing happens between high and low

pressure weather systems. The higher pressure tends to flow towards the lower pressure.

In the absence of any outside influence, the direction of this high to low pressure flow would be direct—the shortest possible course.

However, we have to take into account the earth's spinning on its axis.

CORIOLIS EFFECT

To understand corolis first we need to talk about gyroscopes. A gryoscope works on the principle of conservation of angular momentum. Once it is spun up to speed, the gyro's poles will remain aligned with the earth's poles. This is why gyros are used in lieu of a compass on steel vessels (where the compass readings would be affected by the mass of steel).

The same principle (conservation of angular momentum) is at work with air particles. The actual flow of the air particles is directly from the highs to the lows.

However, from the observer's standpoint, standing (or sailing) on the surface it appears that the wind is bent by the Coriolis effect. In reality, the

Coriolis force imparts an angular motion to the direction that wind flows between areas of high and low pressure.

This force is opposite in the North and South Hemispheres.

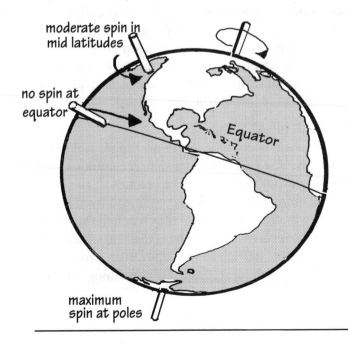

moderate spin in mid latitudes

no spin at equator

Equator

maximum spin at poles

The strongest Coriolis effect is at the pole. There is no Coriolis at the equator.

Note: lows are referred to as cyclones and highs as anti-cyclones in some forecasts.

particles are still going straight; the appearance of their motion is different as the observer is rotating under the particle.

There is more angular motion the closer you get to the poles. The opposite is true as you close with the equator, where there is no angular motion.

This Coriolis force accounts for the difference in rotation of highs and lows between Northern and Southern Hemispheres. In the Northern Hemisphere highs rotate clockwise while lows rotate counterclockwise. In the Southern Hemisphere, it is just the opposite: The highs rotate counterclockwise and the lows rotate clockwise.

EVAPORATION

As the sun's energy is imparted to the earth, the heating process causes evaporation of water from the soil, oceans and lakes.

The process of evaporation involves a *change of state* for the water, going from a liquid to a gas. In this process, heat energy is absorbed and maintained within the gasified water. In effect, this gasified water stores heat energy.

The change of state that occurs to moisture during evaporation and condensation is one of the key elements driving weather.

We all experience this when we step out of the water after a swim. As the moisture on our skin evaporates we feel a coolness. The evaporation process is removing heat energy from our skin.

The amount of moisture that the atmosphere can hold is a function of temperature. The warmer it is, the more humidity you can have—in effect, the more moisture that can be held in suspension.

CONDENSATION

As the air is cooled, it can no longer hold this humidity. The gaseous water then recombines, first into tiny droplets that we see as clouds. If the air is cooled more, these droplets combine to form larger drops, which become rain if they reach the surface.

As these processes take place, the heat which was absorbed in the original evaporation process is given back to the surrounding air, warming it in the process.

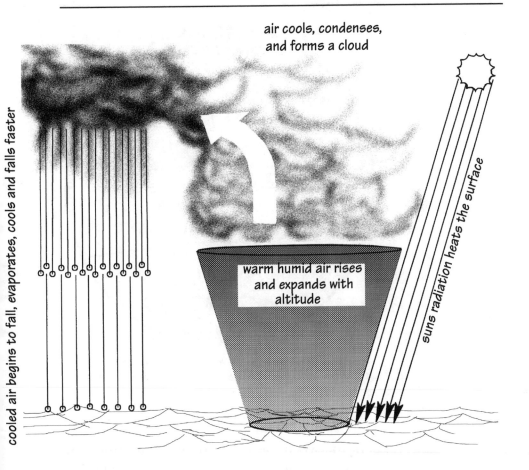

air cools, condenses, and forms a cloud

warm humid air rises and expands with altitude

cooled air begins to fall, evaporates, cools and falls faster

suns radiation heats the surface

What we have here is a delayed transfer of the sun's energy—first warming the liquid to a gas and then, when the gas recondenses, giving the heat up to the surrounding air mass.

This process provides a critical ingredient in all of the weather phenomena that affect us.

WEATHER ON A GLOBAL SCALE

The processes we've been discussing lead to the formation of two types of weather systems. First, in the polar regions, the cool, dense, relatively dry air forms high pressure domes called the polar highs. Then, in tropical areas we find warm, light, moist air forming low pressure areas.

The general pattern of world wide weather: Warmed air rises at the equator, flows to the mid-latitudes and poles, sinks forming high pressure systems, and then flows back towards the equator with a rotational bias picked up from Coriolis effect.

Air masses with different characteristics tend to remain isolated.

In between these two regions, at around 30 degrees latitude, there is another area of subsiding air, only this one is warmer and much more moist than that which falls over the poles. This is called the subtropical high pressure area.

Recall now that air masses with different characteristics tend to remain isolated.

In the summer weather systems move toward the pole—in the winter they move toward the equator.

Between the polar high and the subtropical high are shear lines, usually referred to as polar fronts. These typically are found around 60 degrees latitude.

During the summer, the sun's energy helps the tropical lows and subtropical high pressure systems move poleward, away from the equator. During the winter the opposite happens; systems move away from the poles and towards the equator.

Because different air masses tend to stay isolated, these systems maintain their different characteristics, while flow between them takes place along a definite path. This flow between the systems, and the rotational energy within the systems, is what forms the wind.

We can briefly summarize these wind flows as follows: The high pressure of the polar high flows towards the polar front. The top (poleward side) of the subtropical high flows towards the polar front. The bottom (equator side) of the subtropical high flows towards the low in the Intertropical Convergence Zone (ITCZ).

The Coriolis force from the earth's spin deflects the direction of flow from a straight pole-to-equator direction to one that has a clockwise or counterclockwise direction.

The tradewinds, which are such an integral part of our cruising plans, are the result of this process and come from the subtropical high pressure systems.

Polar high pressure air flows toward the polar front.

The top side of a subtropical high flows toward the polar front.

The bottom of the subtropical high flows toward the doldrums.

LOCAL WEATHER PATTERNS

If everything worked smoothly and was perfectly balanced, we could draw one weather chart and know what to expect anywhere in the world.

However, variations in the sun's output of energy, changes in evaporation rates, and a host of other factors, many of which are unpredictable, fit themselves into this brew.

The result, as we are all aware, is a constantly changing, sometimes frustrating, and always fascinating mix of different weather.

While the features we've just discussed are measurable on a long-term basis, and have a certain statistical constant, on a short-term micro basis they are always changing.

 In some regions, the high pressure systems are relatively stable, changing only with the seaons. Others, where the highs come and go, expand, contract and change shape as they interact with the weather systems around them.

The low pressure systems typically have an even more vibrant life cycle than the highs, and this is, of course, the genesis of most of our unpredictable weather.

BACKING AND VEERING WINDS

Wind direction is always spoken of as where the wind is coming from. So a west wind is coming out of the west (blowing west to east). A southeast wind is blowing from the southeast and towards the north-west.

When the wind direction is changing in a clockwise direction, it is said to be veering. When it switches in a counterclockwise direction, it is said to be backing.

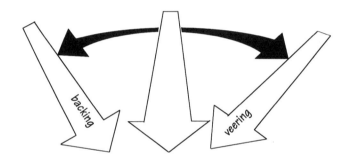

WIND FLOW IN HIGHS AND LOWS

Wind flows from the high pressure towards the low pressure.

Highs rotate clockwise north of the equator and counterclockwise south of the equator.

Lows rotate counterclockwise in the Northern Hemisphere and clockwise in the Southern.

As we've already mentioned, the wind flows from high pressure towards low pressure. The apparent direction is bent by the earth's rotation.

In addition, both highs and lows rotate about their centers in one fashion or another.

When you look at the surface wind flow between a high and a low, the flow is outward from the center of the high, with more angle on the direction as you get closer to the poles. Closer to the equator, in the tropical regions, the Coriolis effect is so reduced that flow is almost directly along the lines of pressure.

A low flows inward, toward the center, again with an angle imparted by Coriolis. In high latitudes the Coriolis angle is quite pronounced.

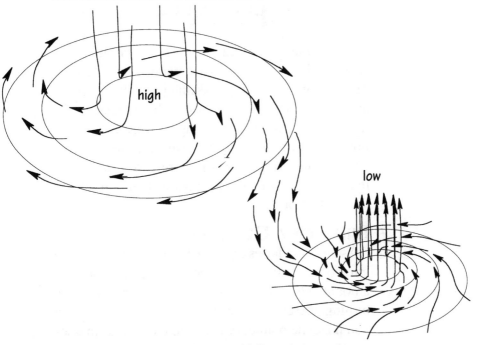

High pressure is cool and dense and falls and then splays outward. It tends to flow toward low pressure, which is typically warmer and rises in the central core. Above is the Northern Hemisphere view, below the Southern.

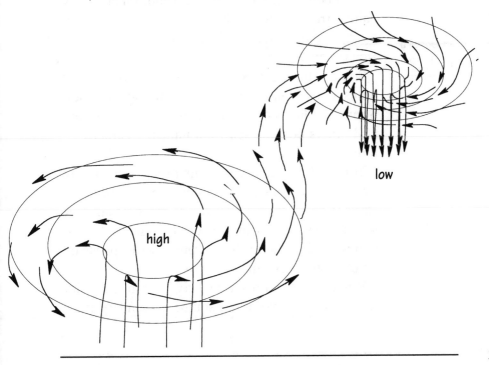

FRONTS

Fronts mark the boundaries *between* differing types of air masses that do not readily mix. These air masses can be roughly classified as follows: polar air masses consisting of dry cold high pressure air; tropical air masses consisting of warm, moist air flowing out of the tropics; maritime air masses that come from a large area offshore and so are quite moist; and continental air masses that come from the land and are dry.

BIRTH OF A DEPRESSION

As the boundaries of the differing air masses come into contact with one another, there is a substantial amount of turbulence and instability. Throw in some turning energy from Coriolis effect and pretty soon you have the boundary between the two air masses starting to rotate about a common center.

The continued release of energy from the difference in temperature, pressure and humidity of the frontal boundaries, together with additional energy gained from other weather systems aloft, and heat energy from the sun, land and water, create depressions of all shapes and sizes.

The release of energy from differences in pressure and temperature coupled with rotational energy from Coriolis force lead to the formation of a depression center.

Some of these can be quite small, perhaps just 100 miles across. Others can cover thousands of miles. Some will last a day or two, some for weeks, and still others become semi-permanent weather features.

You will frequently see this process occurring over the mid to eastern part of the U.S. A depression starts to form, then moves out over the Atlantic. A warm, moist flow of air from the south feeds the system with heat energy. The depression deepens and quickly becomes a major storm.

When these depressions originate at the polar front— in other words, the southern boundary of the

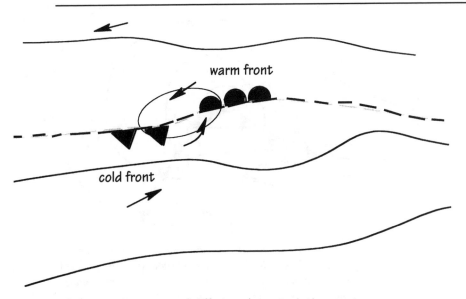

When two air masses of differing characteristics meet, a frontal boundary or shear line between the two develops. In its first stage it looks something like this drawing. Coriolis imparts some twisting to the two masses, and if the front develops into a depression, the spin will create a single, closed isobar as in succeeding drawings. This is a Northern Hemisphere view of the circulation.

polar air mass — they are driven eastward by the circulation on the northern side of the subtropical high (or the southern side of the subtropical high in the Southern Hemisphere).

If you will check back to the drawing on page 36, you will note that these two areas of high pressure — polar and subtropical — are flowing in different directions when they meet at the polar frontal boundary. This difference in direction is what imparts the initial impetus for the fronts to close up and rotate.

The description of frontal activity which follows is quite general. Please keep in mind that there are many variations on these themes. With weather, you never know precisely what is going to happen, until Mother Nature finishes mixing her brew.

Keep in mind that with weather there are no hard and fast rules—only generalities, subject to frequent change!

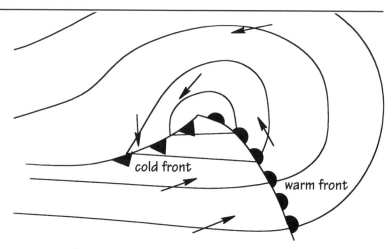

cold front

warm front

The next stage in the formation of a low system is for the isobars to close as is shown above. We now have a warm front leading, with a cold front trailing off behind. Note the shape of the isobars, how they are more or less straight between the warm front ahead and cold front behind. The drawing below is a day or two later, with the cold front starting to catch the warm. Note that the wind arrows flow inward a modest amount towards the center rather than following the isobars.

This is a mid-latitude system. At higher latitudes the wind would be angled more towards the center of the depression.

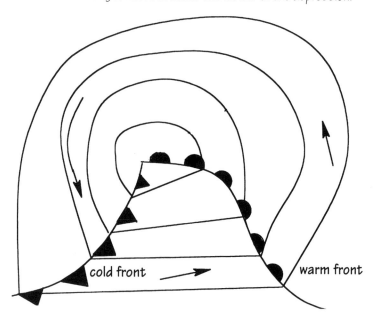

cold front

warm front

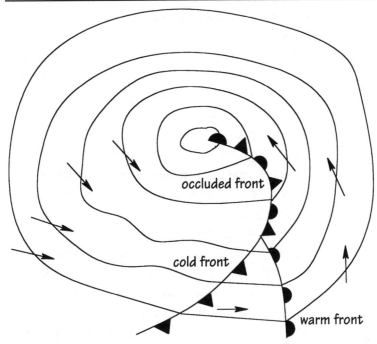

Five or six days into the depression's life cycle and the cold front has now caught up with the warm and overlapped. This is called an occluded condition.

WARM FRONTS

A warm front is the boundary between an area of warm air which has overtaken a cooler area.

Because the overtaking air is warmer, it *rises* up and over the cool air ahead. In the process, the moisture-laden air cools due to the lower temperature

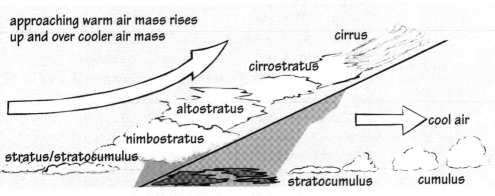

A warm front rises up and over the cooler air mass ahead of it. As the warm air rises it condenses, forming clouds and rain.

levels aloft, the water vapor condenses, and you get clouds and rain.

As the warm front approaches, the first signs you will see are fingers of cirrus clouds indicating the leading edge of warm air which has begun to cool as it comes in contact with the cooler air mass presently on top of you.

As the frontal boundary approaches, the cirrus clouds become thicker, then change to cirrostratus, and then into a heavier altostratus. The next stage as the front gets closer is a change to nimbostratus. However, the nimbostratus are frequently hidden behind a lower level of stratus cloud and rain.

When the rain starts to ease off, and then the nimbostratus begins to appear, you know that the warm front has probably passed you by.

The time it takes for the warm front to pass is a function of its angle relative to where you are, the direction and speed of your vessel, and the thickness of the frontal area.

You can generally look for the following conditions when the warm front passes: rain decreases and becomes patchy, humidity remains high, air temperature rises slightly, pressure steadies, and of course, the wind changes direction.

COLD FRONTS

With a cold front we have cool, somewhat drier air overtaking warmer moist air. Rather than the slow transition experienced with the warm front, the cold front passage is much more abrupt as it forces itself *under* the warm air of the overtaken air mass.

By forcing this warm humid air up, rapid condensation takes place along with a lot more convective (turbulent cloud building) activity.

If you have clear conditions ahead of the cold front you will see a thick, dark band of rain clouds

Signs of a warm front:

❏ Cirrus clouds announces approach.

❏ Cirrostratus, altostratus, stratus and rain.

❏ Barometer drops.

Signs a warm front has passed:

❏ Rain decreases with passage of warm front.

❏ Barometer remains steady.

❏ Wind shifts.

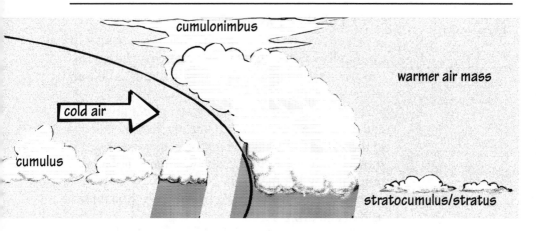

When the cold front approaches a warmer air mass, it forces the warm air up into cooler air aloft. This creates the cloud formations. The change is much more abrupt than with a warm front.

approaching and these will probably be seeded with towering cumulonimbus clouds (however, if you are in overcast conditions the cumulonimbus will be obscured).

The cold front will usually pass quickly, followed by a clear blue sky, studded with sharp-edged cumulus clouds when the cool, dry air moves over you.

As the cold front passes: humidity drops, rain clears, air temperature will drop, barometric pressure will rise, and wind direction changes.

FRONTAL SPEED

The speeds at which fronts move vary dramatically. We'll discuss this in more detail later, but for now, keep in mind that warm fronts typically move slower than cold fronts.

As a rule of thumb, 15 or so knots is fairly normal speed of movement for a warm front and 20 to 30 knots for a cold front (although speeds of up to 50 knots are not unknown for cold fronts).

Cold front signs:

❑ Dark band of rain clouds on approach.

❑ Barometer drops.

❑ Front passes quickly.

❑ Barometer rises.

❑ Temperature drops.

❑ Wind-shifts.

❑ Hard edged cumulus clouds.

The type of fronts we've been discussing are based on what is called the Norwegian model.

The Norwegian model applies to frontal systems over land, most small ocean frontal systems, and some large ocean systems.

Another type of frontal structure, the Shapiro/Kaiser model, also referred to as a bent back warm front, is discussed in detail starting on page 211.

OCCLUDED FRONTS

This speed differential means that a cold front will eventually catch up with the warm front ahead of it.

When this happens, you have what is called an *occluded* front.

The cool air from the cold front behind pushes in and under the warm front. Since much of the energy in the warm front has already been expended in the form of rain, the change in the weather is not as significant as with other fronts.

Moisture left in the warm front is precipitated out as rain and drizzle.

When you consider that both warm and cold fronts are radiating out from a single depression (or low center) it will become clear that the occlusion will start at the depression, then work its way outward as the cold front gradually overtakes the warm front.

As the occluded front passes rain becomes intermittent, the wind drops, the rate at which the barometer is falling will slow up. Air temperature probably remains the same, and the wind should ease.

STATIONARY FRONTS

This is a situation where the driving force for movement has been lost. The front stays mostly in the same place and gradually consumes its energy. Rain slowly gives way to clearing while temperature, the barometer, and the wind stay pretty much the same.

SECONDARY DEPRESSIONS

Once a depression has matured for several days and has become large and slow-moving, it is not unusual to find the shape of the attached fronts extending out and behind the low center.

It may appear as if the entire system is beginning to dissipate. However, occasionally a secondary low will form off these trailing fronts.

The secondary low can pick up some of the leftover energy of the initial fronts, and then gain additional power from a moist, warm inflow from the direction of the equator.

In some cases, this new low will join up with the older low you thought was dying, forming a vigorous, rapidly intensifying weather system.

This is precisely what happened during the infamous 1979 Fastnet Race, when so much damage was done to the racing fleet.

If secondary lows hang around for a day or so, they are usually picked up by the forecasters. However, they will, on occasion, develop very rapidly and be missed by the forecasters. Always keep an eye out for these features as they can be dangerous.

Keep a careful eye out for secondary lows. They can create dangerous wind and sea conditions in less than 24 hours and as a result sometimes are not found soon enough by forecasters.

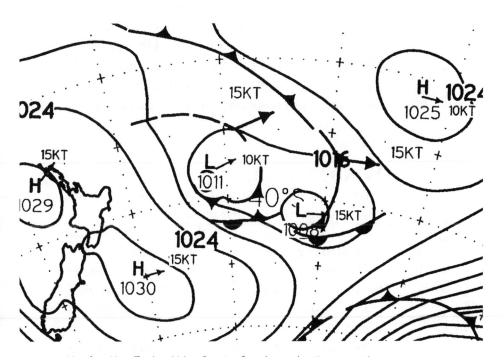

Here's a New Zealand Met Service fax chart showing a section of the South Pacific. There are two lows right in the center of the drawing. The isobar spacing indicates there is not much in the way of surface winds. However, with two shallow lows like this there is always the possibility that they will reinforce one another, so they must be carefully watched.

Another risk on this fax is the high pressure to the west of the two lows. It is bringing cool, dry air up from the south along its eastern side creating what in effect could be a turbocharger for the surface lows.

ONBOARD PREDICTION

So far we've been talking theory. Now let's put this data to practical use and see if we can predict what the weather is going to do.

When we started this book, we discussed how the professional weather forecaster is at a serious disadvantage when it comes to figuring out what is going to happen offshore.

He can have all the satellites and computers in the world, but unless he has on-the-spot data for barometric pressure, wind strength and direction, and humidity details, he is making an educated guess.

On the other hand, you are right on the spot, with all of the critical information at your fingertips. If you add this to what you see on a fax chart, or hear on a high seas broadcast, you are in a much better position than the weatherman to make an accurate forecast.

WIND STRENGTH

Factors affecting wind force:

❑ Speed at which pressure falls over time: faster = more wind.

❑ Spacing of iso-bars: closer = more wind.

❑ Direction of movement of weather system.

Wind strength is a function of a number of factors, chief among which is the pressure gradient. Pressure gradient is a fancy term that means the amount of change in pressure over a given distance.

The greater the change in pressure over time, or the shorter the distance over which the change takes place, the stronger will be the pressure gradient and hence the wind.

Another factor is the direction of movement of the weather system that is bringing you the wind, and where you are relative to the center of the system.

The movement of the weather system augments the wind when movement and wind direction are the same. Weather system movement detracts from the wind when the wind is blowing opposite the direction of travel.

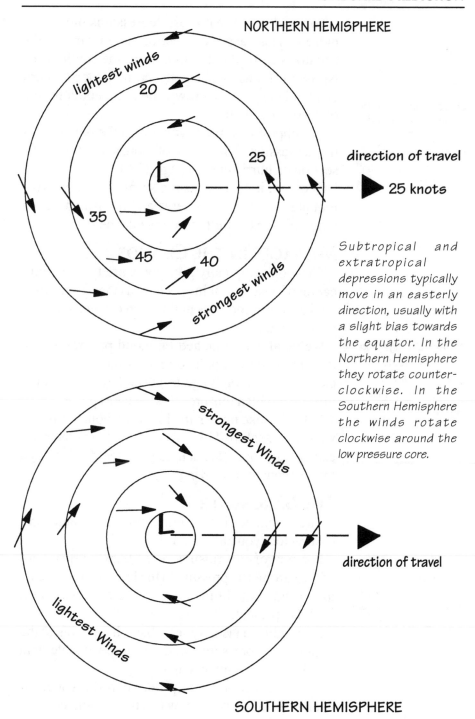

NORTHERN HEMISPHERE

lightest winds

20

25

35

45

40

strongest winds

L

direction of travel

25 knots

Subtropical and extratropical depressions typically move in an easterly direction, usually with a slight bias towards the equator. In the Northern Hemisphere they rotate counter-clockwise. In the Southern Hemisphere the winds rotate clockwise around the low pressure core.

strongest Winds

L

direction of travel

lightest Winds

SOUTHERN HEMISPHERE

You will recall that most depressions move in a more or less easterly direction. If you are on the equator side of the depression (to the south in the Northern Hemisphere and the north in the Southern Hemisphere), the wind will be augmented by the easterly movement.

Depressions moving east:

❑ Strongest winds on equator side of storm.

❑ Weakest winds on pole side of storm.

The opposite is true if you are on the pole side of the depression. (There is a lot more about this in the section on hurricanes on page 328.)

Geographic features can also funnel the wind— mountain ranges, gaps between high islands, even large ships and buildings alongside the shore.

MESSAGES IN THE CLOUDS

The clouds typically give you a pretty good indication of what is coming, as long as they are visible. And even on moonless nights, you can get a feel for what is in the sky.

Note in the log cloud type and direction of travel to develop a pattern for later analysis.

We've already touched on cloud progression in the section on fronts (and there is more data under clouds starting on page 66). The key factor is the time over which this progression takes place.

I like to make note in the log on an hourly basis of what we see aloft. Then, six or eight hours later, we can go back over this data to get a feel for how fast things seem to be moving.

THE BAROMETER

The barometer is the single most important forecasting tool you have aboard.

The barometer is the single most important weather forecasting tool you can have aboard.

For most of our cruising we made an hourly record of the barometric pressure in the log. Then, ten years ago, Linda bought me a recording barometer as a birthday present.

Being able to visually see what is happening to the atmospheric pressure I find far more valuable than looking at raw numbers in the log.

There is a relationship between the speed of change, in other words how fast the barometer is rising or falling and wind speed (except in squash

Latitude	Longitude	Time	Log	Speed	Course steered	BAR.	Wind
		0285		250		30.32	NE 10
		0345		350		30.34	
		0500		797		30.37	NEY
		0600	573.3	250	5.8	30.29	''
3°23'S	53°53'E	0730	79.6	250	5.2		
		1000				30.38	NE 8
		1200	307.6	255	6.2	30.36	
		1515	327.5	255	6.1	30.3	''
		1800	342.8	255	6.2	30.29	
		2000		250		30.32	
		2200		250		30.33	
		0130		''		30.34	
4°13'S	52°32'E	0500	382.5	''	6.7	''	NE 12
		0300		295			
		0400		295		''	''
		0530	422.3		7.3	30.07	
		0550		290		''	

A page from the past—October 22, 1979 and we are en route from Mauritius in the Southern Indian Ocean towards Durban, South Africa. As you can see from the hourly recording of the barometer, we are still in the friendly embrace of a high pressure system. In this part of the world, keep a close eye on the barometer as it is the best warning of "southerly busters"—fast-moving gales that come in from the south.

zones where a low is pushing against a high — which are discussed starting on page 114).

This correlation is related to your latitude. The lower the latitude (i.e., the closer you are to the equator), the more wind you will see from small changes. Conversely, higher latitudes require more of a barometric change to produce a given amount of wind.

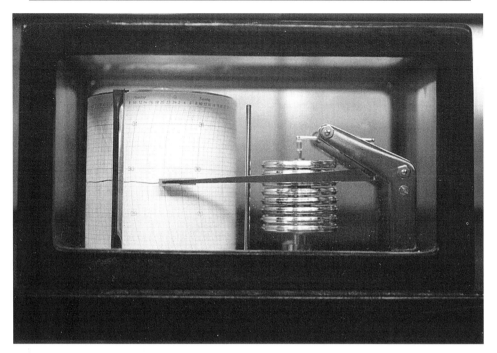

A Weems & Plath recording barometer. This unit runs on a single AA battery that lasts about six months. The paper chart takes a week to go around the drum. Having a visible trace of what the barometric pressure is doing makes it a lot easier to get a handle on the coming conditions.

The wind force that comes from barometric pressure change is a function of latitude. Closer to the poles requires more change for a given amount of wind—closer to the equator small changes in pressure create strong winds.

Keep in mind that the change in the barometer means a change in the wind. If there is no change in one then the other will remain more or less stable.

If you are hove to, waiting out a gale, for example, with the wind blowing at 40 knots and the barometer steady at 996mb, you would expect the wind to remain steady at 40 knots as well, unless you are in a compression zone (for more data on compression zones see page 114).

Barometer mechanisms typically lag the pressure change somewhat. The best way to get an accurate reading is to lightly tap the glass of the case and note the subsequent change, if any.

It is important that the barometer be *accurately calibrated*. This can be done at any airport and most

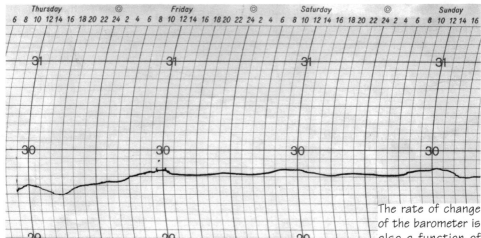

A sample trace of barometric pressure covering a three-day period. Note the low point reached on Thursday afternoon, and then the gradual increase in pressure from there until mid-day on Friday. This shows the passage of a warm front, and as you would expect with the gradual change in pressure, winds were light.

meteorological offices. It should be done at least once a year.

There will be times when you are looking at the weather and you expect an event to happen by a certain time—perhaps you are waiting for a certain low pressure reading as the center of a low moves near.

We find it helpful to mark a target pressure in the log, and sometimes to put a note right on the barometer with the pressure and time it is expected. This makes it a lot easier to keep track of things when you are wet and tired!

When the center of a depression is headed right at you, the barometer will drop precipitously. On the other hand, if you are above or below the depression track, the change in the barometer will be more jumpy but slower in rate of fall and less precipitous.

As the depression passes, the barometer will steady, even out, and then in time begin to rise.

The rate of change of the barometer is also a function of your direction of travel relative to the weather systems. When you are beating towards a system, you will have a rapid rate of closure and so the change in the barometer will be more precipitous. When you are traveling in the same direction as the system, it will take longer for the weather to overtake you and the change in the barometer will be much slower.

A consistent barometer reading means steady wind speed, unless you are caught in a squash/compression zone between a high and low pressure system—in which case the wind can increase while the barometer is steady.

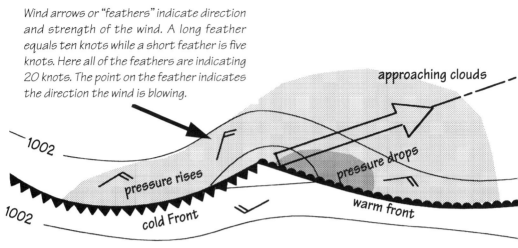

Wind arrows or "feathers" indicate direction and strength of the wind. A long feather equals ten knots while a short feather is five knots. Here all of the feathers are indicating 20 knots. The point on the feather indicates the direction the wind is blowing.

approaching clouds

1002

pressure rises

1002

cold Front

pressure drops

warm front

Here's a recap of the frontal scenario. A front forms between two air masses, the isobars close to form a low, and then a warm front reaches off the low center, followed by a cold front. The closer the isobar spacing on the chart, the stronger will be the wind speeds. The barometer drops on the approach of warm or cold front, and rises after the passage of the cold front.

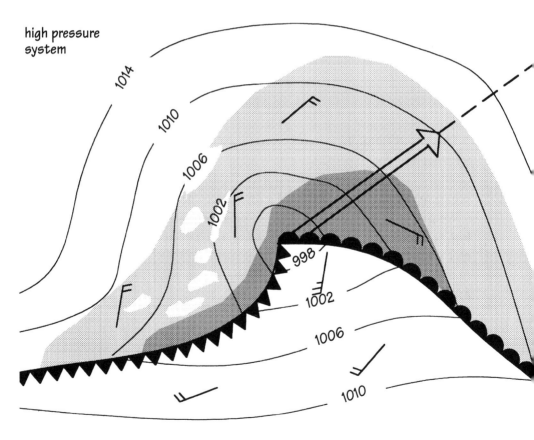

high pressure system

1014

1010

1006

1002

998

1002

1006

1010

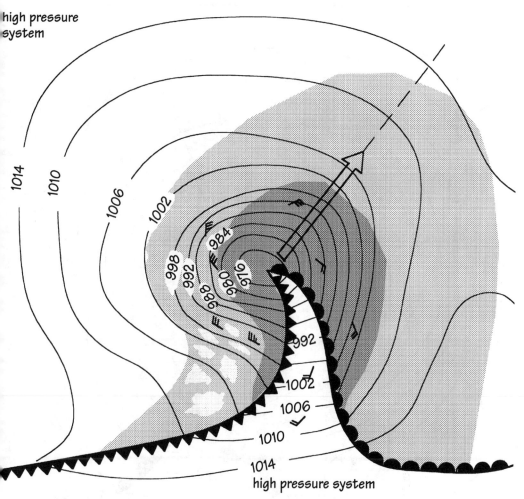

high pressure system

high pressure system

This is what a really deep frontal system would look like as it is nearing occlusion, where the trailing cold front has almost overtaken the leading warm front. The pressure shown would indicate storm-force winds in the higher latitudes and hurricane-strength winds in the subtropics.

You would typically find a high pressure system behind this low, probably with another high either ahead of it on the equator side of the system (to the south in the Northern Hemisphere and on the north side in the Southern Hemisphere).

Clouds (shaded area) ahead of the front start with cirrus, and end, after the cold front, with sharp-edged cumulus. The barometer drops on the approach of the warm front and then, depending on where you are, steadies or continues to drop until the cold front has passed, after which it begins to rise.

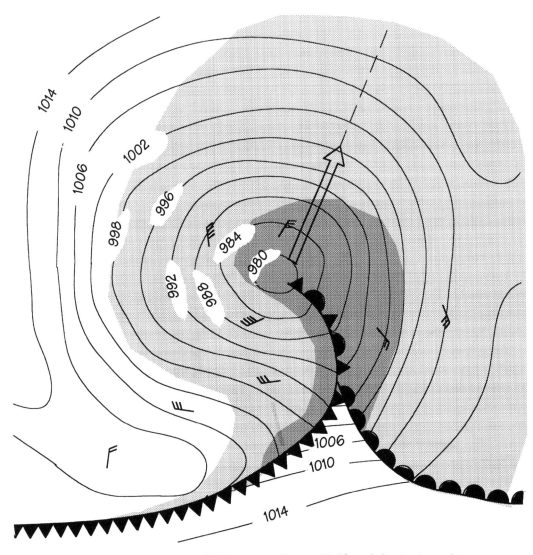

A low can just fill (from an adjacent high) and dissipate, or it can become occluded as shown here. This is where the trailing cold front overtakes the leading warm front. Note that the central pressure in this drawing has risen to 980mb, and the isobar spacing has begun to widen out.

It is fairly unusual to have an occluded front with such tight isobar spacing. The norm is to have them spread out a bit more by this point in a depression's life cycle. Occluded fronts also tend to be slower moving at this stage, and to sometimes have more rain than other scenarios.

ALONG THE SOUTH AFRICAN COAST

One of the toughest places for a shorebound weather forecaster to work is along the South African coast.

Here you typically find weather systems sweeping in from the Southern Ocean, and then following the coastline in a northerly direction.

For the most part, there are few real-time reports with which to predict the weather. So along with a couple of isolated islands down near the Antarctic continent, the main forecasting tool is the weather satellite.

As you know by now, this is not the most accurate or timely forecasting system available.

You can be sitting in Durban, in the north of South Africa, waiting for a clear spot between weather systems coming up from the Southern Ocean, for weeks or even months at a time.

If the weather systems hit land farther south, then the forecasters have a pretty good handle on what is coming up the coast. But frequently these systems are all but unannounced as they stay out to sea.

So what do most cruisers do? They wait for a clear spot, hopefully good for a couple of days, and then go like hell until they reach the next port.

One of the ways you do this is by riding the south flowing Aghulas current. This can give you anywhere from a two-to-seven knot ride in the right direction—so it is worth heading offshore to hitch onto.

However, if a southerly gale runs into this southerly flowing current, huge breaking seas are the result, and these seas have claimed lots of big ships along with the odd yacht.

If you know there's a blow coming, the normal tactic is to head into the shore, cross the 100-fathom line, and get out of the current. This makes the seas much more manageable.

So how do you know that something is coming, in the absence of an adequate radio or fax forecast?

Use your barometer, of course.

Marty and Marge Wilson have recently completed a westabout circumnavigation aboard their Sundeer 64, *Kela*.

When Marty called to fill us in on their current plans, I asked him about the approach in use today for getting down the South African coast.

"The barometer is still the best tool," he told me. "When a gale is approaching, while it is still sunny, the barometer will start to drop. Sometimes the breeze will hold from the north for a while; other times it will stop completely. Your immediate reaction is to stay out in the current and take advantage of the ride. However, you need to get into shoal water fast to get away from the freak waves.

"A half-hour after the wind quit it would come around on the nose, from the south. It would build for a half an hour to fifteen knots or so. Then in another half-hour it would be blowing 30 knots and sometimes a lot more. Between the wind against the current, and the old northerly waves, things would just be chaotic.

"We'd sometimes see the barometer drop four to five millibars in six hours. By the end of this time, we knew we were in for a blow and were trying to get into shore. Occasionally there would be a false alarm, with the barometer starting to drop, and then nothing happening. But you had to go into shore in case it was for real."

It is interesting to note that the same system that Linda and I employed 20 years ago when we were passaging along the same coastline is in use today.

WIND DIRECTION

Trends in wind strength and wind direction, can tell you where you are in relation to the center of a high or low.

Once you have deduced this data, you are then in a position to forecast the wind direction which can be expected in the near future.

The drawings on the next page will give you an idea of what to expect in a variety of conditions. What I find helpful is to make my own drawings when we are tracking the weather. These days, with weather fax, we draw little boats (and I have been drawing boats for a very long time!) on the fax charts.

In the Northern Hemisphere, if you take the wind on your back and point at right angles with your left arm, your arm will be pointing roughly at the center of the low.

In the Southern Hemisphere with the wind at your back, point at right angles to the wind with your right arm, and you will be indicating the low center.

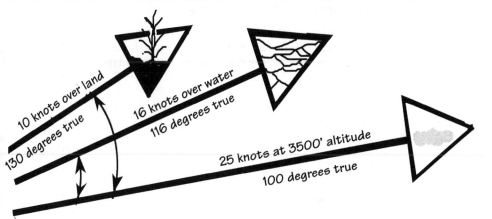

10 knots over land
130 degrees true

16 knots over water
116 degrees true

25 knots at 3500' altitude
100 degrees true

There's a substantial difference in the wind direction and speed over land, water, and at altitude. This is due to the varying friction encountered. Over land, with the most friction, wind speed is reduced, while Coriolis has the greatest impact. Over water, friction is less, so wind speed is up and angle to the isobars from Coriolis is less. At altitude you have the strongest winds and almost no Coriolis force.

GUST FACTORS

It is helpful to know what kinds of gusts can be expected so you can decide whether to set up your rig for the mean wind speed (and then feather through the gusts) or reef down in anticipation of the gusts and be undercanvassed (or motorsail) in the lulls.

Most wind forecasts (voice and fax) are based on the expected *steady state* winds, usually the average speed anticipated over a ten minute period, at a height of about 35 feet (10 meters) above the surface.

Gusts are caused by vertical instability in the atmosphere. This can be due to the sun's heating the nearby land, or areas of warm water triggering updrafts, or the passage of a cold front. Eventually, this leads to mixing with the higher wind speed aloft.

When downdrafts occur they bring with them some of the upper air wind speed, causing the gusts.

Whenever you have squalls about, or have a cold front moving in, conditions tend to be more gusty than with warm fronts or stable air.

Gusts are caused by vertical instability in the atmosphere. This brings stronger winds from aloft down to the surface.

Wind speed range	Gust factor—maximum wind speed	Gust factor—mean wind speed
Day		
7—16 knots	2.0	1.6
17—27 knots	1.8	1.5
28—40 knots	1.6	1.5
Night		
7—17 knots	1.9	1.5
17—21 knots	1.8	1.5
28—40 knots	1.7	1.5

Gusts vary with the weather systems, and between day and night. Here is a rough approximation based on different wind forces. Gust factors are higher in the day due to thermal action and tend to reduce with wind speed. Multiply the average wind speed you have by these factors to get an idea how hard the wind may blow.

Gusts also tend to be stronger during the daytime when solar heating promotes the updraft/downdraft cycle (an exception to this will be when there are squalls, which sometimes are more vigorous in the evening—see more on this subject in the chapter on squalls beginning with page 256).

Gusts generally will increase the wind velocity anywhere from 30% to 70% above mean wind speed. When you consider that the force in the wind goes up with the *square* of the wind speed—so that a 30-knot wind has more than twice the force of a 20 knot wind—you can see why gust factors are worth paying attention to.

Expect stronger gusts:

☐ During the daytime.

☐ If there are squalls about.

☐ With the passage of a cold front.

☐ When you see virga hanging from clouds.

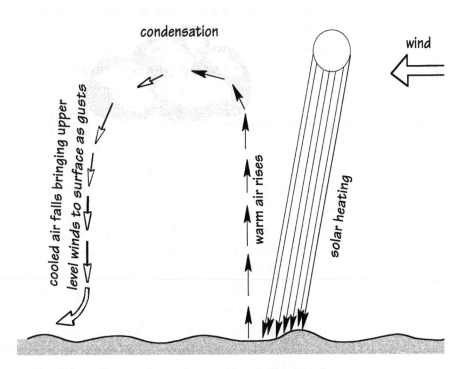

condensation

wind

cooled air falls bringing upper level winds to surface as gusts

warm air rises

solar heating

Wind gusts are the result of vertical instability resulting in the mixing of upper level winds—which are stronger—with surface winds.

This instability can be the result of thermal activity from the sun's radiation, or the mixing of the upper and lower atmosphere as a result of frontal passages.

DATA FROM OTHER YACHTS

It is the norm now on most passages to be sharing your part of the ocean with a number of other yachts.

Often these yachts will check in to a "net" on either ham or SSB frequencies, giving their position, barometer reading, cloud cover, wind strength and direction.

Things to look for when listening to weather reports from other vessels:

❑ Experience of the reporting crew.

❑ Trends in their wind speed, direction, sea state, and barometric pressure.

❑ Cloud types and trends.

❑ Has their barometer been calibrated recently?

If you log this data, you can then begin to construct a highly accurate picture in your mind of what the weather is doing.

Some years ago Linda and I were in Fiji, ready to head for New Zealand. *Beowulf* was new at the time, and we were taking her to Auckland for her interior.

This was the last leg of our trip and we wanted a really good blow as one final test.

We sat in Malololailai for two weeks watching fax charts from New Zealand, Australia, Honolulu, and Rarotonga. All of these fax charts were derived from the same raw satellite data using different computer models—and they all differed substantially from each other.

At the same time, several dozen yachts were en route to Bay of Islands, New Zealand from Tonga and Fiji, all checking in with Keri-Keri radio.

By plotting their locations and reported conditions, it was easy to see what the real picture was—a high pressure was moving in from the Tasman, winds were light and, unfortunately, we expected them to stay that way.

Sometimes there's just one other vessel out there. If it happens to be between you and a brewing weather system, they can serve as an early warning service for you.

One thing for which you do need to make allowances is the accuracy of the other boat's barometer. It may be off several millibars if it hasn't been calibrated making the absolute reading of small value.

However, the *relative reading* — how much the barometer is rising or falling, and over what time period — is still significant.

WHAT THE WAVES TELL YOU

The pattern and size of wind waves and swell are good indicators not only of the weather in your own neighborhood, but also of weather far away.

In the case of weather predictions, the wind waves are not what we are interested in (local wind waves usually have a period—i.e., time between the passing of crests— of five to seven seconds).

What is of interest are the swells. The swells with the longest period are also the fastest moving. They typically move well ahead of an approaching storm. A normal period for swells might be six seconds (ten swells per minute). As these begin to slow

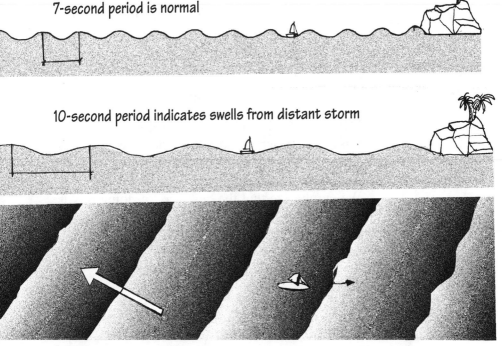

7-second period is normal

10-second period indicates swells from distant storm

the higher you are, the better you can see the wave pattern

down, perhaps to a ten-second interval (six swells per minute), you have an early warning of a major storm system.

If you are anchored, you will hear the swells pounding on the reef or shoreline. The sound alone is enough to alert you.

If there is no interference from the land or ocean bottom, the direction from which the swells emanate will indicate where the storm center is located.

ANOMALIES

The weather more or less goes according to predictable patterns. Typically these are easily understood, and the onboard or shorebound forecaster has a pretty good handle on things.

But we must always keep an eye out for unusual situations that can create unexpected results.

Secondary lows, as we've already discussed, are a potentially dangerous feature.

Another is the formation of small low pressure cells at the edge of the tropics which then with the right conditions turn into severe storms as they move to higher latitude.

An example of this is the Queen's Birthday Storm in June 1994 (which we detail on page 229).

FINDING PRESSURE CENTERS

It is by now obvious that a *key* factor in your tactics is knowing where the center of the depression is relative to your location.

We emphasize that the best way of doing this is using the wind-at-your-back method previously discussed. If you have radio broadcasts or fax charts, it is still worth confirming the low center with this age-old technique.

Watch for dangerous anomalies:

❑ Secondary lows

❑ Tropical lows that could turn into storm or hurricane force winds.

❑ Tropical lows moving into subtropics.

❑ Squash zones between high and low pressure systems.

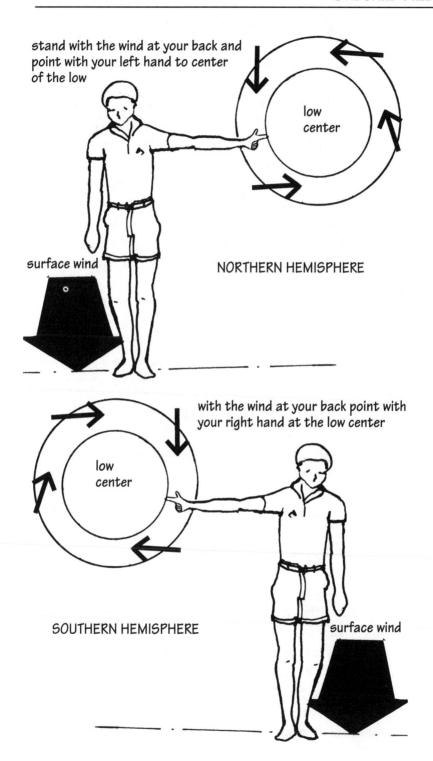

stand with the wind at your back and point with your left hand to center of the low

low center

surface wind

NORTHERN HEMISPHERE

with the wind at your back point with your right hand at the low center

low center

SOUTHERN HEMISPHERE

surface wind

READING THE CLOUDS

The shape and altitude together with the direction and speed of movement of the clouds provide an excellent leading indicator on what is coming, how far away it is, and the type of weather system from which your present conditions are derived.

Let's recap for a minute the process by which clouds are formed.

Moisture-laden air is created by evaporation, powered by the sun. As the warm, humid air rises, it is cooled and condenses to form a vapor, which we see as a cloud.

Recall that differing weather systems vary in both temperature and humidity levels. Warm fronts, for example, are warmer than the surrounding air, and more humid. When this humid air comes in contact with the overtaken cooler, drier air mass, clouds form.

The shape and altitude together with the direction and speed of movement of the clouds provide an excellent leading indicator on what is coming, how far away it is, and the type of weather system from which your present conditions are derived.

GENERAL CATEGORIES OF CLOUDS

For some reason, clouds have difficult names taken from Latin (the result, no doubt, of a plot by meteorologists to make things seem more complicated than they really are).

There are four basic types of cloud names, which refer as much to the altitude at which they are normally found as their shape.

These are:

Nimbus: A ragged looking, typically low cloud usually associated with poor weather. When you see something in the nimbus family, it normally means it is raining or (heaven forbid) snowing.

Stratus: Sheet-like, fairly solid in density, and appear to maintain an even altitude.

Cumulus: Like balls of cotton, well spaced, typically seen in fair weather, unless they extend very high, in which case thunderheads may be developing.

Cirrus: A thin, veiled cloud, almost like cotton candy pulled off a cone, these are excellent leading indicators that something is on its way.

CIRRUS

Cirrus clouds are quite easy to identify with their long, feathery wisps of white vapor trailing aloft.

They are composed of ice crystals and frequently are a feature of the jet stream (for more information on the jet stream see page 182). Cirrus are an excellent precursor of the arrival of frontal weather, or more ominously, rotating storms in the tropics (for more on this subject see the following chapter on hurricanes starting with page 328).

As the cirrus mix with the leading edge of the warm front, "hooks" (tendrils of clouds falling towards the ground) are created on the outer edges of the cirrus clouds.

Cirrus with hooks—the first indicator of an approaching front. (NOAA photo).

And any time you see these hooks, a front is not far behind.

The intensity of the low is usually related to the speed at which the cirrus clouds are moving.

Because they are so high (typically 35,000 feet - 10,000m), if you can detect *any* relative motion the jet stream is cooking along at a 100 knots or more.

If the cirrus appear to be moving rapidly, then the jet stream could be working at as much as 150 to 200 knots.

CIRROCUMULUS

Cirrocumulus clouds are thick collections of ice crystals at high altitudes. They have the appearance of beach sand after it has been lapped by gentle

Cirrocumulus clouds — Frontal weather is on its way. (NOAA photo)

waves. This has long been known as a "mackerel sky."

These clouds are typically associated with the approach of frontal weather.

CIRROSTRATUS

Cirrostratus is another high-altitude (30,000 ft / 9000m and up) cloud system made up from ice crystals. They are typically veil-like, but with more density than plain cirrus.

Again, these clouds herald the approach of a warm front.

Cirrostratus will create halos around the sun and moon. This latter feature is a valuable indicator at night that weather is approaching (when other signs may not be visible aloft).

You can often make out cirrostratus at night when there is a three-quarters to full moon, as they make haloes around the moon.

A mix of cirrostratus and cirrocumulus. (NOAA photo)

ALTOCUMULUS

Altocumulus are like a thin version of normal cumulus clouds. Somewhat broken up on the bottom, they present a typically uniform coverage of much of the sky.

These clouds are the next step in the warm front warning system and are typically found in the 10,000-to 20,000-foot (3000 to 6000 m) elevation.

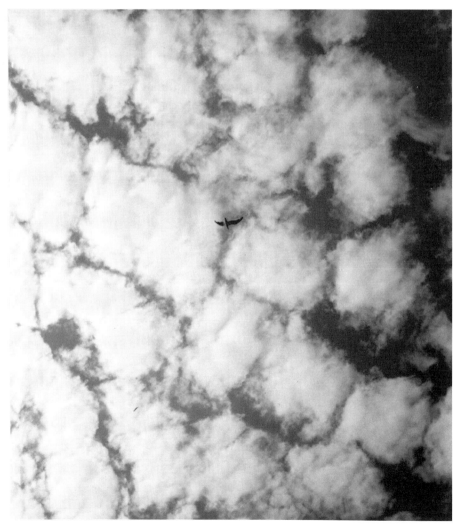

This photo shows broken altocumulus clouds. As the warm front gets closer, this will form a more uniform cloud cover.

ALTOSTRATUS

Altostratus signal that the front is very close and rain is about to start. This is a relative smooth layer of cloud, quite dark in patches.

The altitude of these clouds is typically similar or slightly lower than altocumulus.

Sometimes the sun will shine through the thinner parts of the cloud system with a weak, watery (and to some depressing) light.

STRATUS

Stratus present a uniform low layer of cloud that is typically gray in color, with no shape, looking like a low sheet of smooth cloud. If there are low mountains in the area, sometimes the tops of the mountains are lost in the stratus clouds.

You will normally find light rain or drizzle with stratus clouds and they occur at the end of a front—either cold or warm, or during an occluded front.

NIMBOSTRATUS

Nimbostratus is similar to stratus except that there is a lot more texture to the bottom of the cloud. It is typically found between 700 and 2,500 feet (200 and 750m) altitude, and is associated with heavy precipitation (both rain and snow).

It is common to see smaller, broken sections of nimbostratus clouds hanging below the main cloud base. On occasion these underhanging clouds will appear to move faster than the higher, thicker mass above. They are sometimes referred to as "scud."

Nimbostratus are associated with the passage of the front, and as the sky begins to clear you can usually expect better weather.

Nimbostratus clouds have that heavy, "it's about to open up" look. (NOAA photo)

CUMULONIMBUS

Cumulonimbus have a low base, but they can have extremely high tops (sometimes as high as 40,000 feet/12,000m). These are towering, billowing, visu-

Cumulonimbus clouds like this can reach to 40,000 feet or more. They may be isolated, or be embedded in other cloud layers.

ally exciting monster clouds. When found on their own they are indicators of squalls, heavy rain, and gusty winds.

The bottoms of these clouds often have a nimbostratus look to them, dark in places with rain, light in others.

The tops will be bathed in sunlight and brilliant white.

When the tops begin to form a horizontal anvil on the downwind side this is a sign that the cloud is dieing and the resulting downdrafts will be more pronounced at sea level.

Cumulonimbus clouds are often associated with the passage of cold fronts. And, as we said earlier, cumulonimbus often form a squall line some distance ahead of the cold front.

You will frequently find cumulonimbus clouds embedded in other layers of cloud and/or hidden from view by lower level cloud decks.

CUMULUS

Finally, we get to what you see most of the time in the trades, fair-weather cumulus clouds. These are like giant cotton balls, sometimes with bottoms as low as 2,000 feet (600m) but they can be up much higher in dry conditions. They have a soft appearance to them.

Tradewind cumulus clouds, with squalls about in late afternoon.

You will also find cumulus clouds in the cool, clear air behind a cold front. In this case the clouds have a more defined, hard edge look to them. Initially they can be associated with gusty wind and rain showers.

As their shape softens, and the space between them opens up, weather typically eases and showers cease.

Tops can rise in both cases to 15,000 feet (4,500m).

Fair-weather cumulus in the trades. Note how thin the clouds are. This shallow development indicates conditions are not right for thunderstorm activity.

NAME & SYMBOL	HEIGHT (FEET)	HEIGHT (METERS)	THICKNESS	DESCRIPTION
Cirrus (Ci)	20,000-40,000	6,000-12,000	Usually couple of thousand feet (few hundred meters)	Typically indicates an approaching frontal system
Cirrostratus (Cs)	20,000-40,000	6,000-12,000	Usually couple of thousand feet (few hundred meters)	Typically indicates an approaching frontal system–may be accompanied by haloes around the sun
Cirrocumulus (Cc)	29,000-40,000	6,000-12,000	Thin	Same as above but without haloes
Altocumulus (Ac)	7,000-20,000	2,000-6,000	Usually couple of thousand feet (few hundred meters)	Bands are often seen ahead of fronts–the castellated types are associated with thunder
Altostratus (As)	7,000-20,000	2,000-6,000	Thick–up to 10,000 feet/3,500 meters	Indicates closeness to precipitation area of frontal system
Nimbostratus (Ns)	300-2,000	100-600	Thick–up to 15,000 feet/4,500 meters	Associated with precipitation–tops merge with altostratus
Stratus (St)	500-2,000	150-600	Thin–from 100 feet/30- to 100 feet/300 meters	May cover low mountains
Stratocumulus (Sc)	1,000-4,500	300 - 1,350	Thin–from 500 feet/150 meters-3,000 feet/900 meters	May indicate the approach of heavy rain in some cases. In others, only light drizzle.
Cumulus (Cu)	2,000-5,000	600 - 1,400	May be thick–from 4,000 feet/1,400 meters-15,000 feet/4,500 meters	Is some indication of atmospheric instability–strong vertical currents in large clouds-gustiness at surface level
Cumulonimbus (Cb)	2,000-5,000	600 - 1,400	Very thick–from 10,000 feet/3,000 meters to as high as 50,000 feet/15,000 meters	Very turbulent cloud, accompanied by heavy showers, with some hail, lightning, and thunder

THE EXTRATROPICAL FORECASTING PROCESS

As our cruising grounds change, we come into contact with the weather forecasting services of different governments. While these vary to some degree, there is a modicum of uniformity. This is the result of a set of standards promulgated by the World Meteorological Organization (WMO).

These standards define minimum time cycles for the dissemination of general information and storm warnings.

Members of the WMO also agree to geographic boundaries for their broadcast products. These boundaries are arbitrary, and obviously the weather does not respect them.

It makes sense to try to determine from your local weather sources at what point they hand off to the next national authority. The local met service will be able to give you this information.

At the same time, check on schedules and how weather systems with the *potential* for problems are handled—*especially when these occur along boundaries between national forecasting agencies.* (See the chapter on the Queen's Birthday Storm for more data on this subject— page 229.)

NATIONAL WEATHER SERVICE'S MARINE PREDICTION CENTER

In the U.S. extratropical forecasts for both east and west coasts originate from the Forecast Branch of the NWS Marine Prediction Center in Camp Springs, Maryland. It is a small office, with a permanent forecast staff of 20, who work 24 hours a day, seven days a week to bring us the current and projected weather.

Dave Feit, chief of operations for the center, filled us in on some of the details of the prediction process. "The first step in any forecast is to look at all the ship data and determine if there are any obvious errors. We get between 2500 and 3000 reports from ships every six hours on wind speed and direction, wave height, barometer, and sea surface temperature. These observations are done on a voluntary basis although some countries may require their ships to report. The system under which the ships report was set up after the *Titanic* disaster (Safety of Life at Sea Agreements — SOLAS).

"These ship observations come in continuously typically via Inmarsat or coastal radio stations, although they are taken every six hours," Dave continued, "and they are compared to a numerical model we produce on our computers. We may have a ship report from 33 degrees North latitude and 70 degrees West longitude, which is showing a barometric pressure of 1018 when the model says it should be 1008. This is flagged, and then we try to analyze what has happened. Frequently in a situation like this it is a case of the watch officer transposing the numbers. But sometimes we say, 'By God, he is correct' and we adjust our analysis to the ship's data.

"Maybe it's a situation where there are a series of ships off the East Coast sitting under a high pressure system. All are reporting south winds of 15 to 20 knots, except for one who is showing north winds. We know that the oddball has made a mistake. We have a history with each ship — they are usually on a voyage for six to eight days — so we get a feel for the quality of their reporting.

"When we see mistakes in reporting, we correct the isobars on the surface analysis charts to what we think the conditions really are. *But we will sometimes leave the wind arrows pointing the way the ship reported.* This is the only way we have to get a message to them that they have messed up."

Forecast breakdown:

- Coastal—within 25 to 60 miles of the coast, mainly for recreational use.

- Offshore—60 to 250 miles offshore, for commercial fisherman, shipping and yachtsmen.

- High seas—for commercial shipping and yachtsmen.

It is important to keep this last bit of advice in mind the next time you look at a surface forecast. You can put a degree of trust in the isobars, but when the wind arrows don't seem to make sense, remember that the forecasters may be sending a message to someone!

Along with ship and buoy reports, the forecasters use a scatterometer in a polar orbiting satellite to measure wind strength based on back scatter of the radar return from the sea surface. Computer models of the area then tell them which direction the waves are going and the wind is blowing—but of course, as we mentioned earlier, this can be off 180 degrees at times.

UPPER LEVEL CONDITIONS

The atmosphere is incredibly complex and difficult to model. To have any shot at doing this accurately, the forecasters need measurements of what is happening at different levels in the atmosphere.

On land, these *soundings* of conditions are taken by balloons which are sent aloft, at 0000 hours and 1200 hours (UTC). This is true for all members of the World Meteorological Organization, and takes place on a coordinated basis throughout the world. One of the mandatory levels at which the wind, temperature, and humidity data are measured is 500 millibars.

At sea the forecasters don't have this luxury. There are a few balloon-equipped ships and, of course, on island locations balloons are sent aloft. But for the most part this data is derived from satellite-based soundings at certain infrared wavelengths of moisture profiles. Aircraft flying at jet steam levels also send back reports. Finally narrow beam satellite soundings are taken for various parts of the forecast area, and then fed into the computer model.

COMPUTER MODELING

Dave Feit indicated, "There are 12 to 15 well-established computer models in use around the world today. These are constantly being updated and improved, and one of the ways in which they vary is how they are initialized."

He went on to state, "Initialization of the model is the most critical part of the whole thing. If we don't get the initialization right, if we don't get everything balanced, then we are starting with a false atmosphere, which gives us an unreliable forecast.

"We use between 25 and 50 vertical levels in the atmosphere."

I asked Dave which computer model he used and was surprised at his answer. "We use a variety of programs and then compare the results. It is important to understand the strengths and weaknesses of the different models. Some do better in one area than another.

"The primary computer model we pay the most attention to is the medium range forecast model or MRF. We run this once a day on a Cray 90 super-computer. It is not well suited for short-range forecasts as it takes a long time to get the data loaded into it. For the short-range forecasts we use the Aviation Model. This is actually the MRF, but it is used with initial data and out for a short period of time.

"We find that we can get marginal forecasting results out at eight to ten days and quite good results in the four-or five-day range. However, you do have to understand the characteristics of the model. You might see a series of lows off Baja California in the summer and you would know that this was not a realistic result. You would then go and check the European Medium Range Forecast Model or the Navy Model and look at their results.

"You can have a situation where three or four models are all saying the same thing and all are wrong. And you can have a scenario where they are all giving different answers and one is right."

A typical timeline on the forecast cycle for an individual forecaster (computer work is prepared for the forecaster by Central Computer Operations):

- ❑ 0000—Begin process, review data.
- ❑ 0120—Get first cut of computer-generated data.
- ❑ 0140—Second batch of data is output and manual (human) analysis begins based on ship and whatever other data is available. Review previous computer forecasts.
- ❑ 0245—Aviation model loading cutoff time. Start computer analysis run.
- ❑ 0310—Manual sea-state analysis issued.
- ❑ 0315—Aviation model spits out bad data that it cannot use.
- ❑ 0320—Begin fax transmission of surface analysis.
- ❑ 0330—The aviation model has balanced input data and begins run. Each day's projection takes 15 minutes to calculate.
- ❑ 0430—Issue high seas text forecast via USCG transmission and WWW.

☐ 0600—Medium Range Forecast model begins processing, culling out data it does not like, and then running forecasts.

☐ 0730—96-hour computer model is complete. Data is analyzed, compared to other models, human decisions are made and synoptic charts are drawn.

☐ 0900—Issue 48-hour surface forecast.

☐ 0915—48-hour sea state forecast is issued.

☐ 1430—Fax chart is broadcast.

"Sometimes when we initialize the computer, we'll make a series of different runs with a variety of slightly varying initial data. Temperature, pressure, wind speed, or location may be varied. We then look at the end results. It may be that in a certain situation the answers all turn out pretty much the same. At other times, very small variations in the initialization have big impacts on the forecasts."

Joe Sienkiewicz, one of the marine forecasters, filled us in on more detail on the modeling process: "We use six hour forecasts from the operational computer models as a first estimate as to the initial state of the atmosphere. The global observations are then used to tweak the previous computer model forecasts in the right direction, which makes for relatively consistent model forecasts. Highly sophisticated operational forecast computer models that simulate the atmosphere are then run using the analysis determined from a combination of the observed data and previous model forecasts."

Joe Sienkiewicz, lead Marine Forecaster, working on the morning Pacific regional chart and text package. Forecast text is shown on the left screen and a satellite image on the center with model output overlaid. On the right screen is model output data. These monitors are tied to the central computer server and can call up any of the data or images on any of the screens.

FORECAST CYCLE

The forecast areas are broken up into the Atlantic and Pacific regions. For each area there are two forecasters working. One does the offshore forecasts and the other the coastal analysis. They work independently but coordinate where the weather overlaps.

Interestingly, with all of this computer power available, the surface forecast charts are drawn by hand.

In the U.S. the standard is to issue surface analyses via fax four times a day (every six hours). Text forecast are also broadcast four times a day, in this case covering the 36-hour prognosis.

The 48-hour forecast fax charts are broadcast twice a day, while the 96-hour forecast is sent out once a day.

The forecaster's work cycle:

❑ Prepare surface analysis.

❑ Do written forecast to be broadcast over coastal, high seas radio, and Inmarsat.

❑ Record voice analysis to be broadcast over WWV.

❑ Prepare fax charts (either by hand or with computer).

Each fax chart is signed by the forecaster that prepared the analysis and chart. By watching who is doing the charts over a period of time, you get a feel for how good they are at picking out different situations. Most have slightly different styles and over time a pattern will emerge. In this case, Scott Prosis is completing the 1800 UTC Pacific surface analysis.

Here is the beginning phase for the 1200 UTC Atlantic forecast. Jim Nolt, Marine Forecaster, is beginning his analysis by reviewing ship's observations and a computerized first scan (underlaid on the light table) of what the computer thinks the isobars should look like.

How good is the medium-range forecast?

"My gut instinct is that it is pretty good in most cases and in some cases amazingly good. In the blizzard of 1996 for example, we were right on at 96 hours. But after all, it is a 96-hour forecast and you have to worry—there are spurious things that happen and things which are missed." Dave Feit

BUDGET ISSUES

As taxpayers in the good old U.S.A., we are generally outraged at the way most of the money we send to Washington is wasted. One of the few areas I can see where the taxpayer gets real value is with the marine weather services.

From time to time there have been attempts at cutting the budget of the marine branches. The same folks who bring us 1.5 trillion dollars worth of programs want to save the country money by cutting a couple of forecasters and eliminating fax transmissions.

If you are a U.S. citizen, let your congressional representatives know just how important and cost efficient are our weather services. Consider the cost of a couple of Coast Guard search-and-rescue missions, or a missed storm, and you have enough money to transmit all of the marine weather faxes for years!

WHEN YOU'RE AT SEA

In spite of our comments about forecasters' mistakes, the bottom line is that today most national weather services do a remarkably accurate job of telling us what is going to be happening.

However, we need to continually keep in mind that, in the end, a lot of black art is still involved in this entire process. That implies human skill, and where you have human skills, you sometimes have human error.

Then there is the issue of the information with which the forecasters have to work. In many cases you don't have to be off very far in your initialization of those computers before the end results are heavily skewed.

A standard part of every 24-hour cycle at the Marine Prediction Center is a review of the previous day's forecasts and how they have turned out.

Dave Feit is to the right while the forecaster responsible for the Northern Pacific is giving the head's up.

When we are at sea, we need to be constantly aware that the forecast may or may not be correct. The most prudent course of action is to look at the situation, consider what the worst outcome might be if the forecast has missed something, and have a fallback plan if the worst appears to be about to transpire.

Remember, you are on the spot, you have the real data, and with barometric pressure, wind velocity, direction, and changes in cloud pattern, you can do an excellent job at predicting the future on your own.

If the professional forecast does not agree with your conditions, it is almost always best to assume the worst. Prepare for it, take evasive action if required, and go with your own prognosis until the forecasters come up with a product that matches the conditions you have.

WHO ARE THE FORECASTERS?

In the process of writing this book we came to know a number of forecasters from different countries around the world. They all shared one common interest—trying to out-guess Mother Nature. Given the complex and demanding nature of this pursuit, it is not surprising that it seemed that most of these people were passionately devoted to this endeavor.

We thought it might be of interest to digress for a moment to talk about the background of one forecaster who works so hard at providing these services.

Lee Chesneau is a good example of the type of person you find working a forecast desk at the Marine Prediction Center. We'll let Lee tell you in his own words: "I first got interested in weather when I was exposed to a severe lightning storm in my early childhood years in New York City. My family then moved to Miami, Florida when I was

The life of a marine forecaster is rarely dull—Mother Nature sees to that. Here Lee Chesneau checks satellite images, upper level vorticity, and what the Medium Range Forecast model says about the next 48 hours while he talks on the phone to a counterpart in the Tropical Prediction Center.

starting elementary school. Hurricanes were a big deal in South Florida, and when Hurricane Donna struck the Florida Keys in 1960, it caused significant wind and flooding damage to the Miami area and forever ignited the spark that led to an incurable fever for weather forecasting.

"I used to hang around the National Hurricane Center as a young teen and got to know many of the hurricane forecasters. Their encouragement provided additional motivation for me to earn a meteorology degree and pursue a career in weather forecasting.

Lee graduated in 1972 from one of the top universities for meteorology, the University of Wisconsin, and received a commission in the U.S. Navy. After a

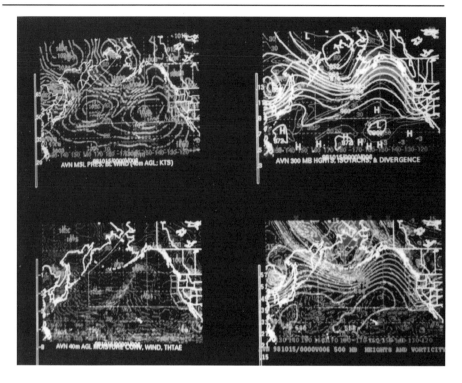

Talk about cool tools! Lee can display four different images at once on any of his three computer screens. This way he can compare different programs or different levels of the atmosphere (as in this view). These are available as loops, so the forecaster can see what the computer thinks is going to happen every six hours or so into the future.

The only problem with all of this data is knowing what to use and what to toss out. That is where the real-world experience of forecasters like Lee comes in. If you are trained on land-based weather it will take some time before you are proficient about what is happening at sea.

couple of years in Viet Nam on an aircraft carrier he finally started doing what he was trained for. "My official tours in the Navy took me to Rota, Spain, where I learned intimately about weather in the Mediterranean (and, incidentally, met my beautiful Spanish wife). I also served in Norfolk, Virginia, in the Meteorology and Oceanography Center, and aboard the USS Guam, another aircraft carrier, as Meteorology Officer.

Lee can call upon a variety of satellite images in all sorts of different visible and invisible wave lengths to confirm or refute what the computer models are telling him.

This is one of the most valuable tools, since it is a real-time definition of what is happening. Using early warning signs such as moisture vorticity (before cloud images are visible) Lee can figure out what is happening with the upper level troughs and if there are the ingredients for substantial surface development.

Lee left active naval service in 1979, and went to work in private industry for Oceanroutes, Inc., where he was exposed to forecasting and routing on a global scale. He also spent time in Anchorage, Alaska with NOAA's NESDIS satellite service, then went back to the U.S. Navy in Pearl Harbor, Hawaii as a civilian ship router where Lee "tracked weather patterns and ships over two-thirds of the globe in both North and South Pacific oceans, including the Northern and Southern Indian Oceans, and the Antarctic regions."

If you spend time with the professionals in this business, as we were privileged to do in writing this book, you will be impressed by the breadth of their knowledge and dedication. They typically work long, intense hours. Why do they do it? It seems to be a mixture of the challenge, helping others, and the thrill of watching weather systems develop—especially something like what you see on the adjacent page!

"It was in Pearl Harbor that I began to see the importance of direct interaction with the end consumer. I got to answer questions of Masters and their licensed crews about routing techniques and heavy weather avoidance. After a couple years in Hawaii, I accepted a position with the NWS in Seattle, WA with the NWS's Ocean Services Unit and spent 5 years with the Ocean Services Unit in Seattle, Washington. I primarily issued marine warnings and forecasts for coastal and inland waters in western Washington state and offshore waters (60 to 250 miles) off Washington and Oregon. This also included bar forecasts of Grays Harbor and the Columbia River. Other marine events such as tidal flooding (associated with astronomical high tides in conjunction with low pressure systems crossing western Washington) were part of the warning and forecast process, along with dangerous surf conditions affecting beachfront areas.

"With the evolution of the modernized NWS marine program, specifically involving high seas warnings and forecasts, SSB radiofacsimile broadcasts, and offshore forecasts, functions which were previously performed at local NWS forecast offices were transferred to the National Meteorological Center(NMC) and I moved back here in 1989."

Lee worked on a series of modernization programs at the MPC including upgrading the high frequency facsimile broadcasts to where they now broadcast surface and 500mb analysis and forecast out to 96 hours. (Even longer range forecast products are currently under development.)

Like many other forecasters, Lee is involved with teaching—both to professional mariners at the Maritime Institute of Technology and Graduate Studies (MITAGS) and with seminars at boat shows and on special weekends for cruising sailors.

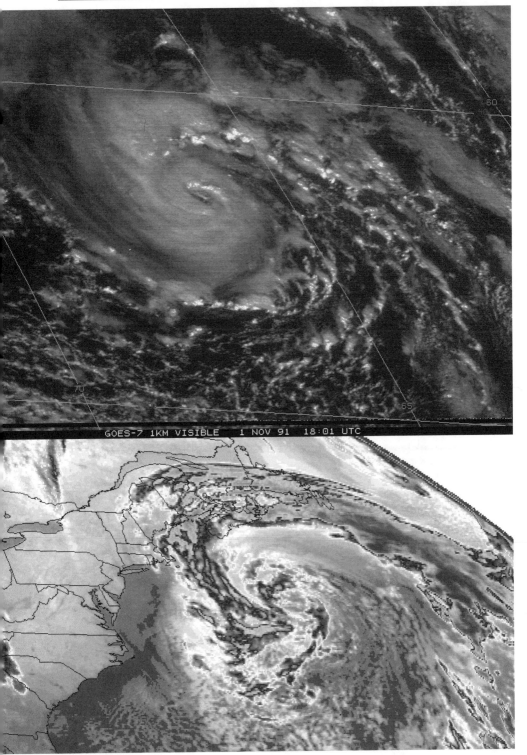

GOES-7 1KM VISIBLE   1 NOV 91 18:01 UTC

SURFACE FORECASTS

We've touched on the use of external forecasts, the problems that forecasters have in interpreting their somewhat limited data, and the time constraints in the system. Remember that sailing lore is replete with examples of forecasts that are 180 degrees wrong, a day late, or miss a good blow entirely.

It is worth repeating that it is always better to make your own analysis of what is happening, based on firsthand data. The weather fax or radio report should be considered as *just one bit of data* and used or modified after evaluating what your senses tell you.

COMMON TERMS

At the risk of repeating ourselves, let's revisit some common terms used with *surface forecasts* (and examine a few new ones) that you will see on fax charts and hear on broadcasts.

These symbols indicate the type of frontal on the weather fax charts, and the direction in which it is moving.

The point or round edge is oriented in the direction of movement. With the examples alongside, the movement would be to the top of the page.

Frontogenesis refers to the birth or formation of a front that occurs when two adjacent air masses with different densities and temperatures meet.

Frontolysis is just the opposite—the weakening or dissipation that happens when two adjacent air masses lose their contrasting properties (e.g. the density and temperature).

A *warm front* is the leading edge of a relatively warmer surface air mass that separates two different air masses. The differences in temperature and moisture are maximized in the frontal zone between the different masses of air.

Ahead of a normal warm front in the Northern Hemisphere, you will usually find that winds are from the southeast and that as the warm front passes the winds will shift to the southwest.

A *cold front* is the leading edge of a relatively cooler surface airmass that separates two airmasses in which there are major differences in temperature and moisture. In the Northern Hemisphere, winds ahead of the front will typically be southwest and shift into the northwest with frontal passage. In the Southern Hemisphere, the winds ahead of the cold front will usually be northwest and go to the southwest with the frontal passage.

Stationary front refers to a front that has not moved significantly from its previous analyzed position for a period of 24 hours or so.

An *occluded front* occurs as a union between two fronts when a cold front overtakes a warm front. This process usually leads to the dissipation of the front in which there is no longer a difference (gradient) in temperature and moisture.

A *ridge* refers to an area of high pressure, usually sticking out from a corner of a high pressure system—shown as a solid line on the chart. Sometimes these ridges will have strong winds associated with them, especially around the areas where the isobars have significant curvature.

——— ——— ——— ——— ——— ———

Troughs are a similar situation where an isobar makes a sharp bend (usually like a "u") around a low center. These typically have weather similar to the low or the fronts with which they are associated.

A *Col.* is an area between two pressure systems where there are no isobars. These are areas of very light winds, sometimes with thunderstorms if there is sufficient cold air aloft.

The lines on fax charts are called *isobars*. This is a fancy term for a line of equal pressure. The pressure is shown in millibars (mb), also called hecapascals hPa, and is usually drawn at 4mb (hPa) intervals.

You will hear lows described (or see them annotated) as *shallow* (usually with a central pressure above 1000mb), *moderate* (with a lowest pressure of 980 to 1000mb) or *intense* (with a barometric pressure below 980mb).

If the center of the low has its pressure rising, it is said to be *filling*. If the pressure is falling it is called *deepening* or *intensifying*. If two lows are associated within a single system, it is said to be *complex*.

If a low is said to be *rapidly intensifying*, this means an expected drop in surface pressure of at least 24 millibars within 24 hours.

An *anticylone* is another term for a high pressure system (rotating clockwise in the Northern Hemisphere and counterclockwise in the Southern).

A *cyclone* is another term for a low (rotating counterclockwisecounterclockwise in the Northern Hemisphere and clockwise in the Southern Hemisphere).

An *extratropical low* is a low pressure center (depression) that is outside of the tropics. Tropical cyclones occasionally evolve into extratropical lows losing tropical characteristics they initially had in the process (for more data on this see Tropical to Extratropical Transition of Hurricanes on page 471).

The term *new* may be used to forecast the position of a high or low pressure center where the center is expected to form by a specific time. For example, a surface synoptic chart might show a new low pressure center with an "X" at the location it is expected to form in 24 hours. This will be followed by the word *new*, and the date and time in UCT when the forecast service expects the low to be on the surface.

When you see or hear about a *developing gale* this refers to an extratropical low (in other words a low which is out of the tropics) that is expected to have areas of gale-force winds of 34 knots by a certain time period. If this occurs on a current surface fax chart, the weather service expects the gale-force winds within 36 hours. When developing gale is used on the 48-hour surface prognosis, the gale is expected within 72 hours. If you see this on a 96-hour prog chart, the gale is expected within 120 hours

A *gale* means an extratropical low or an area of sustained surface winds (one minute or longer duration) of 34 knots or greater.

A *developing storm* is an extratropical low from which storm-force winds of 48 knots or greater are projected by a certain time period. The time frames are the same as with a developing gale.

A storm refers to an extratropical low or an area of sustained winds (one minute) of more than 48 knots.

On marine forecasts there are several versions of fog used. Normally, the term *fog* is seen in the context of visibility cut to less than three miles, but more than one half a nautical mile.

The term *tropical wave* refers to a disturbance with a potential for development into a hurricane. These waves are typically shown as north-to-south-running heavy dashed lines.

Dense fog is where visibility is less than one half of a mile.

Finally, here are some generally used definitions for sea state. The combination of wind waves and swell is generally referred to as *seas*. The *primary swell* direction is that heading for the main swell system in a given area. Significant wave height is the average height (trough to crest—bottom to top) of the one-third highest waves.   *Swells* are wind waves that have moved out of wind generation area. Swells show a regular and longer period than wind waves.

RADIO FORECASTS

Radio reception is affected by:

❑ Sun-spot activity.

❑ On-board sources of interference.

❑ External static.

❑ Antenna gain.

❑ Time of day.

❑ Frequency.

Any time you are using a radio to receive high-frequency signals, voice or fax, you are subjected to the vagaries of the air waves.

Your ability to hear a given station will vary with the time of day, your distance from the station, frequency chosen, the level of sun-spot activity, and any interference on or near the broadcast frequency.

If this sounds like a lot of variables, you are right. That is why it is important to have a variety of stations to listen to as you travel. It may take several tries over a number of days before you find good reception.

Keep in mind that what you receive well in one location may be lost when you are 500 miles farther down the track.

As broadcast times, areas of coverage, and frequencies change, be sure you have the most up-to-date schedules for the region in which you will be cruising.

ANTENNA SELECTION

By far the most important factor in being able to hear weak stations is the type of antenna being used. The very best is a half-wave dipole. Next would be a long wire (i.e., a backstay) and, finally, some form of a whip.

The best antenna for reception is a half-wave dipole.

ONBOARD INTERFERENCE

If you have low levels of onboard static from electronics, engines or motors, these will mask weak signals. This is especially true with weather faxes where you don't always listen to the signal strength. If a weak signal is masked by onboard noise, no chart is received, and while it is common to blame this on atmospheric problems, the real issue may be homegrown.

The best way to determine if there is an onboard noise problem is to tune the radio to a weak signal, using earphones to listen, with every circuit on the boat turned off.

Then, turn on each electrical circuit, running whatever is on that circuit—one item at a time. Be sure to run all electrical motors, main engine, and any generators. If there is a problem, this process will find it.

To check onboard interference:

- ❏ *Turn up volume on weather fax receiver so it is easily heard.*
- ❏ *Turn off all electrical circuits, and shut down engines and generators.*
- ❏ *Bring one item at a time back on line while listening to audio signal.*

BAND CONDITIONS

Long-range radio waves travel by means of bouncing off the ionosphere layer. The angle and distance of the bounce is a function of how energized the ionosphere is by the sun. During periods of active sunspot generation, the ionosphere is really cooking, and radio propagation is good. When the sunspot cycle is low, propagation is poor. Since the sun activity typically runs in 11-year cycles, it is easy to know how this affects what you are doing—although solar flares will affect radio propagation for short periods of time.

At different times of the day, you will find better propagation on one frequency than on another. What works, and what doesn't, varies with your distance from the broadcasting station.

The key is to experiment. If you don't hear the broadcast on a given frequency, try different frequencies. If nothing at all is heard, wait until the next forecast a few hours later and try again.

RECEIVING VOICE FORECASTS

When Linda and I started cruising what weather forecasts we could find were always voice — either on the single-sideband (SSB), short wave radio, WWV or via ham.

Reception varied, and the data came at us so fast that it was frequently impossible to get all of it written down.

Tape record voice weather forecasts so they can be played back and listened to at leisure.

Then we purchased an inexpensive battery-powered tape recorder, and life became a lot simpler. We would make a recording of the forecast and transcribe it at our leisure.

If you have a weather fax aboard, you may still find voice forecasts of value. Instead of having to interpret the fax data on your own, the reader on the other end of the airwaves does the job for you. Even when you are doing your own interpretation, it is nice to get a second opinion (maybe there's a feature you missed).

NETS AND WEATHER RELAYS

There are a number of ham nets around the world that take the position and current conditions for cruising yachts on passage in their region.

The location and conditions being encountered are frequently far more valuable than forecasts based on a theoretical computer model.

However, you have to quantify the quality of the

reporting. If the vessel checking in is reporting bad weather, this could mean 25 knots or 50 knots, depending on their experience level and what they consider nasty. You need to sort out between true wind speed and apparent. If the boat is beating, or reaching, then the wind speed read on the anemometer will be higher than the true wind speed if the boat were stopped.

Just the opposite is true when sailing off the wind—apparent wind is then less than true wind.

You also need to take barometric pressures with a grain of salt, unless the barometer on the reporting vessel has been recently calibrated. However, as we have said before, what is critical is the rate of change of the barometer, not the absolute reading.

We like to listen in over a period of days, and then develop a feel for the *quality* of the data being reported by different boats. We make a check-in sheet each day, with boat name, position and conditions. Once we have the data, we reassemble the check-in data geographically so that positions that are close to each other can be compared.

Many of the ham nets have shore stations who are skilled in analyzing weather data, and have a variety of information at their fingertips from the Internet.

However, you need to get a feel for the quality of this reporting as well, and that only comes with time and talking with other folks.

Figuring out marine weather is an acquired skill at which some shore-based stations are better than others.

Always quantify the quality of the weather advice being broadcast. Weather radio nets, and data from other vessels may not be totally reliable.

THE WEATHER FAX

The weather fax can give you all sorts of information—from synoptic charts of current surface and upper-air condition to 24-, 48-, and 96-hour prognosis charts. You will also find data on sea state and surface sea temperature, along with satellite images.

Most important are upper-level synoptic charts—an extremely valuable tool (see the next section, beginning on page 118, for more data on this subject).

The only problem is that some of this data is based on computer models, satellite radar and infrared images, with a scarcity of real-time ship or buoy reports on wind direction, speed, or barometric pressure. As such, sometimes it is not as accurate as we would all like it to be. Yet the weather fax remains one of the very best tools we can have aboard for using and/or avoiding the weather.

So you have to keep your eyes open, and compare your present wind direction, strength, and pressure to what is shown on the chart. If there's a difference between your conditions and the fax, obviously you have the accurate data and what is shown on the synoptic chart is incorrect. The next question to answer is; What causes the difference?

DEDICATED FAX OR COMPUTER?

There are two ways to go with fax receiver. One is to have a dedicated set like the Furuno #208. This set has its own receiver, usually uses a separate antenna, and has a memory loaded with the current frequencies of every fax station in the world.

It allows automatic recording with a timer of multiple stations and frequencies. It also has a feature that will look for the strongest signal of a given station—selecting from among the three or four frequencies in its memory. This works well when

Weather faxes are only one part of the total picture. Always take what they show with a grain of salt. If local conditions are different it is better to believe what you are experiencing rather than what the fax shows.

conditions are good, but in marginal conditions, the set will often lock onto noise, rather than a fax signal.

In marginal conditions, we leave the external volume turned up so that we can hear what is going on with the audio signal. As the fax broadcast has a very definite sound to it, you can easily tell if the receiver has locked onto a strong signal or just interference of some sort.

The alternate way to go is with a portable computer, a special modem, and a connection to an all-band receiver, ham or SSB rig. (For more data on this see the section on forecasting tools starting on page 560).

This approach has the advantage of allowing you to manipulate the images with the computer once they are received.

We've sat next to another yacht, with both of us receiving the same signal, and then compared images, and those on the computer have always looked better than our fax-paper versions.

However, there are several problems with this approach. To begin with, there is frequently a conflict between the ham/SSB schedules and fax times. So a choice has to be made. Next, the computer-based systems are inherently more complex and difficult to operate. We'd guess that at least two-thirds of the yachts we've met with computer-based systems don't use them because of this difficulty.

Our own advice is to use a dedicated set if you can afford it — and we'd put this extra cost ahead of a lot of other gear commonly found aboard cruising yachts.

Using a weather fax in marginal conditions:

- Turn up volume and listen to the signal.
- Try alternate frequencies.
- Try alternate times.
- Shut down all on-board electrical systems to see if there is a noise problem.

AT THE BEGINNING OF A PASSAGE

To make the best use of fax data on a passage, it is our habit to run the fax for several weeks prior to departure. We start out with the primary station, and leave it on for 24 hours or so. This ensures that we will get the current schedule of times and coverage, and gives us a feel for what time of day is best for reception.

Once we have this data in hand, we'll switch to a secondary station and repeat the process.

Then, we like to program the fax timer so that the charts in which we are most interested are recorded automatically. We run these for a couple of days to make sure we've got the time and band conditions right, and to get a feel for the flow of the weather.

Occasionally, you will find that the synoptic charts are right on the money. But more often than not, they will be off by quite a bit. However, even inaccurate fax charts provide some useful information. This information can help you interpret what you are experiencing. Perhaps a front has speeded up or tightened its pressure gradient, and that is why you are seeing more wind.

Before starting a passage:

❑ *Check out prima-ry fax station for 24 hours.*

❑ *Check out sec-ondary station for 24 hours.*

❑ *Verify charts against current conditions.*

SYMBOLS

Fax chart symbols are pretty much standardized. However, there will be a bit of variation from time to time, especially where the charts are hand drawn as opposed to computer generated.

It makes sense to check in with the local meteoro-logical bureau to ascertain their current standards.

Following are a series of commonly used symbols (in addition to those at the beginning of the chapter) found on your fax-charts.

Clear SCT BKN OVC Obscure Missing

When there is a reporting station at sea level you will find one of the above symbols near the wind arrow or on the end of the wind arrow. These indicate the cloud conditions observed.

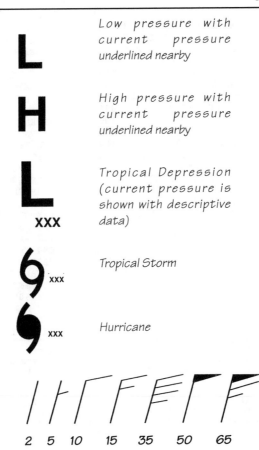

L *Low pressure with current pressure underlined nearby*

H *High pressure with current pressure underlined nearby*

L **xxx** *Tropical Depression (current pressure is shown with descriptive data)*

xxx *Tropical Storm*

xxx *Hurricane*

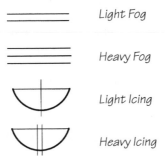

| 2 | 5 | 10 | 15 | 35 | 50 | 65 |

Wind feathers indicate the strength (in knots) and direction of the wind. The head of the arrow (without feathers) points in the wind direction. A single small barb is five knots. A single long barb is ten knots. A flag is 50 knots (the feather to the right is for 65 knots). When the head of the feather has a circle this indicates the report is from a ship or buoy.

Light Fog

Heavy Fog

Light Icing

Heavy Icing

NOAA NATIONAL WEATHER SERVICE WASHINGTON D.C.
RADIOFACSIMILE SCHEDULE TRANSMITTED VIA
U.S.C.G. BOSTON, MASSACHUSETTS (NMF) 08 SEP 98

TIME	AREA	CHART	TIME	AREA	CHART
0230Z		TEST PATTERN	0925Z	2	06Z SFC ANAL PART 1
0233Z	1	00Z PRELIM SFC ANAL	0938Z	3	06Z SFC ANAL PART 2
0243Z		SCHEDULE PART 1	0951Z	6	SATELLITE PICTURE
0254Z		SCHEDULE PART 2	1002Z	2	RETRANSMIT 0925Z
0305Z		REQ FOR COMMENTS	1015Z	3	RETRANSMIT 0938Z
0315Z	1	00Z SEA STATE ANAL	1028Z		END TRANSMISSION
0325Z	2	00Z SFC ANAL PART 1	1430Z		TEST PATTERN
0338Z	3	00Z SFC ANAL PART 2	1433Z	1	12Z PRELIM SFC ANAL
0351Z	5	SATELLITE PICTURE	1443Z	4	96HR 500 MB VT 00Z
0402Z	2	RETRANSMIT 0325Z	1453Z	4	96HR SFC VT 00Z
0415Z	3	RETRANSMIT 0338Z	1503Z	5	SATELLITE PICTURE
0428Z	4	00Z 500MB ANALYSIS	1515Z	1	12Z SEA STATE ANAL
0438Z		END TRANSMISSION	1525Z	2	12Z SFC ANAL PART 1
0800Z		TEST PATTERN	1538Z	3	12Z SFC ANAL PART 2
0805Z	1	06Z PRELIM SFC ANAL	1551Z		END TRANSMISSION
0815Z	1	24HR SFC VT 00Z	1720Z		TEST PATTERN
0825Z	1	24HR WIND/SEA VT 00Z	1723Z	2	RETRANSMIT 1525Z
0835Z	1	24HR 500MB VT 00Z	1736Z	3	RETRANSMIT 1538Z
0845Z	4	36HR 500MB VT 12Z	1749Z	4	12Z 500MB ANALYSIS
0855Z	4	48HR SFC VT 00Z	1759Z	4	12Z SEA STATE ANAL
0905Z	4	48HR SEA VT 00Z	1809Z		END TRANSMISSION
0915Z	4	48HR 500MB VT 00Z	CONTINUED		ON SCHEDULE PART 2

NOAA NATIONAL WEATHER SERVICE WASHINGTON D.C.
RADIOFACSIMILE SCHEDULE PART ONE TRANSMITTED VIA
U.S.C.G. PT. REYES, CALIFORNIA (NMC) 08 SEP 98

TIME	AREA	CHART	TIME	AREA	CHART
0245Z		TEST PATTERN	1100Z		TEST PATTERN
0248Z	7	SATELLITE PICTURE	1104Z		SCHEDULE PART 1
0259Z	5	SATELLITE PICTURE	1115Z		SCHEDULE PART 2
0310Z	1	00Z SEA STATE ANAL	1126Z		REQUEST FOR COMMENTS
0320Z	2	00Z SFC ANAL PART 1	1137Z		PRODUCT NOTICE BULLETIN
0333Z	3	00Z SFC ANAL PART 2	1148Z	9	RETRANSMIT 2304Z
0345Z	2	RETRANSMIT 0320Z	1158Z	6	RETRANSMIT 2314Z
0358Z	3	RETRANSMIT 0323Z	1208Z		END TRANSMISSION
0410Z	1	00Z 500 MB ANALYSIS	1415Z		TEST PATTERN
0420Z		END TRANSMISSION	1418Z	1	96HR 500 MB VT 00Z
0815Z		TEST PATTERN	1428Z	1	96HR SFC VT 00Z
0818Z	8	24HR SFC VT 00Z	1438Z	5	SATELLITE PICTURE
0828Z	8	24HR WIND/SEA VT 00Z	1449Z	6	SATELLITE PICTURE
0838Z	1	48HR 500 MB VT 00Z	1500Z	8	12Z SEA STATE ANAL
0848Z	1	48HR SFC VT 00Z	1510Z	4	12Z TROPICAL ANALYSIS
0858Z	1	48HR SEA VT 00Z	1520Z	2	12Z SFC ANAL PART 1
0908Z	7	SATELLITE PICTURE	1533Z	3	12Z SFC ANAL PART 2
0919Z	2	06Z SFC ANAL PART 1	1545Z	2	RETRANSMIT 1520Z
0932Z	3	06Z SFC ANAL PART 2	1558Z	3	RETRANSMIT 1533Z
0944Z	5	SATELLITE PICTURE	1610Z	1	12Z 500 MB ANALYSIS
0955Z	2	RETRANSMIT 0919Z	1620Z		END TRANSMISSION
1008Z	3	RETRANSMIT 0932Z	CONTINUED		ON
1020Z		END TRANSMISSION	SCHEDULE		PART TWO

FREQUENCIES: DAY = 8682, 12730, 17151.2, 22527 KHZ
NIGHT = 8682, 12730, 17151.2, 4346 KHZ
CARRIER FREQUENCY IS 1.9 KHZ BELOW ASSIGNED FREQUENCY

Here are a couple of typical fax broadcast schedules—the top is from the US Coast Guard station in Boston and the lower from the USCG in Point Reyes, California. While these schedules are available on the Internet and in various books, the best way to get them is to turn on the fax.

Note that the time of the fax broadcast schedule is usually constant (although the rest of the schedule may change on occasion).

SAMPLE FAX CHARTS

Following are a series of fax charts that we have digitized from those we have actually received aboard a vessel at sea. These will give you an idea of the quality available.

We find that satellite images are most useful near the equator, and when getting a feel for tropical disturbances. In this image you can see remnants of a tropical depression off the coast of Baja California, between the 120 and 130 longitude lines.

The image opposite was received a few pages later in the transmission. This one shows more detail along the Pacific Coast. Note the frontal cloud band closing in on Northern California.

Later on, in the section on a passage between Nuka Hiva in the Marquesas and San Diego, California, (on page 423), you will see a greater selection of what you can expect in the way of faxes—the good and the bad when you are at sea.

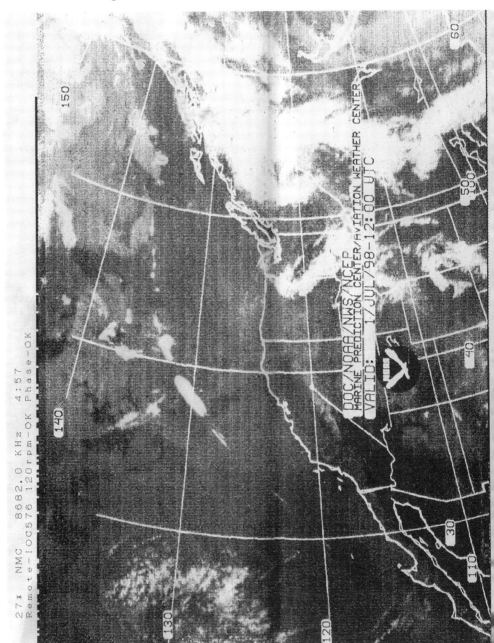

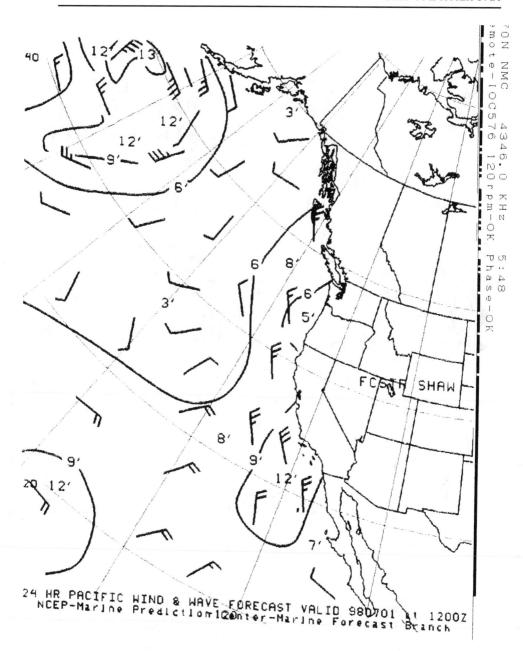

A 24-hour surface wind and wave forecast. Wave heights are shown in feet. International charts have wave heights shown in meters. This gives you a rough idea of what to expect. However, the detailed prognosis ("prog") charts are more valuable as you can check the barometric pressures against current conditions to get a feel for timing.

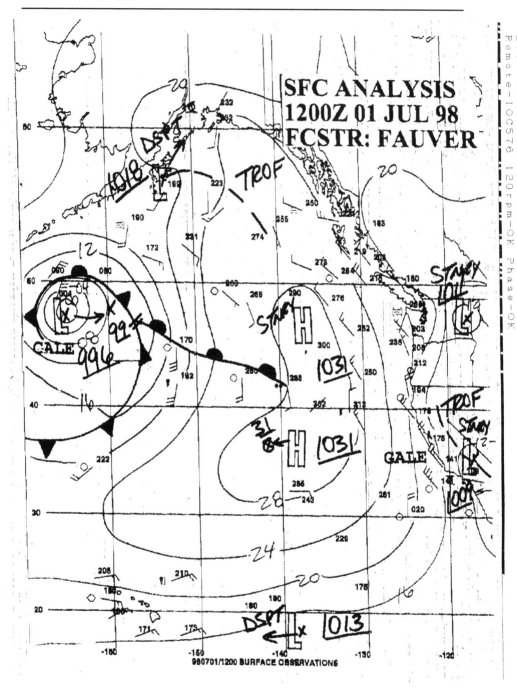

A typical surface chart. In the U.S. wind arrows indicate surface wind strength and direction. Many other countries just put in the isobars, and leave the strength/direction analysis to you.

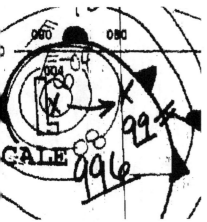

Here are a series of blowups from the fax chart on the left. This is the low center on the middle left of the chart. Notice there is an "x" in the center of the low, with an arrow pointing east to another "x". The second "x" is the projected position of the low in 24 hours. The handwritten 996 represents the projected pressure at that point.

The segment below is from the coast. It shows a stationary ("STNRY") trough ("TROF") of low pressure just in from the coast. This low pressure, working with the high to the west, is what is causing the gale conditions along the coast.

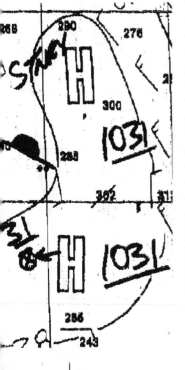

The segment to the left is from the center of the fax chart and represents the middle of the Pacific High. Note there are two high centers. The upper (northern) is stationary ("STNRY"). The southern high center is projected to move somewhat west to the "x" within the circle.

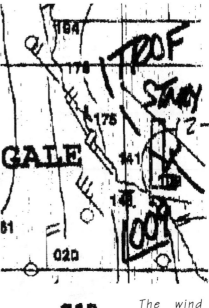

The wind feather (left) indicates wind speed (20 knots) and the last two whole digits plus tenths of barometric pressure (in this case 1020.0mb)

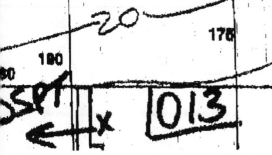

This segment (left) is from the bottom middle of the fax. It shows a dissipating ("DSPT") low. The 1013mb center is shown by the arrow to be moving west.

107

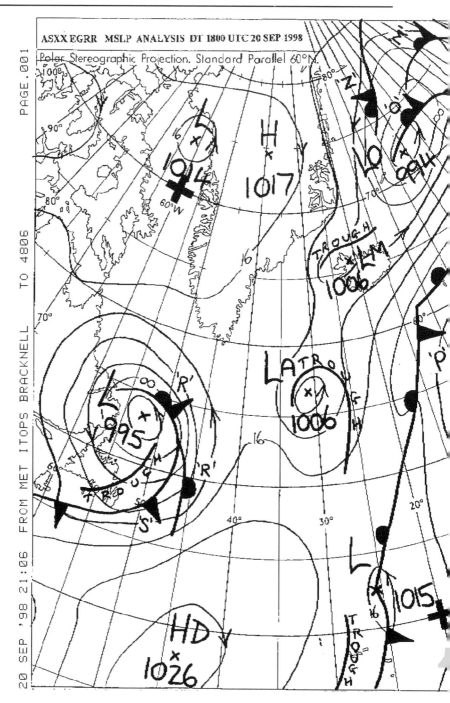

A United Kingdom surface chart. The biggest difference compared to the U.S. charts is the lack of wind feathers. However, they do provide a "geostrophic wind scale" that you can use (see the lower right hand corner).

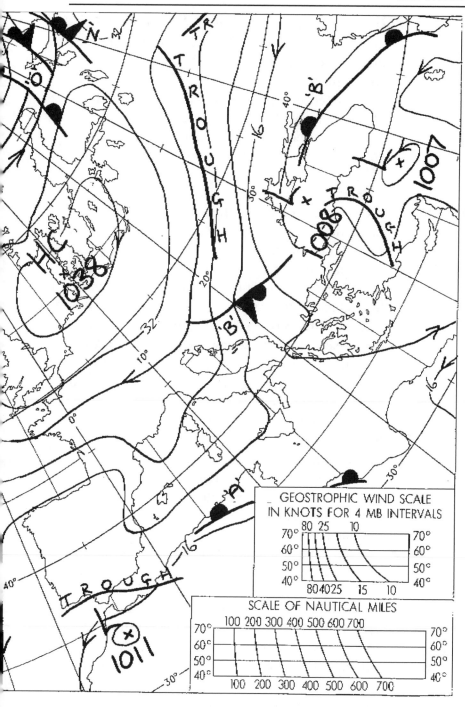

This chart covers all of the Central and Eastern Atlantic, down as far as the Mediterranean Sea. Forty-eight hour and 96-hour prognosis charts are also broadcast.

INTERPRETING SURFACE FAX CHARTS

You already know that the closer the isobar spacing, the stronger the winds. There will be wind arrows placed on the chart signifying direction and wind speed in most cases. But some charts are drawn simply with the isobar lines. In this situation, you can use the graph on the corner of the chart (if you can read it), or data similar to the table on page 113.

Here are some other issues to consider:

The isobars drawn on the charts are averages of the actual pressure lines. As such, they tend to smooth out the kinks over small distances. However, the wind you experience still has those kinks!

If there is terrain in the area—such as mountains, high islands, or large expanses of flat land—this may not be reflected in the fax chart. However, all of these features do affect how the wind blows. Land with its increased surface friction reduces wind speeds, but some geographic features compress and accelerate wind flow.

When you have solar heating and thermals building over land, a sea breeze will develop that may fight or reinforce the larger scale pressure gradients. Again, this usually does not show up on the fax charts, nor does the tendency for winds to flow downslope from mountain valleys during the evening (*katabatic* wind).

When there is significant curvature in the isobars wind will accelerate around the *corners* of a high by as much as 15% to 25% above what the isobar spacing would normally indicate. Around a low pressure system, the curvature correction is just the opposite—it reduces wind speed by 15% to 25%.

If the isobars curve gently, then little or no correction is required. If they have an abrupt change in direction, then more correction is required.

Issues which may not show up on fax charts:

❑ Compression against high terrain.

❑ Reinforcement by afternoon (thermal-based) sea breezes.

❑ Reinforcement by evening land breeze.

❑ Significant curvature in isobars (in highs wind is increased.

❑ With lows corners in isobars decrease wind.

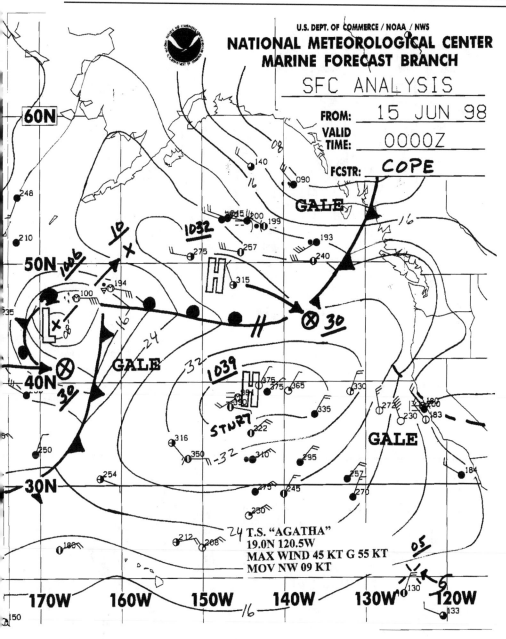

Here is another a typical NOAA fax chart for the Eastern Pacific. Note that most of the wind feathers have circles on their ends, indicating these are conditions reported by buoys or ships. As the high presses up against the coast near San Francisco, there's a tightening of the isobars indicating that some breeze is likely. The forecaster has been kind enough to indicate a gale is in progress!

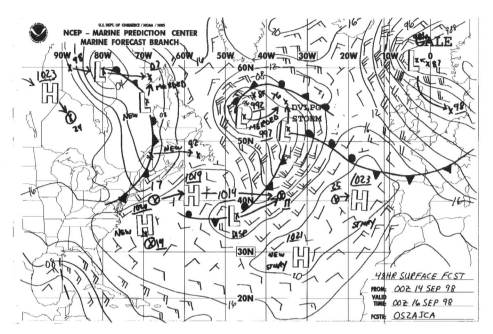

These are 48- and 96-hour surface prognosis faxes. While they must be taken with a grain of salt, they are useful for planning purposes. We mark colored Xs to indicate where we expect to be at the projected time of the chart, and then see how the weather is going to look. These are more complex to look at than the simplistic prognosis chart presented earlier, but the data is more valuable.

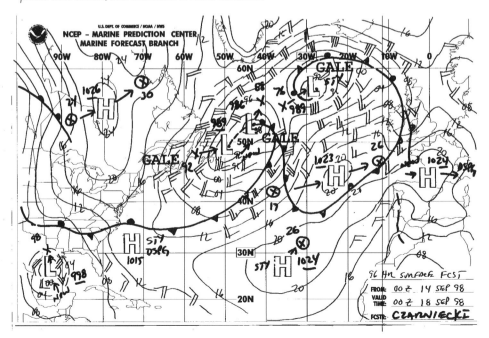

LATITUDE	DISTANCE (NAUTICAL MILES)												
	20	25	30	35	40	45	50	60	80	100	150	200	300
10°										133	89	67	44
20°							136	113	85	68	45	34	23
30°				131	115	102	92	77	57	46	31	23	15
40°			119	102	89	80	72	60	45	36	24	18	12
50°		121	101	86	75	67	60	50	38	30	21	15	10
60°	132	105	88	75	66	59	53	44	33	26	18	13	9
70°	122	98	81	70	61	54	49	41	31	24	16	12	8
80°	118	93	79	67	59	52	47	39	29	24	16	12	8
90°	115	92	77	66	57	51	46	38	29	23	15	11	8

You can use this chart to calculate the wind speed expected based on the standard 4mb spacing between isobars. Measure the distance between isobars in nautical miles, then look up your latitude. For example, if there is 150 miles spacing at 30 degrees latitude, you would expect steady winds of 31 knots (gusting higher of course). Between the latitudes shown, interpolate that at 35 degrees and 150 miles spacing, the wind speed would be 27.5 knots.

Coriolis, changing the direction of wind flow, acts as a drag on the wind. As a result, the closer you get to the poles, where Coriolis is strongest, the closer the spacing of isobars must be for a given amount of wind.

The opposite is true as you close with the equator, where Coriolis is weak or non-existent. Very wide isobar spacing will create extremely strong winds.

DEG LAT	20°	30°	40°	50°
1	78 gust 116	54 gust 80	42 gust 62	36 gust 52
2	39 gust 58	27 gust 40	21 gust 31	18 gust 26
3	26 gust 39	18 gust 26	14 gust 20	12 gust 18
4	19 gust 30	14 gust 20	10 gust 15	9 gust 13
5	16 gust 23	10 gust 16	8 gust 13	7 gust 10

Here's a different way of looking at things—in this case, measure the distance in degrees between 4mb isobars, and then enter the table for your latitude.

COMPRESSION ZONES

As lows and highs do their dances across the oceans, their speed and spacing is constantly changing. Since lows typically move faster than highs, they frequently overtake a high pressure system moving at a more stately pace somewhere to the east.

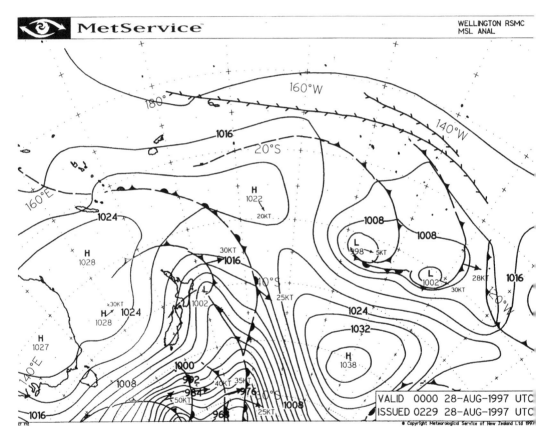

A classic squash zone between a high, in this case to the east of New Zealand, and a huge depression moving in from the Tasman Sea between New Zealand and Australia. This would not be a good place to be sailing right now! The high is indicated as stable; i.e., not moving. So the storm-strength winds in this region are going to continue for some time. Remember that in this situation the barometer will remain steady as the isobars squash together and the wind increases.

When this occurs the isobars on both high and low are compressed. The compression or tightening of the isobar spacing significantly increases the pressure gradient and wind speed.

If you find yourself sailing along someday with a steady barometer and a rising wind, the odds are you are sailing parallel to an isobar line in a compression zone.

TROPICAL AND SUBTROPICAL LOWS

It is worth repeating that subtropical lows that appear quite innocuous and of relatively high pressure can quickly mature into significant storms. Obviously, these need to be watched with the greatest of care.

When these lows move out of the tropics or subtropics they import energy from cool, dry high pressure weather with which they come into contact. When this occurs, a small, harmless indication of low pressure can create gales in the tradewind belt in a matter of hours.

❏ Compression zones account for a large percentage of severe weather encountered by cruisers.

❏ In a compression zone there will be little or no change in the barometer as the wind increases.

Watch tropical lows with care, especially when there is dry, cool high pressure air with which they could come into contact.

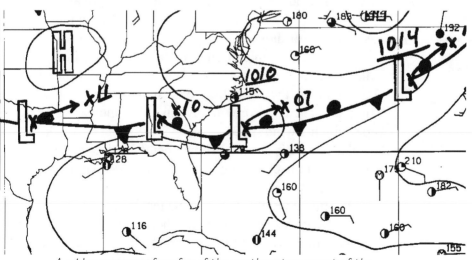

A mid-summer surface fax of the southeastern coast of the U.S. The subtropical low and associated front sitting off Georgia and the Carolinas will bear close watching. The warm waters of the Gulf Stream will provide energy, and if some cool, dry air from Canada works its way south, you could have a serious blow on your hands.

ISOBAR CURVATURE AND WIND SPEED

Before we leave the subject of interpeting fax charts we should come back to the question of isobar curvature and wind speed.

Because of Coriolis forces, the shape of the isobars tend to accelerate and decelerate wind speeds.

This is an area which is often missed by forecasters, so you will want to keep an eye on wind speeds in these areas as they are likely to vary substantially from what you read or hear on the forecasts.

You may want to search out these areas for more wind if things are light, or to find patches of lighter winds when the breeze is a bit strong.

The details of the principle are relatively simple.With depressions, curvature which is cyclonic (i.e. in the same direction as the low is rotating) reduces wind speed. If the curvature is anticyclonic, this will increase the wind speed.

With highs the opposite is true. Anticylonic curvature (i.e. in the same direction as the high is rotating) increases wind speed and cyclonic curvature reduces wind speed. This sounds more complicated than it really is, as a quick glance at the following sketches will show.

There are a couple of other factors that enter into this. One is the pressure gradient. The steeper the gradient, i.e. the closer the isobar spacing, the more impact the curvature will have in either increasing or reducing wind speed.

The second is latitude. The higher the latitude, the more the impact and the lower the latitude, the less impact there will be.

One final thought. You may be tempted to ignore these "wrinkles" in the isobars when cruising if they do not affect your safety or comfort. However, keep in mind that very substantial gains in boat speed can be had when winds are light by playing these correctly.

Isobar curvature rules for depressions:

❑ Curvature which is in the same direction as wind flow reduces wind speed.

❑ Curvature which is against the direction of wind flow (i.e. a "hollow" in the isobar) increases wind speed.

Isobar curvature rules for highs:

❑ Curves which tighten in the same direction as wind flow increase wind speed.

❑ Curves which are the reverse of wind flow (hollows in the isobars) reduce wind flow.

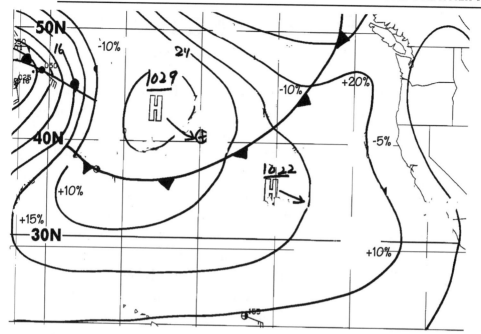

The North Pacific high is a semi-permanent feature which moves, bulges, and contracts. When you are sailing to or from Hawaii the ripples in the isobars can have a major impact on your passage. If you are racing, how you play these will determine how well you place.

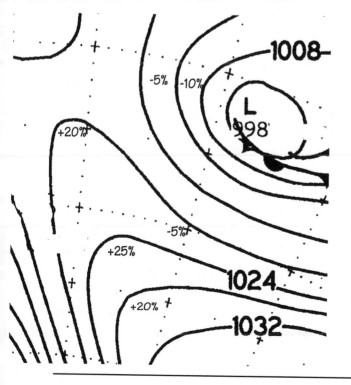

Southern Hemisphere example (lower left)—In this case, we have a high pressure to the south interacting with a modest low on the equator side.

The high ridge sticking out towards the northwest will have substantial acceleration around the corner, and then slight deceleration where the curvature reverses a little to the southwest. The areas between these two systems will see increased wind from compression, but that is a different issue.

FORECASTING IN THREE DIMENSIONS

The key to success-ful analysis, fore-casting, and tactics is understanding the structure of weather. Knowledge of how the upper atmosphere relates to the surface is central to this. Even without a weather fax this knowledge will help you puzzle out the message in the sky, barometer and sea state.

Up to this point we have talked about weather mainly as a two-dimensional phenomenon. This is the way we see it on the surface fax charts just discussed and, of course, how we experience it on land or water.

But a moment's thought will make it clear that the weather we experience is at the bottom of the earth's atmosphere—and that there is lots going on above us that affects everything below.

This three-dimensional concept is key to all forecast models. If you understand it, and then work with it in the form of 500mb fax charts, you will be far ahead of where you are when using only surface charts.

What follows are the basics of weather in three dimensions. This is material that is not ordinarily covered in marine (or popular) texts, yet forms the very core of every successful forecasting system. It is what the race-winning routers use, what the professionally-trained government meteorologists base their forecasts on, and what all ship routers employ before sending off recommendations to their ship captain clients.

We urge you to study this material at length, until you fully understand it. While it may take several passes through this section of the book, we promise that, when awareness finally hits you, when you have reached the stage of enlightenment as it relates to upper levels of the atmosphere, nothing on the sea will ever seem the same again—and you will passage with an understanding of weather that will add immeasurably to your safety and comfort.

3-D LOW STRUCTURE

With a low pressure system, the closer you come to the center, the lower the atmospheric pressure. Because this pressure is low relative to the surrounding area, air from regions of higher pressure rushes in to try to balance things out.

If the low were a two-dimensional structure, shallow in height (the way it appears on a surface fax chart), over a relatively short period of time the pressure differential between highs and lows would even out, there would be no wind, and the weather would always be stable.

This simplistic view is what we have discussed in the section on fronts (page 40).

Now think of the surface low as a giant vacuum cleaner, one of the old canister styles that is placed on end (vertically). When the air is sucked into the vacuum cleaner it has to exhaust somewhere. If you cover the vacuum cleaner's exhaust at the top with your hand, no suction can occur because there is nowhere for the air being sucked in at the bottom to escape.

This is precisely the same thing that occurs with a surface low. It needs a place to vent out what it sucks in at the surface. In order for the low pressure system to deepen and grow stronger, a mechanism is required to vent the high pressure rushing in.

This venting mechanism is provided by the upper atmosphere. When properly established, the upper atmosphere not only vents the surface low, but by providing additional suction over the top of the surface low, works to promote its development.

In fact, most surface low pressure systems start as upper-level disturbances.

As the surface low goes through its life cycle, the central pressure continues to fall for a period of time, before stabilizing and beginning to fill.

With a fax, and the ability to receive upper level charts, you can assess risk factors at any given time. Long before the forecasters have put anything on the surface charts you can detect the possibility of severe weather—if certain trends continue.

This advance warning is invaluable for preparation. It gives you significantly more time in which to maneuver out of the way.

Making an early jog in your course—as insurance based on upper level analysis—can result in a substantial reduction in your weather risks.

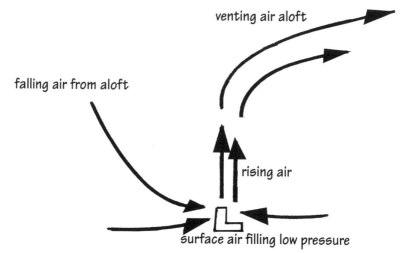

Surface air converges around the low center, then rises up to where it diverges out. Note the upper-right arrow is bent around to indicate it is diverging out with the upper level wind flow (if the arrow were straight it would imply diverging into the upper level wind, which it cannot do).

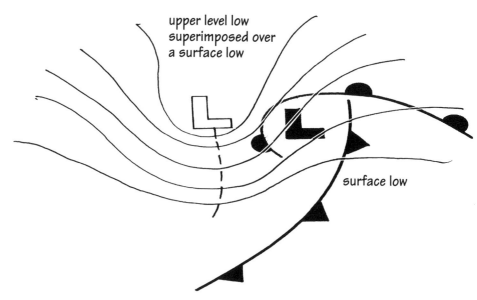

The upper-level low is shown here to the west of the surface low (the surface low has a cold and warm front attached to the center). Note the relationship between the two systems. The upper-level low is to the west of the surface. This is what it would look like in the early phase of development.

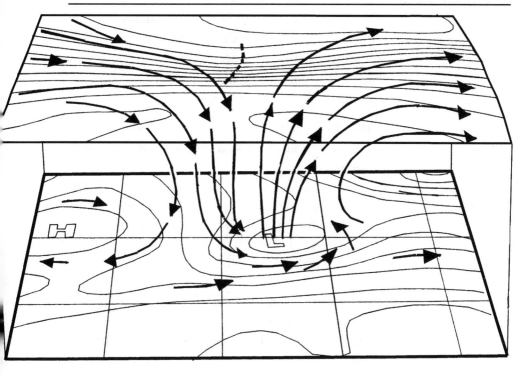

Here is another view of the way surface convergence and upper level divergence work with low pressure systems.

To begin with, a vacuum at upper altitude provides a place for the surface low to vent. If the upper altitude venting is faster than air is coming in at the surface, the central pressure of the surface low drops. Surface wind then accelerates inward (converges) trying to balance out the lower pressure.

The size, shape, wind speed, and orientation of the upper-level divergence gives us clues as to how the surface low will behave.

This cycle is directly related to what is happening in the upper atmosphere.

The stronger the venting, the faster the pressure falls, and the stronger the surface winds are around the surface low pressure center.

When the upper atmosphere no longer provides venting action, the surface low fills, the pressure of the central area rises, and winds decrease.

If we can get a handle on the mechanics of this upper-air process, we are a long way towards understanding what is likely to happen at the surface—both in the near term, and out a day or two in the future.

DIVERGENCE

Let's talk now about a process meteorologists call divergence.

If the upper levels of the atmosphere are diverging, or spreading out, they are in effect reducing the pressure in the region from which they have diverged. As divergence takes place, air is pulled up from the surface to try to balance out the upper-level pressure drop. This will create a surface low, or strengthen one which already exists.

The manner in which this upper-level divergence takes place—the shape and speed of it—is directly related to what we see happening at the surface.

If there is rapid divergence, then there will be a rapid pressure fall in surface weather features. On the other hand, if divergence is weak, an existing surface low will end up unable to vent itself and eventually fill and dissipate.

Fortunately the process by which this divergence takes place is reasonably well understood and reported in upper level fax charts.

3-D HIGH STRUCTURE

In the case of a surface high pressure system just the opposite is happening. The surface high pressure is the result of a heavy column of air sitting over it. This means air is colder, and therefore more dense (heavier) than the warmer and lighter air of the core of a low.

This high pressure structure is maintained into the mid levels of the atmosphere.

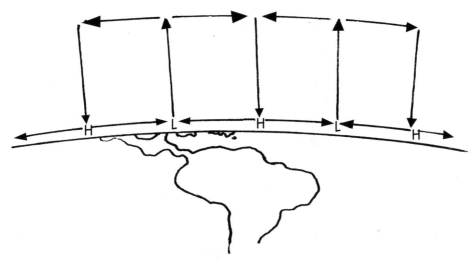

The atmosphere is made up of a series of highs and lows, each a product of divergence and convergence. As you can see here, the surface winds converge on a low, rise up, diverge outward, and eventually converge and drop down to form a surface high.

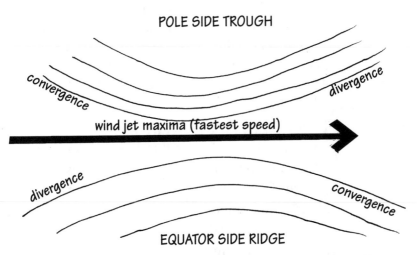

Here's a another view of the way the upper atmosphere sorts itself out. We start out with a high-speed wind jet. On the poleward side there is cold air which, being more dense and therefore heavier, is lower in height for a given pressure.

On the equator side, the air is warmer, so the heights for a given amount of pressure are higher.

For the cold, pole side, the winds diverge on the downwind side and converge on the upwind side. On the warm side, the winds diverge on the upwind side and diverge on the downwind side.

CONVERGENCE

The colder, denser air converges, and then because it is denser than the surrounding atmosphere it falls. This convergence process is what creates our surface high pressure systems. The converging dense air falls to the surface and then diverges out from the center of the high.

Of course this higher pressure air has to go somewhere. It diverges away from the center of the high — in other words moves outward — and then converges on the center of a surface low, at which point it is vented back up into the upper altitudes where it diverges away from the central core of the low and eventually forms a high to converge around at upper altitude.

This is the process which keeps the earth's atmosphere in balance which we described in the first section on what creates the weather (page 29). The vagaries of this process are what give us the clues to project what our surface weather is likely to do.

By understanding this process we have excellent indicators of when real trouble is possible — giving us valuable advance warning with which to prepare ourselves.

UPPER-LEVEL WESTERLIES

In general, it can be said that the upper-level winds in the mid to high latitudes flow in a west-to-east pattern. The speed of this flow can vary from 20 to 30 knots to hundreds of knots if the jet stream is involved. The speed of flow is a function of temperature contrasts aloft. The more contrast, the more wind speed (we'll discuss this in more detail a little later in the section on the jet stream, page 182).

If this wind flow was constant in speed and direction, there would probably be no need to read this book.

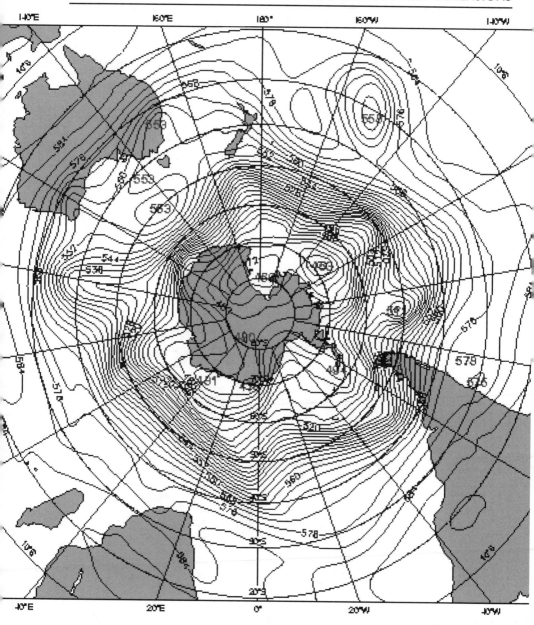

This is a polar view of the earth's weather, looking at things in the Southern Hemisphere. This is a 500mb height chart (which we'll discuss in more detail in the following pages). What we want to show right now is the meandering nature of the upper - level westerly winds, clearly show in this view.

However, these upper-level wind flows act much like a river or stream of water on a smooth surface. They move this way and that, driven by a variety of forces—principally temperature differential and Coriolis.

MEANDERING UPPER-LEVEL WINDS

On first impression these upper level meanders appear chaotic. But if you study them over time, a rhythm begins to appear. The winds bend and flow in waves, and the shape of these waves gives rise to areas of divergence and convergence.

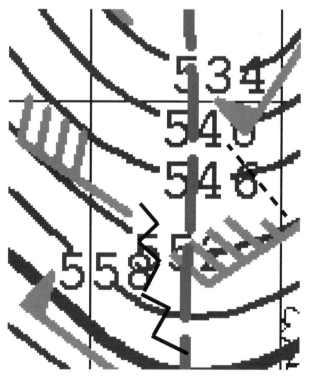

Here's a detail of the previous chart. A trough is shown with the dashed line. This is an area of warmer air.

To the east of the trough and west of the ridge, you will find divergence. Conversely, to the west of the trough and east of the ridge will be convergence.

As the winds flow around the waves towards the poles, Coriolis force increases as latitude increases. This larger Coriolis force bends the winds around until they are headed back toward the equator.

As the wind moves towards the equator Coriolis decreases and the upper level flow tends to straighten out and then head towards the pole.

The shape of these wind flows may be wave-like, and then there will be periods when flow is straight. The amplitude of the waves varies as does the distance between the crests. But through all this there is a certain almost repetitive rhythm.

RIDGES AND TROUGHS

As this river of wind meanders its way around the world, ridges of warmer air with lower pressure and troughs of colder air with higher pressure are formed. The shape, wind speed, and movement of the troughs and ridges has the biggest influence on our surface weather.

There are a couple of general rules about upper-level ridges and troughs and surface features. First, there is usually divergence downstream of troughs and upstream of ridges.

As we've said earlier, these areas of divergence are associated with the development of surface lows by acting as an upper-level vacuum—creating convergence or inward rushing wind at the surface.

Upstream of troughs and on the downstream side of ridges you typically have convergence. This convergence is associated with surface high pressure systems where the upper-level convergence sinks to the surface, and then diverges outwards from the center of the high.

This pattern of upper-level meandering winds with associated troughs and ridges is what gives us the surface flow of lows followed by highs followed by lows.

Troughs and ridges are terms which help define a constant pressure surface—i.e. the altitude at which a pressure will be found—in this case the pressure of 500mb.

How do you tell a trough from a ridge?

❑ Ridges are areas of higher heights of constant pressure surface and indicate warmer temperatures.

❑ Ridges are anticyclonic in curvature—clockwise in the Northern hemisphere and counterclockwise in the Southern.

❑ Troughs are areas of lower heights and colder temperature.

❑ Trough curvature is cyclonic—counterclockwise in the Northern Hemisphere and clockwise in the Southern.

❑ Ridges bring warm air up from the equator.

❑ Troughs bring cold air down from the polar regions.

UPPER-LEVEL CHARTS

All of the data about the three-dimensional aspect of the atmosphere comes together in one handy resource—the 500mb contour charts.

These upper-level charts are far and away the most valuable forecasting tools with which we can work. They are the key to what the weather will be doing at the surface in the near future, and are the best warning that exists for dangerous extratropical storm development. There is simply no better forecasting tool available to the mariner.

We'll start out with a basic description of these upper level charts—and then move onto some detail.

500mb charts provide by far the best indication of severe weather, and surface wind speeds, along with the direction and track of surface storms.

500MB FAX CHARTS

The most common upper level chart is what is called the 500mb level. This is the altitude at which the barometer reads half of what it does on the surface, or about 18,500 feet (5,600m).

The upper-level winds move at much faster speeds than what we see on the water, so don't let all those barbs on the arrows scare you.

Several factors are important to keep in mind: First, upper-level winds sometimes act as steering currents for surface weather features. The stronger the winds aloft, the faster the surface weather features will move.

If you have a large surface high pressure system with little or no 500mb movement above it, the high will tend to be stable. On the other hand, if the 500mb level has fast-moving winds over or near the surface high, surface system may clear out quickly followed by the inevitable low.

As we discussed earlier in the book (page 76), the upper level charts are typically produced from a computer model of the atmosphere.

The 500mb level of the atmosphere is important for a number of reasons.

❑ Above this level only vertical atmospheric motion interacts with the surface. Horizontal flow has no impact on the surface.

❑ It is high enough that it is not impacted by what is happening at the surface.

❑ It is the level at which vorticity (spin) is easily measured (vorticity is a key element in the creation of weather systems on the surface).

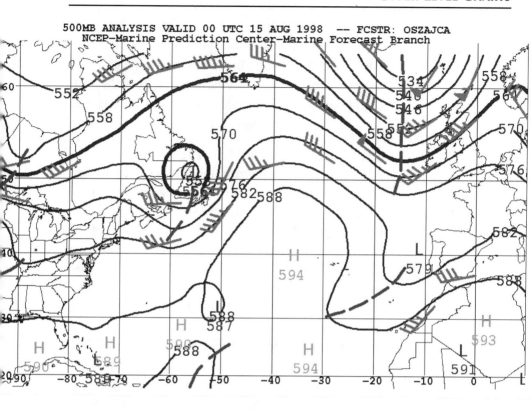

500MB ANALYSIS VALID 00 UTC 15 AUG 1998 -- FCSTR: OSZAJCA
NCEP-Marine Prediction Center-Marine Forecast Branch

(Chart 1) *This mid-summer 500mb chart (18,500 foot/5,600 meter altitude for the Atlantic region is fairly typical. Note the upper-level lows off the east coast of Canada and the one farther south on the 50-degree longitude line at 30 degrees latitude. Both could cause trouble at the surface. Except for the area just to the west of the United Kingdom, wind speeds are moderate for this altitude, indicating easy sailing at the surface level.*

As discussed in the section on gust factors (see page 113), the relationship of the upper level winds to the surface winds tends to be closer after the passage of a cold front, when there is a lot of vertical turbulence in the atmosphere and mixing of upper- and lower-level wind fields.

When you are looking at the upper-level winds, the pattern from chart to chart is quite important. It is the pattern that gives you a feel for how things are developing, and what the wind speeds and directions are going to look like a day or so hence.

As with the surface fax charts, if you keep these on a clipboard, in chronological order, you can begin to get a feel for the rhythm of the weather.

THE PROFESSIONAL'S VIEW

Getting to know the pattern of upper level weather features is the key to projecting what is going to happen in the future on the surface.

In the process of researching this book we've had numerous discussions with forecasters around the world. When we were discussing the 500mb data with Dave Feit, Chief of the Forecast Branch of the NWS Marine Prediction Center, he suggested we look at a paper two of his forecasters had written on the use of 500mb charts.

Joe Sienkiewicz and Lee Chesneau have been kind enough to allow us to incorporate portions of their work on 500mb charts in this section. They have also been helpful in answering innumerable questions and supplying us with sample fax charts. If you come away from this section with an understanding of the 500mb phenomenon and how it affects surface conditions, it is in no small part due to the efforts of Joe and Lee.

SURFACE WEATHER REVIEW

As we've been discussing, surface weather charts depict isobars, high and low centers, and a variety of weather fronts with which by now you have some familiarity.

The general perception is that lows are associated with bad weather and highs mean light winds near the center with generally fair weather. But there is more to it than that.

The three-dimensional characteristics mentioned earlier make the weather process somewhat more complex—but at the same time this provides the tools we need for analysis and forecasting. And most important, we have a means of analyzing the risk factors to which we may be exposed.

If you look at a surface map and think that the low over Chicago today will be over New England tomorrow and affecting your vessel off the Eastern Seaboard of the U.S. the day after, you are forecasting by continuity.

By continuity, we mean moving the existing state of the atmosphere (lows, highs and fronts) around the earth without taking account of all the processes involved in creating those states. In the early part of this century that is the way meteorologists first forecast storm systems, and is the basis for most of the two-dimensional-based forecasting rules you will find in this book.

Surface weather represents everything that is going on in the atmosphere above the surface.

Without the use of upper-level fax charts, this is all we can do. But once we have data on how the upper atmosphere is behaving, we add a new dimension to this equation.

We know that the atmosphere is incredibly dynamic, and that the surface pressure responds to changes in the atmosphere aloft and the pressure aloft responds to those below. The life cycle that storms go through—birth, sometimes growing in strength, and eventually spinning down and dying— is a direct result of interaction between the lowest level in the atmosphere and mid and upper levels—and an excellent measure of this interaction is the 500mb height field

WHAT IS A 500MB CONTOUR?

When you measure the atmosphere at the surface of the earth, pressure is used to quantify what is going on. But when you move up, where the atmosphere is free to move vertically as well as horizontally, a different form of measurement is required to quantify what is occurring. This is where the concept of a constant pressure surface comes in.

The following 500mb charts have been specially annotated to make them easier to read. The trough and ridge lines are heavier than normal. The surface low tracks are not usually shown on 500mb charts.

A constant pressure surface is simply an altitude, expressed on fax charts as meters, at which a given pressure exists.

The 500mb level is a constant pressure surface approximately midway up in the troposphere (the lowest layer of the earth's atmosphere). The pressure exerted by the air column above this level is exactly 500mb. The vertical height of this surface above the earth varies, but as we said before, gener-

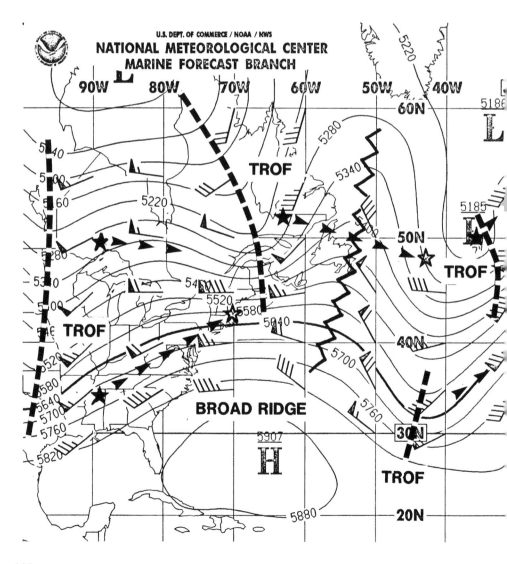

ally averages 5,600 meters although it can vary from roughly 4,700 meters in an extremely cold (more dense) atmosphere to nearly 6,000 meters in a very warm (less dense) atmosphere.

The solid contours shown on the U.S. 500mb charts represent geopotential height in whole meters—not isobars which are lines of constant pressure (as are used at the surface).

The 500mb level is a constant pressure surface approximately 18,000 feet (5,600 meters) above sea level.

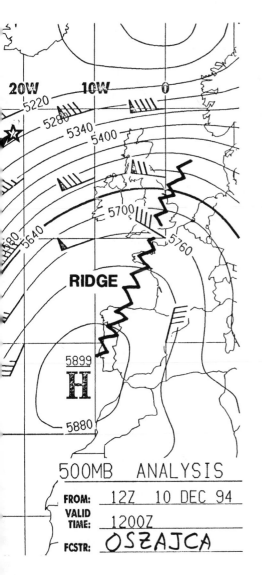

(Chart 2) *The 500mb analysis for 12Z December 10, 1994. Short wave troughs are shown by a dashed line. Zigzag lines indicate ridge axes. The location of surface low pressure centers at 12Z December 10 are indicated by a star. Projected 24-hour tracks of lows are shown by arrowheads, and the observed position of low centers at 12Z December 11 are shown with an open-faced star.*

The number 5640 on the chart means 5,640 meters. In effect you are looking at a topographic map of the 500mb pressure surface level.

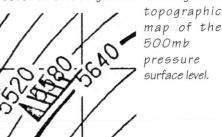

500MB ANALYSIS

FROM: 12Z 10 DEC 94
VALID TIME: 1200Z
FCSTR: OSZAJCA

On some charts the last digit is left off. Thus 5460 becomes 546 as in the example alongside.

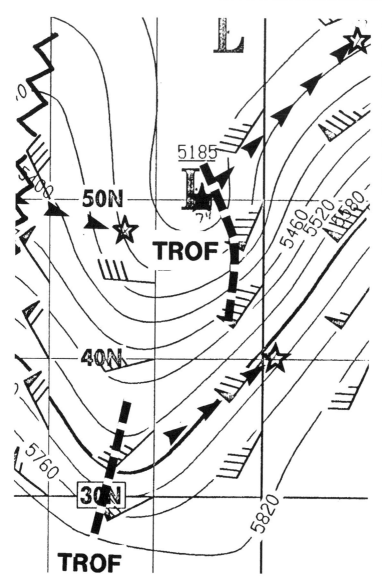

The star represents the forecast position of the through 24 hours hence. The solid arrows show the projected line of travel.

(Chart 3) Here's a blowup of a section from the middle of Chart 2 on the preceding page. The contour lines represent the geopotential height of the 500mb barometer reading. The 5820 just above the bottom is 5,820 meters. The flags on the wind feathers equal 50 knots, while the long barbs equal ten knots and the short barbs five knots.

An open 5185 low, where there is no closed height contour and no closed circulation. is in the middle of the chart.

The 500mb heights are higher in warmer air masses (less dense) and lower in colder air masses (more dense). As a result, the heights of the 500mb geopotential lines are generally lower towards the poles and higher towards the equator. In Chart 2 on the previous page, look at the height differences from the contour at 30 degrees N, 30 degrees W—5820—and south of Iceland near 60 degrees N 20 degrees W—5220 (approximately 600 meters difference). This is due to their difference in latitude and the relative temperatures in the two regions. It is obviously going to be colder in Iceland than down around 30 degrees North latitude.

500mb contours are higher above the earth in warm air and lower in cold air.

The closer the 500mb height contours are together, the stronger the horizontal and vertical temperature contrasts and the faster the wind speed (the wind at this level is for the most part parallel to the height contours). In this regard, you read these upper level charts in a manner similar to surface charts with isobars.

A simple rule of thumb: The tighter the height contours, the higher the wind speed, and the stronger the temperature difference below 500mb. In Chart 2, a strong band of southwesterly winds extends from near 30 degrees N, 40 degrees W to northern Scotland is a good indication that a moderate to strong surface front exists in this area.

Closer height contours indicate stronger temperature contrasts and higher winds at altitude.

From the distribution of height contours, you can infer the speed of the 500mb winds as well as the temperature contrasts that exist at this altitude.

Meteorologists call wind speed *maxima* (maxima refers to a region of wind that is faster than surrounding areas) at the 500mb level jets or jet streams.

Generally speaking, the greater the differential in height of the contours on the 500mb chart, the stronger the wind field at the 500mb level.

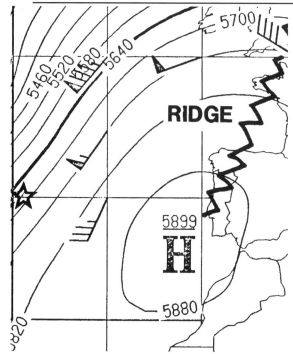

(**Chart 4**)*A 5899 closed high with a ridge extending to the northeast can be seen just west of the Strait of Gibraltar.*

RELATIVE HEIGHTS

Ls and Hs on these upper level charts represent areas of relatively higher and lower heights of the 500mb pressure level.

(On the surface, as you know, the Ls and Hs represent pressure. This is a little confusing because the actual pressures at the 500mb chart are high where you have the lowest height contours as this is the coldest air and therefore lower than the surrounding air mass. Conversely, areas that are higher in height are lighter and therefore the pressure is less.)

An L or H with a closed height contour around it implies that the high or low has a closed circulation with the wind circulating around it.

Troughs are areas of relatively lower heights of the 500mb pressure contour and are U- or V-shaped in the contours. Trough axes are indicated on 500mb charts by dashed lines. For example, if you refer back to Chart 2 (on page 133), a trough extends from just east of Hudson Bay to the Canadian Maritimes. A more complex area of troughing can be seen in the mid-Atlantic with one trough along 35 degrees W and a second between 40 degrees and 50 degrees W south of 40 degrees N.

Ridges are areas of higher heights for the 500mb pressure contour, and are shaped like an upside down U or V, and are indicated by a solid zigzag line. On chart 2 and in the detail above a strong ridge

trough

ridge

extends north-northeastward from off the African Coast to the British Isles. A broader, flatter ridge can be seen off the southeast U.S coast extending to between 50 degrees W and 60 degrees W.

On the charts distributed over radiofacsimile by NMC (Point Reyes) and NMF (Boston), the 5,640-meter height contour is enhanced in bold and troughs and ridges are always indicated. However, many other countries transmit their faxes without this data, leaving it to the user to make their own annotations.

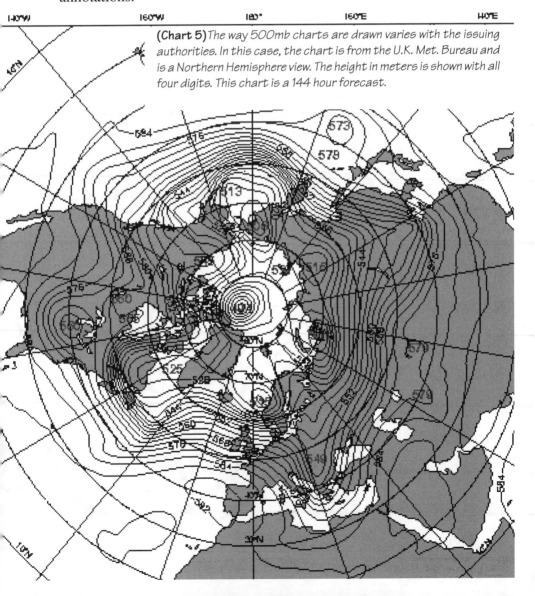

(Chart 5) The way 500mb charts are drawn varies with the issuing authorities. In this case, the chart is from the U.K. Met. Bureau and is a Northern Hemisphere view. The height in meters is shown with all four digits. This chart is a 144 hour forecast.

5,640-METER HEIGHT CONTOUR

The 5,640-meter height contour is considered one of the most important heights of the 500mb pressure.

A series of generalizations about this level is in use by marine meteorologists around the world.

RULES OF THUMB

In wintertime the 5640 contour is an excellent indication of the southern extent of surface winds of force 7 westerlies or greater. In summer the 5640 height contour is more representative of force 6 surface westerlies.

The surface storm track is usually 300 to 600 nautical miles poleward and parallel to the 5640 height contour.

Fronts (cold fronts, in particular) and surface storm centers move at approximately one-third to one-half the 500mb wind speed.

The surface wind speed of a low, especially in the west to southwest quadrant (the cold air behind the cold front) in the Northern Hemisphere and west to northwest quadrant in the Southern Hemisphere — is approximately 50 percent of the 500mb wind speed.

5640mb height contour "normal" conditions:

❑ *In the winter, indicates southern extent for Force seven westerlies.*

❑ *In the summer, represents southern extent for Force six westerlies.*

❑ *Surface storm track is on the poleward side of the 5640 contour.*

Wind speed indications:

❑ *Cold fronts and associated lows move at 33% to 50% of the speed of the 500mb winds.*

❑ *Surface wind speed is typically 50% of the 500mb wind speed—especially behind a cold front.*

The heavier line represents the 5640 meter height contour on most 500mb fax charts.

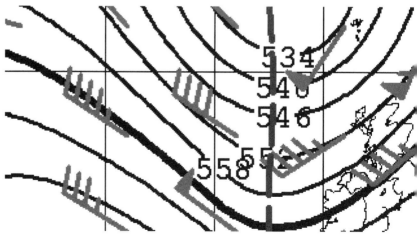

500MB ATMOSPHERIC WAVES

If you could look at a time-lapse movie loop of the 500mb height contours over the Northern or Southern Hemisphere for a year, you would see a westerly circulation undulating northward and southward in what appears to be waves of troughs and ridges passing around the globe.

The bigger waves appear to stand still or move slowly for a period of time and then either break down or move westward. When a larger wave moves westward, it is said to retrograde.

The smaller waves move quite rapidly from west to east and tend to enhance or flatten as they pass through the larger waves.

LONG WAVES

The bigger waves are called long waves or long wave troughs and have a wave length between 50 to 120 degrees of longitude and number from approximately three to seven around the world. These waves are responsible for the overall weather patterns or storm tracks. For example, prolonged drought or excessive storminess over an area is a result of the long wave pattern.

The long wave pattern tends not to fluctuate significantly for a period of 10 days or more, and the period between crests can be as long as several months

It can be difficult to pick out the long waves on the Mercator projection charts distributed on most radiofacsimiles. This is due in part to the type of projection and extent of the area covered by these charts. A hemispheric chart projection of the 500mb pattern for a period of a week to ten days is more useful for this purpose.

If you watch these charts over time, you will begin to see a pattern where troughs tend to reoccur. These are usually long wave troughs.

Long waves typically are stable, or move very slowly in a westerly direction. They are responsible for long term surface weather patterns such as droughts or excessive periods of rain.

SHORT WAVES

The smaller wave troughs that travel rapidly in the westerly flow are called short wave troughs or simply short waves and are associated directly with specific surface low pressure systems.

They tend to have a life cycle of less than a week and rotate through the longer wave troughs. Their size tends to be on the order of 700 to 1,800 nautical miles (1,000 to 2,500 kilometers) in scale.

These short waves can flow in almost any direction, but typically a west-to-east flow is common, although poleward-and equator-oriented directions are seen as well.

Short waves—also called troughs—can flow in any direction and are typically associated with surface lows.

WAVE INTERACTION

The long and short atmospheric waves interact like wind waves and swell. When wind waves and swells are in phase, wind waves tend to enhance the swell making for significantly higher amplitude seas. When out of phase, the wind waves tend to dampen the swell.

Similar interactions occur in the atmosphere. When in phase, short waves help to enhance the longer wave pattern and are themselves enhanced or gain amplitude—resulting in stronger surface lows and higher surface winds.

When out of phase, the short waves can dampen the long wave pattern and, in turn, the short wave amplitude can be reduced (flattened) with surface lows being more benign and lower surface winds.

Long and short waves interact and can reinforce each other or dampen each other.

PICKING OUT WAVES

Being able to pick out long and short waves is very much a function of pattern recognition. To do it properly takes lots of practice. Following are several charts which are marked for long and short waves. These charts are available from the Internet at various sights. If you are serious about this subject, the more time you spend practicing before you go to sea, the better off you will be.

For strong surface low development to occur:

❑ A 500mb trough axis (of cold air) is required roughly a quarter-wavelength to windward (typically west).

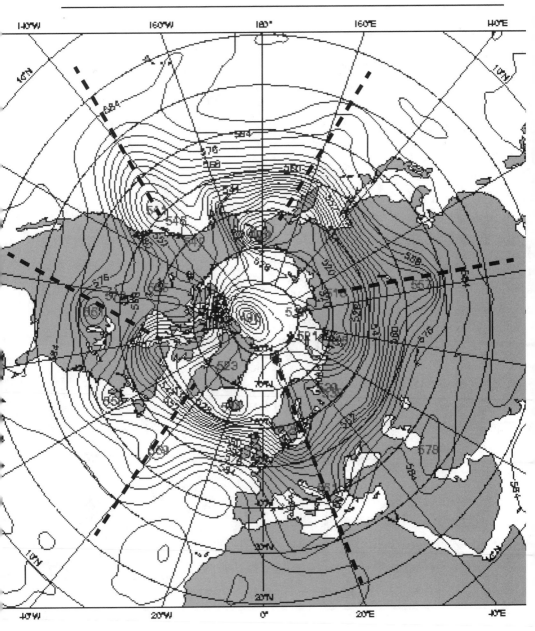

Long wave troughs are typically identified by their wide separation, typically 50 to 120 degrees of longitude. Long waves determine the patterns in the weather, but do usually affect the surface by themselves. it is the short waves that have the biggest impact on surface features, especially when they get into phase (rotate through) the long waves.

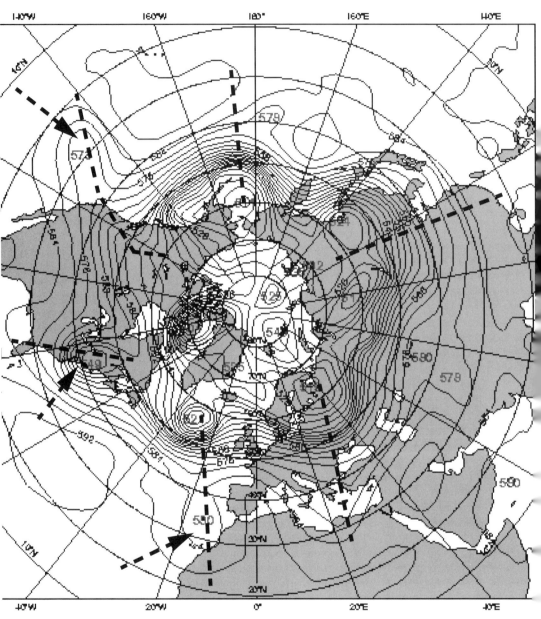

Three days later and the position of the long waves has changed slightly, but the same six waves circle the Northern Hemisphere.

One of the ways you can identify a long wave is with an extension towards the equator. These extensions look like lobes. Several are marked with arrows on the chart above.

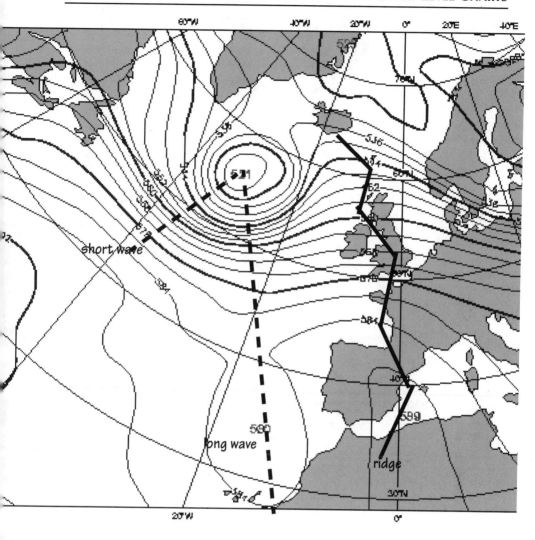

This detail of the North Atlantic is for the same time period as the chart above.

Note the short wave to windward (to the west) of the long wave. As this wave moves along towards the east it will eventually get into phase with the semi-stationary long wave. When this happens expect vigorous surface development.

The ridge (shown by the zig zag line) to the east of the long wave trough will tend to stack up the short wave trough, causing it to amplify towards the equator. This again is a sign of potentially substantial surface development to come in the near future.

Note how the spacing of the isoheight lines tighten to the west of the short wave trough axis. This tightening of the lines indicates an acceleration of wind speed which in turn would call for a deepening of surface features associated with this trough (especially as it rotates into phase with the long wave to the east).

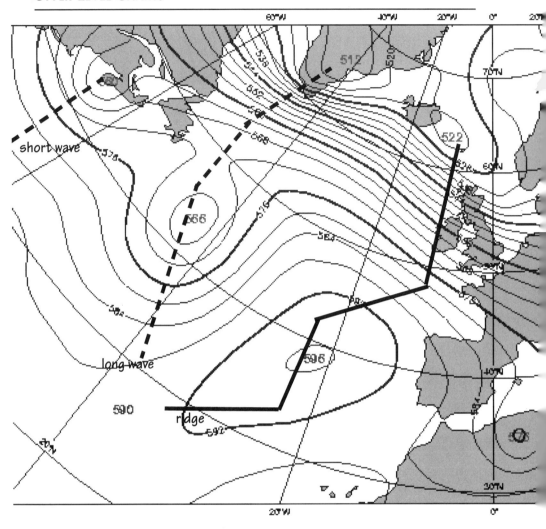

Here we have a long wave coming down from Greenland, with a ridge to the west, and short wave trough well to the east.

There does not appear to be any immediate concern for severe surface development. However, when the short wave to the west rotates to the east there could be some excitement when it aligns with the long wave trough.

Another issue which needs to be watched is the potential for trouble in the tropics. The long wave is shown all the way down to 27 degrees N. This is starting to get into the area where it could influence tropical development, if conditions were right a little closer to the equator.

SHORT WAVES AND SURFACE LOWS

For the development of a mid-latitude surface low, the short wave trough axis at the 500mb level must be offset to windward toward cold air, relative to the surface low.

A typical initial distance is a quarter-wave-length separation between the surface low and 500mb trough at the early stages of development. This offset means that there is a divergence of air aloft and the air spreads out. The divergence provides the venting system for the surface low which we discussed in the beginning of this section.

The offset that occurs between the surface low and the upper-level trough (with the upper-level trough to the west) is an indicator that good venting can take place. This is a prerequisite for strong surface development.

The venting needs to occur more rapidly than surface air can rush in, thus providing the mechanism by which the surface low pressure drops and surface winds increase.

On the other hand, if the upper-level trough is aligned over the surface low, the colder air directly aloft tends to sink, blocking the venting action from the surface, leading to the eventual dissipation of the surface low and its related winds.

Now let's take a look at the 500mb and surface pressure patterns associated with a developing Atlantic low pressure system in the fall of 1994.

The four panels, 24 hours apart on the following pages, show the development of a short wave trough (dashed line) and surface depression as they move off North America in strong west-to-east flow. The low then strengthens to a storm over the central North Atlantic.

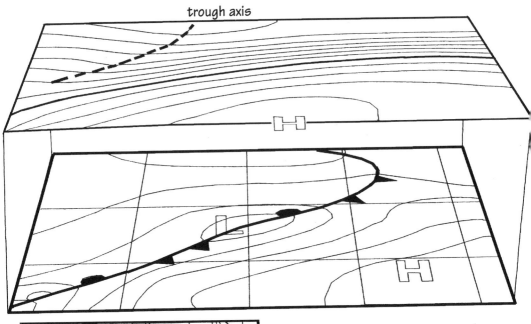

trough axis

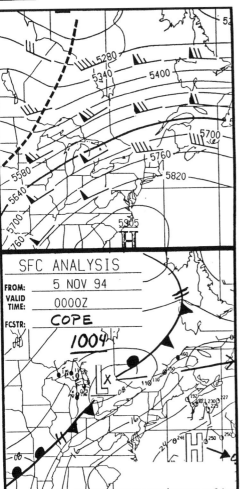

SFC ANALYSIS

FROM: 5 NOV 94
VALID TIME: 0000Z
FCSTR: COPE

1004

This perspective view (above) gives you a feel for the relationship between these two charts. Note, however, that the vertical distance shown between the two surfaces is out of proportion. The dashed line represents the 500mb trough axis.

In reality, if the separation between these two levels were in scale, they would be separated by the thickness of a pencil line.

In this first series of fax charts the 500mb short wave trough (middle fax) is still west of the Great Lakes with the 1004mb surface low (shown on the lower fax chart) over southeastern Ontario.

The surface low is approximately half-way between the 500 mb trough axis and the 500 mb ridge over eastern Canada—a quarter-wavelength.

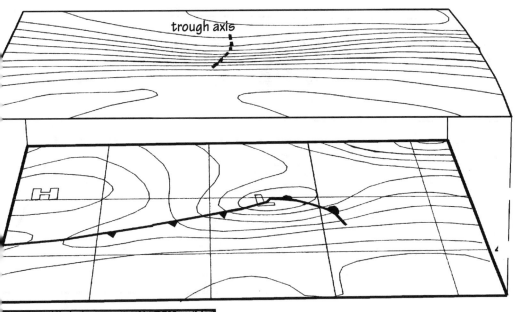

trough axis

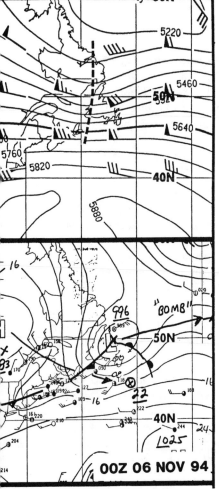

5220
5460
50N
5640
5760
5820
5880
40N

16
996
BOMB
50N
16
22
40N
1025

OOZ 06 NOV 94

Twenty-four hours later, the short wave trough is over the Canadian Maritimes with a 996mb surface low just crossing the coast of Newfoundland.

The 500mb short wave has flattened as it crosses over the top of the ridge to the south. The surface low has deepened 8mb over the past 24 hours, and the distance between the 500mb trough axis and surface low has closed by about half the original distance.

To indicate that this low is expected to deepen explosively over the next 24 hours, the forecaster has written the word "bomb" along the expected track of the low in the lower panel. (The Marine Forecast Branch now refers to lows deepening 24mb in 24 hours as "rapidly intensifying" as opposed to "bombs").

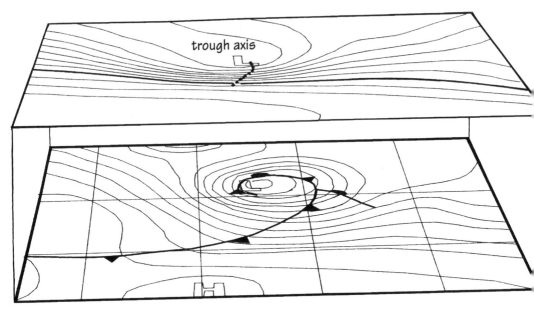

trough axis

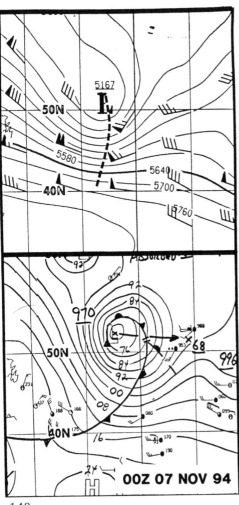

5167

5580

5640

5700

5760

50N

40N

970

996

50N

40N

OOZ 07 NOV 94

On this third day of the cycle explosive deepening has indeed taken place. The surface low has deepened 26mb over the past 24 hours. The 500mb short wave trough has amplified (become more U- or V-shaped or extended north to south).

We no longer have just a 500mb trough but now have a 5167-meter low center just to the west of the surface low. The upper-level low is beginning to "close off," meaning height contours are beginning to encircle the low at 500 mb.

The closing off of the 500mb low indicates the closed circulation has grown with height from the surface to 500 mb level.

Closing off is a good indication that the surface low is beginning to slow. Some offset of the trough still exists to the west suggesting that the surface low will still deepen a little more.

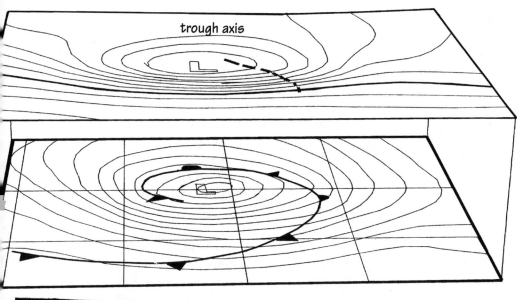

trough axis

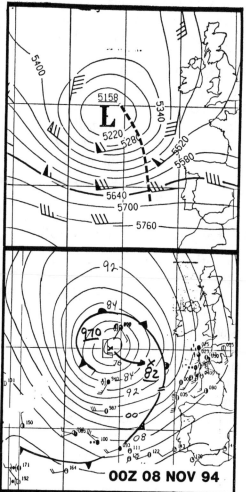

5400
5158
L
5220
5280
5340
5520
5580
5640
5700
5760

92
84
970
84
82
92
00
08

00Z 08 NOV 94

On the fourth day of the cycle, November 8, the surface low and 500mb low are vertically stacked with little or no offset of the upper-level trough.

This indicates that the atmospheric column has become more homogeneous in temperature and moisture content.

The surface low has matured to 968 mb at and is beginning to fill or weaken. A well defined closed circulation now extends to the 500mb height and beyond into the higher levels of the atmosphere.

SHORT WAVE TROUGH LIFE CYCLE

In the preceding sequence we have seen three stages in the life cycle of a short wave trough. First is the developing phase where the 500mb short wave trough is upstream—typically to the west of the surface low. This trough increases its north/south orientation with time.

The westerly offset of the 500mb trough axis relative to the surface low decreases with time. The 500mb trough moves over the surface low and the surface low deepens.

The second or closing-off phase is shown in the third panel as height contours begin to encircle the newly formed 500mb low and close off the circulation. The circulation has become closed from the surface to 500mb—in other words, they have become, in a sense, directly connected—and the surface low slows its forward motion.

In the mature phase, the 500mb low is vertically stacked above the surface low. There is no more deepening and the depression begins to fill.

To summarize, this low pressure system in 72 hours moved from the Great Lakes to 20 degrees W (halfway to Europe!), deepening 36mb in the process. The rapid speed of motion was a direct result of the 500mb flow being oriented in a west-to-east direction.

HORIZONTAL OFFSET AS AN INDICATOR

Any time you see a horizontal offset between a surface low and an upper-level trough or wave to the west at the 500mb level, the potential exists for strong winds.

Always take this as an indicator that things could happen at the surface in a hurry.

Because of the high potential for venting the surface low pressure system that these offsets bring, development at the surface can be extremely rapid.

It is this process that creates the meteorological bombs that have caused so many problems over the years.

Stages in the life cycle of upper-level trough:

❑ Trough lags to west behind surface low.

❑ Offset relationship becomes more vertical as the surface low becomes stronger.

❑ Upper-level circulation closes off.

❑ Upper-level closed low and surface low are vertically stacked—depression begins to fill.

Horizontal offset between 500mb troughs and surface lows are the best indicator we have for potential severe storm development.

The fact that this storm development can happen so rapidly, sometimes in a matter or 12 hours, means we all should be keeping a very close eye on these relationships, and the key to this is watching the 500mb fax charts.

SHORT WAVE TROUGH INTERACTION

Let's follow the 500mb wind maxima through the life of two short wave troughs as they interact.

The 500mb and surface analyses for every 12 hours from 1200Z October 12 to 0000Z October 15, 1994 are shown for this mid-Pacific development in the next series of surface and 500mb charts.

In the series of charts which follow the shaded areas indicate the regions of maximum wind force.

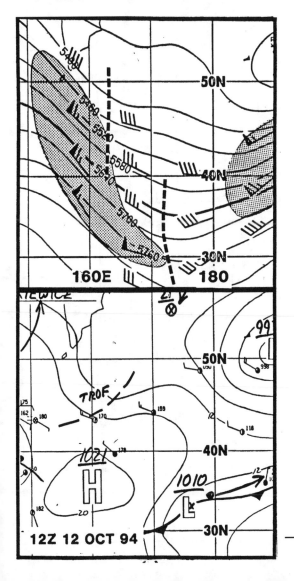

At 1200Z October 12, a benign looking 1010mb low can be seen at 33 degrees N, 176 degrees E (on the lower chart) with a weak short wave 500mb trough at approximately 172 degrees E (on the upper chart)—there is some offset to the east with height, so further deepening is expected of the surface low.

Upstream, south of Kamchatka, is a moderate northwest flow of 65 knots and a fairly flat (i.e., not much shape) short wave trough (second dashed line) along 163 degrees E.

Energy at 500 mb is poised to push southeastward from the second short wave toward the 1010 mb surface low (this push towards the equator is referred to as a "dig").

If you were only looking at the surface fax you would not expect much in the way of deepening of this surface low. But with the 500mb chart in hand, you are aware that the potential for deepening exists—and a careful eye on the weather should be maintained for the next 24 hours.

By 0000Z October 13, the two short waves have begun to get into phase with each other, as indicated by the two dashed lines beginning to line up. They have increased their V or U shape over the past 12 hours. Some short wave ridging (upside down U curvature of the height contours) had also occurred to the east as indicated by the zigzag line.

The surface low has deepened 10mb—nearly 1mb per hour during the past 12 hours.

All of these factors—the change phasing of the two short wave troughs, the deepening shape of the trough on the north/south axis, and the ridging to the east are signs that better venting will take place. This in turn means that the surface low will continue to deepen.

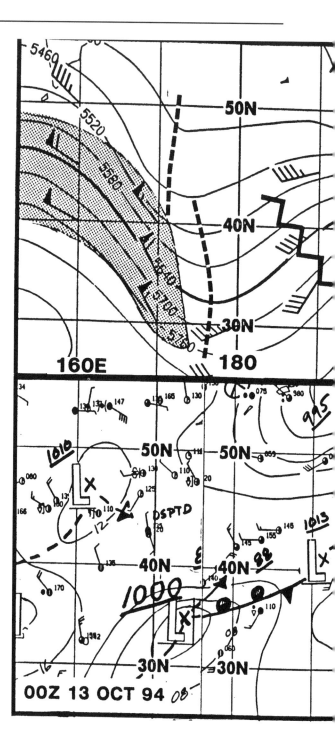

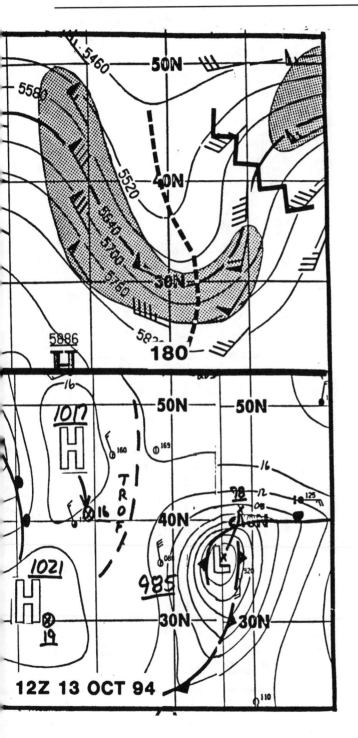

Twelve hours later the surface low has deepened another 15mb to 985mb and the pressure gradient has dramatically tightened in the northwest quadrant of the low.

Storm-force winds should be expected at the surface in this region.

At 500mb the wind maxima has now spread to the east of the trough. An 80-knot maxima exists in the northwest flow along 40 degrees N. The trough axes are aligned—and only one dashed line is shown on the chart—as the two short waves are now in phase.

At 0000Z October 14, the open trough at 500 mb has closed off as a 5436-meter low. Circulation from the surface now extends up to 500mb height.

The 500mb wind maxima continues to grow to the east of the storm as the low moves slowly northeastward. The low is now vertically stacked from the surface to above 500mb and has nearly completed its deepening.

One ship observed a 50-knot northeast wind north of the storm system.

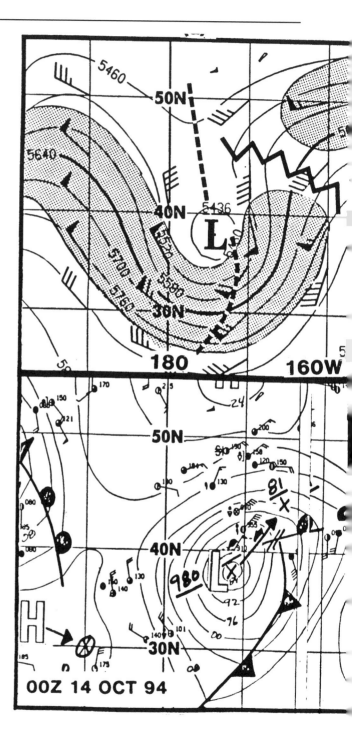

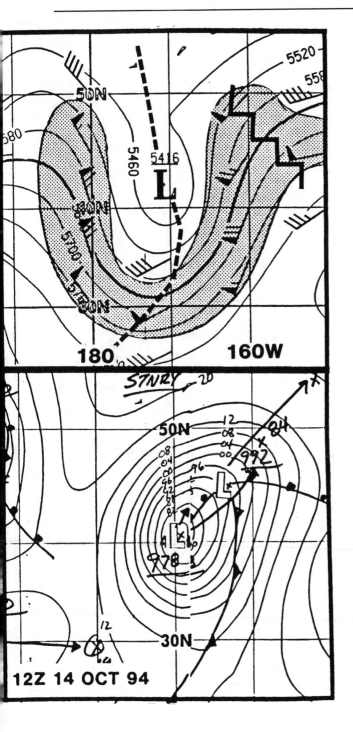

By 1200Z October 14, although the 500mb low is at 5416 meters—20 meters lower than in the previous 12 hours—the closed contours have opened up. The 500mb low is lifting northeastward while the surface low is elongated toward the northeast as indicated by a second surface low shown near the intersection of the warm and cold fronts.

The wind maxima at 500mb is evenly distributed east and west of the 500mb trough but is growing on the east side, so the 500mb low is beginning to open up and lift out.

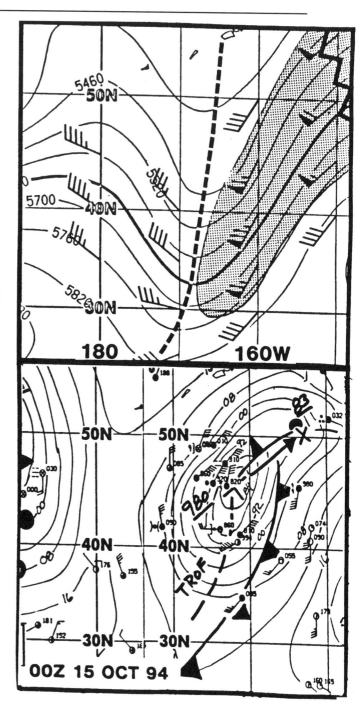

Twelve hours later the 500mb low has opened up and dissipated. The 500mb wind maxima to the west of the system is gone and the bulk of the wind energy is now east of the northeastward-pointing short wave trough axis.

The surface low is elongating northeastward—the direction toward which the strongest 500mb winds are blowing.

This surface storm system will continue to be significant in terms of wind and seas for another 24 to 36 hours, but at least at this point we know that the situation should not get any worse.

In review, the greatest deepening in the surface low took place during the first 36 hours (the initial three sets of fax charts) as the two 500mb short wave troughs began to get into phase, and the strong wind maxima began to extend around the base of the 500mb short wave trough.

The depression is vertically stacked at 0000Z October 14 with the closed 500mb low right over the surface low and wind maxima continuing to strengthen east of the 500mb trough axis.

Little or no deepening should be expected after this point. In the final two frames, we see the wind maxima weaken west of the system and strengthen to the east of the 500mb trough axis, the closed 500mb low opens up to a trough and the surface low begins to weaken and elongate northeastward.

This sequence is fairly typical for the formation of a low and evolution of the 500mb trough and associated wind maxima.

Consider for a moment trying to forecast this situation without the help of the 500mb charts.

If you were to look at the 1010 surface low on the 1200Z October 12 chart, you would see nothing to indicate dangerous storm potential. Twelve hours later, at 0000Z on October 13, the low has deepened to 1000mb. The 10mb drop in 12 hours is a pretty good sign that something is going on—and in the absence of a 500mb fax, you would infer that an upper level trough was acting with the surface low. But the surface chart still gives no real hint of the potential of what is to come.

Twelve hours later, with the 1200Z October 13 chart, you see that a pretty good-sized depression is in your area. Central pressure has dropped another 15mb to 985, a sure sign that the low is deepening. As these systems frequently mature over a 48- to 72-hour period, it is safe to assume that an even lower central pressure and more wind are on their way.

When short waves get into phase with each other, this indicates a deepening of the trough and the risk of strong winds at the surface.

Using only the surface charts for this weather scenario, you would have little warning of the risk of the impending storm.

With the 500mb charts you would know at least 24 hours in advance that the potential was there for a real blow and so be able to take appropriate action to place yourself in a favorable part of the storm system.

ZONAL PATTERN

Surface fronts and lows embedded in upper level zonal flow move at one-third to one-half the speed of the upper level winds.

Now that we have gone over the behavior of 500mb short wave troughs and surface lows, let's take a look at some typical 500mb flow patterns.

Rapid west to east wind flow where the 500mb height contours are aligned west to east is called zonal flow (see Chart 10 below)).

Any short waves embedded in zonal flow tend to move rapidly from west to east. It is not unusual to see associated surface lows or fronts move 35 to 50 knots. A good rule of thumb: A low or front embed-

(Chart 10)

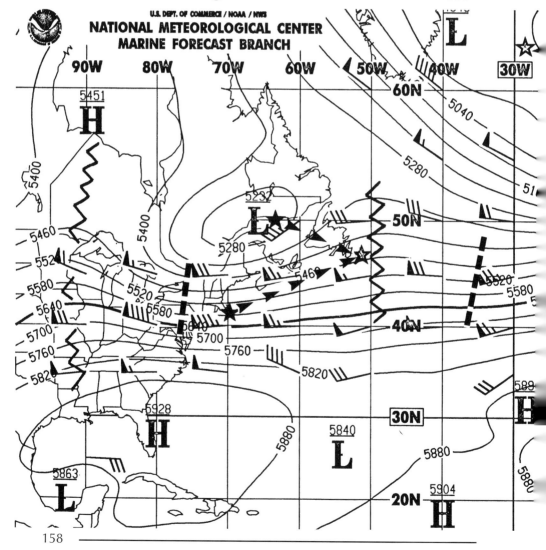

ded in zonal flow in winter will move, on average, between 30 to 50 percent of the 500mb wind speed.

In the 500mb chart below westerly flow at 500mb extends from central North America across the Atlantic to western Europe with a 90-knot maxima over Ohio and near 50 degrees N, 20 degrees W.

Merging streams of flow—cold air from the pole and warm air from the equator—create strong temperature and height contrasts, making for stronger winds aloft.

Fronts embedded in these areas may move as rapidly as 40 to 45 knots. Zonal flow patterns tend to be unstable and short-lived. They usually break down rapidly into a more pole-to-pole oriented pattern.

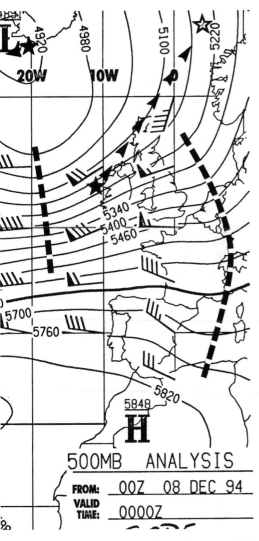

STREAMS OF FLOW

Notice two distinct ribbons or streams of flow in this chart. The dominant flow is west to east from North America to Europe. The second stream, to the north, drops southeastward from Greenland and merges just west of Europe with the more southerly stream.

Merging streams create areas of constricted height contours, generating higher 500mb wind speeds, and strong temperature differences.

Think of this as the northern stream supplying very cold air and the southern stream supplying relatively warm air and moisture. It is not unusual to see as many as three streams at 500mb.

This is similar in concept to what can cause a tropical low to turn into a subtropical bomb (see "The Queen's Birthday Storm" on page 229 for more data on this phenomenon.).

159

MERIDIONAL PATTERN

When a transition from a zonal to a more amplified or pole to pole pattern is taking place (this pole to pole flow is called meridional), a strong surface storm will usually develop. The faster the change from zonal to meridional, the greater the chances for a real blow at the surface.

Chart 10 on the preceding page is two and a half days earlier than the more amplified pattern shown in Chart 2 on page 133. The surface low center off the New England coast in Chart 10 moves east northeastward at nearly 30 knots to the southeast of Newfoundland where it merged with an older low (nearly vertically stacked) located over the Gulf of St. Lawrence. The resultant surface low strengthened rapidly to 975mb by 0000Z December 09 (the day before Chart 2) and the 500mb pattern was amplified.

Another low on Chart 10 is embedded in strong 500mb southwesterlies off Ireland, and it moves northeastward at 35 knots across Scotland to the Norwegian Sea on Chart 2. A third low nearly vertically stacked under the closed 4891-meter 500mb low off Iceland drifts west towards 30 degrees W.

In a meridional pattern the contours have more amplitude (north-south orientation) than in a zonal flow (the earlier six panels of fax charts from the North Pacific, starting on page 151, are indicative of meridional pattern). Meridional patterns tend to move cold air towards the equator and warm air towards the poles—providing the difference in air mass makeup which is necessary for substantial surface level winds.

In meridional pattern, surface lows and 500mb short waves will move more toward the pole or equator than with a zonal pattern.

Look at the 24-hour tracks in the December 3, 1994 fax on the next page (Chart 11). The surface

Meridional pattern flow moves cold air from the poles towards the equator and warm air from the equator towards the poles.

The clash of these air streams helps to provide the "interesting" weather on the surface.

low at 47 degrees N 169 degrees W moved north-eastward at 30 knots to just off Kodiak Island. The low and short wave trough west of California moves southeastward. The surface low, associated with a closed low north of Japan, moved slowly northeast-ward. A large ridge extends from Alaska to west of Hawaii and northerly flow east of the ridge brings cold air southward from interior British Columbia and Northwest Territories out over the waters west of the Pacific Northwest. Southwesterly flow is moving warm moist air from south of 30 degrees N near 170 degrees E northeasterly toward Alaska. These troughs and ridges are all part of short waves caught up in a meridional pattern

The concept of different streams can also be seen on this chart east of Japan. The northern stream weakens as it moves over a ridge along 160 degrees E. The southern stream is stronger west of 170 degrees W and less amplified than the northern stream. Farther east the northern stream is stronger in the northerly flow east of 140 degrees W with a weaker southern stream trough near 35 degrees N, 140 degrees W.

The stream concept is important because the inter-action between short waves embedded in different streams — and, in particular, where the short waves phase together — are areas for potentially significant surface low development.

Remember that the 500mb field is in motion. Therefore, it is a good idea to look at the 500mb forecasts to see how the pattern is expected to evolve.

It is not unusual to have a progressive meridional pattern where short wave troughs and ridges, although they are amplified, continue their eastward progression.

The 500mb height field is always in motion. To get a feel for what the future is bringing watch the 24-, 48-, and 96-hour 500mb fore-casts.

If short waves embedded in differ-ent streams begin to phase together, there exists the potential for signifi-cant surface storm development.

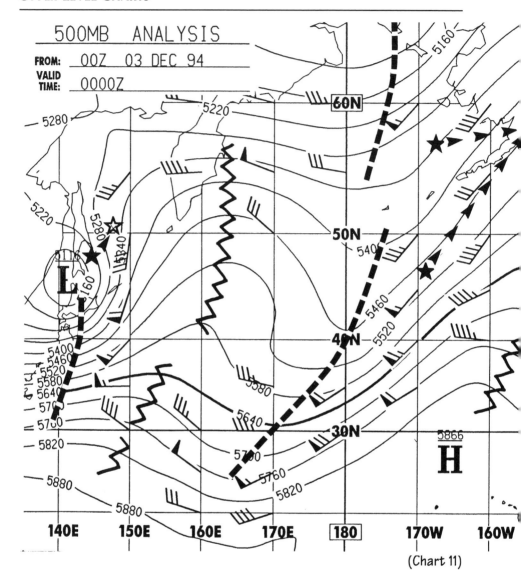

(Chart 11)

TOPOGRAPHIC INFLUENCES

Atmospheric waves are influenced by mountain ranges. In the Northern Hemisphere, for example, waves hitting the Rocky Mountains tend to be diverted in direction. This is probably a major reason for some of the differences in Pacific and Atlantic Ocean weather patterns.

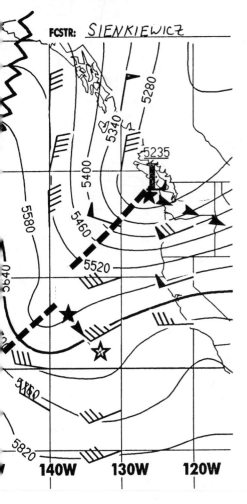

U.S. DEPT. OF COMMERCE / NOAA / NWS
NATIONAL METEOROLOGICAL CENTER
MARINE FORECAST BRANCH

FCSTR: *SIENKIEWICZ*

In the Southern Ocean there is much less land mass to interfere with atmospheric waves, until you run up against the North and South Islands of New Zealand and the Andes Mountains at the southern tip of South America.

New Zealand's notoriously bad weather off the South Island is probably the result of atmospheric waves hitting the land mass.

This is also probably the reason that weather to the west of Cape Horn is relatively worse than in other parts of the Southern Ocean.

When you are sailing in the South Pacific and Indian Oceans, particularly at the deeper latitudes, you will notice that the zonal flow is more stable than that which we find in the Northern Hemisphere. This is probably the result of the lack of land mass in that part of the world.

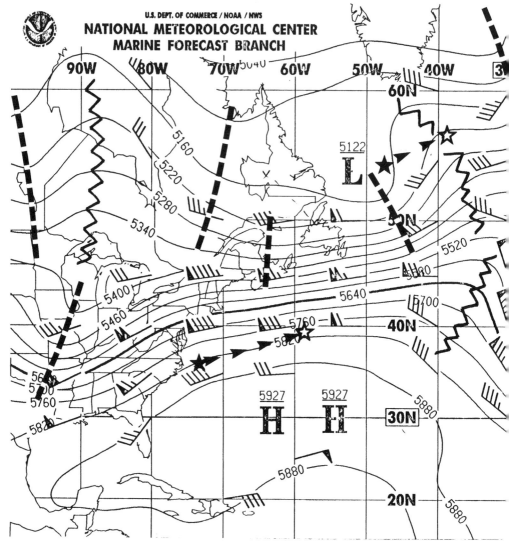

(Chart 12)

RIDGE BLOCKING PATTERNS

A high-amplitude ridge that blocks the west-to-east progression of the westerlies is called a blocking ridge. Chart 12 (above) shows a blocking pattern with a large ridge blocking the westerlies over Western Europe and the Eastern North Atlantic.

In a blocking pattern, short waves will be steered poleward, or poleward with an easterly bias around the blocking ridge.

If the amplitude of the ridge is large enough, then short wave troughs approaching from the west may try to undercut or drive under the block. The short

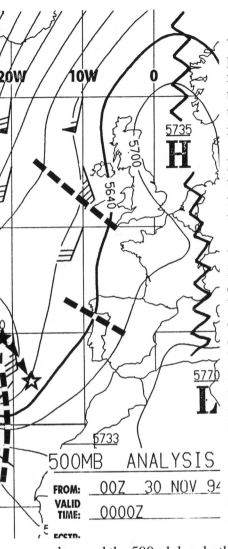

500MB ANALYSIS

FROM: 00Z 30 NOV 94

VALID
TIME: 0000Z

ECSTD.

waves continue to pound at the blocking ridge, forcing it up with their energy (so that the upper levels of the ridge go up in altitude).

Eventually, enough height is attained so that the short waves are then able to slip in under the ridge.

In this fax, the split in the westerlies can easily be seen near 50 degrees N, 25 degrees W. The 5450-meter closed low near 39 degrees N, 24 degrees W is a result of the westerlies trying to undercut the blocking ridge. Due to the strength of the northwest flow to the west and northwest of the 500mb low, the low is said to be "digging" (moving) to the southeast. Thus, the surface low and the 500mb low both move southeastward.

Closed lows that form to the west of a blocking ridge and dig southeastward tend to be fairly strong. It is not unusual to have surface winds at 45 to 50 knots to the west and southwest of the surface low associated in this manner with a blocking ridge of high pressure.

Two lows, one near Iceland (which is difficult to see) and the other south of Greenland are moving northeastward and north-northeastward due to the blocking ridge to the east. Blocks may last 10 days or more.

Short waves running into blocking ridges tend to move laterally (usually towards pole and equator) or try to drive under the ridge.

To the west of blocking ridges, upper-level eastward-moving lows will tend to close off. These typically lead to stronger surface winds than when the closed low is formed at the end of a cycle.

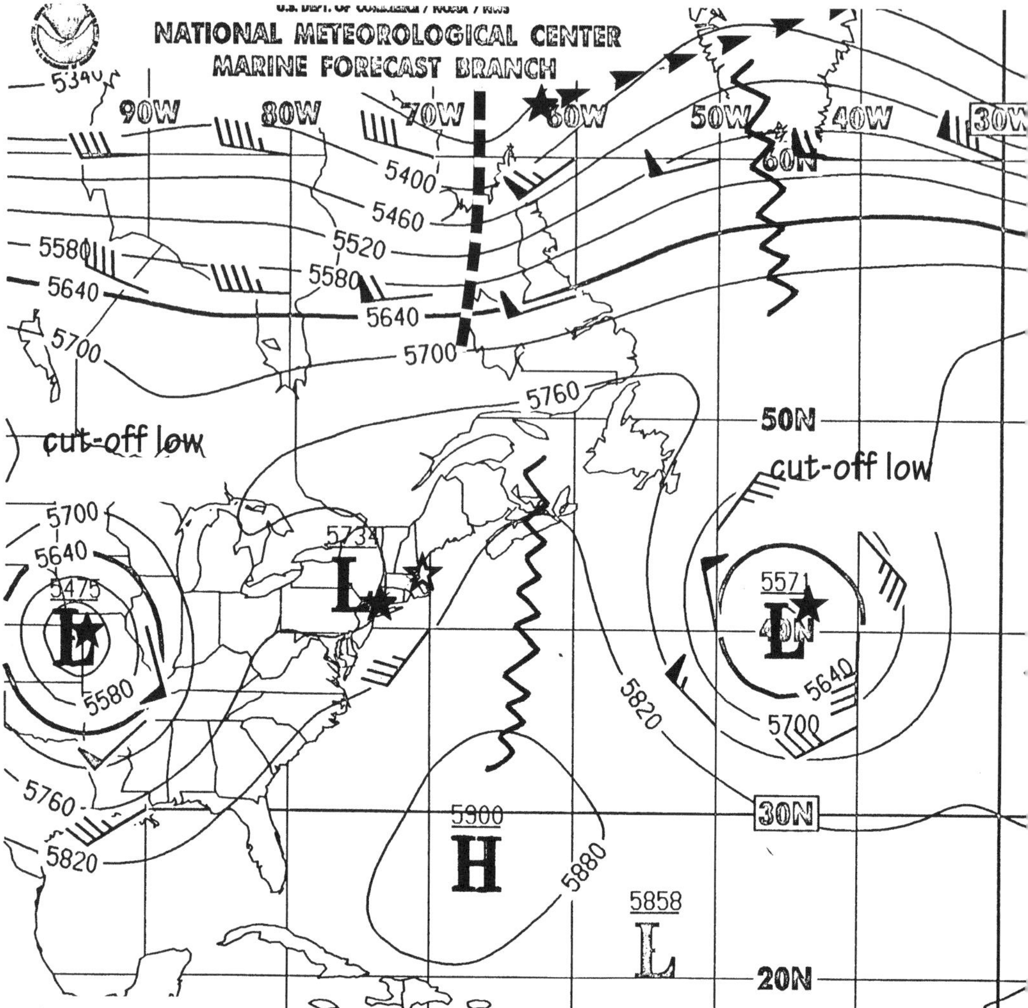
U.S. DEPT. OF COMMERCE / NOAA / NWS
NATIONAL METEOROLOGICAL CENTER
MARINE FORECAST BRANCH
90W
80W
70W
60W
50W
40W
30W
60N
50N
30N
20N
5400
5460
5520
5580
5640
5700
5760
5820
5880
cut-off low
cut-off low
5734
L
5475
5571
5640
5700
5580
5900
H
5858
L

(Chart 13)

Cut-Off Lows

If a 500mb pattern becomes amplified enough in its meridional flow then it is possible for a low to form on the equator side of the upper level westerlies and become "cut off" as shown in Chart 13 above.

In a cut-off low, a cold pool of air aloft is trapped out of the normal flow. Between this upper-level cut-off low and the surface a significant difference in temperature—far more than normal—is in place. This temperature differential gives rise to unstable conditions with lots of rain, thunderstorms and squalls.

Eventually, through the process of rain, the cold pool energy is eroded and the cut-off low dissipates.

It is in the early stages of a cut-off low that the

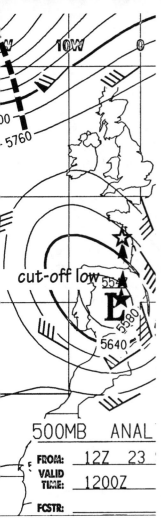

500MB   ANAL

FROM: __12Z   23__
VALID
TIME: __1200Z__

FCSTR: _____

greatest risk for strong surface winds exists. Once the cut-off low has been around for three or four days it typically does not have the energy to create as great a problem at the surface.

The closed circulations associated with the lows over eastern Kansas, the mid-Atlantic (40 degrees N,45 degrees W) and Spain on this chart are cut off from the main stream of zonal westerlies north of 55 degrees N.

Weak ridging separates the higher-latitude westerlies from the three cutoffs. Cut-offs tend to remain stationary and persist for several days.

They may be accompanied at the surface by strong winds (in particular, in the north to northwest flow to the west of the developing low), showers and thunderstorms.

Also, it is not unusual to have strong easterlies to the north and northeast of the center due to the strong pressure gradient between the cut-off and strong surface high to the northeast or east.

Cut-off lows either gradually weaken or are picked up by the higher latitude westerly flow when the pattern amplifies and turns meridional again and the capping ridge (a capping ridge is a small area of higher heights poleward from the cut-off low) breaks down. Cut-off lows tend to occur most in the spring and fall when the westerlies migrate towards the poles and equator.

The preceding charts are just samples of several basic 500mb patterns. At any given time a variety or combination of patterns may exist over an ocean basin. You need to keep your eyes open and check the pattern of the 500mb charts over time.

Upper level cut-off lows:

❑ Bring a pool of colder than normal air with them.

❑ The cold air aloft increases the temperature gradient making for highly unstable conditions.

❑ Have more rain and snow associated with them than with other systems.

❑ Typically last three to four days.

❑ Strongest winds are found in first couple of days of development.

❑ Local upper-level ridges usually start the cut-off low process.

❑ When "capping" ridges move on, cut-off lows dissipate.

.

500mb patterns can vary within a given region. For example, it is not unusual in the Pacific to have strong zonal flow over the Western Pacific with a meridional, or even a blocking, pattern over the Eastern Pacific.

MAKING USE OF 500MB CHARTS

One way to use the 500mb charts is to set up a display of both surface and 500mb analyses along with the 48- and 96-hour forecasts in the nav area. We find that putting the surface and 500mb charts on different clipboards is a big help.

You may want to use a highlighter pen on the wind maxima associated with each trough expected to affect you.

One issue to look at is the wind maxima to the west. Is it evenly distributed around the short wave trough, or stronger to the east of the short wave trough? In other words will the trough dig towards the equator, lift out towards the pole, or just stay steady state in the overall flow?

Take a look at the previous forecasts you have accumulated. Are there any big changes from the earlier series of surface and 500mb analysis and forecasts to the current series?

Remember that the 500mb pattern and specific short waves are linked and associated with the motion and life cycle of surface storm systems.

Look at the progression of the 500mb pattern from analyses time to 48 hours and then to 96 hours. Is the pattern becoming more meridional, zonal, or blocked over the next four days?

Next, look at specific short waves and associated surface-level features that will be affecting you over the next several days. You may want to mark the position of surface lows on the 500mb chart to see how the surface low relates to the 500mb short wave trough (does the trough offset with height or is the system vertically stacked?).

The bottom line is that you will begin to see, through repetition, how the 500mb pattern and surface pressure fields are linked. Pattern recognition will give you a better idea as to how and why storm systems develop and move the way they do.

WHEN ISOHEIGHTS ARE MISSING

You will find that some countries broadcast their upper-level charts with only wind arrows showing

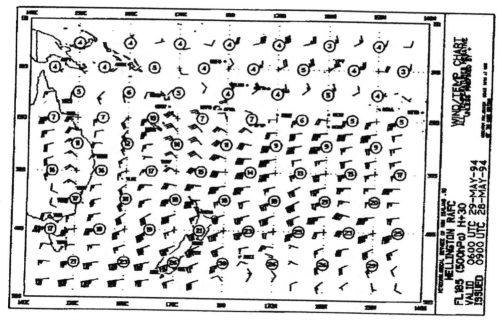

rather than isoheights.

These are not as easy to use, but if you study the wind-arrow patterns—both speed and direction—you will develop a feel for the troughs, ridges, zonal and meridional flows.

These charts frequently have temperatures indicated. You can create your own height fields by connecting similar wind arrows, the same as if you were connecting like pressures when drawing up a surface synoptic chart.

IN THE TROPICS

Upper-level atmosphere dynamics in the tropics are very subtle in nature. Small changes in pressure gradient have a much larger impact than at higher latitudes.

As a result, 500mb charts are of marginal use once you slipped much below 20 degrees or so of latitude.

Occasionally, if there is a really big trough pushing towards the equator at the 500mb level, it might drop down as low as 18 degrees. But more often, 25 degrees is about as close as these come to the equator.

Keep in mind that these "digs" towards the equator are bringing dry, cold air into a region of warm, moist air. This is precisely the mixture required for a meteorological bomb.

In some parts of the world the only upper atmosphere charts available are for aircraft, as in the case above. This New Zealand chart is for flight level 18 or 18,000 feet—we know this as the 500mb level.

The wind arrows have temperature alongside and by connecting the wind arrows of equal speeds one can construct a layout of equal height contours.

Forecasting 500mb Behavior

There are a number of generalizations that we can make about the behavior of zonal and meridional features at the 500mb level.

Zonal to Meridional Transition

First, with zonal flow, if the strongest winds are found upstream, i.e. to the west, you can assume that the zonal flow is about to break down into meridional. The greater the disparity between upstream and downstream winds, and the faster the winds, the more vigorous will be the ensuing trough.

This transition usually takes from 24 to 72 hours. Twenty-four hours later you are likely to be seeing the start of vigorous activity on the surface.

Meridional Behavior

If winds are strongest on the windward (usually west) side of a trough axis it indicates that the trough will dig south and strengthen.

When winds are stable around the trough axis it usually indicates the trough will remain stable for a period of time and that the surface low will deepen a bit more.

If the winds to leeward (usually east) of the trough axis are strongest, then look for the trough to lift out and open up (i.e. flatten out) and for surface low centers to fill.

Trough Axis Orientation

The axes of troughs typically show a rotation as they go through their life cycle. The poleward end of the trough will appear to be relatively stable while the equator side will rotate downwind. This is a clockwise rotation in the Northern Hemisphere and counterclockwise in the Southern.

Meteorologists refer to this as positive (with the equator side to the west) and negative (with the equator end to the east) tilt.

The best way to learn how to predict what is going to happen at the 500mb level is by studying wind speeds and how they vary relative to the pole and equator, and on one side or the other of the troughs and ridges.

There are consistent patterns in this behavior, and the more you study these wind speeds, the better you will be able to recognize what is going to happen over the next few days—based on today's wind flows.

You usually find that with positive tilt the surface low is developing, while with negative tilt the surface low is winding down and filling.

CUT-OFF LOW TRIGGERS

When you have a vigorous transition from zonal to meridional flow, and when the trough begins to lift out or flatten, it will sometimes leave a cut-off low behind (if the meridional amplification is stronger than normal).

When this occurs, as we indicated earlier, the cut-off low is likely to hang around until it winds itself down by dissipating its energy with rain, or until another trough comes along and picks it up.

LONGER TERM WEATHER PATTERNS

You will see, from time to time, long-term weather patterns that manifest themselves in the 500mb flow.

Our recent El Nino event was one such example. In this case, the normal winter storm track at 45 to 50 degrees was displaced towards the equator to a track of 35 to 40 degrees.

If you had been used to watching the 500mb charts you would have easily recognized this pattern.

USING CLOUD PATTERNS

If you do not have access to upper level charts, there are certain cloud signs you can look for. These cloud signatures are also good for confirming what you see on the faxes.

To make use of this system you need to be familiar with what "normal" cirrus cloud movement looks like, and how it looks when moving at high rates of speed.

The best thing is to practice tying the cirrus cloud movement to what you see on the fax charts.

As we go through these rules keep in mind the offset shown in the previous drawings and 500mb/surface fax charts.

If you have the ability to receive satellite images of water vapor, these can be used to indicate location of the 500mb level and the activity which is taking place therein.

If you loop the cloud images, you can see both zonal and meridional flow.

Note that water vapor images are visible before clouds start to form, and thus are an excellent leading indicator of what is about to happen at the 500mb level.

Practice using cirrus cloud signatures to check the 500mb forecasts, and develop a feel for using these as a leading indicator in case you do not have reliable upper level fax charts.

These jet stream clouds are typically uniform in shape and not ragged looking.

If the cirrus flow is moving from the pole toward the equator, this indicates that you are under the windward side of the of the trough. As the surface low is probably a quarter wave length to leeward (east) of you, there are no immediate areas of concern. However, if you are chatting with someone on the radio well to the west of your location, and they indicate pole to equator high speed cirrus movement, and then your barometer starts to drop, you are probably in for a pretty good blow.

On the other hand, if the cirrus are moving from the equator towards the pole, this indicates that you are on the downwind side of a trough and the windward side of a ridge. In this case, the troublesome offset to windward is in place, and conditions are primed for a vigorous surface development.

If the cirrus flow is zonal, i.e. west to east, and it begins to change so that the cirrus flow is more oriented towards the equator, this is an indictor of zonal to meridional transition. Again, this is a signal of surface low development to follow.

A key factor in all of this is the speed of the cirrus clouds. The faster they appear to be moving, the more vigorous is likely to be the surface development. Speed is a relative term, and when you are looking at clouds at the 500mb height and above, 100 knots will look pretty slow. This is why it is necessary to study cloud movement under a variety of conditions, and tie it to your surface experience. Over time you will get a feel for the warning signs.

Before we leave this subject we should touch on a few other cloud issues.

If the progression of cirrus to thickening lower clouds takes place rapidly (or more quickly than you are accustomed to seeing), this can be taken as a sign that the storm system is developing rapidly — and fast development often leads to stronger surface winds.

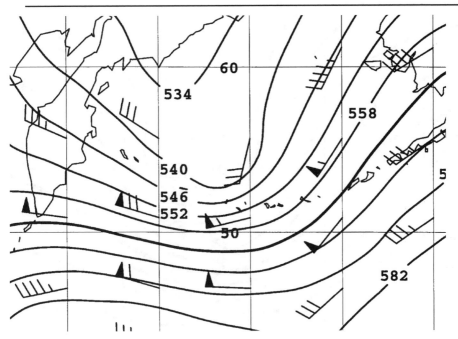

When the winds upwind of the trough are stronger than downwind as in these two details of 500mb charts, expect the trough to dig towards the equator and amplify. This implies surface low development. In the situation presented here, the charts are 24 hours apart. You can see that the trough is more developed in the bottom (later) chart, and there is even more difference in the wind speed between the upwind and downwind side of the trough axis.

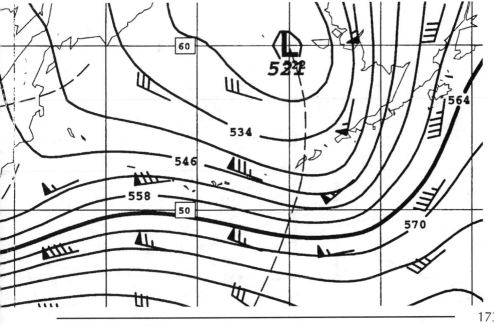

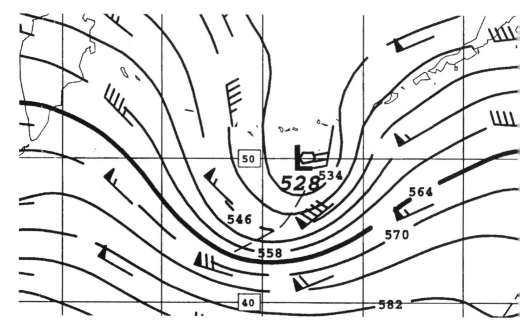

A further 24 hours later and the wind speeds are starting to pick up on the downwind side of the trough axis. This implies that the trough will begin to weaken and that surface features will soon begin to fill and wind down.

Below is a different system. In this case the winds upstream are stronger than downwind, so you would expect the trough to strengthen and cause development on the surface.

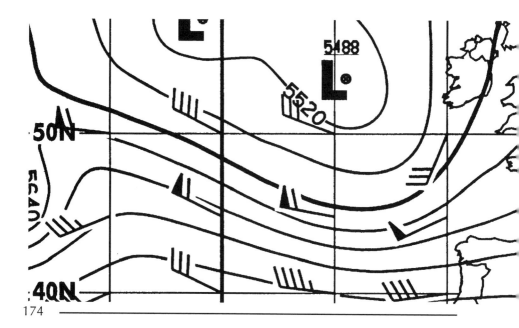

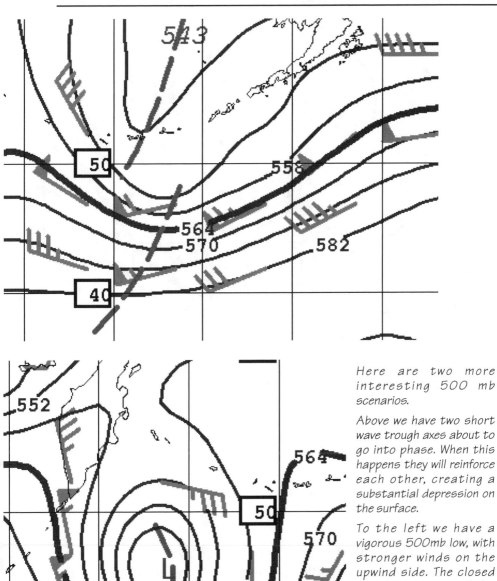

Here are two more interesting 500 mb scenarios.

Above we have two short wave trough axes about to go into phase. When this happens they will reinforce each other, creating a substantial depression on the surface.

To the left we have a vigorous 500mb low, with stronger winds on the upwind side. The closed circulation around the 5360 meter height would normally indicate that the surface low will fill. However, you would also expect at this point to have stronger winds on the leeward side rather than the windward, as shown here. The safest thing is to assume further deepening of the surface low.

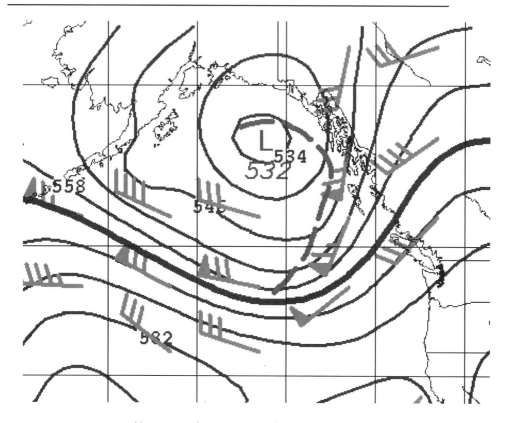

Here is another situation where the isobars have closed in the trough center. Winds are almost even between upwind and downwind sides, so it is probably reasonable to assume more or less stable 500mb conditions, with some further deepening of the surface low as the equator side of the trough axis rotates towards the east.

TROUGH AXIS ROTATION

It is worth repeating that the rotation of the trough on its axis is one of the keys to predicting surface behavior. When the equator side of the axis is pointing upwind, towards the west, the surface low is starting to develop. As the equator side of the axis rotates downwind, to the east, the surface low deepens. Once the trough axis has swung around, the surface low usually begins to fill and weaken.

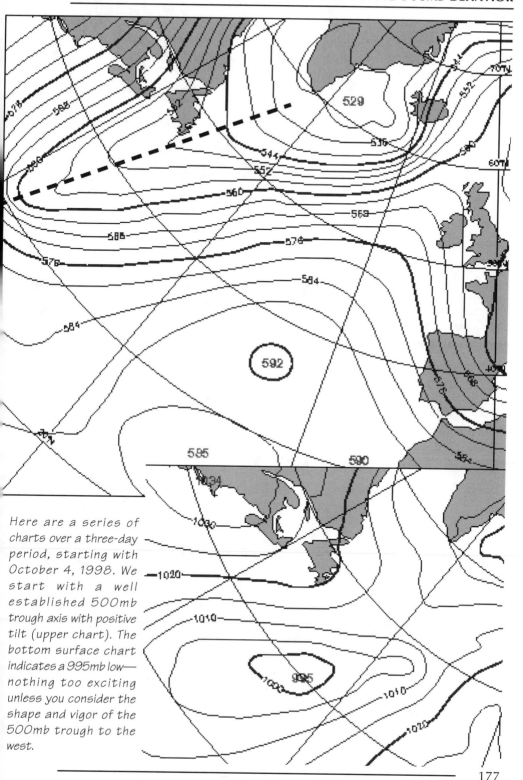

Here are a series of charts over a three-day period, starting with October 4, 1998. We start with a well established 500mb trough axis with positive tilt (upper chart). The bottom surface chart indicates a 995mb low—nothing too exciting unless you consider the shape and vigor of the 500mb trough to the west.

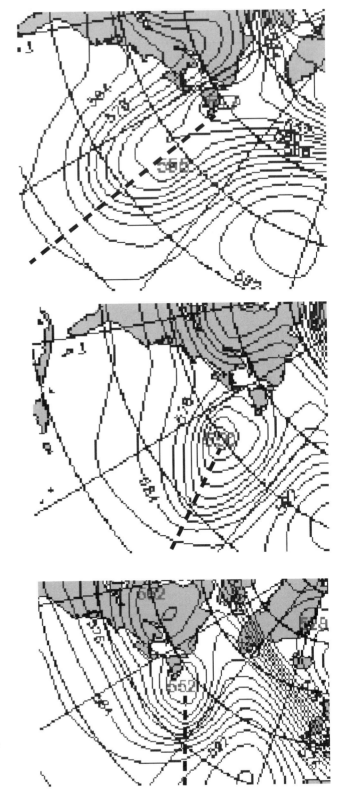

Twenty-four hours later (October 5th) and the trough axis has rotated to the east. Given the rotation of the trough axis and the shape of the trough, you would assume that the surface low was continuing to deepen to the east.

October 6th and the axis has rotated even more to the east, with the isobars now closing around the central low.

This would indicate that the surface low was about finished with its growth in strength and would shortly begin to fill.

October 7th and the trough axis is now significantly rotated to the east. The 500mb level closed low has started to rise a bit, and you could probably infer that the surface low was beginning to fill. Note the blocking ridge to the east. This could extend the surface gale conditions until it breaks down or moves east.

500MB RECAP

As you realize by now the 500mb charts are the most essential ingredient in understanding what is about to happen with the weather and what the risks really are of severe surface weather. They are a wonderful tool, and despite all the technical jargon you've just endured, they are not that difficult to understand.

We cannot overemphasize how important it is to get a feel for the patterns that exist at the time and place of your passage. The longer you study the patterns, the better you will be able to pick your departure time, and the better job you will be able to do with your tactics.

If you have access to the Internet, in most countries you will be able to download the 500mb charts every 12 to 24 hours. You can visit the local Met office, or if you have a weather fax (and this is one of the best reasons for having a fax aboard) run it for a week or two before you depart.

It is worth repeating that the key here is in recognizing the patterns that exist when you are getting ready to go. Because these patterns are relatively long-term, they show up well over a period of a couple of weeks.

We want to close this section with a recap of some of the rules you will need to keep in mind.

SURFACE TO 500MB OFFSET

Offset between the surface and 500mb waves indicates storm potential.

As the 500mb wave moves towards the surface low, the surface low deepens and intensifies.

As the 500mb trough begins to close and form a 500mb low, the surface development will be at a maximum.

Once the 500mb low has formed a closed isobar, and is over the surface low, surface conditions will begin to improve.

In the Northern Hemisphere: If the trough runs from the northeast to the southwest, this is an indicator that divergence is stable and there will not be rapid intensification at the surface.

If the trough runs from southwest to the northeast it is probably unstable and there exists the risk of rapid intensification.

In the Southern Hemisphere: If the trough axis runs from the southeast to the northwest the odds are that the situation will remain stable. If the trough runs from the northwest to the southeast then the situation is potentially unstable.

ZONAL TO MERIDIONAL FLOW

Zonal (west-to-east) flow is unstable. When you see zonal flow it is an indicator of the potential for dangerous weather.

As zonal flow breaks down to meridional flow, rapid development of surface lows can occur. The faster the change from zonal to meridional, the nastier surface conditions are likely to be.

CUT-OFF LOW DEVELOPMENT

A low cut off from the normal meridional or zonal flow brings with it a dangerous pool of cold air.

In the early stages of the break away from the parent stream, risks are high for rapid development of surface wind and rain.

While the cut-off lows can exist for many days after the greatest surface wind, risks exist in the first three or four days of their development.

RIDGE BLOCKING

Where a high pressure ridge is blocking long or short waves, if a closed low forms you may have strong surface winds.

These typically will occur on the west side, towards the equator, from the blocked low.

CONFIRMING 500MB PROJECTIONS

Since 500mb charts are drawn by computer, the results do not always fit the real world. The more data that is available, the better the computer analysis works. Forecasters usually check the computer output by looking at the water vapor wave length on satellite images. The water vapor leaves a trail which indicates 500mb activity before anything can be seen in visible or infrared wave lengths.

The less balloon sounding data available, the more important these water vapor images become.

By getting on the Internet and looking at satellite images which cover your sailing area and that to the west, you can confirm the 500mb charts. When there is a difference, go with the satellite image.

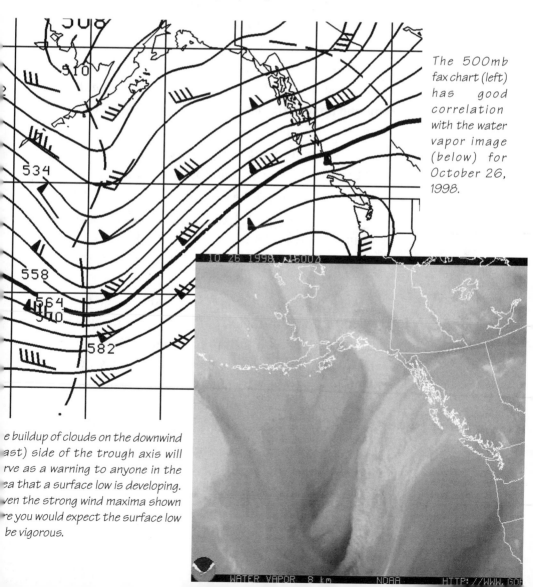

The 500mb fax chart (left) has good correlation with the water vapor image (below) for October 26, 1998.

e buildup of clouds on the downwind ast) side of the trough axis will rve as a warning to anyone in the ea that a surface low is developing. ven the strong wind maxima shown re you would expect the surface low be vigorous.

THE JET STREAM

The jet streams are typically thought of as high altitude phenomenon (around 40,000 feet or 12,000 meters).

These fast-moving currents of air are the result of extreme temperature gradients between polar air masses on one side and warmer air masses towards the equator on the other.

During the winter they move toward the equator, and during the summer towards the poles—the same as with the 500mb flows.

Every jet stream will generate a storm, it is just a question of where and when.

Because we are dealing with a three-dimensional atmosphere, in which everything affects everything else, the high-altitude jet streams are inexorably bound up with the activity at the 500mb level we've just been discussing.

In some parts of the world where 500mb charts are not available, you will almost always find 200 or 250mb data at airports as this is primarily used by jet aircraft in their route planning. In New Zealand, for example, they broadcast a 250mb chart over the same frequencies as they send the marine surface charts.

Below 30 degrees of latitude if you see upper level clouds, it is usually the result of jet stream interaction with local moisture.

For the mariner, there is some added data to be gleaned from this region of the atmosphere, but the best information is still to be found at the 500mb level, where the signatures of various waves, troughs, and ridges are more pronounced and easier to read.

The same rules we've just discussed for 500mb signs apply equally at the 250mb (jet stream) level.

JET STREAM COMPONENTS

There are three main components of the jet stream. The warmest is the subtropical jet. This brings the warm, moist air up from the tropics. It is a key component in the power-generating equation.

The middle flow of the jet stream is known as the polar jet. This is, as its name implies, typically farther north. When it stays north, conditions in the mid-latitudes are benign. When the polar jet begins to undulate towards the equator, the cold air it is bringing with it comes into contact with the warmer moist air from the subtropics, and the potential for rapid weather development at lower levels improves.

The third flow of the jet stream is called the arctic jet. This is the coldest, driest airflow.

The equator-to-pole and pole-to-equator flows of these upper-level streams are one of the key balancing components for the earth's atmosphere.

The three main components of the jet stream are:

❑ The subtropical jet (coming up from the equator.

❑ The polar jet from the mid to higher latitudes.

❑ The arctic jet from the highest latitudes (coldest and driest).

THE JET STREAM IN WINTER

During the winter, the jet stream is an indicator of unsettled weather under and to the north of its axis.

If you are sailing during the winter in the tropics, the jet stream will hold little of interest. However, if you are making a passage from the temperate climate toward the tropics, you will want to be well to the equator side of the jet stream when you depart, with enough time to get well away before any troughs or waves move into your area.

The temperature contrasts between the various jet streams is what caused the westerly flow aloft. The more contrast in temperature, the faster the wind.

CLOUD SIGNATURES

As we've discussed in the 500mb section, keep an eye peeled aloft for fast moving cirrus clouds. These are the best surface indicator we have of jet stream activity.

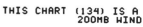

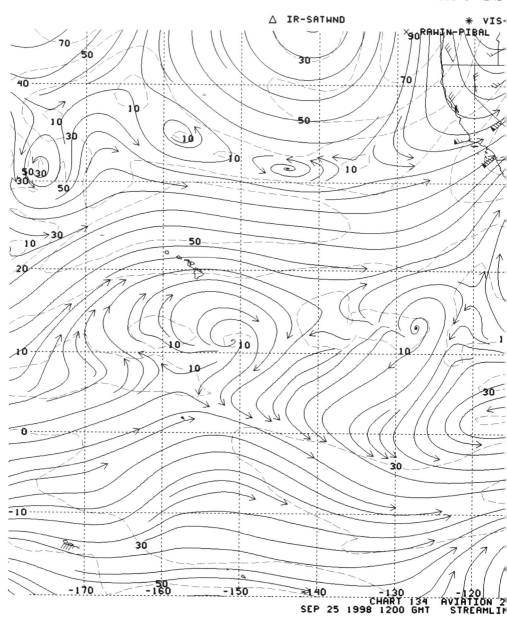

A 200mb chart for September 25, 1998 (1200Z), issued by the Tropical Prediction Center. Note the essentially zonal flow across the Pacific mid-latitudes—both north and south of the equator.

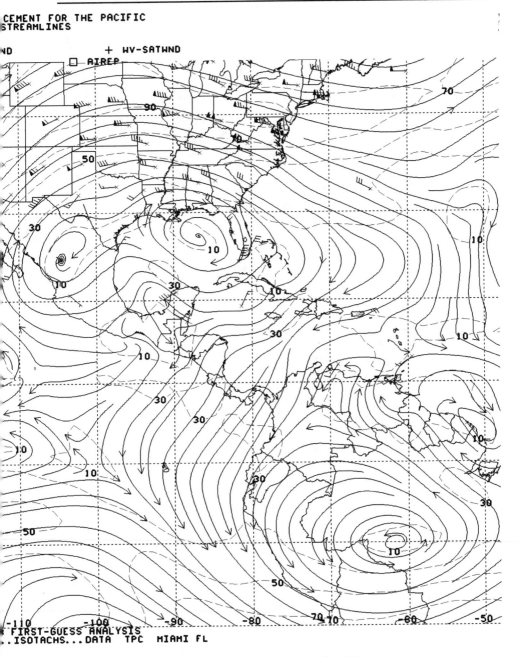

As this is a marine chart, most wind arrows are left off. However, you can infer temperature gradient and therefore wind strength by the closeness of the contour lines. In the Pacific Northwest, for example, flow is turning toward the northeast and is accelerating (shown by the close spacing of contour heights).

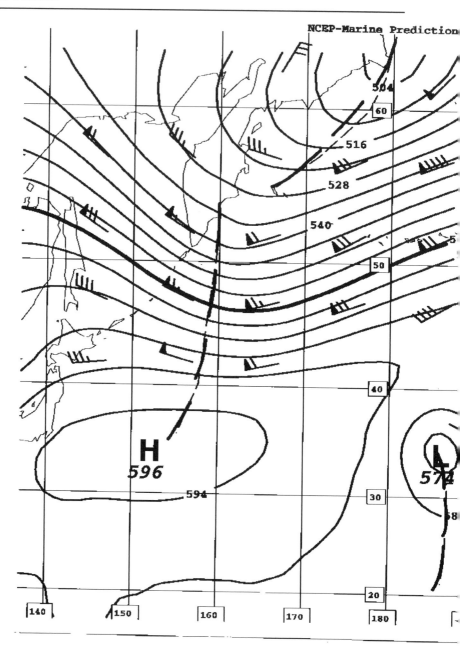

NCEP-Marine Prediction

500mb chart for the same time period for comparison purposes. Note the strong zonal flow over the Central Pacific. The two short waves shown on the west side of the chart will bear watching. If they get into phase with the southerly wave, bringing warm air to meet the colder air mass of the northerly wave, rapid development will occur on the surface.

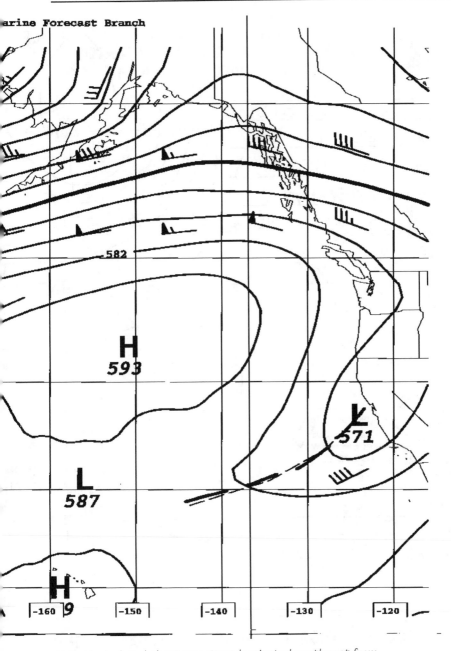

Note the isolated short wave trough oriented southwest from
the San Francisco Bay area (35 degrees N/125 degrees W). If
there were more of a height contour, this could be something to
watch carefully. However, with the moderate temperature
differential indicated by the two widely separated height
contours, this should remain benign.

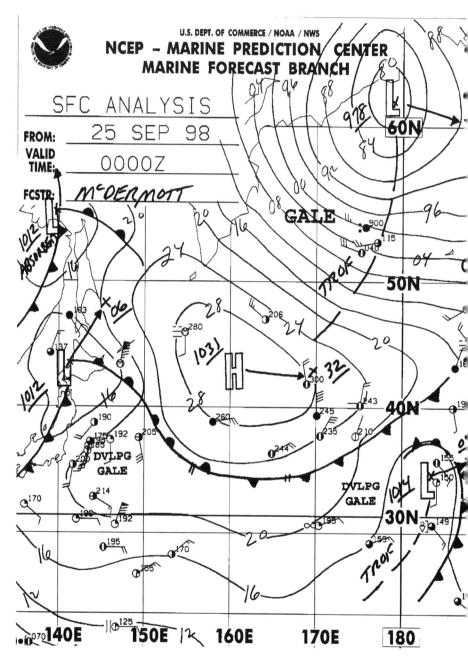

A surface chart for the same time period. Two interesting features are on this chart. The first is the enormous storm system at the top of the chart in the Gulf of Alaska. The 500mb trough is almost directly above it so it should start to fill and wind down over the next day or so.

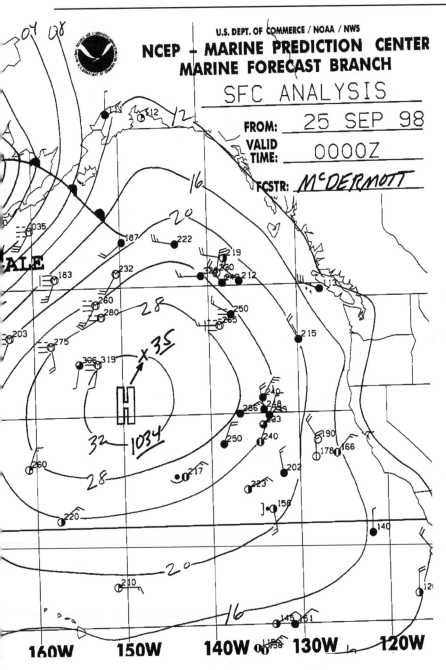

*The other issue is the surface trough at 33 degrees N and 178 degrees W.
By itself it looks harmless enough. But go back and check out the 500mb
trough to the west. When this overtakes the surface, rapid development
could occur—especially if it is in phase with the short wave to the north.*

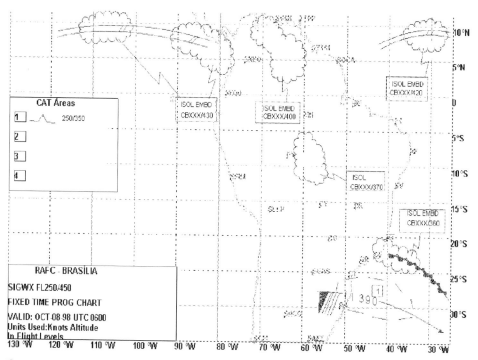

These are South American aviation charts (from Brazil and Argentina). These indicate surface fronts, and upper level cloud features which are indicative of vertical instability. These are not ideal for surface forecasting, but sometimes they are all you can get.

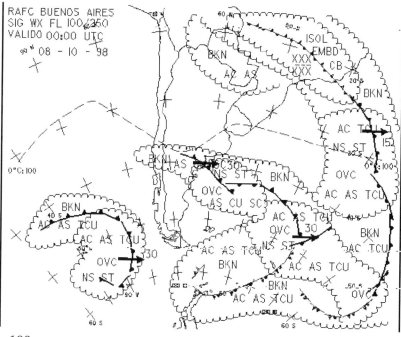

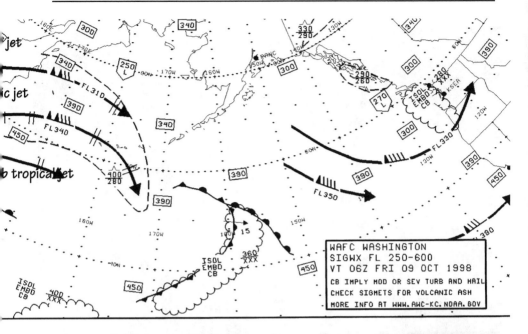

WAFC WASHINGTON
SIGWX FL 250-600
VT 06Z FRI 09 OCT 1998
CB IMPLY MOD OR SEV TURB AND HAIL
CHECK SIGMETS FOR VOLCANIC ASH
MORE INFO AT WWW.AWC-KC.NOAA.GOV

Here are two examples of U.S. aviation charts for altitudes 25,000 to 60,000 feet. On the upper level chart you can see a moderately strong jet with the area to the west and south of the Aleutian Islands showing a pronounced dig to the south. You can probably infer from this equator dig that there will be a 500mb level trough forming in this area.

The bottom chart is a detail from two days later. Notice how the jet shown with an axis on the 140W longitude line has amplified toward the equator from the upper chart. This is a sign that there is probably a 500mb trough below this that is doing something similar, and that there will be a surface low developing rapidly to the east of the trough axis.

Aviation charts like this are not as informative as 500mb charts, but when the latter are missing they will help to fill in the gaps.

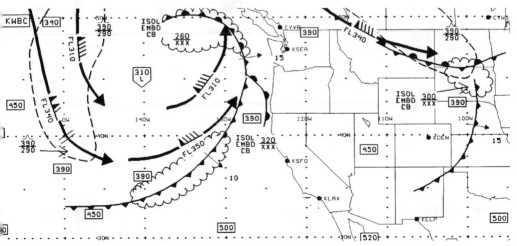

There are always signs of an approaching warm front, well ahead of any change in the barometer. The sunset (above) gives fair warning of the front's approach some 30 to 50 miles away. The lower photo was taken after the barometer has already begun to fall.

Low Pressure Tactics

Everything we've talked about so far is a foundation for what comes next—low pressure tactics. With an understanding of the forces that drive lows and their associated fronts, and how the winds work around the center, you can position yourself to take advantage of the changing winds—or at least mitigate the discomfort and/or risks that may be associated with them.

Let's take a minute and recap the basic behavior of lows.

Lows (or depressions as they are also called) circulate in a counterclockwise direction in the Northern Hemisphere and clockwise direction in the Southern Hemisphere.

They generally (but not always) track in an easterly direction.

There is a warm front attached to the low center, which is followed at some distance by a cold front, also attached to the low center.

Sea level winds are angled inward, toward the center of the low, while the winds at altitude, where surface friction is not an issue, follow the isobar lines. This accounts for the difference in direction you see between lower cloud layers and the surface wind.

The direction of the center of the low can be determined by placing your back to the wind and pointing with your left arm at right angles (or more accurately at about 100 to 110 degrees) to the wind in the Northern Hemisphere, and with your right arm in the Southern Hemisphere.

And, as we've already discussed, you can also track the progress of the low as it approaches by cloud sequence and with the barometer.

Extratropical low check list:

☐ Circulates counterclockwise in N. Hemisphere.

☐ Circulates clockwise in S. Hemisphere.

☐ Track generally in an easterly direction.

☐ Warm front attached to center is followed by cold front.

☐ Surface winds angle in 15 to 20 degrees toward center from isobars on surface fax charts.

☐ Winds aloft follow isobars.

☐ Find center with back to wind and point to left in N. Hemisphere and point to right in S. Hemisphere.

"NORMAL" DEPRESSIONS

There is no such thing as a normal depression. They all need to be watched with care. However, our own experience has been that the vast majority of the lows have been moderate in intensity and duration.

For the most part, they've lasted less than 18 hours, with winds rarely exceeding 35 knots.

Of course, there have been the exceptions!

N. HEMISPHERE WIND DIRECTION

If you are *directly* on the track of the low, the wind direction stays the same as the center approaches, typically blowing from the southeast to south southeast. As the depression *center* passes, there is a switch in wind direction of almost 180 degrees to the northwest.

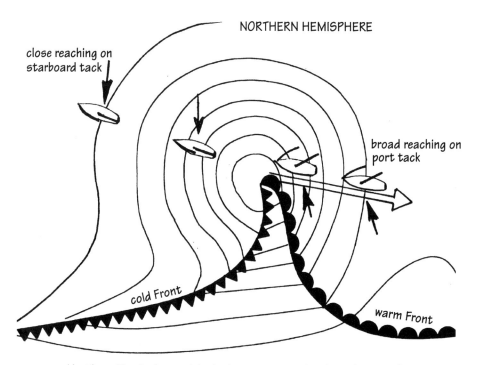

Northern Hemisphere, with the low center coming directly toward your position. You start out with the wind on port tack, then as the center passes it goes to starboard forward of the beam.

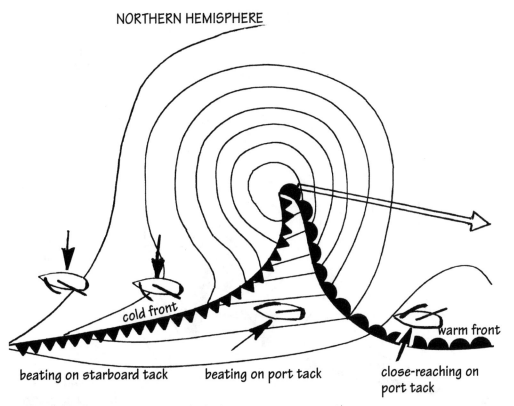

NORTHERN HEMISPHERE

cold front

warm front

beating on starboard tack   beating on port tack   close-reaching on port tack

Northern Hemisphere with the low center to your north—you start out close-reaching to beating on port tack, then the wind goes further forward after the warm front passes. After the cold front passes, the wind shifts to the north and you are beating to close-reaching on starboard tack.

When the center of the disturbance is north of you the wind starts out in the south to southwest, and then eventually clocks around to the northwest as the low moves past. An abrupt veering (clockwise shift) in wind direction usually comes as the cold front passes.

If the low center is to your south, you will have east to southeast winds ahead of the system, swinging to the northeast and then northwest as it passes.

NORTHERN HEMISPHERE

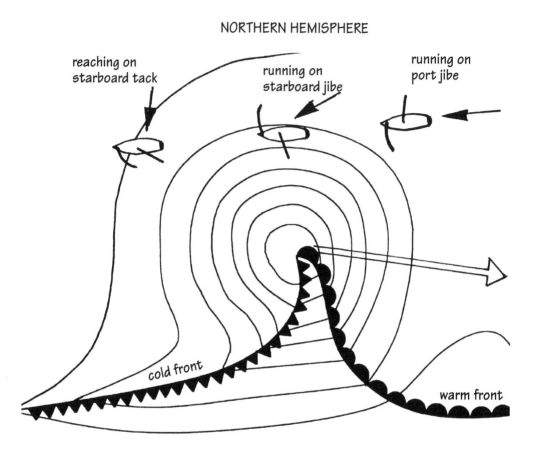

reaching on
starboard tack

running on
starboard jibe

running on
port jibe

cold front

warm front

In the Northern Hemisphere, with the low center to your south,
the wind starts out behind you, then backs (goes counterclockwise) as you pass the center, until you are reaching on
starboard tack after the low center has passed.

S. HEMISPHERE WIND DIRECTION

Down south of the equator, everything is backwards. (Would you believe that in Australia and
New Zealand, the toilets flush backwards, light
switches are the opposite of the Northern Hemisphere, and in the days of dial telephones they dialed
counter-clockwise However, this doesn't seem to
affect their sailing abilities!)

If you are directly on the track of the depression, the wind starts out of the north quadrant and stays there until the system has passed, when it switches to the south quadrant.

If you are on the north (equator) side of the depression, the wind starts out of the northwest to north, and then switches to the southwest as the system passes.

When you are to the south (pole side) of the depression, the winds start up in the northeast, gradually swinging around to the southeast as the center passes and eventually going to south southeast.

SOUTHERN HEMISPHERE

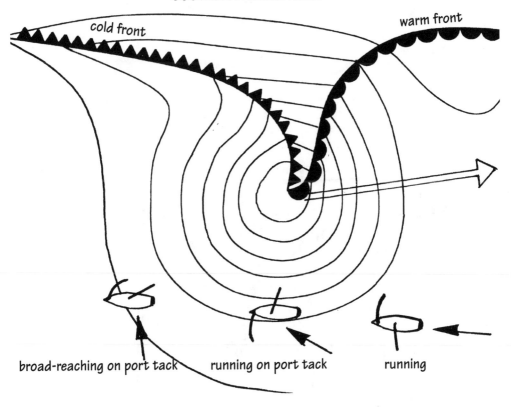

Winds circulate clockwise around the low center in the Southern Hemisphere. When you are sailing to the south of the low, on the pole side, you have fair winds as shown here.

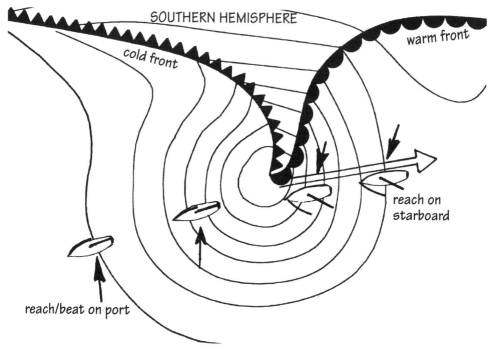

Sailing through the center of the low you have the wind on starboard to begin with and then on port after the center passes. Being to the north of the center (below), the equator side, guarantees you a dead beat.

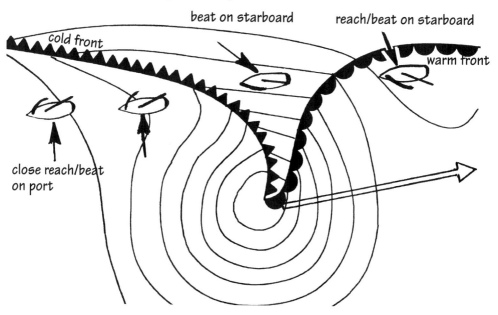

WIND STRENGTH

As we have discussed, wind strength is a function of the pressure gradient (isobar spacing) *and the direction of movement* of the weather system.

This means that on one side of the system, the speed of travel is added to the wind strength and on the other it is deducted.

In the Northern Hemisphere, the south or equator side of the low has the most wind and the north side the least.

In the Southern Hemisphere, it is the north side of the depression (again the equator side) that has the most wind and the pole (south) side of the system has the least.

You always want to keep an eye out for isobar compression caused by mountains or other weather systems (a high) into which the low is bumping.

If you have a weather fax aboard you will want to keep a close eye on the 500mb charts. These will give you the best leading indicator of the possibility for rapid development of extratropical storm systems. There is no better tool available to the mariner for forecasting than these upper-level charts.

Finally, gustiness needs to be factored in. As previously discussed, this is generally higher during the day, and after the passage of the cold front portion of the system.

SEA STATE

More important than the depression itself is the likely sea-state. This is a function of fetch (the distance over which the wind has been blowing), the strength of the wind and time it has blown, water depth, and any current that may be present.

Keep in mind that as the low system passes and the wind shifts, a new set of waves will be created that will cross the first system at roughly right angles.

Sometimes these waves reinforce each other in

N. Hemisphere: wind strength issues:

- South side of east-moving low has the most wind.

- North side of east-moving low has the least wind.

S. Hemisphere wind issues:

- North side of east-moving low has the most wind.

- South side of east-moving low has the least wind.

General wind strength factors:

- Gustiness is greater in the day, especially in the afternoon and after a cold front has passed.

- Watch for compression of isobars between a slow moving high and fast moving low.

- Keep an eye out for secondary lows.

- Watch tropical lows moving out of tropics.

- Monitor 500mb charts for warning signs!

NORTHERN HEMISPHERE

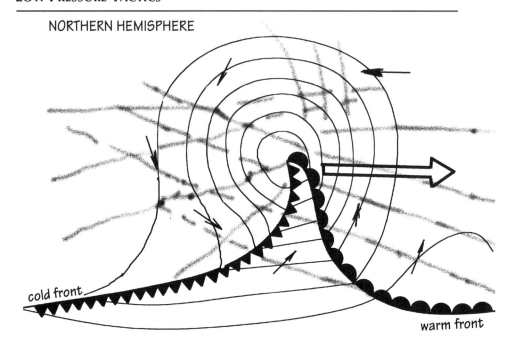

cold front

warm front

This confusing drawing is an attempt to show what the sea pattern is like after the cold front has passed and a major wind shift—usually 90 degrees or so—has taken place.

The crosshatched area above and to the left of the cold front is where the most disturbed seas will be found. Note that this sketch does not show any swells from other systems which are probably in the area as well.

unusual ways that may create large, breaking seas.

It is also worth remembering that if the wind drops rapidly after the system passes, there is the potential for very large, unstable waves to be created.

BASIC DECISIONS

What we are leading up to is the basic decision on where to position yourself relative to the low center.

Along with the weather and sea-state data, you will be thinking about how well prepared the vessel and crew are to cope with what may be coming.

After all this has been factored in, the next thing to do is to look at the likely track of the weather system, your position relative to where the center is currently located, and the speed and direction of movement you have at your disposal.

Generally speaking, positioning yourself on the poleward side of the storm center (the north side in the Northern Hemisphere — south side in the Southern) means you will have the least wind.

You will have the most wind on the equatorial side of the system (the south side in the Northern Hemisphere — north side in the Southern Hemisphere).

UPWIND DESTINATIONS

When it comes to an upwind destination, a low system is your friend. The variety of wind directions within the circulation pattern, if properly used, reduces or eliminates the need to tack back and forth.

Take, for example, a trip from Northern Europe back to the East Coast of the U.S. To minimize or eliminate head winds, you could go the tradewind route, dropping down to the Canaries and then taking the trades to the West Indies, before heading up to your final destination. But this takes the better part of six months, allowing for seasons, and is a very long way to sail — if you don't want to cruise in the Caribbean.

On the other hand, you could make a summertime passage directly across the North Atlantic. "Yuck!" you say. "I don't want to beat all the way there!"

However, if you stay to the north of the depressions as they track across the Atlantic in their west-to-east progression, you have the wind behind you.

Of course, if the depressions get to your north, you will have head winds.

Going from the Eastern Seaboard of the U.S. to Europe, just the opposite is true.

Here, you want to be south of the depressions to keep the wind behind you. If you get on the north side, you will have easterly head winds.

Your ability to play these systems to advantage has a lot to do with how far in advance you commit to a strategy, and how fast you can move to put that

Approaching low considerations:

- ❑ Condition of boat.
- ❑ Experience level of crew.
- ❑ Onboard preparation for gale or storm conditions.
- ❑ Position relative to low center (poleward side for least wind).

How far should you position yourself from the center?

This is a complex question. It is partially based on meteorology, sea room, and the issues discussed on the list above.

One of the key ingredients in the decision is the speed at which you can change location, if you suspect the situation is going to get out of hand.

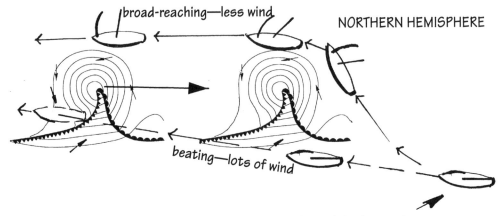

In the Northern Hemisphere (above) for fair winds heading west stay on the pole (north) side of the lows. The equator (south) side will have head winds.

In the Southern Hemisphere stay to the south (again pole side) of the low for fair winds going west. The equator (north) side has head winds.

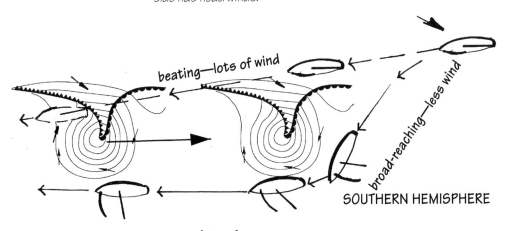

strategy into play.

The faster your boat, the more options you have. Whitbread and BOC racers sometimes sail at right angles to their course or even away from the final destination in order to properly position themselves for the coming low.

If you are on a smaller, slower vessel you may have little flexibility other than to try to pick a course that you hope will keep you in the correct part of the weather.

What Linda and I do is to look at the fax chart,

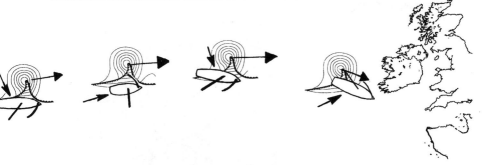

Heading to Europe from the East Coast of the U.S. almost guarantees a series of depressions en route. The key is to stay below—on the equator side—of these weather systems, so that you maintain fair winds.

make any allowances we think are required for the weather we actually have (as opposed to what the meteorologists think we have), and then plot a projected course for the low and ourselves.

I find the easiest way to do this is with a piece of tracing paper (the kind I draw boat sketches on) placed over the fax chart. Sometimes we will use the yellow Post-it notes on our navigation charts to signify where the low will be at various intervals and where we want to be with the boat.

And sometimes, despite all our efforts, things do not work out according to plan. We find ourselves heading into lots of wind and big seas, the boat is getting banged around, and we are not making a lot of progress.

Our approach when this has happened has been simple — we stop.

Generally speaking, if we heave to and wait half a day or so, the front will pass and the wind will swing to a more favorable direction.

Why beat up crew and boat for a few miles when you just wait it out, knowing wind direction will change?

When encountering adverse wind and seas from a low pressure system, it is usually best to heave to and wait until a freeing wind shift arrives.

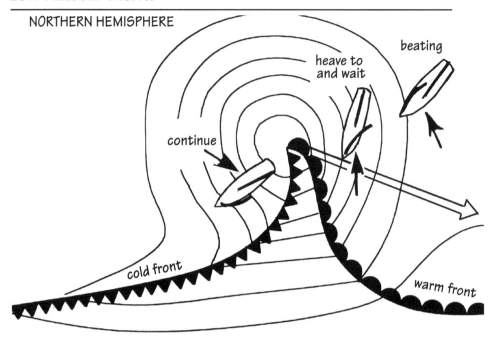

NORTHERN HEMISPHERE

Why tack back and forth on a dead beat when you can heave to, wait a few hours, and wait for the wind to shift to a more favorable angle?

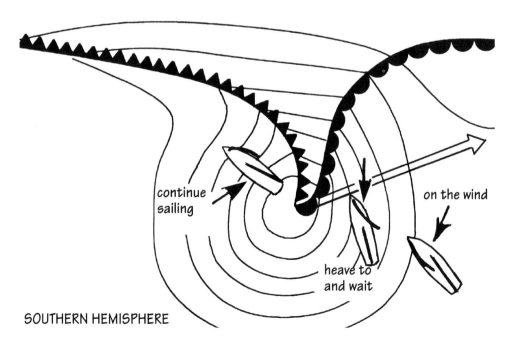

SOUTHERN HEMISPHERE

FAVORED TACK

If your destination is upwind, and you don't want to wait for the low to pass and bring you freeing winds, there is always a *favored tack* on which to approach the system.

Although the optimum solution will vary with existing wind conditions, what you expect the weather to do, and the progress you can make against the seas, it is generally best to approach the low on the tack that takes you closest to the expected favorable wind shift.

Let's say you are head southwest from Bermuda to the Virgin Islands. A low is working its way towards you on an easterly course.

As the leading edge of the circulation around the low hits, you have southerly winds shifting to southwesterly winds.

By staying on port tack and heading first southwest and then west, you are on the best course to get into the more favorable northwest circulation behind the low center. You stay on port tack until you can lay your original course on starboard tack.

Another way of looking at this is to stay on port tack until the new (backing) wind from the northwest heads you down to your original southwesterly course, so it can be sailed on starboard tack.

Let's look at what happens with the opposite tactics. If you approach the low on starboard you will be driven south and away from the favorable shift behind the low. You may even miss it entirely if you head too far south. Eventually the starboard tack will be lifted back onto course, but by this time you will probably have sailed a much longer distance and be close-reaching to get back on course as opposed to the beam-reaching course of the boat which attacked the low on port.

With a low center approaching and head winds expected:

- ❑ Stay on the tack which takes you closest to the favorable wind shift expected as the front passes.

- ❑ N. Hemisphere— usually approach the front on port tack, then switch to starboard on wind shift behind front.

- ❑ S. Hemishpere— approach on starboard tack and switch to port as shift behind front passes.

Bermuda

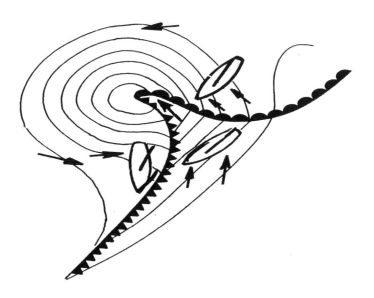

Puerto Rico

If you can't position yourself on the favored side, then approach the low close-hauled, heading in the direction which will get you to the favorable wind angle as quickly as possible. In this example, the boat is caught on the equator (wrong) side of the low as it approaches. It stays close-hauled on port, then tacks to starboard and continues southwest towards the West Indies and (hopefully) some high pressure tradewinds.

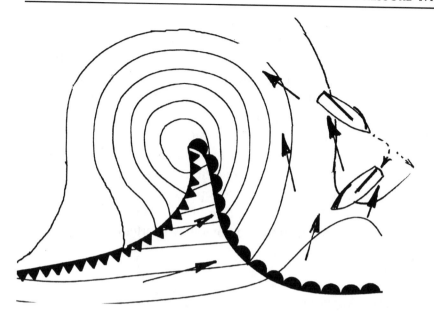

Here's the same situation, only this time the low is approached on starboard tack. This takes you away from the favored lift (and away from your destination). When you finally do tack over onto port, you are still being headed. You will continue to be headed until the depression has passed by.

RUNNING BEFORE A DEPRESSION

When you are sailing in the same direction as the depressions, you have more options with strategy.

To begin with, there is more time in which to take action as the relative approaching speed of the weather system is reduced by your boat speed. If the system is moving at 20 knots, and you are going at seven, then the speed of closure is just 13 knots. If you and the weather system were on a collision course, you would add the speeds together, giving a closure speed of 27 knots.

The key factor is to make sure you have the depression positioned so that you maintain favorable winds as the depression overtakes and passes.

If you fail to accomplish this goal and end up with head winds, usually the best thing to do, once again, is heave to and wait for the weather to calm down.

Heading east with a depression approaching:

❑ Move south of center in N. Hemisphere.

❑ Move north of center in S. Hemisphere.

Heading west:

❑ Move to north of center in N. Hemisphere.

❑ Move to south of center in S. Hemisphere.

As boat speed increases you have better ability to use these systems to your advantage.

By hanging on as long as possible in the favorable quadrant you not only make good progress, but avoid a new weather system that is almost surely following behind.

Taking this to an extreme, in a vessel like *Beowulf* we have the ability to average 13 to 15 knots in most broad-reaching conditions. This means we can hang onto a single weather system for days at a time, reducing the exposure to the unknown coming up from behind and obviously shortening our passage time.

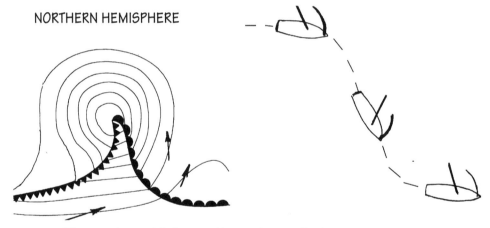

NORTHERN HEMISPHERE

When running east before weather systems, adjust course so that the low center passes on the poleward side of your boat.

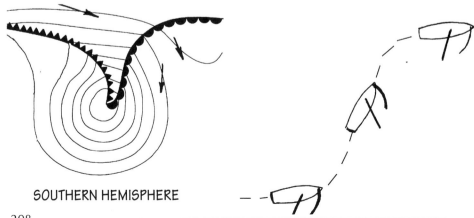

SOUTHERN HEMISPHERE

FAVORED JIBE

Most boats are happier on a broad reach rather than on a dead run. The higher the speed potential of your boat, the more this is the case.

In light to moderate winds it frequently makes sense to jibe downwind. Generally, you more than make up for the extra distance sailed with increased boat speed.

When you are running before a depression, or using the downwind circulation of a depression this

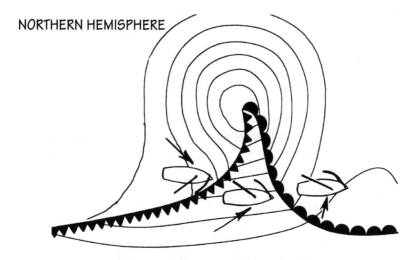

NORTHERN HEMISPHERE

Running with a depression there is a favored jibe, on which the wind angle is more on the quarter. As the depression approaches, maintain best speed by heading a bit towards the equator (unless you are sailing at hull speed). As the front approaches and the breeze increases, sail a more downwind angle. Then jibe against the shift that comes with the passage of the cold front.

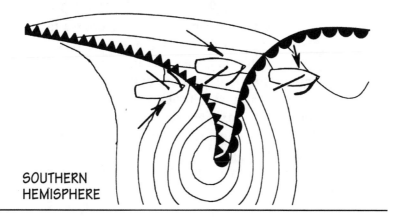

SOUTHERN
HEMISPHERE

that is coming at you, the wind shifts that occur can be used to keep you sailing at a fast angle *without sailing extra distance*.

Once again, the rule is to stay on the course that takes you closest to the next favorable wind shift.

Let's go back to that East Coast of the U.S. to Europe passage. Staying below the track of the depressions so that the wind is behind you, keep the breeze on your starboard quarter as the low center tracks to your north. The wind will be veering clockwise towards the northwest as the low passes.

Ahead of the front, in lighter winds, keep speed up and sag off the wind. Head up to the southeast if required. As the breeze picks up with the approaching front, adjust course back to leeward, increasing boat speed in the process.

When the front passes, jibe over onto port and continue on course.

If the breeze is strong enough, to the point where you are already close to hull speed, rather than heading up to keep speed and angle high (as you would in light airs), let the wind go dead behind you, while you maintain your course.

One consideration is always wind strength. Generally, when sailing off the wind you want more rather than less breeze. Getting too close to the center will reduce the wind you have to play with and have the shift take place rather quickly, which reduces its effectiveness.

Being too far away from the center also reduces the wind, with the wind shifts being more moderate.

REACHING ACROSS DEPRESSIONS

There will be times when the course takes you across the prevailing track of depressions.

When this happens it is difficult to avoid the significant swings in wind and wave direction, frequently almost 180 degrees, which are a part of crossing the axis of a depression at right angles.

Our own approach when faced with this situation is to either speed up and cross ahead of the system, or heave to and allow it to pass before carrying on.

In moderate winds, jibing before a depression when on favored side of low center for following winds:

❑ Maintain course for best speed with approach of low.

❑ As breeze increases sail further off the wind maintaining best speed.

❑ With passage of front and accompanying wind shift, jibe back onto favored course.

BENT BACK WARM FRONTS

Before leaving the subject of large-scale weather features we want to come back to the issue of extratropical storm structure.

The process described in our section on extratropical weather (starting on page 40) is based on what is known as the Norwegian Cyclone Model. This has been the standard since the early part of this century, and is what you still find in all of today's weather texts.

For the most part, this type of storm structure analysis works. But there are situations where the three-dimensional structure of a storm system can vary considerably from the Norwegian model — with significant differences in the distribution of wind and seas around the depression center.

This has been the subject of much research (and debate) for the last decade, and is the focus of what is known as the Shapiro/Kaiser extratropical cyclone model. What is not debatable is the fact that, under certain conditions, a different type of frontal structure can develop with far more severe wind and seas than the norm.

Pressure drops as great as 65mb within 24 hours have been recorded with this type of storm, with huge areas of hurricane strength winds.

During the North Atlantic Halloween storm in 1991, the area of peak winds was several hundred miles in diameter, with buoy measurements of significant wave height in the 50-foot (15.3-meter) range and maximum wave height in the 99-foot (30.4-meter) range.

The odds are that 60 to 70 percent of all severe extratropical storms exhibit this structure when they are over the ocean. Although the fax charts do not show it, the Queen's Birthday Storm (discussed on page 229) is probably this type of structure.

The Shapiro/Kaiser model of frontal structure is considerably different than the traditional "Norwegian" model which has been in use most of this century.

There are significant differences in the distribution of wind and seas around the depression center, and in the speed at which this type of storm system develops.

Because of the power of these storms, and the difference in the distribution of wind around the core, different avoidance tactics are required before the storm and different sailing tactics are required within the storm system.

FRONTAL STRUCTURE

The bent back warm front is what the Norwegian model refers to as an occlusion (see page 46 for more data).

The next eight panels show a Northern Hemisphere storm. For the Southern Hemisphere you would mirror these images, with winds circulating clockwise around the core (rather than counterclockwise as shown here).

Lee Chesneau, Senior Forecaster at the Marine Prediction Center explains, "This is a phase in the development of a maturing extratropical cyclone where the cold front slides under the warm front and as that happens the warm front wraps around the cyclone core — back into and over the cold front. Tremendous mixing of cold and warm air masses occur—the worst of which is before occlusion."

The frontal structure starts out with a normal open wave appearance. However, early into the storm's development a bent back warm front develops around the core of the depression.

This bent back warm front is an extension or continuation of the original warm front, rather than a new structure. The cold front may detach from the warm front in the form of a fracture. In the vicinity of the fracture the temperature gradient is minimal and a very gradual wind shift from the south to southwest in the Northern Hemisphere and north to northwest in the southern hemisphere is experienced.

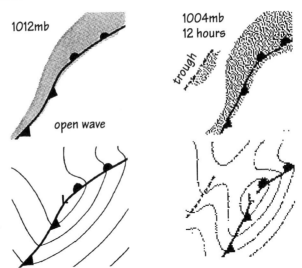

In the beginning phase, a bent back warm front scenario looks much like the situation we are used to viewing—except for the rapid fall in central pressure over time. In this case, in the first 12 hours pressure falls 12mb. Note the trough which starts the frontal process going.

In the next two drawings, the central pressure continues to fall as the warm front sweeps around the central core towards the cold front on the equator side of the storm.

The central pressure continues to fall rapidly. In the next 12 hours there is a 12mb fall, or 1mb per hour. In the succeeding period the pressure drops 15mb (1.25mb per hour).

It is this incredibly fast development, from moderate conditions to hurricane force winds, in this case within 36 hours, which makes these storms so dangerous.

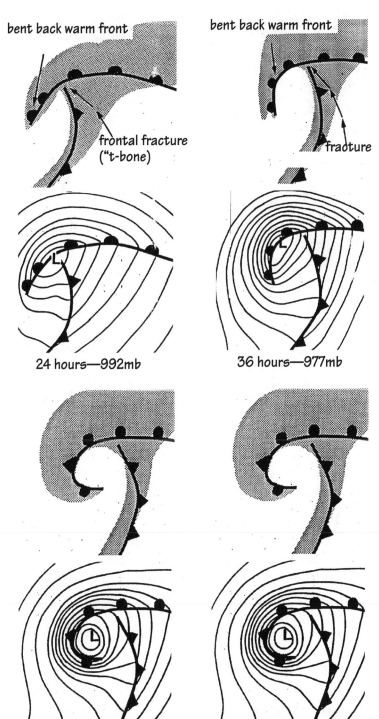

bent back warm front

frontal fracture
("t-bone)

bent back warm front

fracture

24 hours—992mb

36 hours—977mb

48 hours—962mb

60 hours—946mb

Notice how when the cold front develops it does so off the warm front rather than off the central low pressure area as we have seen in previous models.

At 48 hours, just two days after starting to form, the central pressure is now down to 962mb and still falling. At the 60-hour mark, pressure is down to 946—a drop of 16mb in the past 12 hours. (Frontal model drawings courtesy of the Marine Prediction Center.)

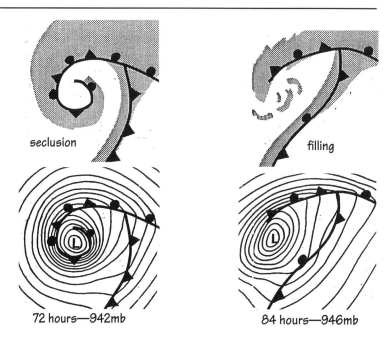

seclusion

filling

72 hours—942mb

84 hours—946mb

By 72 hours the rate of fall of the central pressure has slowed significantly, and thereafter the low begins to fill. Notice how the warm front has become occluded at this stage.

There is, in effect, a pool of warm air sitting over the low center (to an altitude of about 10,000 feet/3,000 meters), with extremely cold air immediately above.

Only in this case this frontal fracture, or "T-bone" as it is sometimes called, is in the early stages of the storm.

At this stage the warm front drapes *over* the low pressure center, and then as it matures, the warm front bends back, around the depression center.

WARM CORE

One of the unusual characteristics of these storms (as compared to what has been considered a conventional extratropical depression) is their warm core. There is, in effect, a pool of warm air sitting over the low center (to an altitude of about 10,000 feet/3,000 meters), with extremely cold air immediately above.

This structure, while verified by aircraft fly-throughs, is subject to some debate. What we can say for sure is that there is a lot of precipitation going on that is providing heat to this region of the storm—and that the very intense temperature gradient from this warm bottom/cold top structure provides the conditions required for extreme convective (thunderstorm) activity.

With conventional extratropical storms you have a cold-core center aloft. With tropical storm centers you have a warm core aloft.

SATELLITE IMAGES

Satellite images of these storms show rapid changes in cloud structure with very fast expansion of cloud mass as the depression deepens. The mature depression may resemble a tropical cyclone in cloud structure, with several coils of cloud bands spiraling around the center.

In some cases a tropical cyclone-like "eye" has been observed in the satellite images around the core of the depression.

WIND-FIELD STRUCTURE

The wind field around the central low pressure area of these storms is considerably different than with conventional extratropical depressions.

For one thing, it has been found that there are areas of moderated intensity in close proximity to the core—in some ways like what is found with tropical storms.

Forecaster Joe Sienkiewicz says that the data they have from buoys and aircraft indicates the strongest winds are near the bent back warm front. Before the storm has matured, these can be strongest on the poleward side of the system. Then, as the system matures, the winds bend around the developing warm core until they meet up with the cold front on the equator side of the storm.

Joe indicates that as the warm front curves back around the center, the wind backs from the northeast to the northwest, to south right near the center. In the Southern Hemisphere, this would be southeast to southwest, with cold air coming in from the north.

The very intense temperature gradient from the warm bottom/cold top structure provides the conditions required for extreme convective (thunderstorm) activity.

Conventional extra tropical storms have a cold core center aloft—tropical storm centers have a warm core aloft.

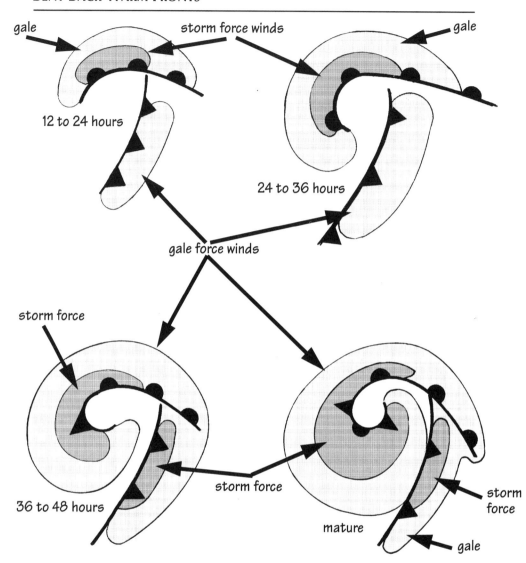

gale

storm force winds

gale

12 to 24 hours

24 to 36 hours

gale force winds

storm force

36 to 48 hours

storm force

storm force

mature

gale

Here are a series of drawings of how the wind field has been seen to develop in these bent back warm front storms. Note how the maximum force winds (dark shading) wrap around the center and spread out towards the equator. The area of gale force winds (light shading) can extend as far as thousand miles across.

These systems tend to have lighter winds in the central core area, not unlike the eye of a hurricane. However, these central core areas are much larger than found in tropical storm systems

Joe goes on to say that sometimes right under the low there is not much wind. But there is a strong boundary at the front, on the other side of which are horrendous winds and seas. In the early stages of the storm, this is typically on the pole side of the system.

WARNING SIGNS

Conventional warning signs are hard to use with a storm system like this. The rapid development means that as the barometer is dropping, the wind is increasing—and you obviously know at this point without checking the barometer that the weather is extreme. Joe Sienkiewitzc indicated he has seen pressure drops of as much as 18mb in six hours with these types of storm structure!

So what do we watch for? As you might have guessed, the 500mb chart is probably the best warning system. If you see in a series of forecasts a significant series of short-wave troughs, with a V'd structure, this is a precursor to the type of storm structure we are discussing.

Another sign is convective activity. Because of the warm-core/cold-top structure, these storms have far more thunderstorm action than what is normally associated with the development of an extratropical low pressure system.

If you have the ability to download satellite images directly (see page 565 for more data on satellite direct receivers) you can watch for a rapid expansion of cloud mass. When these lows explosively deepen they produce huge areas of cirrus clouds in a matter of hours.

So if you are in the vicinity of a deepening low, and there seems to be excessive thunderstorm activity for the your location and time of year, this is a sign that something unusual may be occurring. Note that this thunderstorm activity tends to take place in and around the center of the forming depression.

What to watch for:

- Look for a significant series of short wave troughs on the 500mb charts.

- If wind flow downwind of trough axis is strongly confluent, i.e. the isoheights are coming together, this is favorable for bent back warm front formation.

- If wind flow is strongly diffluent, i.e. spreading apart on the downwind side of the trough axis, this is more favorable for a Norwegian model front.

- Watch for more thunderstorm activity than usual for season and location.

- If you are in the vicinity of a deepening low (barometer is dropping) be even more alert for unusual signs.

- Watch for rapidly building cloud masses on satellite images.

AVOIDANCE TACTICS

The best avoidance tactic is to stay out of the areas of potential risk during the equinoctal and winter gale seasons, when these system seem to be most prevalent.

If you are caught, the decision on what to do is not quite as simple as with conventional storms (conventional depression structure tactics are covered in the previous chapter).

For one thing, as the storm matures it appears as though strongest winds are to be found on the poleward side. This is the side which would normally be considered navigable. However, if you are close to the storm center, near the frontal boundary and ahead of the storm, you are subject to very strong northeasterlies in the Northern Hemisphere (southeasterlies in the Southern).

If you are some distance away from the frontal boundary, again towards the pole, then this may be the safest side of the storm as the wind gradient is not thought to extend as far towards the pole as it does towards the equator.

Given the uncertainties of these weather systems, the extreme pressure gradients, wind fields, and rapid development, the best tactic may be to stay as far away from the center of the storm as possible.

Given the uncertainties of these weather systems, the extreme pressure gradients, wind fields, and rapid development, the best tactic may be to stay as far away from the center of the storm as possible.

Keep in mind that given the size of these storms, there is extreme fetch in which the seas can build—sometimes upwards of a thousand miles in the quadrant with northwest winds in the Northern Hemisphere (southwest winds in the Southern Hemisphere).

CHRISTMAS 1997

During the Christmas period of 1997 there was a major bent back warm front storm in the Pacific which is a good example of the potential for rapid development and danger in one of these systems.

The following fax charts cover a period of just 48 hours with a series of synoptic charts going from a benign looking open low structure with central pressure of 997mb to a huge storm system with a pressure of 944mb spanning a thousand miles of ocean.

This explosive development is typical of the bent back warm front structure.

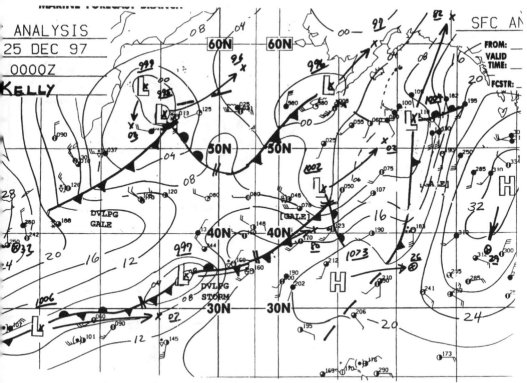

December 25, 1997, 0000Z (top chart). An innocuous looking low, labeled developing storm at 34 degrees N 175 degrees E, gives no hint of what is to come on the surface. Central pressure is 1002mb. 1800Z (below left) and the pressure has dropped to 1001mb. Still nothing to get excited about except the "DVLPG STORM" label.

0000Z on the 26th (bottom right) and things have started to explode! Central pressure in six hours had dropped to 985mb—a drop of 16mb in six hours. This is an excellent example of why it pays to monitor the fax on a frequent basis when you are in risk areas.

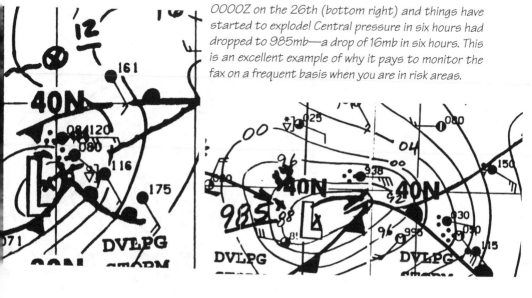

Six hour later, at 0600Z on the 26th (upper chart) and the pressure has dropped to 968mb, another 19mb. The relationship of the fronts is still quite open, but the area of storm force winds is spreading rapidly.

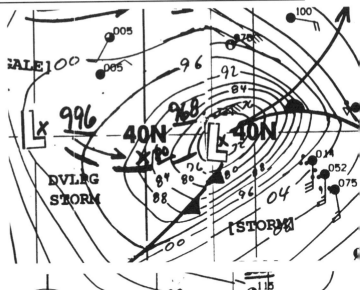

1200Z (middle chart) and the pressure is down to 960mb. The drop has slowed, but is still greater than 1mb per hour. The frontal structure at the surface is beginning to assume the look of a bent back warm front.

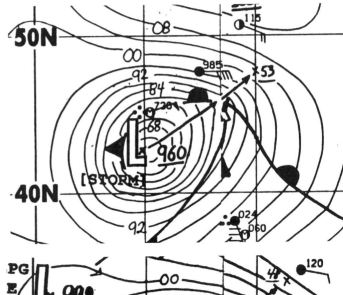

1800Z (bottom chart) and central pressure is down to 944mb. That's a drop of 16mb in the past six hours. The fractured frontal arrangement is now plainly evident.

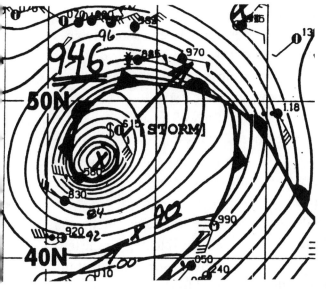

OOOZ on the 27th. Central pressure is now stabilized and has risen slightly to 946 mb.

Note that the strongest winds are shown in the north (pole side) quadrant, while winds to the south, what would normally be considered the dangerous side of the storm, are somewhat less.

Six hours later (below), at 0600Z and central pressure is still at 944mb. The storm force winds have now enveloped the area to the south (equator side) of the storm center. Note the lighter winds in the core itself. Ship reports of conditions make these charts more than a forecaster's guess—this is the real thing. Gale force winds now cover a diameter of 1000 nautical miles.

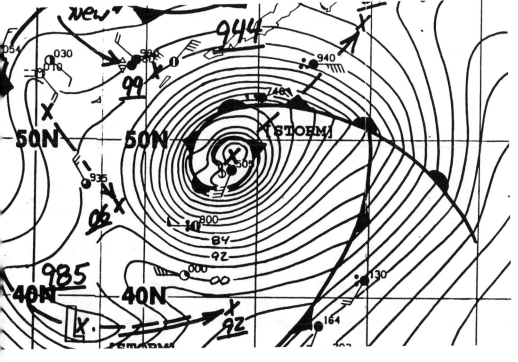

This type of storm system features rapid development of the cloud signature and expansion of cloud mass.

Following are two sample charts from the National Weather Service's Marine Prediction Center. These are used to identify cloud signatures and help forecast bent back warm front events.

You cannot be expected to use these in the same manner as a professional who works with them on a daily basis, but they will give you an idea of the cloud signature, and what to watch for.

CLOUD SIGNATURES

If it is necessary to traverse areas of the world subject to this type of storm structure, it soon becomes apparent that some form of early warning device is essential. Keeping a close eye on the weather service faxes is of course the ideal solution. This means watching the upper level as well as surface charts.

But forecasters occasionally miss the start of these systems, and if the human side of the equation misses, then the weather faxes won't show the problem until it is too late.

With satellite direct reception equipment you have a leg up on the situation. Watching for the telltale cloud signature will give you a warning at the same time as the land-based forecaster, without the lag time for land-based analysis and dissemination. Given the speed at which these storms develop, even a six-hour head start on the situation can be critical.

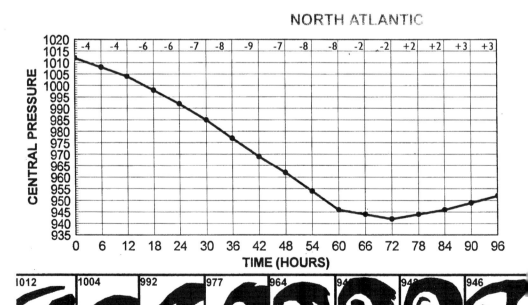

NORTH ATLANTIC

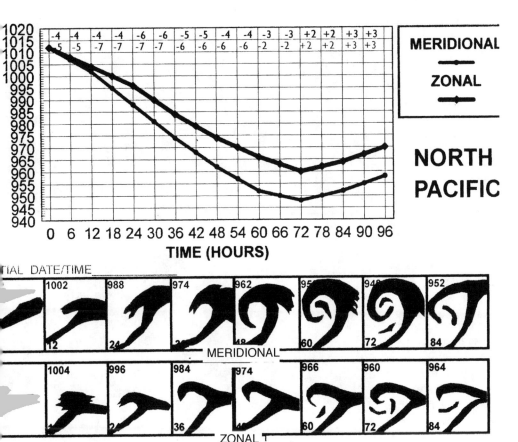

This system is based on the evolution of the back edge of the comma head shape in the clouds, as compared to the main mass of clouds on the equator side of the storm (called the "baroclinic band" by the professionals). The shape of these clouds indicates the strength of the storm, internal structure, and degree of development.

The cloud patterns for the Pacific and Atlantic vary, as does the life cycle of the storm. Atlantic systems are shown on the previous page. This panel shows Pacific storms based on a meridional or zonal pattern at the 500mb level.

The key to using the system is to make an analysis every six hours, so the trend of the storm is captured on paper.

The December 25, 1997 storm reviewed in the previous pages was not well predicted by the computer models of the 500mb level. However, surface level data and these cloud images gave the forecasters the tools they needed. This first image is from 0600Z.

These images are enhanced infrared. The dark areas are the cold cloud tops.

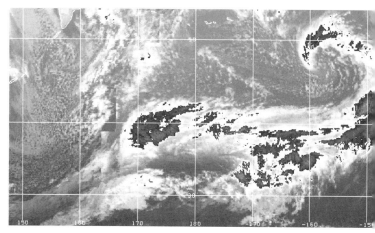

The second image is for six hours later, and just 12 hours after the first synoptic chart which shows no hint of the ferocious brew Mother Nature is cooking.

1800Z on the 25th. and the central pressure is at 1001mb. The early development of the "comma" shape of the cloud structure is clearly visible in these images. Had you seen these yourself you would have known to take immediate evasive action.

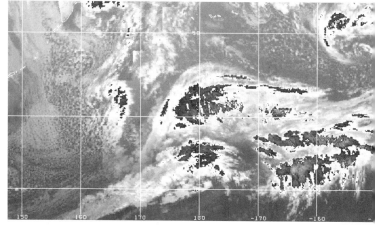

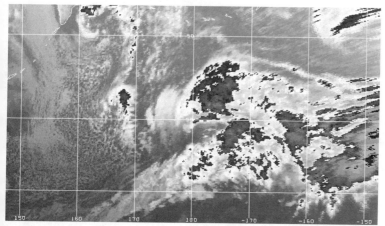

OOOZ on the 26th and the central portion of the storm continues to develop. The surface synoptic charts are showing a 985mb low.

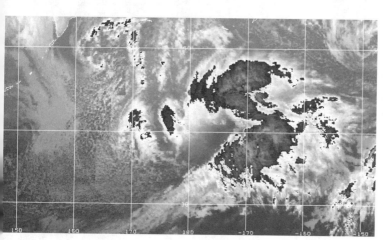

0600Z and the central pressure has dropped to 968mb.

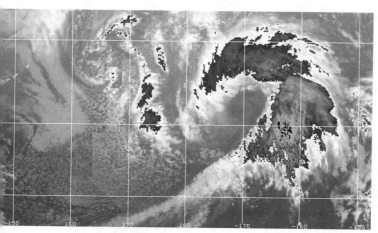

1200Z on the 26th and things are now very well organized on the synoptic chart with a central pressure of 960mb.

The cloud signature development of the past 24 hours is your best way to know the potential severity of this blow.

1800Z on the 26th of December and the comma head shape of the storm is now very well defined. Central pressure is down to 944mb and the storm covers almost 20 degrees of longitude.

The close-up view (below) is from 0000Z on the 27th of December. Central pressure is at 946 and the storm is fully mature. Keep in mind that the images you have looked at so far cover only 42 hours—less than two days.

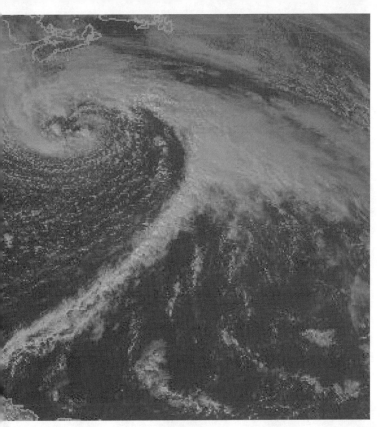

When you consider the awesome power and speed with which these storms develop it is only natural to feel some degree of appre-hension—perhaps even some fear. For those who earn their living upon the sea with schedules to maintain and fish to catch, these storm systems are a part of what is a potentially dangerous existence. By being aware of the development process profes-sional mariners can take early avoiding action.

With those of us who use the sea for our pleasure the situation is different. By picking our seasons conserva-tively and then waiting for the proper weather window, the odds of an encounter can be reduced to an accept-able level—something like the risk of a severe automobile accident. And if worrying about car accidents doesn't keep you home, then bent back warm fronts shouldn't either.

...tober 20th, 1997 ... the Atlantic ...aboard. This ...stem produced ...e force winds from ...va Scotia to 28 ...rees N, a distance ...roughly 1000 ...utical miles. Storm ...rce winds were ...served within 300 ...utical miles of the ...ter!

...te the classic ...mma signature ...uds of a bent back ...rm front ...stem—this could ...confused with a ...opical system ...cept for the ...itude. The open ...re of the comma ...ape is over the ...face low center.

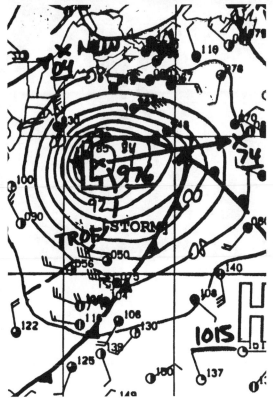

If you take time to watch the weather patterns, and avoid tight schedules so that you can pick the right day to leave on a passage, adverse weather can usually be avoided. Using this approach you will find the vast majority of cruising weather pleasant and passages enjoyable, with the incentive of an idyllic anchorage in which to take a short row once the anchor is down.

QUEEN'S BIRTHDAY STORM

It would be nice to be able to say that weather always conforms to a certain pattern, and that the forecasters always get it right. But as you know by now, this is not the case.

Most of the time, maybe even 99 percent of the time, by picking your seasons, and listening to the forecasts, everything will go smoothly. But that still leaves the one percent of the time when things go wrong.

The passage to New Zealand from Fiji and Tonga is one in which you expect to see at least one gale. You are headed south (from Fiji) or southwest (from Tonga) and the weather systems are coming up the Tasman with a northern track. The combined speed of approach between you and the depressions, and the passage distance of 1,100 to 1,200 miles means a meeting is almost unavoidable. We all understand this, prepare for it, and take what is usually a rather brief gale in stride.

When you leave New Zealand for the tropics, the situation typically improves. Now you are typically heading the *same* direction as the weather systems, so the speed of approach is much reduced.

You can sit in Auckland or the Bay of Islands waiting for the right moment—one with a nice big high just starting to push its way up from Australia, usually on the back of a low—and then take off knowing you've got three to five days to get into the tropics and away from the next depression coming along from farther south.

JUNE 1, 1994

That's exactly the scenario that presented itself at the beginning of June 1994. This was right in the middle of the season for those yachts leaving New Zealand's oncoming winter for a bit of sun and fun in the tropics.

This storm represents an excellent opportunity to analyze a major weather system precisely because it impacted so many vessels.

There is lots of anecdotal evidence from yachts within the storm, those just outside of it, and weather professionals who have studied it extensively.

We'll start out with a basic recitation of what happened, then move on to a "conventional" dissection of the events. Finally, we'll look at the storm from a 500mb view (which was not available to the participants), and then in the context of a bent back comma structure—which it appears was the structure of this storm system.

We are indebted to Bob McDavitt of the New Zealand Met Service for digging out the fax charts shown here and for his help in reconstructing what follows. Bob has written an excellent primer on South Pacific weather, called the *Met Service Yacht Pack* (see the bibliography at the end of the book for how to order). It is clear and concise, and if you are planning on heading to the South Pacific, you will find it immensely helpful.

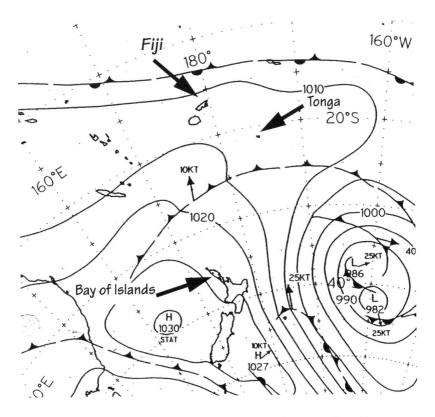

This is a classic "go for it" weather scenario for a fast, comfortable passage to the tropics. The low to the east (right) has passed a couple of days previously, bringing behind it a large high pressure system. The leading edge of the high brings southerly quadrant winds, making for a nice broad reach for the sail up to the tropics. One of the keys is to get away early and keep moving before the northerlies, on the backside of the high, arrive in the area.

With this large a high you normally have three to four days of fair winds before the breeze goes on the nose.

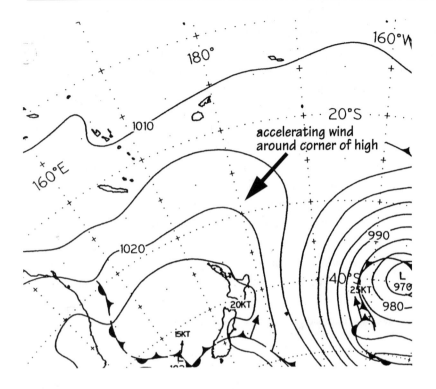

June 2, and things are still looking good. There's likely to be an acceleration of the wind around the northeast corner of the high, as the wind makes the turn. This will make for boisterous sailing, but nothing dangerous.

The low to the east is receding rapidly and will allow the following high center to move over the North Island bringing with it light winds. This is probably too late to be leaving as the light, slow start will allow the back side of the high to catch up before hitting the tradewind belt—and this means a long, uncomfortable beat to the Islands.

The *surface* fax charts from the New Zealand Met Service show a perfect set up for leaving. If Linda and I had been waiting to sail we'd have picked this moment to clear customs and head north.

At this point in time, a whole series of yachts are en route to Tonga in a cruising rally, and others heading for Fiji.

Two days later, with conditions still ideal along the track north from New Zealand, a depression starts to form between Vanuatu and Fiji.

Any <u>time</u> you see a closed isobar (or a low center) in the tropics it is cause for concern.

That single closed isobar shown on the chart looks pretty innocuous all by itself. The question, and the risk factor, lies in what will happen if the low moves south and begins to be influenced by cool, dry air from the high latitudes well to the south, riding the high towards the tropics.

In many cases nothing at all will happen. The low will fill within a day or two and that will be that. Maybe boats within 50 to 100 miles of the depression center will see a few squalls and a disturbance in the tradewind flow for a few days.

Nadi Weather in Fiji issued an easterly gale warning on the third at 0715 — but there was nothing urgent in the warning — no hint of what was to come.

Yet a warning is there for anyone with a weather

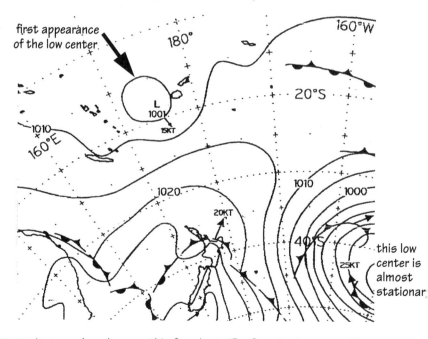

There are two warning signs on this fax chart. The first is the tropical low centered between Fiji and New Caledonia. The second is indicated by the low that had been moving east on the 40th parallel. Note how it has only moved a small amount to the east in the past 24 hours. This holds the high in place, while the breeze between the two systems accelerates from the south (the low is rotating clockwise—the high counter-clockwise). The strong flow of wind from the south has the potential to bring with it cool, dry air, one of the main ingredients to turn a tropical low into a sub-ropical "bomb."

fax to see—any time you see a depression in the tropics, it must be watched with care and the worst assumed, until you know otherwise with a degree of certainty.

THE LOW DEEPENS

By noon on the fourth, the low has moved to 25 degrees south—now in the subtropics—and is deepening rapidly. A classical warm front leads off to the east from the center, trailed by a cold front. NZ Met Service issues a storm warning—five hours <u>after</u> the first EPIRB has been set off aboard one of the passaging yachts.

Always assume the worst, and have a contingent plan ready—in case the tropical low matures into something potentially dangerous.

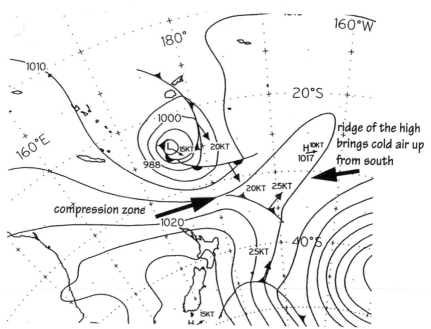

June 4 is a critical day from a tactical standpoint. The low is deepening and has run up against the high pressure system being held in place by the now stationary low well to the east. If you are caught in the area between the two weather systems, the wind will be increasing rapidly, yet the barometer reading stays the same. This is because the isobars are being crushed together between the low and high—increasing the pressure gradient with a steady barometer.

In the absence of a weather report, the increase in wind and steady barometer are enough to indicate a compression zone between two weather systems. You can find the low center by taking the wind on your back and pointing with your right arm. The next step is to move as fast as possible to the west of the probable southeasterly storm track.

This system is running into the high to the south, with a long ridge of high pressure pointing to the northeast, feeding cool dry air into the low and accelerating the maturing process as the warm air from the center of the depression rushes aloft.

Whenever you have a tropical or subtropical low and a nearby source of cool, dry air the risk of rapid intensification exists.

Between noon on the third and noon on the fourth the central pressure of the low drops from 1001 mb to 986mb, making this a classical "bomb" scenario. Winds around the core at this point are estimated to be in the 50-knot range. Certainly uncomfortable, but nothing a well found yacht can't handle.

Twenty-four hours later the depression had deepened to a low of 979mb and had moved to a position of 30 degrees South latitude, 180 degrees longitude.

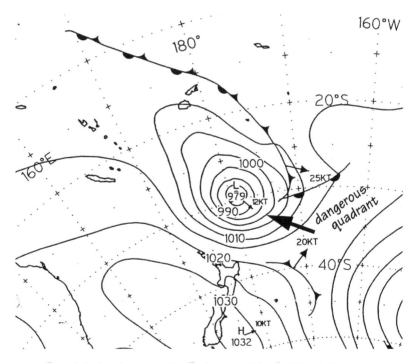

June 5, and the low between New Zealand and the Fiji Islands has deepened to 979mb. It is still squashed against the high to the south, which in turn is still held in place by the stationary depression to the east.

Winds in the dangerous quadrant are estimated at hurricane force. If caught in that part of the storm one should be on port tack, close-hauled. If on the track, or to the west, the wind should be on the port quarter, broad-reaching to the west and away from the center.

The wind in the dangerous quadrant of the storm has been variously estimated at between 65 and 100 knots. Seas were estimated to be in the 35- to 50-foot (10 to 14 m) range.

Between Saturday and Monday, 18 yachts in difficulty made mayday calls or set off their EPIRBS. Seven yachts were lost, 21 people were rescued, and three people lost their lives.

TACTICS

Of the yachts that found themselves in difficulty, the majority were to the east of the depression track—in the dangerous quadrant. Several were to the west, but within the area of strongest winds.

The difference between a survival situation and an uncomfortable couple of days was probably less than 150 miles in position along the east-west axis.

Why, then, did so many people get caught in the wrong part of the storm? I hesitate to be a Monday morning quarterback. I wasn't there, and looking at the fax charts which we've reproduced here, it seems fairly obvious what was happening. Yet Linda and I know all too well how hard it is to think straight when you are getting the tar kicked out of you by the weather, and are cold, tired, and probably more than a little frightened.

The official forecasts did not pick up the severity of the situation until the low had already deepened. Yet the risk factor—that incipient low on the third of June— was there for everyone see.

All of the classic rules for determining the center of the depression and its direction of travel were operable.

Many of the boats were checking in with Keri Keri Radio in the Bay of Islands. The written forecasts made no mention early on, so perhaps people took this at face value, rather than with a judicious degree of skepticism.

The difference between survival and an uncomfortable 48 hours while waiting for the blow to pass was less than 150 miles in distance.

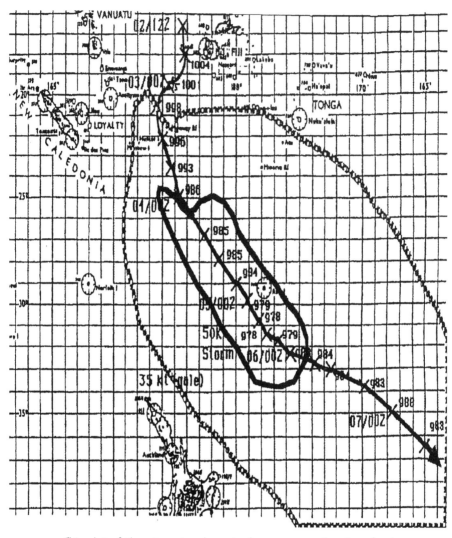

This plot of the storm track, central pressure, and region of gale and storm-force winds is from Bob McDavitt's Met Service Yacht Pack. The region of storm-force winds, following the low center southeastwards, is relatively confined.

The key to security is that you have to start taking evasive action, _before_ you are forced to do so. If you wait until the storm is already upon you, then there are significant risks from wind and confused seas when crossing the storm track.

It's hard to sail at right angles to your course when you are only a little concerned, but in this case it would have paid big dividends!

Another factor making it difficult to get a handle quickly on the situation was the high pressure to the south. As the low pushed into this, a classic "squash zone" was set up between the two pressure systems. For the boats caught in this area, the barometer and wind direction would have remained steady, while the wind speed increased rapidly.

Still, the very fact that the wind was increasing in this fashion with a steady barometer and direction is a warning in itself.

Reading between the lines of the various reports, and thinking about our own experiences, several things stand out for us.

The first is the unwillingness we all have to make major adjustments off-course. To look at a potential risk (as opposed to an actual risk) and then head off at 90 degrees away from the rhumb line, is a difficult decision to make. Yet that is precisely what would have made the difference early on in this situation. And in the context of a safe passage, what difference does a day or two off-course make anyway?

Of course this would be taking you downwind from the final destination — in this case Tonga. So the prospect of having to beat or close-reach into the trades due to giving up ground to the west would have made this decision all the harder.

Another issue is communications. A lot of boats probably relied upon, and took comfort from, the efforts of Keri-Keri Radio to relay the New Zealand Met service broadcasts. When you're on these nets you have a chance to hear what everyone else is doing and experiencing. There are schedules between groups of boats as well. If everyone seems to be doing one thing, even it is wrong, it is sometimes hard to break away from the herd. Yet that is exactly what this sort of a situation calls for.

Issues that can lead to the wrong weather tactics:

- Trying to maintain a schedule.

- Reluctance to head away from final destination.

- Not choosing an alternate destination when this would reduce passage risk factors.

- Taking comfort from others using the same tactics when they are based on wishful thinking and not conservative logic.

- Reliance on outside forecasts when they are at odds with local conditions.

- Failure to maintain a log of wind direction and force, cloud progression and the barometer (so you can figure out what is happening).

WHAT SHOULD HAVE HAPPENED?

The classic tactics for dealing with this type of situation bear repeating.

First, determine where the storm center is by taking the wind on your back, and then pointing at between 100 and 110 degrees with your right arm (in the Southern Hemisphere — left arm in the Northern).

Next determine if you are on the dangerous side or safe side of the storm. If you are in a squash zone, with constant wind angle and barometric pressure, this must be done with outside reporting data (SSB weather reports, faxes, or reports from other vessels).

If you are on the favorable side, in the Southern Hemisphere stay on port tack, reaching away from the storm center. If you are caught on the unfavorable side, bring the wind as far forward as possible on port tack, motorsailing if necessary, to try to beat away from the storm center.

This depression moved in the normal southeasterly direction (for a Southern Hemisphere depression). As such, the optimum course if caught to the east of the track, in the dangerous semicircle, would have been as close to east as possible. For those on the west side of the storm center, the optimal course was west to northwest.

The worst situation would be running before the storm if you were to the east, as it approached. Running would take you directly into the track of the depression, not a particularly pleasant outcome.

A METEOROLOGIST'S VIEW

In working through this material on the Queens Birthday Storm, a number of questions arose in our minds. The issue of the normal warning signs that should have been present has already been touched upon.

Southern Hemisphere storm tactics when faced with an extratropical low:

❑ Determine storm center by taking wind on your back and pointing with right arm.

❑ If in the dangerous quadrant, bring wind on port bow and beat or motorsail as fast as possible.

❑ If in navigable quadrant, bring wind on port quarter.

❑ Avoid starboard tack as this brings you towards the path of movement and storm center.

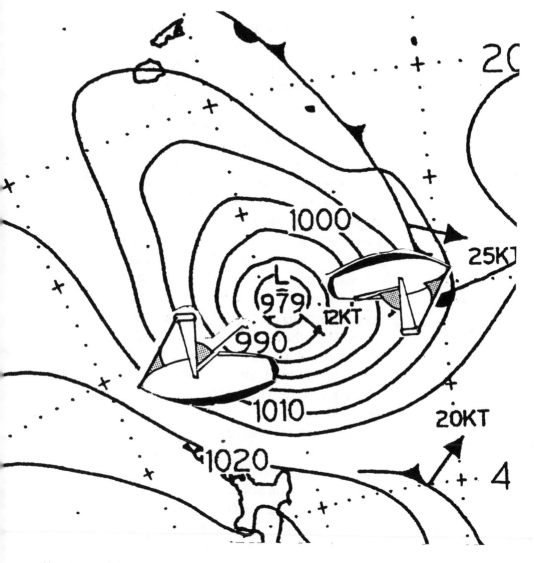

Here is an enlargement of the center of the depression. In the Southern Hemisphere wind circulates around a low center in a clockwise direction. Since the storm is moving in a southeast direction, the speed of advance is combined with circulation wind, making the southeastern quadrant far more dangerous than the southwest (where speed of travel is subtracted from wind force).

In the dangerous side of the storm the normal tactic is to bring the wind on the port bow, and beat—or motorsail—as fast as possible at right angles to the storm's track. On the "safe" side of the storm, you are still on port tack, only now the wind is on the quarter when you are heading at right angles away from the low center.

I posed a series of questions to Bob McDavitt who was involved in both the forecasting and then subsequent analysis of what went wrong.

The first issue was wind strength. Bob writes: "I suppose that some of the sailors would have seen momentary gusts of 90 knots on their anemometers... that is consistent with sustained winds of 60 knots. 60-knot sustained wind is consistent with the waves of 10 to 12 meters and period 9 seconds. I remember reading somewhere that the RNZAF (Air Force) Orions have stress/strain meters in their wings that measured some sort of record number of twists, and these aircraft were measuring the 3000 foot wind at around 70 to 90 knots at peak... again consistent with gusts of 90 knots and sustained winds of 60 knots at the surface.In the "Marine Scene" magazine of July 1994 there is an article by Lloyd Klee which quotes that the Orion dropped a sonar buoy which told them that the surface winds were gusting to 80 knots."

Bob goes on: "The surface maps, drawn at the time without benefit on any measurements of the pressure near the center, estimated wind speed of 55 knots—so if the actual winds were 60 knots (sustained) then the central pressure must have been slightly lower than estimated."

The next question I asked Bob was about warning signs, or lack thereof. "North of the squash zone both clouds and barometer should have been giving those standard warning signs—but the recollections of survivors seem to start after that period."

There has been some controversy about the weather reporting cycle. I asked Bob if there was a mix-up on the meteorological end, or if the data was there and missed by the sailors. "The first gale warning was issued at 0715am Friday June 3 by the Fiji Weather Centre. There is a meteorological border at 25 degrees South—for a while we had Fiji issuing one on 40-knot gales around the centre and New Zealand issuing a gale warning on winds 40 knots in the squash zone.These warnings would be written to be consistent with each other. As soon as the cyclone centre slipped past the 25 degrees South border, New Zealand took responsibility for issuing the warnings and issued a storm warning for 55-knot winds—that was done at 2:30 p.m. NZ Time Sat 4 June. The first EPIRB went off at 9:11am NZ time on June 4. The result is that during the critical warning time, in this case on the Friday, the forecast winds were for 40 knots (with no mention of them rising). It looks like most of the sailors (and radio operators) interpreted conditions as being good-for-40 knots, hence the surprise when the 60 knots arrived.

"(Some people think) warnings were issued too late—but that's just an impression and not true. It may have been an impression got by someone who was not able to get the Fiji / New Zealand High Sea warnings, but was trying to read the weather maps. Certainly the Friday weather maps showed a low that looked very tame. Those who had got the High Seas (radio) warning spent the Friday waiting for it to arrive. (From the log of *Swanhaven*: 'Not too bad so far, although the prediction is for more to come.') But the Friday warnings just didn't go high enough for what actually arrived on Saturday."

REALITY—*HEART OF GOLD*

Jim and Sue Corenman have been cruising aboard the Carl Shumacher-designed *Heart Of Gold* for a bunch of years now. They've been through the usual milk run in the South Pacific, crossed the Indian Ocean, and are presently in Greece. Before deciding to go cruising, they both had raced extensively.

We knew that the Corenmens had been in this blow, and figured that if we could track them down they'd have some interesting comments.

Just as we were getting ready to go on the press with the book, we got through via a ham-based e-mail system. Jim's comments, just as we received them, follow:

From here on in the book from time to time you will see e-mail or weather reports. These are shown in a different type style.

From: KE6RK@pak.win-net.org
To: Dashew@setsail.com
Date: Thu, 17 Sep 1998 22:07:31 UTC
First, the general scenario: We left Mexico in March'93 and did the usual trip through the South Pacific and had an uneventful 5-day trip from New Caledonia to New Zealand in November'93. Our plans took us to Tonga for the next season so we decided to sail with the Tonga regatta in order to meet some new folks—most of our cruising friends had sailed off elsewhere.

The regatta was scheduled to start at noon on Saturday (May 28) with a skipper's meeting and weather briefing on Friday. Bob McDavitt did the weather presentation. At that time it had been blowing hard from the north or northwest for a week or two, 25-35 kts as I recall, and lots of folks (not just the rally) were waiting for a break in order to head north.

Bob showed the extended surface progs which indicated the low pressure finally moving off and high pressure filling in over NZ, providing modezzzzrating winds shifting SW and then SE as the fleet sailed north. He said there was nothing adverse on the horizon, and the low pressure that (we found out later) had been hanging around Vanuatu was not mentioned if it was known about at all.

"...the low pressure that (we found out later) had been hanging around Vanuatu was not mentioned if it was known about at all."

On Saturday it was still blowing 30+ from the northwest, and the regatta organizers canceled the official start and told folks to depart when they were comfortable doing so. We elected to wait a day for the forecast shift to the west, but most of the boats were local and had the usual send-off mob so they dutifully departed and sailed 25 miles north and anchored until the weather moderated.

We departed mid-day Sunday, wind was still 30 knots but westerly as promised, shifting SW and easing a bit during the first 24 hours. Skies were still grey and grim. It was a sloppy, windy reach at first but the boat sailed fine with a reefed main and working jib (a Schumacher 50 with plenty of keel). The wind continued to shift aft and moderate as promised, and most of the fleet got going on Monday.

The first indication of trouble was a surface chart (00z June 2) which showed a small wiggle in the isobar near Vanuatu, not a comforting sign. I think the prog chart that followed showed a closed low. We did a quick analysis and figured if something did blow up it would likely head southeast and we would probably beat it, but we certainly weren't motivated to slow down. As the wind eased and shifted aft we unreefed and changed to a reaching jib to keep the heat on, averaging 200–210 miles per day in the continuing sloppy seas.

We arrived off Tongatapu Friday night, hung around in the lee until daylight and were tucked into the anchorage before the wind started picking up on Saturday. Gallant Cavalier (a 45-footer) arrived just after we did, they had left Saturday and kept going. No one else arrived until Tuesday. It was spooky, and we couldn't help thinking back to the old joke about the s**t and the fan.

We had a chance to talk to nearly everyone who was in the storm including most of those who were picked up by the rescue services, either in Tonga or later in NZ. We've thought a lot about this and have drawn a few conclusions.

First, there is no substitute for boat speed, particularly the ability to keep the boat going fast and comfortably in heavy weather. We agree with you on the importance of waterline length and keep-

"The first indication of trouble was a surface chart (00z June 2) which showed a small wiggle in the isobar near Vanuatu, not a comforting sign. I think the prog chart that followed showed a closed low. We did a quick analysis and figured if something did blow up it would likely head southeast and we would probably beat it, but we certainly weren't motivated to slow down."

ing the beam moderate, but I suspect we put a lot more emphasis on keel and righting moment, as without that it is hard to keep the boat fully powered up in sloppy conditions.

The story of *Destiny* underscores the need to keep the boat moving. They had left a few days earlier, but hove-to for a couple of days prior to the storm when the boat was struggling in the rough weather associated with the last of the NZ lows. They got going again just in time to be one of the first boats lost to the storm. The boat (a Norseman 447) was heavily loaded and I suspect this was a factor.

We've also spent a lot of time studying the weather, both the forecasts around the time of the storm and also the mechanics of weather in general. In fact that storm was my personal trigger to get a lot more knowledgeable about the mechanics of forecasting.

Could NZ Met have provided more warning? In particular, were there any indicators a week earlier when departure decisions were being made? The answer, I think, is a definite "maybe".

There were clearly things worthy of consideration. The first was a weak low-pressure area that had been hanging around Vanuatu for a week or more. Nadi Met had been putting it on their tropical surface chart (Nadi has responsibility for the tropics, 0-25s), but the Nadi chart is not well distributed... it is printed in the Fiji Times and that's about it.

They do encode it into numerical fleet code and send it to NZ via telex to be sent via Morse, but NZ does not get a copy of the chart itself and I don't think they do anything with the fleet code other than send it. I asked repeatedly that NZ Met consider sending the Nadi chart along with their fax charts and the response was NZ could not justify spending the money to get it daily via

"...there is no substitute for boat speed, particularly the ability to keep the boat going fast and comfortably in heavy weather".

"That storm was my personal trigger to get a lot more knowledgeable about the mechanics of forecasting."

telephone fax (about $1 per day). And Nadi had no money at all and felt their obligation was met by telexing the coded chart to NZ.

Nadi Met does a good job with what they have, which is almost nothing. We had a nice visit to there in August'94 and looked at their charts, they tracked the depression carefully but don't have the resources to do much in the way of forecasting, and if they did there is no distribution for it.

The second thing worthy of note was a fast-moving upper-level trough that extended into the tropics. This was clearly the trigger for the whole event, yet has been virtually ignored. I did not pick it up at the time, only months later when I was digging into the storm and the mechanics of weather forecasting. I discussed this with Bob McDavitt in late'94 back in NZ and there is no question as to what happened.

The problem is that weather is a three-dimensional phenomenon and understanding the upper-level mechanics is essential, but represents a level of complexity that neither met professionals nor authors of weather books want to get into.

The obvious question is why NZ Met didn't pick up the combination of a weak tropical low and an approaching upper-level trough. I think the answer is that it wasn't caught because the computer model didn't pick it up, because computer models don't do well in the tropics and the low may not have been in the model at all. And if the computer didn't pick it up then the forecasters aren't going to pick it up...this is the 90's, after all. The other factor is that it was a low-probability event. We've seen the same combination two or three times in the following few years when we were watching the Australian charts, and none produced a bomb. And the met services take it as

> "The second thing worthy of note was a fast-moving upper-level trough that extended into the tropics. This was clearly the trigger for the whole event, yet has been virtually ignored."

> "The problem is that weather is a three-dimensional phenomenon and understanding the upper-level mechanics is essential..."

their job to forecast the most-likely scenario, not the unlikely-but-worst-case one.

Did anyone else sound a warning? There are a couple of folks who say they did, Arnold ZK1DB was doing weather from Rarotonga at the time and gets the Nadi chart from the Raro airport, he had mentioned the weak low in the context of it making him nervous, but nothing more specific. And ditto Pete Sutter who copied the Morse fleet code and drew the Nadi chart. But nobody was watching the upper-level stuff, and weak lows hang out in that area a lot, maybe half the time in the spring and fall, so "keep an eye on it" warnings are so common as to be useless.

So my conclusion after six months of study was that there were warning signs that could have been seen maybe a week in advance, but they were not things that the met services are going to pick up: too subtle, too low a probability, and the computer models don't work well in the tropics. But to a cruising sailor, a low probability of a Very Bad Event is something that ought to be considered. The problem is that picking up the warning signs requires fax charts which governments are increasingly less willing to provide, and a knowledge of weather mechanics that is beyond the interest level of all but a small handful of cruisers. The prevailing attitude is "Don't make me think, just tell me the answer".

"...nobody was watching the upper-level stuff, and weak lows hang out in that area a lot, maybe a half the time in the spring and fall, so "keep an eye on it" warnings are so common as to be useless."

DETAILS

Given the wonder of an e-mail service that is free to someone who is cruising (courtesy of the world of Amateur Radio), I sent Jim several specific questions which have been nagging me since I first heard about this storm.

Thanks for the note back. We left Bonifacio this morning and are currently en route to Menorca, spinnaker up with a

lovely 15-knot Easterly. After a week-
long Mistral it is most welcome, and we
hope it lasts a few days.

To answer your specific questions:

*1-Were there warning signs (swell,
barometer, cloud progression, wind
speed, and direction)?*

I think there was virtually no early
warning by these conventional signs. It
was heavily overcast and had been for a
week or more, due to the series of south-
ern-ocean lows that had brought extended
heavy weather to NZ. The low itself was
initially tight and fast-moving, and was
upon the fleet before the baro or wind
showed much of anything.

*2-How about the forecast data (synoptic,
500mb warnings from Nadi or NZ Met and
timeliness of same)?*

There was virtually nothing prior to the
wiggle on the June 2 chart and even that
went largely unnoticed. NZ was sending
500mb charts but they were aviation
charts with wind birdies, not isobar
lines and are hard to interpret in terms
of troughs. I also don't believe they
were sending anything past a 24h prog.

It turns out that there were better
southern-hemisphere 500mb charts from
Australia that I later found very useful
for tracking upper troughs and looking
for patterns. But that is beyond the
ability of any but the most keen of sailors. And the weak low was on the Nadi
charts but, as I mentioned, not distributed.

So knowing what we know now, and if we
had been tracking the short-wave troughs
on the Australian southern-hemi charts,
then maybe we would have seen the warning
signs a week ahead. And probably with
enough confidence for a personal decision but not enough to stand in front of
a group and advise them not to go.

*3-Did you pick up the closed isobar which
showed up on June 3 (innocuous, but something to be watched)?*

Yes. I actually picked up the wiggle on

"It turns out that there were better southern-hemi-sphere 500mb charts from Australia that I later found very useful for tracking upper troughs and looking for patterns."

"The bottom line is that cruisers need to learn enough so that they can make sound, independent decisions, and recognize when advice may not be sound or fit their situation. We can't depend on others to think for us."

the 00z June 2 chart which I took as an ominous sign, but at that point we (and most of the fleet) were 3 days into the trip. It was much too late for a decision to delay departure, the only choice was which way to head. Keri-Keri radio unfortunately dispensed some advice which turned out to be inappropriate, to stop or head west and let the depression pass to the north. The problem that John missed is that there was strong high pressure over NZ and the south side of the depression was the killing zone. The wild card was the high pressure over NZ. Absent that, it would have been a "textbook" depression and the conventional advice would have been correct for the reasons you suggest. But the high pressure was a huge factor.

I personally think squash zones are to be avoided almost above anything else, almost every story of a non-hurricane storm involves a high-pressure squish.

In the absence of the high pressure to the south my inclination would be to sail at right angles to the storm track, which means either NE or SW depending on where I was and which side I thought was favored.

The bottom line is that cruisers need to learn enough so that they can make sound, independent decisions, and recognize when advice may not be sound or fit their situation. We can't depend on others to think for us.

The other side of this is that information needs to be available, in the form of fax charts and text analysis. Governments are reluctant to spend money distributing information for which they perceive no demand. A great example is the US Navy - they spend a lot of our money generating some first-rate weather information, then won't spend the few extra dollars to make it available via radio. But if boaties become more knowledgeable, and start asking for more information, maybe it will come.

4-Where were you relative to the storm track?

North of, by about 200 miles, simply a result of being able to keep the boat speed up in sloppy conditions.

5-What wind/sea conditions did you experience? Did these seem normal given the barometric readings?

Until Saturday (when we were in the anchorage) everything seemed completely normal given the baro and the surface charts, i.e. cold, overcast and sloppy, confused seas. I don't believe the small closed low on Thurs.-Fri had much discernible effect outside its immediate area, and from what we heard the depression was moving fast enough that it kept pace with the seas that it was generating. On Saturday it blew like stink in Tonga as the low passed to the south.

This storm is a tough one, because there is, in my opinion, very little to point to in terms of lessons. The disabled boats ran the spectrum and included a Westsail 32, a couple of capable racer-cruisers and a cat, and the boats that had no trouble included all the same. The ones that worried me the most, a couple of 50' home-built ferro boats, did just fine. By conventional standards NZ Met did an adequate job and met their obligations, and if folks like Keri-Keri put out some bad advice, they are volunteers and always said they weren't professional forecasters.

We feel strongly that cruisers don't pay nearly enough attention to performance under sail, and happily trade whatever performance they have for minor comforts paid for in windage and weight. And everyone wants an accurate weather forecast, but few are willing to put any effort into getting it. But these are not thoughts that many folks want to hear and we tend to keep them to ourselves.

Regards, Jim Corenman, s/y *Heart of Gold*

"We feel strongly that cruisers don't pay nearly enough attention to performance under sail, and happily trade whatever performance they have for minor comforts paid for in windage and weight."

To make the following charts easier to read, we have added heavy dashed and zig zag lines to indicate troughs and ridges.

May 31 (local time). There's a ridge over the East Coast of Australia with a lobe extending to the North which could become a cut-off low at some point. The trough over Western Australia will bear watching, but should not affect the New Zealand to Tonga area for three or four days—in theory.

500MB VIEW

As you know from the preceding text none of the participants in this storm had access to 500mb charts. Aircraft (flight level 250) data was broadcast from the New Zealand Met Office, but the reality is that there was little to show on these faxes that would help interpret the surface fax charts, or give early warning of an impending storm system.

With Jim Corenman's comment about what Australian 500mb faxes might have shown in hand, we went to the Aussie Met Office and asked if they might have some historic records. Two weeks later we had the following series of 500mb charts which shed some interesting light on the subject.

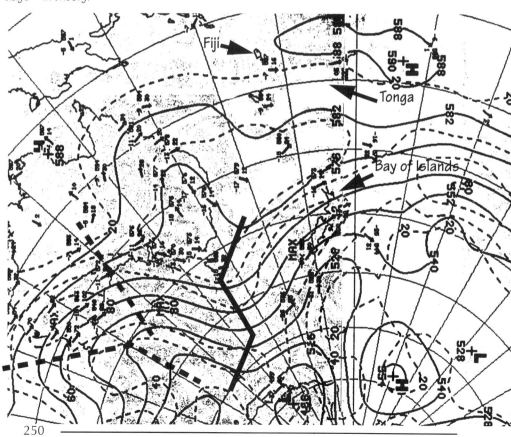

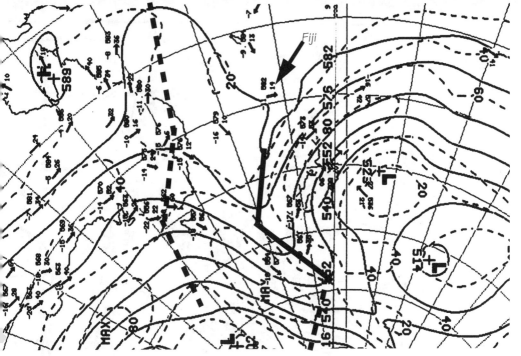

June 1 (above) and there is a ridge just west of New Zealand with a trough starting to amplify over Eastern Australia. The lobe of the trough which now extends well into the tropics should be of concern. Given the normal tropical instability, any time you see an upper level feature like this below 25 degrees (this one goes to 15) you need to think about what it is doing on the surface. June 2 (below) and the trough has weakened, but still extends over Fiji. So far we have seen nothing in these charts that would have held us in port—but we would be keeping a close eye in the Fiji area to see if anything develops on the surface under the trough.

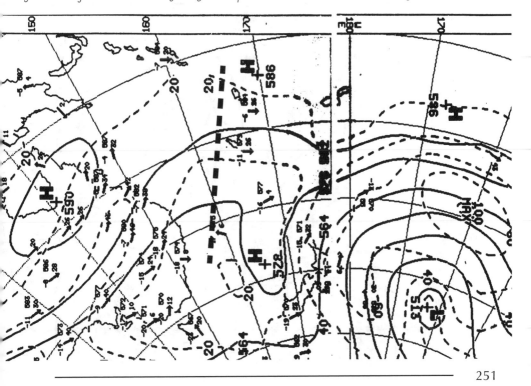

June 3 (top chart) and the trough is still there, and still over Fiji. This is the first day we see the telltale low on the surface charts. If this were taking place at higher latitudes, there would be no concern. But in the tropics, a weak low with a weak upper level trough spells trouble.

June 4 and the 500mb trough is showing as amplified with the ridge to the west strengthening as well. These are both negative developments. The strengthening of the surface low clearly shown on the fax chart of June 4, when matched with this upper level disturbance is a major warning sign. This is the point at which evasive action needs to be taken by anyone potentially in the path of this system.

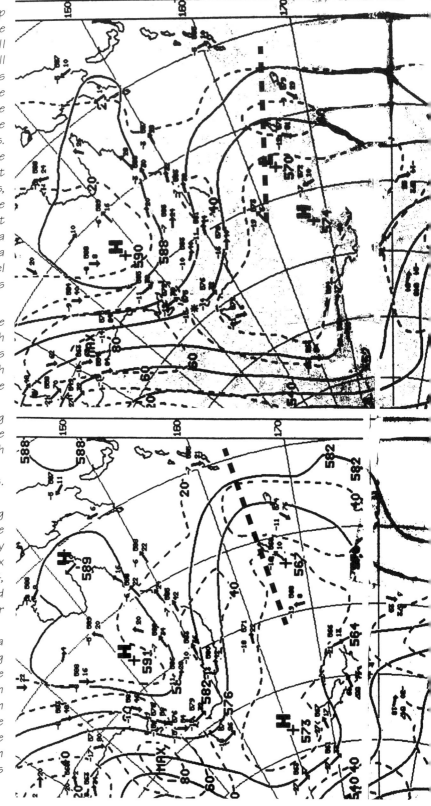

500MB HINDSIGHT

Since these 500mb charts were not available, one might be tempted to dismiss them as irrelevant. But knowing that the Australians broadcast them means that now you have the chance to study them—as well as check them on the Internet before departure.

If you were sitting in the Bay of Islands ready to go, and saw the first of these charts on May 31 or June 1, you probably would have said everything looks OK, especially if the surface high holds.

On June 2 we see a risk feature creeping in—that weak upper level trough into the area around Fiji. Since these frequently lead to tropical disturbances, you would want to watch everything with even more care from here on out.

It is on June 3 that we get the first strong caution signal. The upper level has amplified slightly and the axis is just to the west of where we want to be heading. When you combine this with the first appearance of the surface low you now must admit that there is the potential for the rapid development of a tropical storm system.

This is the point at which you would have wanted to start thinking seriously about evasive action. A jog to the west at this point for 24 hours, while downwind from your final destination, would have been cheap insurance. And if not a jog, then perhaps you could have tried just heaving to until the situation to the north clarified itself.

June 4 and we now have a stronger looking trough (in a tropical context) and the surface chart is showing the tropical system moving into the subtropics. If you had hove to or moved west yesterday, today you would simply move a bit further to the west to be out of the area of major wind force.

Heading away (downwind!) from your destination would be a hard pill to swallow—but it would have paid big dividends.

In reviewing these 500mb charts from Australia you need to keep in mind that in 1994 computer analysis was not nearly as good as today.

The charts are not only difficult to read due to the small size we have reduced them to, but some of the data is probably not totally accurate.

Every year the computer programs which produce 500mb charts get better, and the human understanding of the strengths and weaknesses also improves.

However, even with the problems in the system today, the 500mb charts are probably the best early warning system we have. If you always take action early, many times it will be wasted. But that's juts like buying health insurance—you hope you are throwing away the premiums!

These four drawings are the Southern Hemisphere version of those presented on page 211 in the section on bent back warm fronts.

The light shaded area is where you find gale strength winds while the dark areas are the storm force wind regions.

Put these drawings into the context of the Queen's Birthday Storm and you begin to see that there were really strong winds to the north of the center as well as in the southwest.

How does this affect the tactics which should have been used? It probably doesn't. The key issue is to have been well away the storm's track—either to the west or the east. Either strategy would have kept you free of the region of strongest winds.

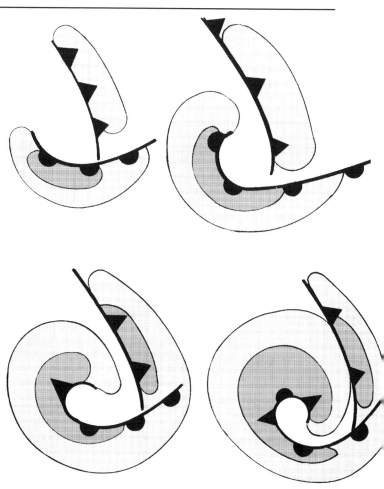

WAS THIS A BENT BACK WARM FRONT?

The rapid pressure drop and cloud signature (reported by Bob McDavitt) make it likely that the Queen's Birthday Storm was a bent back warm front type of structure.

This is anecdotally supported by the fact that the vessels in the southwest quadrant seemed to have more trouble than might have otherwise been expected. Also, several vessels reported a calm "eye" effect which you sometimes find in these storms.

Our first impression, and indeed that of all other observers with whom we've chatted, is that the high pressure to the south created a squash zone between the surface high and low. This is probably what accounted for the problems boats encountered in the nominally safer southwest quadrant. However, in light of the satellite image below we suspect that the structure of the storm, with its difference in surface wind field, may have been the actual culprit (although it is easy to see how the high pressure contributed to the problem).

Bob McDavitt feels that this type of storm structure is actually quite common in the Southern Hemisphere — perhaps more so than in the Northern.

As Bob explains it, "the Norwegian model is formulated by watching the interaction of the polar front in the North Atlantic. But we do not really have a polar front here, not even in the Southern Ocean. There is more room for things to spread out, we end up with the warm below/cold on top scenario quite often."

The bottom line to all of this is that bent back warm fronts are probably more common in this part of the world than in the Northern Hemisphere.

The warning signs remain the same in both hemispheres, both in terms of the atmospheric phenomenon as well as with cloud signatures and water vapor images seen in satellite images.

Keep your eyes open!

SQUALLS

As you move towards the tropics, squalls become a regular feature of passaging. They often bring welcome wind and rain with which you can top off the tanks.

Squalls develop as a result of unstable atmospheric conditions, caused by significant temperature differences in various parts of the atmosphere as you go aloft.

The mechanics are straightforward. At sea the air is warmed by the surface of the ocean, forms a bubble, and begins to rise. As the air rises it eventually condenses, releasing energy in the process that causes the air to rise some more, becoming colder as it goes up and condensing even more, until a large cloud has been built up. The condensed water vapor eventually forms droplets that are too heavy to stay aloft and so they begin to fall. As the water drops fall down through the drier air below some of it begins to evaporate, cooling the air and making it more dense (this cooling process is the same as works with a swamp cooler). The cooled air is also denser so it continues to fall.

The droplets and descending air are the two main characteristics with which we are all familiar with a squall—wind and rain.

LAPSE RATES

You will recall from our earlier discussions that the higher you go in the air, the cooler it becomes and the lower the pressure. The temperature variation is called the lapse rate. The norm is for the air to become roughly three and a half degrees fahrenheit (2 degrees C) cooler for every thousand feet (300m) you go up in altitude.

In neutral (or stable) conditions, with the *standard* lapse rate, there is no incentive for air to rise or fall. When this is the case, there is little vertical development of clouds, weather overall tends to be stable, and squalls cannot form.

If you were to measure the temperature at sea level and it was, say, 80 degrees F, and then go up 1,000 feet above sea level and measure it again it would be 76.5F or 3.5 degrees F less. Keep going up and the air temperature continues to drop.

Now let's interject some surface heating into the equation. During the day the air is heated by the sun at a much faster rate than the ocean surface that heats up very slowly.

However, at night, the air cools rapidly while the ocean temperature remains pretty much the same. With the ocean surface warmer than the air just above it, you have the conditions necessary to start squall activity.

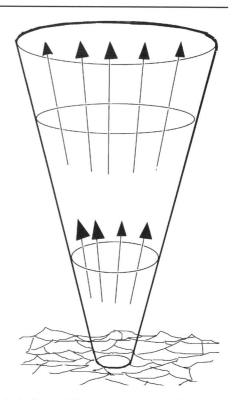

As the warmed air rises it expands, cools, and condenses forming a cloud. Later on, if there is a large enough heat source at the base (the ocean surface or on land), and upper air conditions are cool and dry enough, a squall or thunderhead may develop.

The surface air is heated by the ocean and begins to rise. As we've already seen, this air is warmer than that which surrounds it, so it has a higher pressure and therefore expands. While the air is rising, it does not exchange energy with its surroundings.

This rising, expanding air has what is called a *dry adiabitic lapse rate* as long as it does not condense into droplets. This lapse rate is roughly 5.5 degrees F per 1,000 feet. The two degrees F difference between it and the surrounding air are what propels the column of air upward and outward.

At some point, when this air has cooled sufficiently, the moisture in it begins to condense. The condensation process is known as a change of state — the physical properties of the moisture change from widely dispersed molecules to those that are quite a bit closer together, forming water droplets (a cloud) in the process.

This change-of-state mechanism releases energy, warming the air a small amount in the process. At this point, our pocket of rising air, which now has become cloud vapor, is even warmer than the surrounding environment. There is renewed impetus for it to rise because of the temperature differential between it and the surrounding cooler air. It goes up farther, which drops the temperature even more, with more condensation taking place in the process.

This process of changing into water vapor is called the *wet adiabitic rate.*

UPPER ATMOSPHERE REQUIREMENTS

You can see from the preceding description that humidity as well as heat are the two ingredients of this squall-making process.

Another is the humidity level of the air aloft. The drier the air aloft, the more energy is released by the rising air in its condensation process.

Any time you have variations in sea-surface temperature, this helps to generate pockets of rising air.

This is one of the reasons we find so much squall activity in the doldrums (ITCZ) as there are numerous currents mixing the sea surface with variations of several degrees in temperature. (In addition, as we discussed at the beginning of the book, there is a general upwelling of air in the ITCZ region to offset the sinking air around the poles.)

Boundary layers between high and low pressure systems, especially cold fronts (as we've already discussed), also tend to produce more squall activity. This is because there is a temperature as well as a humidity variation between the two.

SQUALL WATCH

In the context of tradewind sailing you can easily see the squalls forming at night as their tops block out the stars and planets.

Requirements for squalls to develop:

❑ Heat source at surface.

❑ Upper level air which is relatively dry and cool.

❑ Moderate to low wind shear (wind aloft is not too much stronger than on the surface).

Expect isolated squalls:

❑ Late in afternoon or evening if surface and upper air conditions are favorable.

❑ After passage of a cold front.

❑ Later at night.

Another excellent tool is radar, which is discussed in detail starting on page 562. Both size and intensity of the squall can be estimated by the amount of rain clutter and physical size of the radar return.

PREDICTING SQUALL STRENGTH

Generally speaking, the bigger the cloud size (or radar echo) the more wind potential in the cloud. Our own experience is that large horseshoe-shaped radar returns have a higher probability of wind than those which are more circular in shape.

The taller the cloud, the more energy potential it has. Most thunderheads at sea rarely rise above 20,000 feet (6,000 meters). But occasionally you will see a really big one. Those are the guys to keep a close eye on.

You will usually find that if the wind precedes the rain, the wind-speed increase will not be as great as when the rain precedes the wind.

Squalls obviously form during the day. However, the tops of the clouds absorb energy from the sun and this inhibits the updraft of warm, moist air from sea level.

At night, the tops of the clouds radiate heat back into space, which enhances their ability to grow. This is the reason most squall activity takes place at night, generally starting between 2200 and 2400.

As the night wears on, the squalls tend to get a little stronger as the upper atmosphere is cooling, while the sea surface stays at its normal temperature.

Squall-generated wind rarely strikes without warning, and a rapid drop in temperature is almost always a precursor. The bigger the temperature drop, generally speaking, the more wind you can expect.

Finally, you will most probably see the wind on the water as it is coming towards you. The whiter the water, the more wind you can expect.

Squalls will be stronger:

❑ With taller clouds.

❑ When large anvils are present on downwind side.

❑ When rain precedes the wind.

❑ Late in the evening.

❑ When there are large, elongated or horseshoe shaped radar returns of rain.

❑ Just before dawn.

TAKING ADVANTAGE OF THE WIND

Many cruisers are afraid of squalls. However, most tradewind sailing takes place in light airs. And squalls can provide welcome relief in temperature, rain with which you can fill your water tanks, and a nice breeze to help you on your way.

You will find that squalls generally (although not always) move at the same speed as the surrounding tradewinds, on a course to the right of the surface wind 15 degrees or so in the Northern Hemisphere and to the left in the Southern Hemisphere. (In the Northern Hemisphere, if the surface wind was blowing 90 degrees, then the squalls would be moving about 105 degrees. In the Southern Hemisphere with an east wind the squalls would be moving on a course of about 075.) This is due to the Coriolis force of the earth's rotation.

Squall movement:

❑ Typically in direction of surrounding wind.

❑ With a slight bias away from the equator when in the trades.

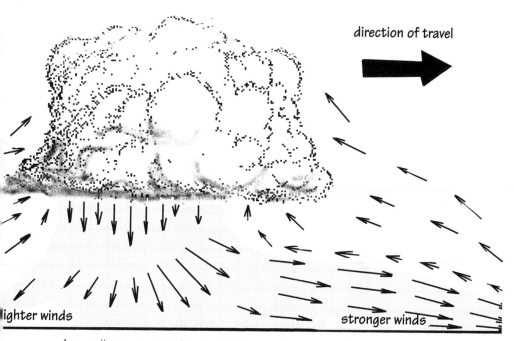

direction of travel

lighter winds

stronger winds

A squall represents the death throes of a cumulonimbus cloud—when it has stopped growing and is about to collapse. The lightest winds are typically on the upwind side of the cloud, while the strongest are on the down wind side.

NORTHERN HEMISPHERE

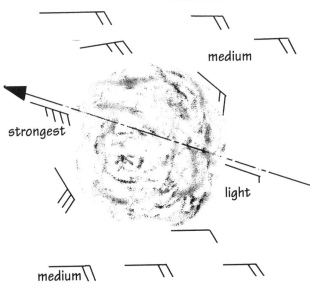

medium

strongest

light

medium

The wind field around a squall system typically has the strongest breeze downwind of the squall and the lightest breeze upwind of the squall. The cells normally track away from the prevailing breeze by 15 to 20 degrees with a bias towards their respective polar regions.

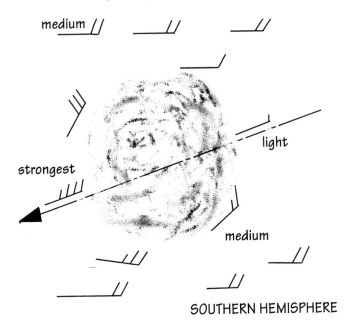

medium

strongest

light

medium

SOUTHERN HEMISPHERE

The wind pattern of the squall is asymmetric to some degree in its distribution around the base of the cloud.

The strongest downdrafts will be found on the leeward side of the cloud where the downdraft is reinforced by the tradewind movement of the cloud. The wind direction is typically veered 15 to 20 degrees from the surface wind, more or less along the track of the squall itself in the Northern Hemisphere (in the Southern Hemisphere the wind from the squall will back relative to surface winds).

The windward side of the cloud normally has the least amount of wind, or sometimes an updraft. In either case, the force of the downdraft is subtracted from the tradewinds.

To recap, there is more breeze downwind of the squall and less to windward.

Another factor is the side of the cloud where you are positioned. There is almost always better wind on the side closest to the equator (to the south side in the Northern Hemisphere and the north side in the Southern Hemisphere).

If you are sailing on a fast boat, it is possible to use the squall to move you much faster than would otherwise be possible. On boats like *Sundeer* and *Beowulf*, for example, we can sometimes stay with a squall for several hours at a time.

The technique we use is to spot the squalls on radar, verify that they are not overly large, and then modify our course to get in front of them.

We start out on port tack in the Northern Hemisphere (starboard in the Southern) and then jibe over as soon as the breeze starts to lighten. As we come back in front of the squall, we watch for a header (i.e., a wind shift forcing our bow back to leeward), and when that occurs, jibe back away from the squall again (towards the equator). This keeps us away from lighter winds on the pole side.

Winds around a squall:

❑ Strongest downwind of cell.

❑ Weakest upwind of cell.

❑ Best wind on side closest to equator.

❑ Weakest wind on side away from equator.

Using squall wind field when trades are light—N. of equator:

❑ Start out on equator side of squall.

❑ Sail intersecting course with squall's track.

❑ When you feel downdrafts and breeze go on port jibe.

❑ As breeze lightens jibe to starboard to get back into stronger winds.

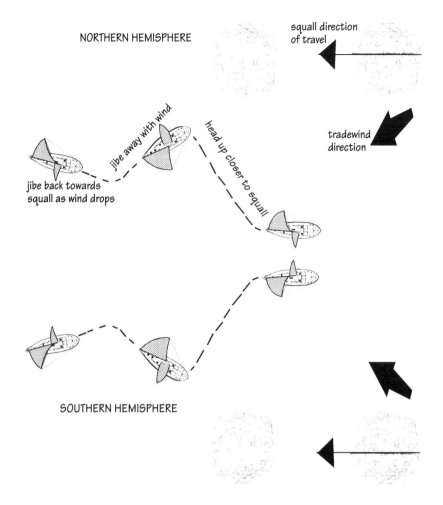

NORTHERN HEMISPHERE

squall direction of travel

tradewind direction

jibe away with wind

head up closer to squall

jibe back towards squall as wind drops

SOUTHERN HEMISPHERE

GETTING AWAY FROM THE WIND

There will be times when you want nothing to do with the squalls. In this case it is generally better to do just the opposite of what we've discussed.

When you see a squall bearing down—either visually or on radar—adjust your course to stay on the light wind side (i.e. on the pole side, away from the equator).

This approach assumes you have the time to get to the pole side of the squall. If you are on the equator side of the storm track, then it is better to head down toward the equator as this avoids the necessity of having to cross the squalls track. This would be port jibe on the Northern Hemisphere and starboard jibe in the Southern.

This photo was taken in the South Pacific. We are caught on the wrong—light wind—side of the squall. The trades had been blowing a steady 18 to 20 knots, and are probably blowing 25 on the opposite side of the rain, while here it is almost calm.

WITHIN THE SQUALL

More often than not you will be overtaken by the squall. The odds are you probably have a jib on the pole or the spinnaker up. Within the squall you may find a substantial windshift as the cloud passes.

The easiest thing we've found to do is run off downwind with the wind shift. This may take you at right angles to your course, but it will only be for a few minutes to half an hour.

When the squall passes the odds are you will be left bobbing, with little wind on the surface. It sometimes takes an hour or more for the trades to re-form in this situation.

If you get knocked down by the increased wind and/or the wind shift, it is sometimes easier to just wait for conditions to moderate — which usually happens within a few minutes — rather than to go through all sorts of heroics trying to get the sails squared away.

Nighttime squall indicators:

❏ Radar return on rain field.

❏ Stars are blocked out by cloud build up.

❏ Tradewinds become fitful.

❏ Squalls tend to be similar during a given weather cycle.

❏ Squalls usually become stronger as the evening progresses.

Imminent warning signs:

❏ Precipitous drop in temperature.

❏ Unexpected rain.

❏ Immediate drop in barometric pressure of one millibar.

DURING THE DAY

This same cloud/squall building process takes place during the day, driven primarily by small differentials in sea surface temperature.

The results are typically not as pronounced as during the evenings, but can nonetheless deliver a nice strong push along your way.

WATCH THE BAROMETER

Along with the warning signs already discussed, big squalls are large enough weather features to show a definite drop in the barometric pressure just before they hit.

LINE SQUALLS

The mechanics of line squalls are the same as with an individual squall. The major difference is that they are usually associated with some form of frontal boundary that provides dry, cooler air over the top of moist, warmer air near the surface.

In the tropics this typically forms with a convergence zone between high pressure systems.

You will also find line squalls in the temperate latitudes, again associated with frontal passages. It is not unusual to find them 50 to 150 miles ahead of an approaching cold front.

Line squalls have to be watched with a bit more care. The mechanism leading to their formation typically indicates that more energy is present to create the updrafts and then the downdrafts. These lead to stronger surface winds than found with isolated squalls.

In addition, line squalls tend to reinforce each other. Exit towards the equator if you are trying to get out of the wind of a line squall.

LAND-GENERATED THUNDERHEADS

Any time you are cruising in hot summer weather, with high humidity and large areas of warm land around, there is a risk of land-generated thunderstorms.

The business end (top) of a cumulonimbus cloud. Note the anvil sticking out downwind. The anvil is a sign that the cloud is finished with the building phase and about to create rain and downdrafts.

The creative process is the same as we've been discussing; only the heat source is different.

Land absorbs the sun's radiation much faster than does the surrounding air (and the ocean). As a result, early on during the day the land starts to radiate heat back to the air near the surface. This air is heated much more rapidly than the process over the ocean, and there is a greater vertical temperature gradient with height.

This allows thunderstorm development on a much faster basis than what you typically find with ocean-heated squalls.

These thunderheads can drift along at a leisurely pace on their own, or be pushed along by some larger-scale air circulation at very high speeds.

Thunderheads that build over land can have significantly more wind in them than the ocean-generated cousins, and these must be watched more closely.

THUNDER AND LIGHTNING

Thunder and lightning are relatively rare in squalls at sea. However, some areas have more than others. The Gulf of Panama, Florida, and the north side of Papua New Guinea are all infamous for their lightning activity.

When you see lightning and then hear thunder, it can be used as a rough estimate of the distance to the storm. By counting the time between flash and thunderclap in seconds, and then dividing by five, you get roughly the distance in miles to the lightning.

MICROBURSTS

Microbursts can occur when:

❑ Upper-level atmosphere is cool and dry relative to normal.

❑ Heat source exists at surface.

❑ There are horizontal shear lines between a cool upper air moving in over a warm lower air mass.

Microbursts are extremely strong downdrafts associated with really big thunderheads. While rare at sea, over land they can occasionally reach 80 to 100 knots in wind strength, due to the much higher buildup of cumulonimbus clouds from land-based heat.

During the summer monsoon in Tucson, Arizona, every couple of weeks there will be a report of severe damage to structures from these occurrences.

They can occur at sea, but almost always there is some warning on the sea and in the sky.

The process that creates microbursts is the same as that which works with normal squalls. The difference comes from a layer of extremely dry air through which the rain drops descend. This very dry air creates more evaporative energy than is the norm, cools more quickly, and becomes denser than the norm. The result is a very strong downdraft.

While normally associated with thunderstorm activity, the rapid approach of a cold front that contributes to upper level instability can also give rise to a microburst.

Springtime (and to a lesser degree the fall), with major temperature contrasts between weather systems, provides the best conditions to generate a microburst.

CLEAR-AIR MICROBURSTS

You might think that microbursts only occur with a cloud buildup. However, it is possible to have strong vertical turbulence in the absence of clouds if there is enough temperature differential as you go aloft and the air is dry. This phenomenon is usually associated with cold air moving in over warmer air, with relatively low humidly in the air mass.

Clear-air microbursts can also be found at horizontal shear lines between two air masses of different density combined with a large difference in temperature over a large-scale area.

A FINAL WARNING

For the most part squalls at sea, especially in the tradewind belts, are not going to be a problem for a well-found vessel sailed by competent crew.

When problems do occur, it is almost always because of a sail-handling error on the part of the crew, coupled with a weakness somewhere in the rig or ship's systems.

The weaknesses in the vessel should obviously be found before you head out. Mistakes by crew, especially if caught by a squall unawares, are understandable. However, *practicing* your sail handling, including reefing and jibing, so that you have the maneuvers down cold day *or* night, will reduce the odds of problems tremendously.

Finally, it bears repeating that there is almost always a sign of severe weather from squalls if you are looking out for it. Don't be caught napping on watch.

AUCKLAND TO RAIVAVAI

So far we've talked about weather pretty much in the abstract. Let's take a few minutes now to look at a live application of what we've been discussing.

It is the Southern Hemisphere winter of 1997 and Linda and I are ready for a break from the land.

We've been finishing up a very arduous book project (the second edition of *Offshore Cruising Encyclopedia*) while *Beowulf* is being fitted with her new interior.

It is mid-May and the two of us have flown to New Zealand to get *Beowulf* ready to go to sea. After a couple of weeks of seatrials, we make the usual round of grocery stores, order 24 loaves of multi-grain bread for the freezer, topoff the fuel tanks, and begin to watch the weather.

TOWARDS THE AUSTRALS

We will be heading east roughly 2300 miles, towards the Austral Islands, a group we've passed by before, but have never taken the time to stop at.

These islands lie 500 miles to the south of Tahiti, so they are somewhat off the beaten track. There is little tourist traffic and only a few yachts visit each year.

With *Beowulf's* speed we are counting on an easy passage — *if* the weather pattern is normal.

We'll wait for a high pressure system to move in from the Tasman Sea, and then leave as its leading edge (southeastern corner) crosses New Zealand.

Linda and I figure that we can ride one high pressure system all the way across, given *Beowulf's* ability to average 300 or more miles a day.

For this tactic to work, the high pressure center must be to the *north* of Auckland. This generates westerly quadrant winds from the bottom-side circulation.

Heading east from New Zealand to the Society Islands the normal tactic is to wait for a high pressure system centered to the north, and then ride it across using the counterclockwise (west to southwest) circulation below the center.

In the summer, when the highs are well to the south, the top-side circulation creates easterly quadrant winds—on the nose for this passage.

AN EL NINO YEAR?

The rule is that highs are supposed to move towards the equator during the winter making our weather scenario practical.

Only 1997 is not a normal year. By the time we arrive in New Zealand, it is starting to look like a major El Nino cycle is under way.

Water temperatures across the Pacific are abnormal, and the high pressure systems are tracking well to the south of where they should be. To add to the confusion, this high pressure pattern is usually associated with La Nina rather than El Nino!

Linda and I have learned never to make commitments that force us to keep a schedule when a long passage is involved.

Under normal circumstances, we would say "OK, the wind pattern is different so let's change our plan."

In this case, we would make our way up to Fiji or Tonga, and then go north to the ITCZ to gain easting for our eventual trip back to California.

However, for the first time ever, we've made a series of dates to meet friends and relatives in French Polynesia—and they have their tickets in hand.

So rather than head north, the easy route, we wait for a high pressure system in a favorable position to take us east to the Australs.

And we wait, and wait, and wait.

Every high pressure is tracking well south, bringing headwinds. If we are to use a high to take us across, we will have to dive down below 45 degrees south, something neither of us relishes at this time of year—even though we have a comfortable pilothouse and large diesel heater aboard.

Eventually, we are forced to abandon the dream of riding one high pressure system all the way and start to look at alternative plans.

USING A FRONT TO START

Between each high is a depression with associated fronts. As the front reaches Auckland, the wind goes to the northeast and then gradually back to the northwest, eventually settling in the southwest for a while before the next weather system.

Of course, we could hitch onto a low and associated fronts, but since they move at 20 to 30 knots, we would not be able to hang onto a single system for the entire passage.

And, being early winter, the fronts are apt to be more vigorous and unstable than one would normally expect in deep winter.

While we are enjoying the quiet of Gulf Harbor, the damp cold of Auckland's winter is beginning to grow a little depressing—especially when we think about palm trees, white sand beaches, and tropical weather!

We have our weather fax set to both the Australian and New Zealand Met service, and each morning we have a series of charts to review. Then we get on the SSB and check in with a local cruiser's net to see what sort of conditions the boats are having on their way to Fiji and Tonga.

A high pressure system is moving slowly across New Zealand and there is a hint that, in the next day or two, we may have favorable conditions for departure.

TIME TO GO

June 8, 0530. We are snuggled under our warmest comforter. Still half asleep, I hear the weather fax chunking away in the pilothouse. The wind is calm, and it seems more humid—good signs for the approach of a warm front.

Linda nudges me: "Maybe we should check the fax—we might need to get an early start."

I get out of bed, fumble my way in the dark to the pilothouse, and see what the New Zealand Met Service has to say.

The stationary high looks like it finally may move off to the east. There's a low, and then another high right behind it.

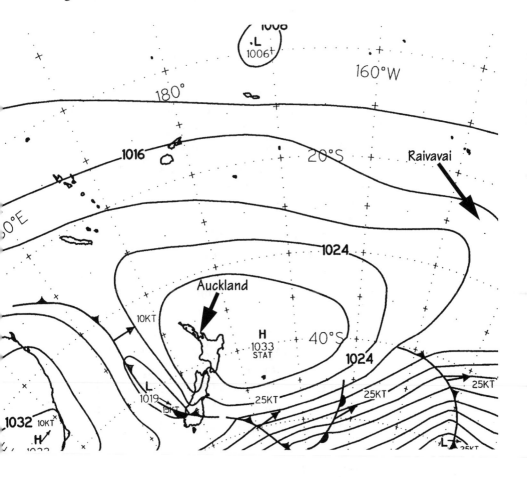

New Zealand Met Service fax for June 8 (all faxes that follow are courtesy of NZ Met Service). A stationary high has its center well to the east of Auckland. There's a small low moving across from the Tasman Sea to the west.

Note the 1006mb low up at the top of the chart. An unusual feature for this time of year, it will bear close watching.

Not exactly what we've been looking for, but at this point our standards are slipping a bit.

I take the fax chart down to Linda and we stare at it. "If we wait for perfect conditions we may never leave," she says. "What about riding the backside of this high, and then if we get headwinds after that, with the next high make a left turn and head for Rarotonga? We can work our way east from Raro when the trades are light."

When the weather is unstable we prefer to be a little undercanvassed.

All we have to do now is make one more trip to the market for our fresh produce, top off the propane tank we've been using, and then clear customs.

We are finally away from the dock! The weather fax this afternoon is looking better. The high is moving east with a weak front coming in behind. Winds are likely to go to the north shortly on the back side of the high, so we head for Kauwau Island to anchor for the night. Our clearance is good for 72 hours, and we can wait a couple of days if necessary.

HEADING OFFSHORE

June 9 and it has been blowing from the northeast all night. The Met Service fax and voice broadcast say the wind should back this morning to the north.

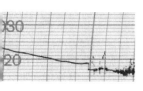

Here's the first section of the barometric trace for this passage. When you see thick lines, as at the right, that is from the impact of head seas (the recording barometer acts as a Richter scale of sorts).

We put reefs in the main and mizzen and work our way out of the anchorage. We are probably way undercanvassed, but with this sort of unstable weather we prefer to be ahead of things.

Once we get clear of Great Barrier Island we can reevaluate and add power to the rig if required.

The breeze is in the mid 20-knot range.

Our plan is straightforward. We'll ride this system as long as possible, heading more or less due east. If the next high brings northeast winds (because it is centered below us, to the south) we'll try to maintain an east southeast track, staying around 40 degrees latitude. When we are south of the Australs, we'll hang a left against the trades and reach due north.

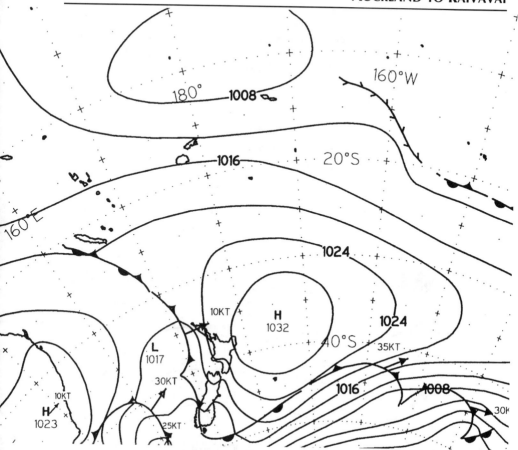

June 9, and the high has started to move east. Note how the isobar spacing on the west side of the center—over Auckland—has tightened. With the wind splaying out from the isobars in a counterclockwise direction (remember, this is the Southern Hemisphere) we have northeast winds at first. As the high moves to the east, these winds will go north and then northwest as the front to the west moves over us.

1300—we are abeam of Great Barrier Island, seven miles to windward. The breeze is north 16 to 18 knots. We shake out the reefs and are making a steady 11 to 12 knots through a confused sea (it is showing the affects of the recent wind shift).

(The following reports are reprinted from Sat C e-mails sent to our web site. The leading numbers represent date, coordinates, heading and speed as reported from the GPS.)

06-10 36.01S 179.23E 093T 09Kt 2049UTC—
24 hours have passed since we left New
Zealand and for our first day at sea we
are doing well. Wind is mainly northwest,
10 to 15 knots. Barometer is steady at
1017—and we actually see the sun from
time to time. We are reaching east. The
fax says there is a slow-moving high over
NZ with a weak trough of low pressure
separating it from our high pressure system.
If we are lucky it will join with our
high and we'll have a southwest swing in
the wind. Just carrying plain sail, and

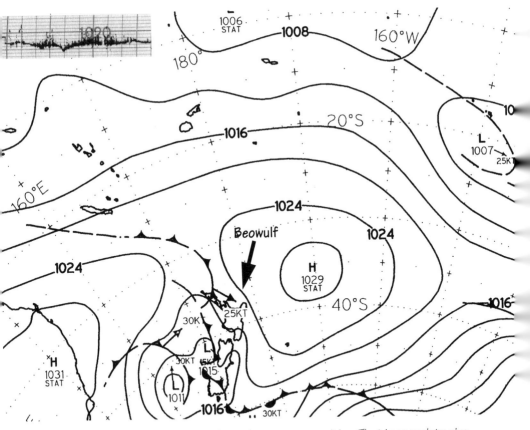

June 10. Notice the slight bend in the isobar near our position. That is enough to give us the northerly winds so that we can reach (rather than beat) on our easterly heading. The front coming up behind promises a shift and increase in the breeze. As it pushes up against the high, a squash zone may be created increasing the breeze. while the barometer remains steady. Our barometer reads about 7mb lower than the fax shows, indicating that the isobars of the high are probably a bit closer than shown.

doing a comfy 10.5/11 knots. Our first day's run is a bit slow at 255 miles, but we are being conservative.

06-11 35.35S 175.51W 090T 12Kt 2005UTC
So much for weather faxes—30 to 40 knots of wind all night from the north. Very lumpy seas. It appears as if we have a squash zone between the front coming in from the west and the slow-moving high to the east. Dropped the mizzen and furled the jib during the night, going with just main. Doing an easy 11/12. Now carrying double reefed main plus working jib. Reasonably comfortable considering where we

We usually take weather faxes and high seas forecasts with a grain of salt—and this one is no exception. It is obvious from the conditions we encountered that the front had a lot more punch than the forecasters expected.

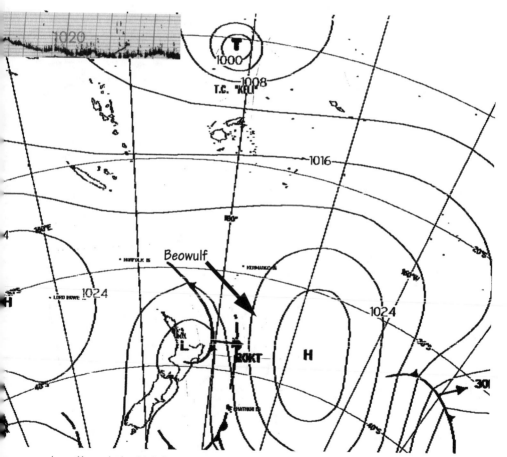

June 11, and the high has moved slowly to the east. Although the isobar spacing does not indicate the breeze we have experienced, it would not take much of a change to create 30 to 40 knots of wind. Notice that the low system to the north of Fiji has become organized and is now down to 1000mb.

When we are in stable conditions, we tend to push the boat and sail aggressively. However, as the weather is as yet quite unsettled, we prefer to have our rig shortened down ahead of the weather—and then motorsail if required in the light spots.

are and what time of year it is. We've been heading northeast rather than east. It looks like we'll be able to maintain this course if we can make enough progress before the tradewinds begin to affect us.

There are lots of lulls tempting us to add sail, but then the wind comes back. I think we will wait till the barometer starts to rise and sea drops a bit. 278 miles passed under our keel in the last 24 hours.

06-12 34.31S 171.09W 056T 10Kt   2140UTC—
Greetings from the one-third point in our passage

Seas have moderated and we have a 10/12

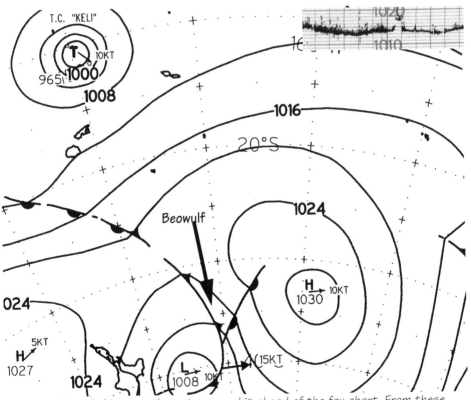

June 12, and things on the water are a bit ahead of the fax chart. From these isobars you would expect northerly winds. However, the breeze has gone to the west, which indicates that the front, shown to our west, has actually passed over us. This is confirmed by a rising barometer. The depression to the north is now a named cyclone—Keli. While is quite far away it still makes us nervous as the normal track would be southeasterly, which could intersect our course at some point.

kt westerly breeze pushing us along at 10 knots. We spent the last 24 hrs with double-reefed main and working jib to keep speed at a comfortable rate for the sea state, so we only put 252 miles on the log.

We are going to take advantage of the nice weather and do a good cleaning today. Looks like next few days will be light following winds and we'll be doing a lot of motoring. Normally we'd complain about the light airs, but around here it is counted as a blessing!

06-13   33.07S   167.07W   086T   10Kt
2033UTC We've just had 24 hours of glorious sailing

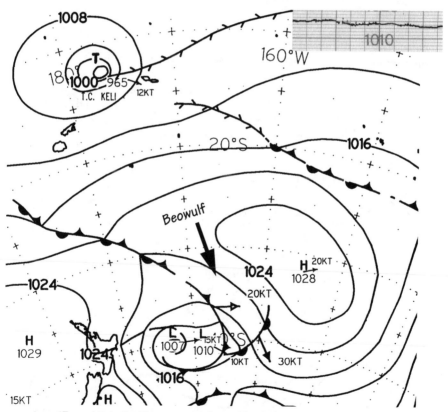

June 13, and it looks like we are pulling ahead of the low as we have northwest winds. This does not make sense, but there is no denying the wind direction. Keli is headed southeast to our northeast track, and we will need to watch out in case she survives her dip into the colder climate.

At this stage of the trip we expect the high pressure system to begin to influence the wind, generating tradewinds from the easterly quadrant.

The question we have to answer is, do we add some north to our course and head toward more stable weather, which guarantees beating, or head more east, which offers the prospect of more unstable but potentially favorable winds. However, on the 15th we are still on the rhumb line!

Fourteen to 16 knots from the northwest, broad-reaching with plain sail plus mizzen jib. Put 265 miles in the bank. Blue skies, calm seas, even WARM. Breeze has lightened now, gone SW and we are motoring due east to get in position for the coming headwinds (from the high following) after the front tomorrow.

June 14th—more of the same, 277 miles today.
0615 30.45S 157.52.W
072T 16Kt 2116UTC—

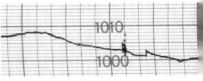

This is what sailors dream about, 28 knots on the quarter, seas from one direction, and we are averaging 16. Top speed has been 27.5, lots of 20+ and we are getting long rides. Our WH autopilot is driving better than we could. Wind is southwest and forecast to go southeast, which would allow us to carry this angle to the Australs. Our only worry is if we are outrunning the high pressure system behind us! The two of us are in fine shape—we both have our sea legs back and are enjoying this wonderful ride. 283 miles on the log for the past 24 hours.

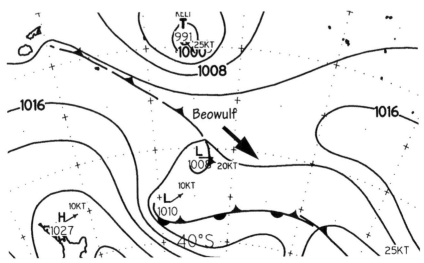

June 15, and the fax is making some sense—finally. We have southwesterly circulation off the back side of the high, so we must be doing something right! There is the prospect of some real breeze if the high behind us shapes up and the isobars tighten. Keli continues on her southeastward track and we are on our northeast track. We expect her to start to weaken, but just in case, we are prepared to heave to or double back to the west if it is required.

Beowulf at speed in the Southern Ocean. She is carrying mizzen jib (foreground) and reaching jib on the canting bowsprit. Main and mizzen are, of course, also set.

06-16   27.39S   153.33W   058T 08Kt
2214 UTC—Spoke too soon yesterday. The
barometer dropped all night as SW wind
increased to 45 knots, gusting to the mid
50-knot range. We gradually reduced sail
to just full main, but carried mizzen
almost until wind started dropping. We
were surfing down the big seas at incred-
able speeds, several times seeing 32 on

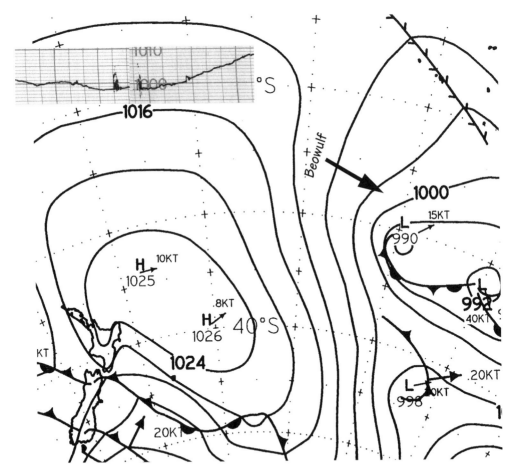

*June 16. You can see where the breeze has come from—we are caught in
a squash zone. However, the dropping of the barometer last night
indicates that the isobars off the low extended more to the west than is
shown on the chart. No matter, we've had a hell of a sail, and it is in the
right direction. Keli appears to have lost her punch and is pretty much
gone from the fax chart.*

the B&G! The boat handled it beautifully, but in retrospect we carried too much sail throughout the day. We will be more circumspect in the future.

We had some hours where we put 16 to 17 knots on the log, but only ended up with 311 miles for the day due to our slow finish.

We now have a rising barometer, puffy cumulus clouds, and a modest southwest wind

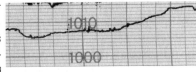

at 20knots. Using just main and small jib we are doing 11. Linda and I are tired from last night's festivities, but Beowulf is in fine shape.

06-18   25.01.S 148.58W   054T 13Kt

0342UTC—We've completed our eighth day at sea and Raivavai is on the horizon. We will heave to later this evening so we arrive at first light. The last 24 hrs have been more of the same—southwest winds in 14/24 knot range. That's what we get for moving the same speed as the weather systems (it is nice to have the ability to pick your weather and then stay with it). While we've played it conservative in the amount of sail carried our daily runs have not been too bad—255,278,252,265,277,283,311 and 304 miles—an average of 278 miles per day.

It's a good thing we're about to arrive too as the pre-baked cookies (chocolate chip) and gingerbread supply from the freezer is almost exhausted. We've been shooting lots of video, and I suspect well have some interesting sailing footage. We've got almost a full moon to guide us on our way tonight, and we'll both probably be up most of the night, exited about the new landfall. The gods willing, our next report will be from anchor, in paradise.

This was the first chance we've had to really push Beowulf hard and to see how she would do in big seas and high winds.

It was an ideal situation with wind waves and swells from one direction.

What we were looking for was an indication of how the bow would react when driven hard into the backside of a wave after surfing at high speed. Would it bury and decelerate rapidly, or lift and continue without a lot of fuss?

Literally thousands of design hours have been spent on this issue. We are happy to report that the bow works beautifully. Beowulf exhibited no tendency to bury her bow or get her decks wet, in spite of being pushed much harder than was reasonable—or prudent.

IN RETROSPECT

With the exception of one night, when we had storm-force winds, this was a very easy trip.

Our original plan, to hang with the leading edge of a high that was centered to our north, was not possible because of the El Nino climatic changes.

When we left we thought we'd have a day or two of the backside of the high's influence, and then we'd have an overtaking low and associated fronts to deal with.

In reality, what happened is that we rode the high/low combination all the way across.

This was made possible by several factors. First, the high continued slowly on its track, averaging roughly 11 to 12 knots, or about the same speed *Beowulf* was maintaining.

Next, where you might expect the faster-moving low to push the high out of the way, in reality a form of symbiotic relationship between the two systems emerged. The isobar spacing did compress, but the high essentially maintained its shape.

Eventually, the low slipped underneath, to the south of the high, and joined another low pressure system. But we were anchored by then and, in any event, it was well to the south of our location.

Another interesting facet of this passage was the development of cyclone Keli. Remember, this was in June, theoretically outside the cyclone season. Keli never became a major storm and petered out before getting close to us. However, it made us quite nervous while it existed, as we'd had a cyclone chase and cross our track, on a similar passage (Auckland to Papeete) ten years earlier. However, that passage took place in February, during the Southern Hemisphere summer.

Most boats would not be able to hang onto the weather systems like *Beowulf.* You need to be very quick to do so. However, this passage is still made successfully ever year by smaller, slower yachts. You will expect to have a sequence of highs and lows, and in an El Nino year might have to sail farther south to avoid inevitable headwinds. If the high-latitude early-winter passage sounds less than pleasant there is always the option of a more direct route to the tropics, with Tonga, Fiji or New Caledonia as a destination.

HIGH-SEAS BROADCAST WEATHER

At the same time we were receiving our weather faxes, we also picked up high seas forecasts from the New Zealand Met Service via our Sat C receiver (these are also broadcast over single-sideband radio).

When we have fax charts available, we usually just give these text forecasts a cursory read, checking for something we might have missed on the fax itself (like the Queen's Birthday Storm warning that was broadcast, but not shown on the faxes).

Rather than intersperse them in the text, we've included them in this section for reference.

```
    ***EGC:    57938   1997/06/09   09:32:21
SAFETY***SECURITE Summary of Storm Warn-
ings for METAREA 14 MARINE WEATHER BULLE-
TIN  FOR  THE  SOUTHWEST  PACIFIC  ISLANDS
AREA EQTR TO 25SOUTH 160EAST TO 120WEST
ISSUED NADI JUN 090600 UTC.
    PART 1 WARNING NIL.PARTS 2 AND 3 SYN-
OPSIS AND FORECAST VALID UNTIL JUN 100600
UTC.TROPICAL   DISTURBANCE   1005HPA   NEAR
08S 173W ALMOST STATIONARY BUT EXPECTED
TO MOVE TOWARDS THE WEST-SOUTHWEST AT 05
KNOTS DURING THE FORECAST PERIOD. CLOCK-
WISE  WINDS  15  TO  20  KNOTS  WITHIN  360
MILES  OF  THE  DISTURBANCE  CENTER.  SEAS
ROUGH AT TIMES IN SQUALLS OTHERWISE MOD-
ERATE.
    FIRST  CONVERGENCE  ZONE  CZ  WITH  POOR
VISIBILITY  IN  OCCASIONAL  RAIN  AND  ISO-
LATED  SQUALLY  THUNDERSTORMS  WITHIN  200
MILES  OF  08S  160E  09S  170E07S  180  08S
175W TO TROPICAL DISTURBANCE 1005HPA NEAR
```

The first of these high seas forecasts is presented in its entirety so you can get a feel for what it looks like. You will note that many areas discussed do not affect us. In the subsequent forecasts we'll put in only the areas in which we are interested.

The tropical portion of the report is issued by NADI weather in Suva, Fiji, and is relayed by the New Zealand Met Service.

These reports are received four times a day on our Sat C modem.

08S 173W TO 10S170W 07S 160W 06S 150W SLOW MOVING.

SECOND CZ WITH POOR VISIBILITY IN HEAVY RAIN AND ISOLATED THUNDERSTORMS WITHIN 200 MILES OF EQTR 170E 02S 180 EQTR 170W 02S150W EQTR 140W SLOW MOVING.WEAK COLD FRONT 20S 160E 25S 163E MOVING EAST-SOUTHEAST 10 KNOTS.WEAK TROUGH 15S 159W 20S 156W 25S 150W MOVING EAST 12 KNOTS.WEST OF COLD FRONT SOUTHEAST WINDS 25 KNOTS. SEAS ROUGH WITH MODERATE SOUTHERLY SWELL.SOUTH OF FIRST CZ AND WEST OF 155W SOUTHEAST 15 TO 25 KNOTS. SEAS MODERATE TO ROUGH. MODERATE SOUTHEAST SWELL.

SOUTH OF 05S AND EAST OF 155W EAST TO NORTHEAST WINDS 15 TO 20 KNOTS. SEAS MODERATE WITH MODERATE SOUTHEAST SWELL.

ELSEWHERE IN THE BULLETIN AREA NORTH TO NORTHWEST WINDS 15 TO 20 KNOTS. SEAS MODERATE. MODERATE SWELLS FROM WEST AND SOUTHEAST.

GALE WARNINGS ISSUED BY METEOROLOGICAL SERVICE OF NEW ZEALAND LTD AT 090930 UTC

GALE WARNING 091

This affects ocean area/s SUBTROPIC, and New Zealand sea area/s KAIPARA

AT 090600Z/091800NZST MONDAY Within 60 miles of the New Zealand coast in and about Cape Reign to Cape Maria Van Diemen: Northeast 35kt, easing below gale about

092100Z/100900NZST TUESDAY.

GALE WARNING 092

This affects ocean area/s FORTIES and SUBTROPIC, and New Zealand sea area/s STEPHENS

AT 090600Z/091800NZST MONDAY Within 40 miles west of a line from New Zealand Cape Egmont to Farewell Spit: Northerly rising to 35kt about 091100Z/2300NZST MONDAY.

GALE WARNING 093

This affects ocean area/s: FORTIES and PACIFIC AT 090600Z/091800NZST MONDAY

Over waters east of 160E: South of line 55S 170E 43S 168W 42S 150W 42S 130W and west of a line 55S 153W 47S 130W 42S 130W: Southwest 40kt.   This area generally slow moving.

GALE WARNING 094

This affects ocean area/s FORTIES, and New Zealand sea area/s MILFORD AT 090600Z/091800NZST MONDAY

Front 40S 167E 43S 166E 46S 166E moving southeast 20kt.Within 180 miles east of front: Northerly 35kt.

ISSUED BY METEOROLOGICAL SERVICE OF NEW ZEALAND LTD AT 090930 UTC SUBTROPIC AREA 25S TO 40S AND 150E/AUSTRALIAN COAST TO 170W.SITUATION AND FORECAST ISSUED AT 090753Z VALID UNTIL 101200Z.

Ridge 37S 170W to high 1033hPa 37S 173W moving east 10kt extends ridge 30S 175E 25S 171E slow moving. Front 25S 164E 35S 169E 40S 167E moving east 20kt. Within 360 miles east of front and south of30S: Expect northerly 25kt with gales as warnings 092 and 091 and heavy northerly swell. Visibility poor in rain within 120 miles of front.Low 1016hPa 35S 165E slow moving. Visibility poor in squally showers and thunderstorms within 180 miles of low

FORTIES AREA 40S TO 55S AND 150E TO 170W.SITUATION AND FORECAST ISSUED AT 090802Z VALID UNTIL 101200Z.

Front 40S 167E to low 1012hPa 45S 165E moving southeast 20kt extends front 48S 175E slow moving. East of front: Expect northwest 25kt with gales as warnings 092 094 and 093 and heavy northwest swell. Visibility poor in rain within 120 miles of front. Second front 40S 153E 45S 159E to low 1000hPa 49S 155E moving northeast 15kt extends front 55S 170E. East of second front and south of 48S:Expect westerly 25kt with gales as warning 093 and heavy westerly swell. West of front and north of 50S: Southwest 30kt. Visibility poor in rain within 120 miles of second front.

PACIFIC AREA 25S TO 55S AND 170W TO 120W.UPDATED SITUATION AT 090600Z AND FORECAST UNTIL 101200Z.VALID UNTIL 100600Z.

FRONT 35S 135W 45S 124W TO LOW 996hPa 50S 130W EXTENDS FRONT 55S 130W ALL MOVING SOUTHEAST 25kt. EAST OF FRONT: EXPECT NORTHWEST 25kt.VISIBILITY POOR IN SHOWERS AND THUNDERSTORMS WITHIN 120 MILES OF FRONT.WESTSOUTHWEST OF FRONT: EXPECT SOUTHWEST 25kt WITH GALES AS WARNING 093 AND HEAVY SOUTHWEST SWELL. RIDGE 30S 134W 35S 154W 38S 170W SLOW MOVING. SECOND FRONT 43S 168W 44S 160W 47S 155W TO LOW 1002hPa 48S 158W EXTENDS FRONT 45S 150W 45S 142W ALL MOVING NORTHEAST 35kt. VISIBILITY POOR IN RAIN WITHIN 120 MILES OF SECOND FRONT AND LOW.

*** EGC: 57956 **1997/06/10** 09:32:04 SAFETY *** SECURITE Summary of Storm Warnings for METAREA 14 MARINE WEATHER BULLETIN FOR THE SOUTHWEST PACIFIC ISLANDS AREA EQTR TO 25SOUTH 160EAST TO 120WEST ISSUED NADI JUN 100800 UTC.

PART 1 GALE WARNING ISSUED NADI JUNE 100750 UTC. TROPICAL CYCLONE KELI (1000 HPA) WAS LOCATED NEAR 09.4S 177.5W AT 100600 UTC. POSITION FAIR. CYCLONE MOVING WEST AT ABOUT 10 KNOTS.EXPECT SUSTAINED WINDS OF 35 TO 40 KNOTS WITHIN 100 MILES OF CENTRE POSSIBLY INCREASING TO 45 KNOTS WITHIN THE NEXT 12 TO 24 HOURS.FORECAST POSITION NEAR 9.5S 178.3W AT 101800 UTC.NEAR 9.8S 179.9W AT 110600 UTC.SHIPS WITHIN 300 MILES OF CENTRE ARE REQUESTED TO SEND REPORTS EVERYTHREE HOURS TO METEO NADI.(MORE FOLLOWS

MARINE WEATHER BULLETIN FOR THE SOUTHWEST PACIFIC ISLANDS AREA EQTR TO 25SOUTH 160EAST TO 120WEST ISSUED NADI JUN 100800

This is the first we've heard of cyclone Keli. It shows up on this Sat C report before we see it on the weather fax cycle. This could be due to a timing issue with the New Zealand Met Service fax preparation, or because we only run our weather fax twice a day—these Sat C messages come in four times per day.

In any event, the notice, even though this is a modest storm and 1300 miles away, is a wake-up call.

288

UTC.(CON'T PARTS 2 AND 3 SYNOPSIS AND FORECAST VALID UNTIL JUN 110600 UTC. MAIN ACTIVE CONVERGENCE ZONE CZ WITH POOR VISIBILITY IN HEAVY RAIN AND SQUALLY THUNDERSTORMS WITHIN 200 MILES OF 10S 160E 07S 170E 05S 175E 03S 180 04S 175W 08S 173W 10S 174W TO TROPICAL CYCLONE KELI NEAR 9.4S AND 177.5W TO 12S 170W 08S 160W 03S 150W EQTR 143W. CYCLONE MOVING WEST 10 KNOTS BUT CZ SLOW MOVING. TROUGH WITH POOR VISIBILITY IN RAIN AND SQUALLY THUNDERSTORMS WITHIN 15S 150W 20S 147W TO TROPICAL DISTURBANCE 1006 HPA NEAR 22S 145W TO 25S 140W. SLOW MOVING. COLD FRONT WITH SHOWERS WITHIN 100 MILES OF 23S 160E 24S 163E 25S 165E. MOVING EAST 10 KNOTS. CLOCKWISE WINDS 35 TO 40 KNOTS WITHIN 100 MILES AND 20 TO 25 KNOTS WITHIN 300 MILES OF TROPICAL CYCLONE CENTRE. (REFER GALE WARNING). ROUGH TO VERY ROUGH SEAS WITH A MODERATE TO HEAVY SOUTHEAST SWELL. CLOCKWISE WINDS 20 KNOTS WITHIN 80 MILES OF TROPICAL DISTURBANCE CENTRE. ROUGH SEAS AT TIMES. A MODERATE SOUTHEAST SWELL. SOUTH OF CZ, EAST OF COLD FRONT AND WEST OF 150W SOUTHEAST WINDS 20 TO 25 KNOTS. ROUGH SEAS WITH A MODERATE SOUTHEAST SWELL. WEST OF COLD FRONT SOUTH TO SOUTHWEST WINDS 15 KNOTS. A MODERATE SOUTHWEST SWELL. EAST OF 150W NORTHEAST WINDS 15 TO 20 KNOTS. ROUGH SEAS AT TIMES WITH A MODERATE EASTERLY SWELL. ELSEWHERE NORTH OF CZ AND WEST OF 150W NORTHWEST WINDS 15 KNOTS BUT 20 TO 25 KNOTS AROUND THE KIRIBATI GROUP (GILBERT GROUP). ROUGH SEAS AT TIMES.

SUBTROPIC AREA 25S TO 40S AND 150E/AUSTRALIAN COAST TO 170W. SITUATION AND FORECAST ISSUED AT 100747Z VALID UNTIL 111200Z. High 1028hPa 31S 150E moving east 5kt. Low 1011hPa 41S 166E moving northeast 25kt. Band of showers isolated thunderstorms vis poor 120 miles wide centered on 34S 160E 37S 166E 40S 167E

The balance of this tropical forecast is of generic interest, in case we should alter our plans and head north. Otherwise, we generally would not bother to read it.

In this subtropical section of the forecast, dealing with the area to our immediate west, there are some tidbits about the frontal system shown on the June 10 weather fax. Note (on the next page) that the system is only moving at ten knots—about our speed.

moving northeast 25kt. Rainband 180 miles wide vis poor east of front 34S 174E 37S 176E 38S 175E moving southeast 10kt. High 1029hPa 37S 170W moving east 5kt.

*** EGC: 57975 **1997/06/11** 09:32:12 SAFETY***SECURITE Summary of Storm Warnings for METAREA 14

MARINE WEATHER BULLETIN FOR THE SOUTH-WEST PACIFIC ISLANDS AREA EQTR TO 25SOUTH 160EAST TO 120WEST ISSUED NADI JUN 110800 UTC.PART 1 STORM WARNING ISSUED NADI JUNE 110715 UTC.TROPICAL CYCLONE KELI (985 HPA) WAS LOCATED NEAR 10 DECIMAL 7 SOUTH179 DECIMAL 0 EAST AT 110600 UTC.POSITION POOR.REPEAT POSITION 10.7 SOUTH 179.0 EAST AT 110600 UTC.CYCLONE MOVING WEST-SOUTHWEST AT ABOUT 08 KNOTS BUT EXPECTED TO CURVE SOUTHWEST LATER.EXPECT SUSTAINED WINDS 55 KNOTS CLOSE TO CENTREAND OVER 33 KNOTS WITHIN 80 MILES OF CENTRE.FORECAST POSITION NEAR 11.5S 177.5E AT 111800 UTC.NEAR 13.0S 176.5E AT 120600 UTC.SHIPS WITHIN 300 MILES OF CENTRE ARE REQUESTED TO SEND REPORTS EVERYTHREE HOURS TO METEO NADI.(MORE FOLLOWS

MARINE WEATHER BULLETIN FOR THE SOUTH-WEST PACIFIC ISLANDSAREA EQTR TO 25SOUTH 160EAST TO 120WEST ISSUED NADI JUN 110800 UTC.

Keli is indicated to be of moderate intensity and generally of only modest concern to us at this point.

The speed of movement, 15 knots in a southeast direction, could pose a problem if the storm were to mature and grow more intense, as it could cross our path.

PARTS 2 AND 3 SYNOPSIS AND FORECAST VALID UNTIL JUN 120600 UTC.ACTIVE FIRST TROUGH WITH POOR VISIBILITY IN HEAVY RAIN AND SQUALLY THUNDERSTORMS WITHIN 240 MILES OF WEST OF 160W AND WITHIN 160 MLIES EAST OF 145W 02S 170E 01S 180 04S 175W TO TROPICAL CYCLONE KELI NEAR 10.7S 179.0E TO 15S 177W 13S 170W 07S 160W 07S 150W 11S 140W 20S 130W 25S 127W SLOW MOV-ING. CLOCKWISE WINDS 20 TO 25 KNOTS WITHIN 360 MILES OF TROPICAL CYCLONE CEN-TRE. HEAVY SWELLS.REFER TO LATEST WARNING ON TC KELI. SECOND TROUGH WITH POOR VIS-IBILITY IN SHOWERS AND ISOLATED THUNDER-STORMS WITHIN 100 MILES OF 19S 155W 25S

147W. WEAK COLD FRONT WITH SHOWERS WITHIN 80 MILES OF 23S 165E 25S 170E MOVING SOUTHEAST AT 15 KNOTS. IN THE BROAD AREA WEST OF 150W APART FROM CIRCULATION AROUNG TC KELI EASTERLY WINDS 20 TO 25 KNOTS WITH GUSTS TO 35 KNOTS AT TIMES WEST OF 180. SEAS ROUGH WITH A MODERATE SOUTHEAST SWELL. EAST OF 150W SOUTHWEST WINDS 15 TO 25 KNOTS TENDING NORTHWEST EAST OF FIRST TROUGH. SEAS MODERATE TO ROUGH WITH A MODERATE SOUTHERLY SWELL. MODERATE NORTHEASTERLY SWELL. ELSEWHERE IN BULLETIN AREA WESTERLY WINDS 10 TO 15 KNOTS. SEAS MODERATE BUT ROUGH IN SQUALLS.

SUBTROPIC AREA 25S TO 40S AND 150E/AUSTRALIAN COAST TO 170W. SITUATION AND FORECAST ISSUED AT 110745Z VALID UNTIL 121200Z.

High 1027hPa 31S 150E moving east 10kt. Low 1013hPa 39S 173E moving east 15kt. Within 150 miles of low in western quadrant: Southwest 25kt. Band of rain and isolated thunderstorms 120 miles wide vis poor east of front 31S 170E 33S 176E 38S 176E 40S 174E moving east 15kt. Band of rain 120 miles wide vis fair east of front 25S 175E 31S 180 40S 177W moving southeast 5kt. High 1030hPa 37S 168W moving east 5kt.

PACIFIC AREA 25S TO 55S AND 170W TO 120W. SITUATION AND FORECAST ISSUED AT 110228Z

VALID UNTIL 120600Z. High 1029hPa 37S 168W moving slow moving. Rainband 100 miles wide vis poor northeast of front 41S 160W 40S 153W 45S 140W 55S 131W moving north 25kt west of 140W and east 30kt east of 140W. South of front between 160W and 145W: Southwest 25kt. East of front to 120W from 42S to 50S: Westerly 30kt. Low 993hPa 30S 133W moving southeast 30kt and deepening. Within 500 miles of low from northeast through south to west: Clockwise winds 25 knots with gales as in

This low (39S 173E) is moving in from the west at 15 knots. If this holds true, it will shortly catch up with us and create a squash zone with high to the east—and this is probably the reason for the 30 to 40 knots of wind experienced during the night.

The rest of this report concerns the areas to our east and is not really of interest at this point.

warning 101 and with heavy swells developing. Rainband 300 miles wide vis poor centered on front 25S 133W 31S 129W 33S 131W moving east 25kt. Rainband 360 miles wide vis poor south of front 30S 136W 33S 131W 33S 125W 32S 120W moving southeast 30kt.

*** EGC: 57999 **1997/06/12** 09:32:38 SAFETY *** SECURITE

Summary of Storm Warnings for METAREA 14 MARINE WEATHER BULLETIN FOR THE SOUTH-WEST PACIFIC ISLANDS AREA EQTR TO 25SOUTH 160EAST TO 120WEST ISSUED NADI JUN 120800 UTC.

PART 1 HURRICANE WARNING ISSUED NADI JUNE 120715 UTC. TROPICAL CYCLONE KELI (965 HPA) WAS LOCATED NEAR 10 DECIMAL 5 SOUTH 179 DECIMAL 7 WEST AT 120600 UTC.

POSITION GOOD. REPEAT POSITION 10.5 SOUTH 179.7 WEST AT 120600 UTC CYCLONE NOW CURVING SOUTHEAST AND EXPECTED TO ACCERELATE TO 15 KNOTS. EXPECT SUSTAINED WINDS OF 70 KNOTS CLOSE TO THE CENTRE. EXPECT WINDS ABOVE 55 KNOTS WITHIN 40 MILES OF CENTER. AND OVER 33 KNOTS WITHIN 100 MILES OF CENTRE. FORECAST POSITION NEAR 12.0SOUTH 178.5WEST AT 121800 UTC. NEAR 14.5SOUTH 176.5WEST AT 130600 UTC. SHIPS WITHIN 300 MILES OF CENTRE ARE REQUESTED TO SEND REPORTS EVERY THREE HOURS TO METEO NADI. MORE FOLLOWS

MARINE WEATHER BULLETIN FOR THE SOUTH-WEST PACIFIC ISLANDS AREA EQTR TO 25SOUTH 160EAST TO 120WEST ISSUED NADI JUN 120800 UTC.

PARTS 2 AND 3 SYNOPSIS AND FORECAST VALID UNTIL JUN 130600 UTC.

T.C. KELI 965 HPA LOCATED NEAR 10.5S 179.7W AT 120600 UTC. TC NOW CURVING SOUTHEAST AND EXPECTED TO ACCELERATED TO 15 KNOTS. EXPECT SUSTAINED WINDS 70 KNOTS CLOSE TO CENTRE WITH VERY HIGH TO PHENOM-ENAL SEAS. OVER 33 KNOTS WITHIN 100 MILES OF CENTRE WITH VERY ROUGH TO HIGH SEAS. CYCLONIC WINDS UP TO 33 KNOTS WITHIN 300 MILES OF CYCLONE CENTRE. ROUGH TO VERY

Keli is now projected to mature and increase to hurricane strength. It is still more than 1,300 miles away. But that southeast course at 15 knots is something to keep a close eye on.

ROUGH SEAS. POOR VISIBILITY IN PERIODS OF HEAVY RAIN AND SQUALLY THUNDERSTORMS WITHIN 200 MILES OF CENTRE. ACTIVE TROUGH WITH POOR VISIBILITY IN HEAVY SHOWERS WITHIN 100 MILES OF EQ 170E 02S 175E 05S 180W 10S 176W 13S 178W TO TC KELI TO14S 177W 13S 170W 08S 163W 05S 160W EQ 156W SLOW MOVING. SECOND TROUGH WITH POOR VISIBILITY IN SHOWERS WITHIN 100 MILES OF 12S 147W 15S 140W 20S 134W 25S 127W SLOW MOVING. COLD FRONT CF WITH SHOWERS WITHIN 60 MILES OF 18S 166E 21S 170E 223S 175E 25S 179E SLOW MOVING. SOUTH OF 20S AND WITHIN 160 MILES WEST OF SECOND TROUGH NORTHWEST WINDS 15 KNOTS. SEAS MODERATE. APART FROM AREA AFFECTED BY TC KELI OVER BROAD BULLETIN AREA EAST OF 170E EAST TO SOUTHEAST WINDS 25 TO 30 KNOTS. ROUGH SEAS. MODERATE EAST TO SOUTHEAST SWELLS.

*** EGC: 58030 **1997/06/13** 09:32:38 SAFETY *** SECURITE Summary of Storm Warnings for METAREA 14 MARINE WEATHER BULLETIN FOR THE SOUTHWEST PACIFIC ISLANDS AREA EQTR TO 25SOUTH 160EAST TO 120WEST ISSUED NADI JUN 130800 UTC.

PART 1 STORM WARNING ISSUED NADI JUNE 130715 UTC. TROPICAL CYCLONE KELI 976 HPA WAS LOCATED NEAR 13 DECIMAL 6 SOUTH 176 DECIMAL 7 WEST AT 130600 UTC. POSITION POOR. REPEAT POSITION 13.6 SOUTH 176.7 WEST AT 130600 UTC. CYCLONE IS MOVING SOUTHEAST AT ABOUT 12 KNOTS. EXPECT SUSTAINED WINDS OF 60 KNOTS CLOSE TO THE CENTRE AND OVER 33 KNOTS WITHIN 100 MILES OF CENTRE. FORECAST POSITION NEAR 15.3S 175.7W AT 131800 UTC NEAR 17.0S 174.5W AT 140600 UTC. SHIPS WITHIN 300 MILES OF CENTRE ARE REQUESTED TO SEND REPORTS EVERY THREE HOURS TO METEO NADI. MORE FOLLOWS

MARINE WEATHER BULLETIN FOR THE SOUTHWEST PACIFIC ISLANDS AREA EQTR TO 25SOUTH 160EAST TO 120WEST ISSUED NADI JUN 130800 UTC. CONT PARTS 2 AND 3 SYNOPSIS AND FORECAST VALID UNTIL JUN 140600 UTC. T.C. KELI 976 HPA LOCATED NEAR 13.6S 176.7W AT 130600 UTC. TC MOVING SOUTHEAST AT ABOUT

Keli is still cooking southeast, and now down to 14 degrees of latitude. It is directly to our north, but almost 20 degrees (1,200 miles) away. Our courses are still converging, but the odds of it sustaining itself in the cooler, high latitudes at this time of year are low.

But if you were in the tropics right now, in the area of Tonga, Nieue or Rarotonga, you would have good cause to be concerned.

Remember, this is in June—well out of the official cyclone season in this part of the world.

12 KNOTS. EXPECT SUSTAINED WINDS 60 KNOTS CLOSE TO CENTRE WITH HIGH TO VERY HIGH SEAS. OVER 33 KNOTS WITHIN 100 MILES OF CENTRE WITH VERY ROUGH TO HIGH SEAS. POOR VISIBILITY IN PERIODS OF HEAVY RAIN AND SQUALLY THUNDERSTORMS WITHIN 200 MILES OF CENTRE. TROUGH T1 WITH POOR VISIBILITY IN RAIN WITHIN 80 MILES OF EQT 165E 05S 171E 08S 180 11S 176W SLOW MOVING. COLD FRONT CF WITH SHOWERS WITHIN 120 MILES OF 16S 179W 20S 179W 25S 177W MOVING EAST 20 KNOTS. SECOND TROUGH T2 WITH POOR VISI-BILITY IN SHOWERS WITHIN 120 MILES OF 10S 151W 15S 138W 20S 128W SLOW MOVING. SOUTH OF T1 AND WEST OF CF SOUTHEAST WINDS 20 TO 25 KNOTS. ROUGH SEAS WITH A MODERATE SOUTHEAST SWELL. IN AREA BETWEEN CF AND T2 WINDS FROM THE EASTERLY QUARTER 20 TO 30 KNOTS. ROUGH TO VERY ROUGH SEAS WITH A MODERATE SOUTHEAST SWELL. ELSEWHERE IN BULLWTIN AREA NORTHEAST WINDS 15 KNOTS.

PACIFIC AREA 25S TO 55S AND 170W TO 120W. SITUATION AND FORECAST ISSUED AT 130223Z VALID UNTIL 140600Z.

Low 968hpa 42S 115W moving southeast 20kt. Within 1000 miles of low clockwise winds 25kt with storms and gales as warn-ing 118 with heavy swell. Visibility poor in rain within 100 miles of front 25s 137w 30s 127w 32s 120w moving northeast 20kt. Ridge 28s 170w to high 1028hpa 32s 155w to ridge 40s 145w 50s 130w 52s 120w all moving east 20kt. Over area northeast of ridge and between 145w and 130w south-erly 25kt. Visibility poor in rain within 100 miles of front 47s 160w 50s 145w 55s 125w moving east 35kt.Southwest of front westerly 30kt and heavy swell and visi-bility fair in showers.Front 30s 175w 40s 165w to first low 1010hpa 41s 167w to second low 1007hpa 41s 173w,front moving east 20kt lows both moving east 15kt. Within 200 miles east of front northwest 30kt and visibility poor in rain.Within 200 miles of first low visibility poor in showers.Within 200 miles of second low in

All of this weather is too far to our south to be of concern.

southern semicircle easterly rising to gale in next 24 hours.

*** EGC: 58058 **1997/06/14** 09:32:47 SAFETY *** <DATA LOST><DATA LOST>

ND ABOVE 33 KNOTS WITHIN 60 MILES OF CENTRE. EXPECT WINDS TO DECREASE FURTHER. FORECAST POSITION NEAR 16.0S 171.0W AT 141800 UTC. NEAR 17.0S 169.5W AT 150600 UTC. SHIPS WITHIN 300 MILES OF CENTRE ARE REQUESTED TO SEND REPORTS EVERY THREE HOURS TO METEO NADI. MORE FOLLOWS

MARINE WEATHER BULLETIN FOR THE SOUTH-WEST PACIFIC ISLANDS AREA EQTR TO 25SOUTH 160EAST TO 120WEST ISSUED NADI JUN 140800 UTC. PARTS 2 AND 3 SYNOPSIS AND FORECAST VALID UNTIL JUN 150600 UTC.

T.C. KELI 987 HPA WAS LOCATED NEAR 15.0S 173.0W AT 140600 UTC. TC MOVING SOUTHEAST AT ABOUT 10 KNOTS. (REFER TO NADI WARNINGS ON THIS SYSTEM). VERY ROUGH TO HIGH SEAS WITHIN 120 MILES SOUTH OF CENTRE. A MODERATE TO HEAVY SOUTHEAST SWELL. ACTIVE TROUGH WITH POOR VISIBILITY IN PERIODS OF HEAVY RAIN AND SQUALLY THUNDERSTORMS WITHIN 280 MILES OF EQTR 167E 05S 180W 10S 170W 15S 167W 17S 172W TO TC KELI TO 17S 172W 15S 167W 10S 161W 07S 157W 07S 155W 08S 150W 10S 145W 15S 135W 20S 125W 25S 120W MOVING SOUTHEAST 08 KNOTS. COLD FRONT WITH SHOWERS WITHIN 120 MILES OF 20S 177E 25S 178W MOVING SOUTHEAST 12 KNOTS. CLOCKWISE WINDS 25 TO 30 KNOTS WITHIN 200 MILES SOUTH OF CYCLONE CENTRE. SEAS ROUGH TO VERY ROUGH WITH A MODERATE SOUTHEAST SWELL.OVER BROAD AREA SOUTH OF 10S SOUTHEAST WINDS 20 TO 25 KNOTS. WINDS TENDING NORTHEAST SOOUTH OF TROUGH BETWEEN 160W AND 170W. SEAS ROUGH WITH A MODERATE SOUTHEAST SWELL. NORTH OF TROUGH AND EAST OF 167W NORTHEAST WINDS 15 KNOTS. SEAS MODERATE WITH EASTERLY SWELL. ELSEWHERE NORTHWEST WINDS 15 TO 20 KNOTS

PACIFIC AREA 25S TO 55S AND 170W TO 120W. SITUATION AND FORECAST ISSUED AT 140215Z VALID UNTIL 150600Z.

Even Sat C has problems. The <data lost> indicates some of the message is missing. Given all that is going on, if we had no other data this would be a major concern. However, these forecasts are sent our four times a day, so six hours later there will be another—and in the interim we have the weather fax data plus our own observations.

Keli has overtaken our longitude by about three degrees but has only dropped down to 15 degrees south. So we still have a separation of 1,000 miles.

Keli's winds have dropped and speed of advance has slowed. It will be highly unusual for the storm to regain strength.

Over broad area east of a line 50s 170w 40s 140w 25s 130w southwest 30kt with gales as warning 128 with heavy southwest swell and visibility fair in showers. Low 978hpa 52s 144w extends front 50s 137w 47s 140w 46s 150w all moving northeast 30kt. Within 300 miles of low clockwise winds rising to gale in next 24 hours with visibility poor in showers and heavy swell. Ridge 27s 170w 30s 160w to high 1025hpa 31s 153w all moving east 10kt. First low 1011hpa 39s 173w moving northeast 10kt extends trough to second low 1006hpa 41s 162w moving east 15kt. Within 300 miles of lows and trough visibility poor in showers. High 1030hpa 45s 180 extends ridge 47s 170w 45s 160w. Between ridge and trough southeast 25kt.

*** EGC: 58083 **1997/06/15** 09:32:38 SAFETY *** SECURITE Summary of Storm Warnings for METAREA 14

MARINE WEATHER BULLETIN FOR THE SOUTHWEST PACIFIC ISLANDS AREA EQTR TO 25SOUTH 160EAST TO 120WEST ISSUED NADI JUN 150800 UTC. PART 1 GALE WARNING ISSUED NADI JUNE 150715 UTC.TROPICAL DEPRESSION (1000HPA) FORMERLY TROPICAL CYCLONE KELI WASLOCATED NEAR 21.0S 163.5W AT 150600 UTC MOVING SOUTHEAST 25 KNOTS. EXPECT SUSTAINED WINDS UP TO 35 KNOTS WITHIN 120 MILES OF CENTRE IN SOUTHERN SEMICIRCLE.SHIPS WITHIN 300 MILES OF CENTRE ARE REQUESTED TO SEND REPORTS EVERY THREE HOURS TO METEO NADI AND METEO WELLINGTON. MORE FOLLOWS

MARINE WEATHER BULLETIN FOR THE SOUTHWEST PACIFIC ISLANDS AREA EQTR TO 25SOUTH 160EAST TO 120WEST ISSUED NADI JUN 150800 UTC. PARTS 2 AND 3 SYNOPSIS AND FORECAST VALID UNTIL JUN 160600 UTC.

TROPICAL DEPRESSION (1000 HPA) FORMERLY T.C. KELI WAS LOCATED NEAR 21.0S 163.5W AT 150600 UTC. DEPRESSION MOVING SOUTHEAST 25 KNOTS. (REFER TO NADI WARNINGS ON THIS SYSTEM). ROUGH TO VERY ROUGH SEAS WITHIN 180 MILES CENTER IN THE

All of this weather is taking place well south of our position and to the east.

Keli is now down to barely a depression, although she is closer to us now— about 800 miles to the north-north-west.

If this were summer, or at the edge of winter, there would be a possibility for a cyclone at this position to maintain its strength and continue southeast towards us. However, it is now too deep into winter, and the energy is not available for Keli to continue into cooler latitudes—thank goodness!

SOUTHERN SEMICIRCLE. A MODERATE SOUTH-EAST SWELL. TROUGH WITH POOR VISIBILITY IN SHOWERS AND ISOLATED SQUALLY THUNDER-STORMS WITHIN 180 MILES OF EQTR 165E 02S 175E 06S 175W 13S 165W 20S 162W TO TROP-ICAL DEPRESSION TO 25S 163W MOVING SOUTH-EAST 25 KNOTS SOUTH OF 20S SLOW MOVING ELSEWHERE.PRESISTENT CONVECTION WITH POOR VISIBILITY IN RAIN AND SQUALLY THUN-DERSTORMS IN AN AREA BOUNDED BY 05S 145W 14S 158W SLOW MOVING. WINDS GUSTING TO 30 KNOTS IN THUNDERSTORM SQUALLS. ROUGH SEAS. CLOCKWISE WINDS 20 TO 25 KNOTS WITHIN 300 MILES OF DEPRESSION CENTRE. SEAS ROUGH. A MODERATE NORTHEAST SWELL IN EASTERN SEMICIRCLE OF DEPRESSION. SOUTH AND WEST OF TROUGH SOUTHEAST WINDS 20 TO 25 KNOTS. ROUGH SEAS WITH A MODERATE SOUTHEAST SWELL. WINDS TURNING SOUTHWEST 15 KNOTS NORTH OF 10S. OVER A BROAD AREA NORTH AND EAST OF TROUGH EAST TO NORTH-EAST WINDS 15 TO 20 KNOTS. ROUGH SEAS AT TIMES WITH A MODERATE EASTERLY SWELL.

PACIFIC AREA 25S TO 55S AND 170W TO 120W.SITUATION AND FORECAST ISSUED AT 150307Z VALID UNTIL 160600Z.

All of this is out of our area.

Ridge 25s 145w to high 1020hpa 29s 130w to ridge 30s 120w all slow moving. Visibility poor in rain within 100 miles of front 39S 147W 42S 138W 47S 132W to low 982hpa 47s 133w to low 990hpa 49s 142w all moving northeast 20kt. Between front and ridge northwest 25kt with gales as warning 140 and heavy westerly swell.Over broad area southwest of front southwest gales as warning 140 with heavy southwest swell and visibility poor in showers. Ridge 48s 170w 50s 160w 42s 155w slow moving. Northwest of ridge southeast 30kt. Visibility poor in showers within 200 miles of low 1010hpa 37s 170w moving northeast 20kt. Low 1008hpa 32s 165w extends front 30s 163w 25s 170w, low mov-ing east 20kt, front slow moving. Within 200 miles east of front visibility poor in rain. North of 28s between 150w and

The low to our west on the fax chart is called out. Note the 20-knot speed. If the high to the east has more body than shown on the fax chart, this could be taken as an early indicator of some breeze as the low runs into the high, catching us in a squash zone.

165w easterly expected to rise to 30kt in next 24 hours.

*** EGC: 58122 **1997/06/16** 21:32:56 SAFETY *** SECURITE Summary of Storm Warnings for METAREA 14

MARINE WEATHER BULLETIN FOR THE SOUTHWEST PACIFIC ISLANDS AREA EQTR TO 25SOUTH 160EAST TO 120WEST ISSUED NADI JUN 162000 UTC. PART 1 WARNING NIL. PARTS 2 AND 3 SYNOPSIS AND FORECAST VALID UNTIL JUN 171800 UTC.

WEAK COLD FRONT WITH SHOWERS WITHIN 60 MILES OF 10S 164E 15S 163E 20S 163E 22S 167E 25S 168E MOVING EAST-SOUTHEAST 20 KNOTS. ACTIVE TROUGH WITH POOR VISIBILITY IN SOME SHOWERS AND ISOLATED SQUALLY THUNDERSTORMS WITHIN 200 MILES OF EQTR 180W 105S 177W 08S 170W 09S 165W 10S 160W 11S 155W 14S 150W 17S 145W 20S 143W 25S 139W MOVING EAST 10 KNOTS SOUTH OF 10S BUT SLOW MOVING ELSEWHERE. EAST OF TROUGH NORTHEASTERLY WINDS 10 TO 15 KNOTS. WINDS TENDING NORTHWESTERLY CLOSE TO TROUGH AND RISING UPTO 25 KNOTS AND GUSTING TO 35 KNOTS SOUTH OF 17S. SEAS ROUGH TO VERY ROUGH SOUTH OF 17S BUT MODERATE ELSE-WHERE. MODERATE EAST TO NORTHEAST SWELL. BETWEEN WEST OF TROUGH AND EAST OF 160W SOUTH TO SOUTHWESTERLY WINDS 15 TO 20 KNOTS. SEAS MODERATE WITH MODERATE SOUTH-ERLY SWELL. WEST OF WEAK COLD FRONT SOUTHWESTERLY WINDS 15 TO 25 KNOTS. SEAS MODERATE TO ROUGH WITH MODERATE SOUTHERLY SWELL. ELSEWHERE IN THE BULLETIN AREA EAST TO SOUTHEASTERLY 15 TO 20 KNOTS. SEAS MODERATE WITH A MODERATE SOUTH TO SOUTHEAST SWELL.

GALE WARNINGS ISSUED BY METEOROLOGI-CAL SERVICE OF NEW ZEALAND LTD AT 162130 UTC PACIFIC AREA 25S TO 55S AND 170W TO 120W. SITUATION AND FORECAST ISSUED AT 161839Z VALID UNTIL 171800Z.

Poor visibility in rain within 90 miles of front 37s 120w 36s 130w to low 989hPa 32s 140w moving ea<DATA LOST>

*** EGC: 58136 **1997/06/17** 09:32:29 SAFETY *** SECURITE Summary of Storm Warnings for METAREA 14

Notice the trough of low pressure and northwesterly winds in its vicinity. If you want to head backwards, against the high pressure trades, by waiting for periodic troughs of this nature you can turn what would normally be a beat into a nice broad reach—or at worst a motorsail in light conditions.

There are no indications on this report of what has given rise to the strong winds on the night of the 15th. Just the hint yesterday of what could turn into a squash zone between the fast moving low and plodding high pressure system.

MARINE WEATHER BULLETIN FOR THE SOUTHWEST PACIFIC ISLANDS AREA EQTR TO 25SOUTH 160EAST TO 120WEST ISSUED NADI JUN 170810 UTC. PART 1 WARNING NIL.

PARTS 2 AND 3 SYNOPSIS AND FORECAST VALID UNTIL JUN 180600 UTC.

FIRST COLD FRONT CF1 WITH SHOWERS WITHIN 100 MILES OF 13S 167E 20S 170E 25S 171E MOVING EAST 10 KNOTS. WEAK COLD FRONT 22S 162W 25S 159W MOVING EAST NORTHEAST 20 KNOTS. TROUGH WITH POOR VISIBILITY IN OCCASIONAL SHOWERS AND ISOLATED THUDERSTORMS WITHIN 150 MILES OF 08S 158W 15S 147W 20S 142W 25S 139W MOVING SOUTHEAST 15 KNOTS. WEST OF CF1 SOUTH TO SOUTHWEST WINDS 15 TO 20 KNOTS. MODERATE SEAS WITH MODERATE TO HEAVY EASTERLY SWELLS. SOUTHERLY SWELL DEVELOPING IN THE NEXT 12 TO 18 HOURS. IN AREA BETWEEN CF1 AND TROUGH WINDS FROM BETWEEN SOUTHEAST AND EAST 15 TO 20 KNOTS. WINDS GRADUALLY TURNING NORTHEAST WITHIN 180 MILES OF CF1. ROUGH SEAS AT TIMES WITH MODERATE SOUTHEAST SWELL. EAST OF TROUGH NORTHERLY WINDS 15 KNOTS. ELSEWHERE IN BULLETIN AREA EASTERLY WINDS 15 KNOTS.

PACIFIC AREA 25S TO 55S AND 170W TO 120W. SITUATION AND FORECAST ISSUED AT 170234Z VALID UNTIL 180600Z.

Front 25s 136w 33s 126w 37s 125w moving east 40kt to complex low with centers 985hpa 36s 129w moving southeast 45kt and 988hpa 31s 142w moving northeast 20kt extends front 36s 138w 37s 125w 37s 120w. East of low centers northwest 25kt with gales as warning 162 and heavy northwest swell. Poor visibility in rain within 240 miles of front. Poor visibility in showers over broad area west of front. Low 969hpa 52s 119w slow moving. Within 600 miles of low clockwise winds. 30kt Ridge 55s 145w 50s 155w 41s 165w to high 1027hpa 36s 172w all slow moving. East of ridge west of a line 55s 135w 40s 145w 28s 149w southerly 30kt with heavy southerly swell.

Nothing here of interest right now, but this frontal activity and reversed wind flow (from the normal southeast trades) bodes well for us as we work our way backwards through the islands in the coming months.

WEATHER AT ANCHOR

So far, we've discussed weather in a voyaging context. However, any time you are anchored in a less than totally protected situation, weather has to be a concern—perhaps not a major one, but something to keep your eye on nonetheless.

The degree of watchfulness is a function of the security of your anchorage. If there is good holding, you are well protected from all quadrants, and fetch in which chop can build is limited, then you can relax, and just check things occasionally.

But as the security of the anchorage is reduced, a more rigorous watch on weather conditions needs to be maintained.

RANGIROA

Eight weeks after Linda and I had visited Raivavai on *Beowulf*, we were sitting at Rangiroa in the Tuamotus.

Rangiroa is a huge atoll with long fetches in all directions. As long as the breeze is from tradewind quadrants (southeast to northeast) you have reasonable protection (although the holding is marginal). Anytime there is a front in the area, you must be very careful as you are suddenly on a lee shore. In addition, if you wait too long to put to sea, your exit may be blocked by poor visibility—these atolls all require eyeball navigation.

So, we were keeping a close eye on the fax each day, as well as watching the sky for signs of any frontal activity.

The following five days worth of fax charts from the New Zealand Met Service are worth a close look. We were watching them because of our exposed situation. In the end, we opted to move on to a smaller atoll, farther to the northeast, before the weather became an issue.

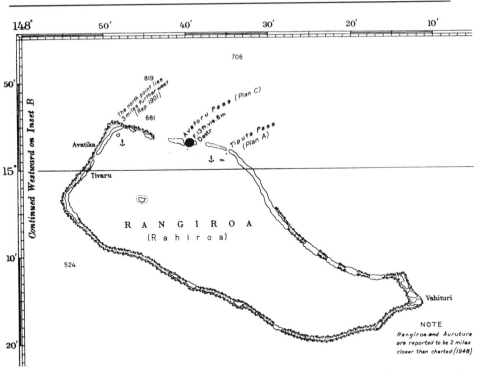

Rangiroa is one of the largest atolls in the world, with lots of
fetch inside of the lagoon in which seas can build when the wind
is from any direction other than the normal tradewind
quadrant.

A weak front did affect Rangiroa marginally and
with our heavy ground tackle we'd have taken it in
stride—but the safest thing to do was to put to sea,
and that is the course of action we always take in
these situations.

Now, however, take a look at the Austral Islands,
and in particular Raivavai where we'd just visited
the previous month. They had winds reported in the
local news to be upwards of 70 knots. Had we still
been there, and caught inside the reef where we'd
been anchored, things would have been dicey
indeed.

In all probability, the only way we'd have kept the
boat afloat would to have been to leave the anchorage well ahead of the *potential* blow, moving north,

towards the equator, and away from its southeast-erly track.

While it is always difficult to give up a comfortable anchorage in the face of a prospective threat, with this sort of weather potential, that would have been the only alternative.

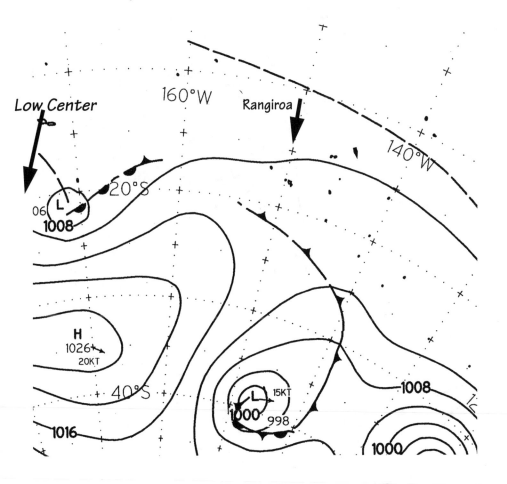

We first started watching this extratropical low when it appeared on August 19, 1997. At 1008mb it did not present much of a threat. However, moving from the tropics to the higher latitudes meant that it could pick up energy from cold air coming up via the high pressure to its south. The 996mb low at the bottom of the chart is a typical winter depression, and at 40 degrees south latitude posed no threat to our cruising grounds.

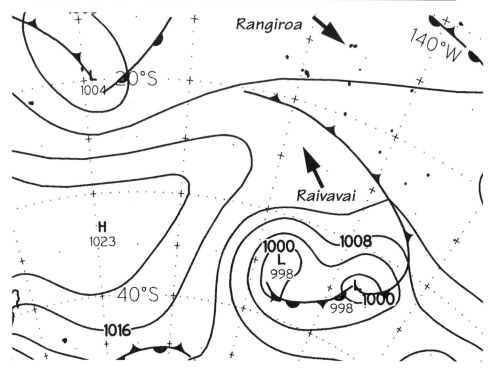

The following day (upper chart) the low had moved southeast and dropped to a central pressure of 1004mb. Twenty-four hours later (bottom chart) on the 19th the low center is now at 986mb with a front stretching out towards Rangiroa.

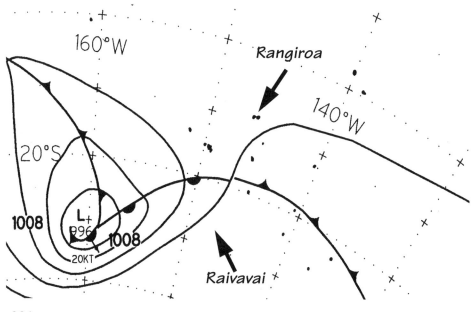

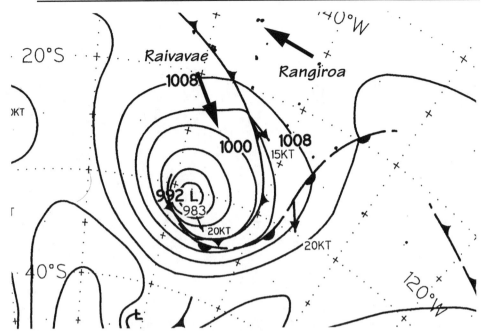

By the 20th of August (upper chart) it was obvious that the low had some real power. You can see the front just to the east of Rangiroa. This will bring westerly quadrant winds, making most of the anchorages within the lagoon untenable. Raivavai to the south is feeling the full brunt of the storm. Between the 20th and 21st Raivavai experienced hurricane force winds. The 19th is the last chance to leave Raivavai for a protected harbor on Tahiti (500 miles to the north) before the storm affects the sailing area.

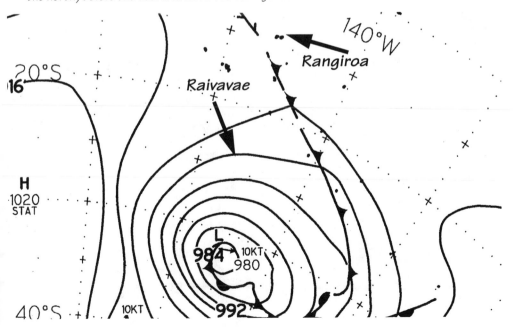

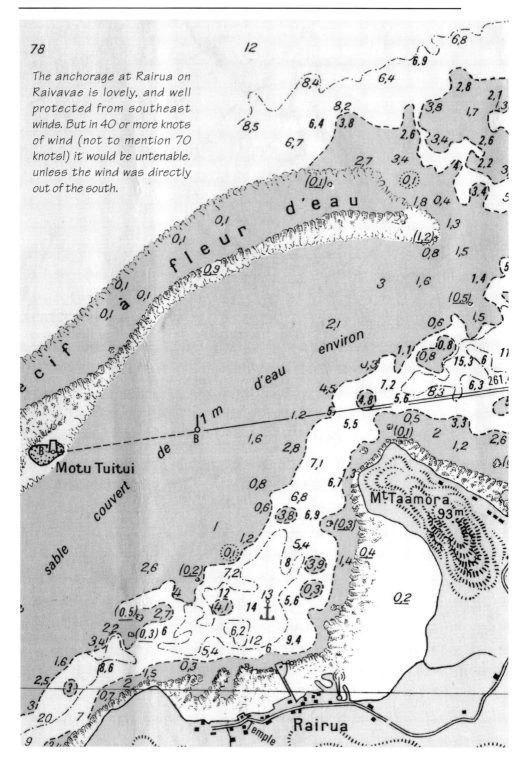

78

The anchorage at Rairua on Raivavae is lovely, and well protected from southeast winds. But in 40 or more knots of wind (not to mention 70 knots!) it would be untenable. unless the wind was directly out of the south.

CRUISING HIGHS

High pressure weather systems hold the key to comfortable passagemaking. This applies to sailors who are looking for wind as well as power boaters who prefer calmer conditions for voyaging.

CIRCULATION ABOUT A HIGH

As we mentioned earlier, in the Northern Hemisphere winds circulate around the center of a high in a *clockwise* direction and counterclockwise in the Southern Hemisphere. This means that if you are on the top of the high—the side closest to the pole—you will have westerly winds, and easterly under the center of the high on the equator side.

Generally speaking, the closer to the center of the high you are, the lighter will be the breeze. There's always more wind towards the edges.

For the sailor, with limited powering range, it is usually advisable to keep to the outer edges of the high, where better winds are to be found. Even though this may mean sailing a longer distance it usually results in a faster passage.

N. Hemisphere highs:

❑ West winds on north side.

❑ East winds on south side.

❑ Southerly winds on west side.

❑ Northerly winds on east side.

S. Hemisphere highs:

❑ West winds on south side.

❑ East winds on north side.

❑ Southerly winds on east side.

❑ Northerly winds on west side.

For those passaging by power alone the center of the high, with its lighter winds and calmer seas promises a smoother ride and lower fuel consumption.

KEEP AN EYE ON DEVELOPMENT

High pressure systems are living, breathing entities that expand, contract, and sometimes move at a pretty good clip. As a result, you need to keep an eye on what they are doing today, and what they're likely to be doing next week.

By tracking the high on a daily basis for several weeks before departure, you can get a feel for its oscillations. A pattern is usually involved, and when you get a handle on this, you're on the way to being in the right segment of the high for the kind of weather you prefer.

I like to drop by the local weather bureau and ask the professionals to acquaint me with the high in question; they've been living with it on a daily basis for years. They are usually glad to give tips on what sort of external phenomenon affect the high (the jet stream, large lows, other highs), and when is the best time to depart.

Once we're on our way, by watching the sky, and keeping track of barometric pressure, coupled with synoptic data on high seas forecasts or weather faxes, we get a pretty good idea of what is happening. And where the high is stable, with only modest oscillations this system works very well.

However, be wary of getting caught up in the windless center, if the high should start to expand or its center move towards your position.

WESTERLY TRADEWINDS

Most people think of high pressure systems and the easterly quadrant "trade" winds they generate as pathways to the tropics, with idyllic downwind sailing.

Before departing on a high pressure dominated passage:

❑ Watch oscillations of stable high or passage of migratory systems.

❑ Check with local meteorologist about normal patterns.

Enroute keep an eye on:

❑ Barometer to avoid getting to close to center.

❑ Movement of center towards your position (bringing light airs).

❑ Isobars turning corners which will bring more wind.

But at some point you have to return home from that downwind destination, and you still have the high to deal with.

Move with us now to the main saloon of the Canadian ketch *Blue Shadow*. She's anchored in beautiful Hanalei Bay on the North shore of Kauai in the Hawaiian islands. A bunch of us have gathered here to compare notes on the North Pacific High and how we plan to use it to speed us on our way home.

On the saloon table are spread a series of fax charts from the past week.

Blue Shadow is heading for Vancouver. She will be able to ride the clockwise circulation all the way home, heading north first, gradually turning northeast, and then east. On the first leg of the passage, they will keep the northeasterly winds on the starboard bow, but within a few days they should have a freeing breeze as they get farther to the north. By the time they've covered 500 miles, the wind will be on the beam, gradually swinging to the quarter and finally a dead run, as they follow the circulation around the high's center towards Canada.

The big tactical question for Fred and his crew will be how close to clip the northwest corner of the high. The great circle route home takes them close enough to the center to risk running out of wind. Since *Blue Shadow* has lots of range under power, she can motor through if required, so her crew has margin for error.

The crew of *Adianne* has a more difficult destination. They are heading to San Francisco. Although geographically closer than Vancouver, the shortest route will take them right through the windless center of the high and they do not have the ability to make it under power. To take advantage of the winds circulating around the high, they are going to have to sail the same course as *Blue Shadow*, and then turn south a few hundred miles from the coast and

Stan Honey's high pressure rules:

- ❑ Within 8mb (two isobar lines) of the high center winds will be light.

- ❑ Can push a little closer if the high is growing (central pressure is increasing).

- ❑ If the 5640 contour on the 500mb chart forms an omega wave (upside-down U) 300 to 400 miles west of the center of the high, the high will tend to strengthen and there will be more wind closer to the center.

- ❑ If there is zonal flow at the 500mb level, the high center will tend to be weak and you should stay further away for better breeze.

It is usually possible to see short term waves in the fax chart streamlines. In Hawaii, these often have a period of three to five days. They appear as inverted troughs. The leading edge is northeasterly and windy. This gradually gives way to lighter east to south east winds. The trick for leaving Hawaii is to figure out the cycle, and then leave when the wind goes just south of east. This gives you two or more days to beat out from the Islands in moderate conditions with a favorable wind angle.

Food for thought—a week's worth of weather faxes are laid out on the saloon table aboard Blue Shadow.

head down to the Bay area. They'll end up with following winds most of the trip, but it will take them at least 22 days to get home.

Aboard *Sundeer* we have an even more difficult destination: Southern California. The most direct route takes us under the high, directly into the teeth of the northeast tradewinds. And even though *Sundeer* is a remarkably smooth boat sailing upwind, the prospect of 2,300 miles of beating meets with little enthusiasm from her crew or your authors. There is, however, an alternative.

Our plan is to take advantage of *Sundeer's* long range under power (2000+ miles) and the calm center of the high. At first we'll head north on a close reach. When we reach the midpoint of the high (about even with the latitude of San Francisco) we'll head due east. In theory three or four days of windless powering will bring us through to the east side of the high from where we'll have a sleigh ride home with northerly winds at our back.

We depart Hanalei with 30 knots of easterly pushing us on our way. Close-reaching on a course of north-by-northeast keeps us moving at a good clip and quite comfortable. After two days of sailing we've covered 480 miles and I'm about to congratulate myself on our plan. Theoretically, in another day or two and we'll turn right towards the coast under power.

The sea state is a good indicator of conditions near the high center. If long period swells are not evident, then the odds are the winds are light around the center.

HIGHS ARE RARELY STABLE

Reality is something else. The high begins to move north, taking its calm center with it. Instead of being able to turn right in a couple of days, we will now have to sail as far north as Oregon to get even with the center.

Blue Shadow is in better shape. Having left before us, they see the high heading north and adjust course to the northeast maintaining their distance from the center. A very quick 16 days after leaving, they are home in Vancouver.

Adianne, on the other hand, is caught by light airs as the center moves over them and their speed drops with the wind. It takes them four weeks to make what should have been a three-week passage.

As our fax charts begin to show the new pattern, aboard *Sundeer,* we realize a change is required in our tactics. In its movement north the high has assumed an egg shape, with the axis pointed north/south. Easterly headwinds will be reduced while this shape is maintained.

We harden up the sails and head almost directly towards home with southeast wind. The next couple of days see us just off the wind, making a steady 230 miles per day. As we approach the midpoint of the *underside* of the high, the wind goes dead on the nose. At this point we light off the engine and maintain course for three days by motorsailing with reefed mainsail.

By day seven there's a perceptible shift to the breeze. As we close with the coast, we begin to feel the northerly winds coming from the east side of the high. Up go the mizzen and working jib as we retire the diesel.

Each day the wind frees more until we're flying our spinnaker on a final sleigh ride towards the barn. After 11 days at sea, *Sundeer's* crew is once again in a calm anchorage.

ON TOP OF THE HIGH

Using the tradewinds from these high pressure systems makes for great sailing. But when you throw in some north or south into your course, you will soon find yourself out of the influence of the high pressure system.

On the polar side of these high pressure weather systems, frontal activity picks up extensively as the polar air masses clash with that within your subtropical high.

BELOW THE HIGH

On the equator side of the highs, at the bottom of the traditional tropical tradewind belts, you begin to run into the doldrums or Intertropical Convergence Zone (ITCZ).

The ITCZ is a band of varying width between the wind circulation of the Northern and Southern Hemispheres. It is typically an area with lots of convective activity (thunder storms), variable wind direction, and fluctuating wind strength.

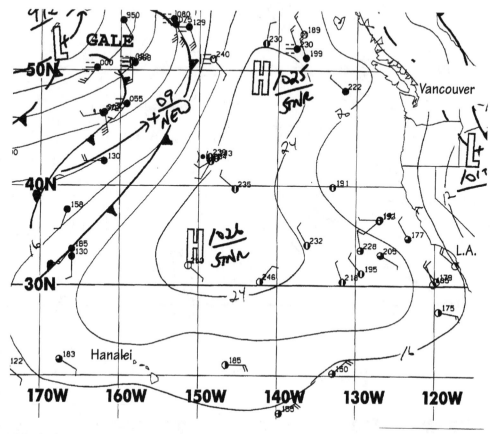

Here's the type of scenario that doesn't look too hot at first—until you consider that low pushing in from the west. The center of the high will probably slide southwest, bringing lighter winds with it.

This is a relatively small center. A boat with good speed in light airs, and some upwind ability can make use of this by tacking into the trades for a couple of days south of the center—and then you are on your way in the center under power and quickly out on the east side of the high with reaching conditions. This is not an option for a slower boat.

Leaving from Hanalei (just to the right of the 160 degree longitude line) you've got close reaching on starboard tack for a day or so until the wind veers (clockwise) around the high.

As you move farther to the north, the wind will be from the south, giving you a nice broad reach. If you are heading to the Pacific Northwest this is a perfect situation. However, for Southern California the choice would be head north, then northeast and power through the center of the high until you come out in the norwesterlies on the east side of the high center.

If you don't have the powering ability to do this, it would be judicious to wait for a better scenario, or go now hoping the low coming in will improve things—and if it doesn't, stop in Seattle for a while.

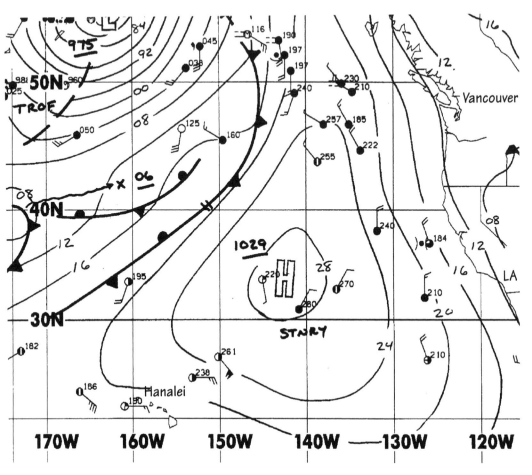

Three days later and we have a great scenario for Southern California as well as the Northwest. The low to the west has pushed across, shoving the high center south. Isobars have tightened and the angles have improved for getting back to the coast. The center of the high will probably slide southwest, bringing lighter winds with it. The bump in the isobar just west of the big island of Hawaii, on the 160W longitude line, is probably caused by an inverted trough coming up from the equator. These inverted troughs tend to accelerate the south east trades near Hawaii.

Leaving the islands, there will be strong southeast trades because the high has pushed down and the isobars are now bent. The curve in the isobars in the vicinity of the Islands will increase the wind 20% or so. Heading to L.A., you might get away with turning east just above the 30-degree latitude line. However, if powering range is limited it would be better to sail up to more like 37 or 38 degrees.

If you are sailing to the Northwest, the low up in the Gulf of Alaska (at the top of the chart) will bear watching. It has now deepened to 975mb and will be moving southeast over the next few days. It will likely intersect your course as you head north.

The location of the ITCZ moves with the sun, heading north in the Northern Hemisphere spring and summer and south in the Southern Hemisphere summer.

The width of the ITCZ also varies. It is typically narrowest where the sea-surface temperature is coolest. The cooler water reduces or eliminates convective (cloud-building) activity.

There are no hard and fast rules about where to cross. The best way to approach this is to look at the conditions as they exist in the weeks leading up to your passage.

It is frequently possible to get through the ITCZ areas with little difficulty. Sometimes just a day of unsettled, showery weather, and then you are into the new hemisphere's tradewind circulation.

Linda and I have now crossed the ITCZ five times, and each time has been a little different. But we've never had more than two days of unsettled weather, and the average is more in the 12-to 18-hour range.

The doldrums (ITCZ) follow the sun. North in the Northern Hemispheres summer and south in the Southern Hemisphere summer.

UNFRIENDLY HIGHS

While high pressure system cruising is usually associated with moderate winds and pleasant sailing, this is not always the case.

As we mentioned earlier, where the isobars of a high make sharp bends, a significant acceleration of the wind is likely to exist.

Likewise, when a high and low come together, with the faster moving low pressing up against the slower moving high, the isobars can be compressed and substantial winds can result.

Without external forecast data, this type of situation is difficult to predict, except by certain, subtle, local signs. You are rarely aware that a low is about to create problems as the barometer and sky show only the influence of the high pressure system.

With a fax aboard, if you see a low pressure system climbing the back of a high, you know to watch out.

TROPICAL FORECASTING

Predicting tropical weather is in many ways more difficult than predicting weather at higher latitudes. Subtle changes in the ebb and flow of the atmosphere have much greater impact closer rather than further away from the equator. Small changes in barometric pressure in the tropics account for much stronger winds than are the norm in the subtropics or out of the tropics entirely.

Complicating the issue is a lack of on-the-spot reporting. There simply are not as many buoys and ships reporting in, and there are fewer aircraft flying in the tropical areas to report back the high altitude conditions.

TROPICAL PREDICTION CENTER

For the tropical waters surrounding the United States (including the Caribbean,

Central America and Mexico) the Tropical Analysis and Forecast Branch of the National Hurricane Center is responsible for forecasting and analysis.

They are responsible for up to the latitude of 30 degrees North, where the Marine Prediction Center takes over.

Forecasting tropical weather is in many ways a more difficult proposition than that which occurs in the higher latitudes.

Christopher Burr is Chief of the Tropical Center and was kind enough to take some time from a very busy summer to fill us in on some of the details on how they predict the weather.

"Lack of ship reports is a bit of a problem for us. We get less than half of what the Marine Prediction Center gets, and we cover a greater area. As a result we have to rely more on computer models and our own expertise."

"We look at satellite images in the infrared and visible spectrum as well as at water vapor images. We also use the Department of Defense polar orbit-

The tropics are barely stable, atmospherically speaking. You have in place heat and moisture, two of the three ingredients necessary for convection and the beginnings of a storm.

All that is required is a spark to set the system rotating.

This spark can be provided by an edge of the jet stream looping towards the equator, or an upper level trough digging towards the equator.

Because the situation is so unstable only very small inducements from the upper atmosphere are necessary to start a tropical storm brewing.

ing satellites to send us scatterometer data on the surface which is very helpful when we don't have ship reports."

The computer process used at the Tropical Predication Center is similar to that used by the Marine Prediction Center (page 76). They also use the Medium Range Forecast model and pull it off the aviation forecast early for their surface analysis. In addition, they use the "NOGAPS" (U.S. Navy Operational Global Atmospheric Prediction System) model.

The fax charts which are broadcast are drawn on a computer, then checked of course by the analyst.

I asked Chris about the techniques they used with hurricane forecasting. "We use the Dvorak technique to forecast intensity and a variety of computer models for movement and development until the storms are within range of aircraft." (The Dvorak technique is covered starting with page 366).

An issue which has always been of interest is the process used to tell where and when a hurricane is going to start cooking.

"We look for areas of scattered to moderate convection, and then keep an eye on it. Using infrared imaging with enhancement techniques we measure the temperature of the cloud tops. This tells us where the areas of convective activity are likely to be. What we are looking for is solid areas of convective activity, not just little thunderstorms."

TROPICAL SYNOPTIC CHARTS

As you move into the tropics there is a reduction of Coriolis force from the earth's rotation. As a result, the wind tends to follow more directly along the isobars. Isobars are spaced further apart than at higher latitudes, so you often find tropical weather maps with streamlines, representing *wind flow*. Keep in mind, as we've mentioned before, that the closer you get to the equator the greater the wind strength for a given isobar spacing. Isobars which would produce a fresh breeze outside of the tropics will produce gale force winds within the tropics.

```
N ATLANTIC N OF 7N TO 31N W OF 35W INCLUDING CARIBBEAN SEA AND
GULF OF MEXICO

SYNOPSIS VALID 0000 UTC SUN SEP 20.
FORECAST VALID 1200 UTC MON SEP 21.

WARNINGS.
0300 UTC SEP 20...HURRICANE GEORGES 15.8N 55.8W MOVING W
280 DEG AT 16 KT.  MAXIMUM SUSTAINED WIND 130 KT GUST 160 KT.
TROPICAL STORM FORCE WIND WITHIN 175 NM N SEMICIRCLE AND 150 NM
SE AND 125NM SW QUADRANTS. SEAS 12 FT OR GREATER WITHIN 325 NM N
AND 200 NM S SEMICIRCLES. FORECAST HURRICANE 17.4N 65.0W.
FORECAST MAXIMUM SUSTAINED WINDS 130 KT GUSTS 165 KT. TROPICAL
STORM FORCE WINDS WITHIN 175 NM N SEMICIRCLE. 150NM SE AND 125
NM SW QUADRANTS. SEAS 12 FT OR GREATER WITHIN 325 NM N AND 200
NM S SEMICIRCLE.REQUEST 3 HOURLY SHIP REPORTS WITHIN 300 NM OF
CENTER.

0300 UTC SEP 20...TROPICAL STORM HERMINE 29.1N 90.6W MOVING NNE
AT 3 KT. MAXIMUM SUSTAINED WIND 35 KT GUSTS 45 KT.
TROPICAL STORM FORCE WINDS AND SEAS 12 FT OR GREATER WITHIN 50
NM NE AND 75 NM SE QUADRANTS. AT 1200 UTC SEP 20 TROPICAL
DEPRESSION INLAND 30.1N 90.3W. MAX WIND 30 KT GUSTS 40 KT.
FORECAST TROPICAL DEPRESSION INLAND 33.7N 87.5W. WIND 20 KT
GUSTS 30 KT.

SYNOPSIS AND FORECAST...
ATLC EXCEPT AT NOTED IN WARNINGS WITHIN 425 NM N AND 300 NM S
SEMICIRCLES OF GEORGES WIND 20 TO 33 KT SEAS 8 TO 12 FT.
FORECAST ATLC AND CARIBBEAN EXCEPT AS NOTED IN WARNINGS WITHIN
425 NM N AND 300 NM SEMICIRCLES OF GEORGES WIND 20 TO 33 KT
SEAS 8 TO 12 FT. AT 0600 UTC SEPT 20...N OF 29N BETWEEN 66W AND
77W WIND INCREASING SW TO S 20 KT SEAS BUILDING TO 8 FT.
FORECAST N OF 29N BETWEEN 65W AND 74W WIND SW 20 KT SEAS 8 FT.

CARIBBEAN E OF 75W WIND E 20 KT SEAS TO 8 FT. EXCEPT AS NOTED
PREVIOUSLY...FORECAST LITTLE CHANGE.

CARIBBEAN N OF 17N W OF 82W WIND SE 20 TO 25 KT SEAS 10 FT.
FORECAST CARIBBEAN N OF 18N W OF 84W WIND SE TO S 20 KT SEAS 8
FT.

GULF OF MEXICO EXCEPT AS NOTED IN WARNINGS WITHIN 120 NM OF
TROPICAL STORM HERMINE WIND 20 TO 33 KT SEAS TO 10 FT. FORECAST
N OF 27N BETWEEN 85W AND 90W WIND S TO SW 20 TO 25 KT SEAS 10
FT.

GULF OF MEXICO ELSEWHERE E OF 93W WIND 20 KT SEAS TO 8 FT.
FORECAST ELSEWHERE E OF 91W WIND S TO 20 KT SEAS TO 8 FT.

REMAINDER FORECAST WATERS WIND LESS THAN 20 KT SEAS BELOW 8 FT.

FORECASTER FET
```

A typical high seas forecast broadcast with voice and via Inmarsat to go with the surface analysis on the opposite page. The written analysis and fax charts are done by the same forecaster.

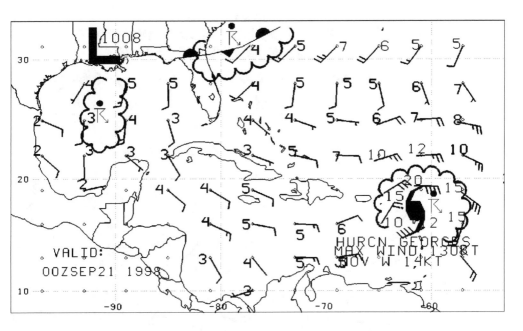

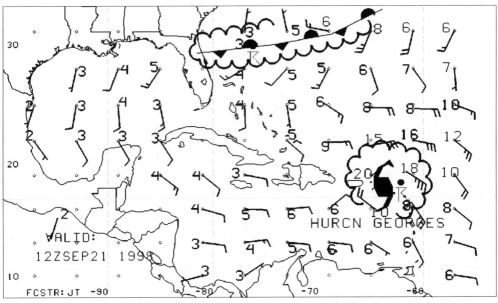

A typical surface forecast, with current conditions as well as
those expected 12 hours forward. Wind feathers have sea
height in feet indicated at the foot of each feather.

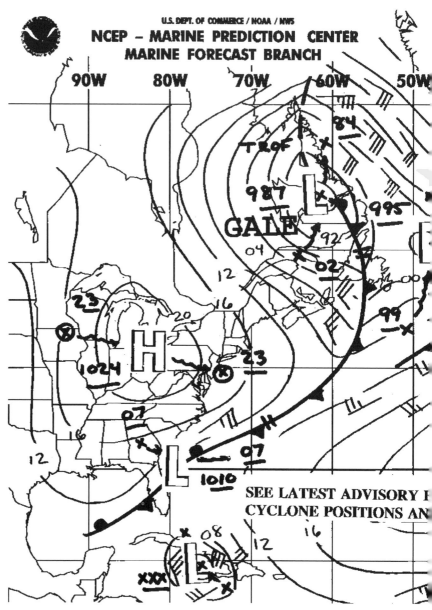

Strictly speaking, this fax chart is more for extratropical weather than that found in the tropics. Yet there are clues here to what may happen in the tropics. Of particular concern is the potential for steering any hurricanes which may be brewing. In this case, there is a well established surface high pressure projected out four days from the current time period.

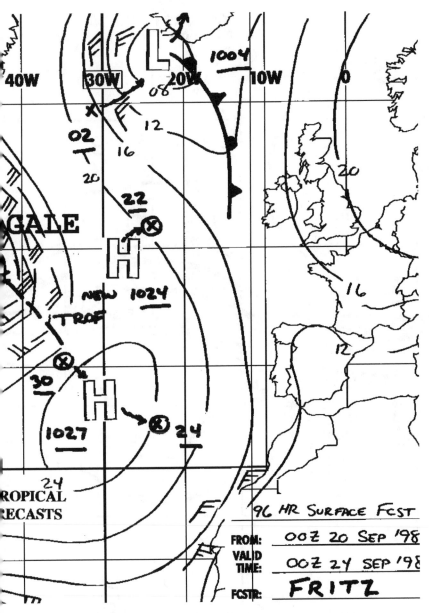

You next want to look at the 500mb charts to see what is happening at higher altitudes (for more data on 500mb charts see page 170). If the upper atmosphere is relatively calm conditions are good for hurricane formation. Steering currents will parallel the surface high for any storms that develop or currently exist.

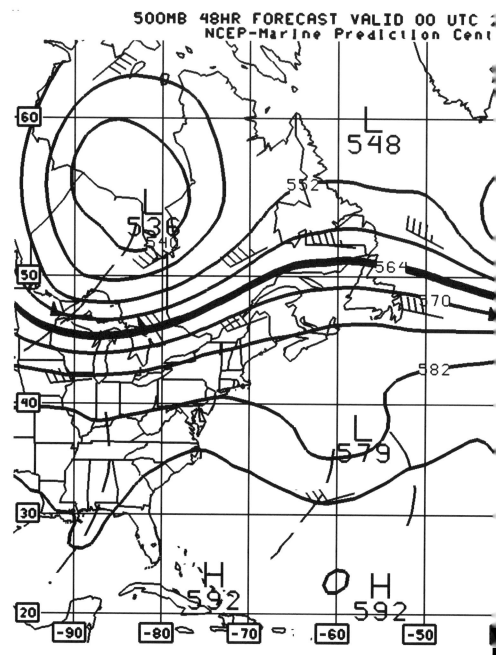

A 48-hour 500mb prognosis. Note how the tropical and sub-tropical areas have stable high pressure conditions and relatively light winds. These are favorable signs for hurricane development.

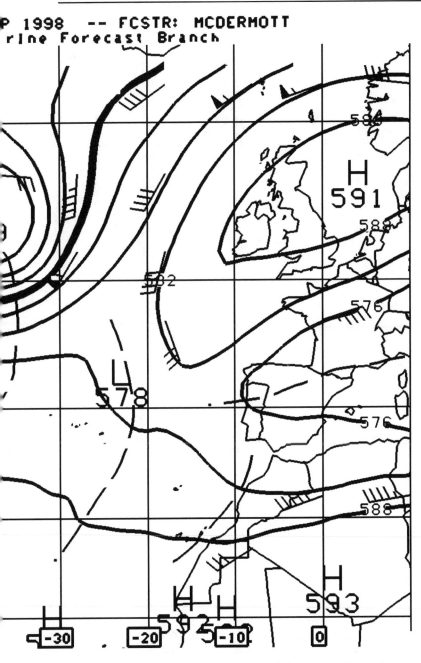

P 1998   -- FCSTR: MCDERMOTT
rine Forecast Branch

Our feeling is that it is better to stay out of the tropics during the hurricane season. However, if you do spend time here in the summer months, keep an eye on the 500mb charts.

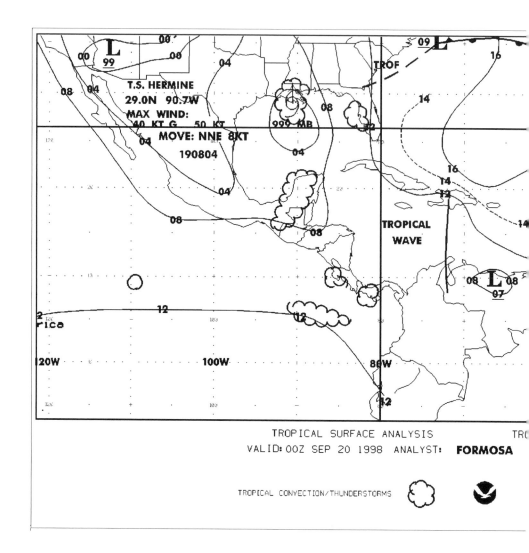

Now we get to the meat of the tropical forecasting issues. This is a typical tropical fax chart, covering from Africa to the Eastern Pacific. There is one well developed storm shown (Georges) and by the two previous fax charts we know that there is a good chance it will continue on its westerly course.

The odds are normally that a storm like Georges will then curve around the high pressure system and begin to head up the East Coast of the US, if the storm lasts that long. The reality for Georges turned out to be different—it headed straight north and slammed into Mississippi.

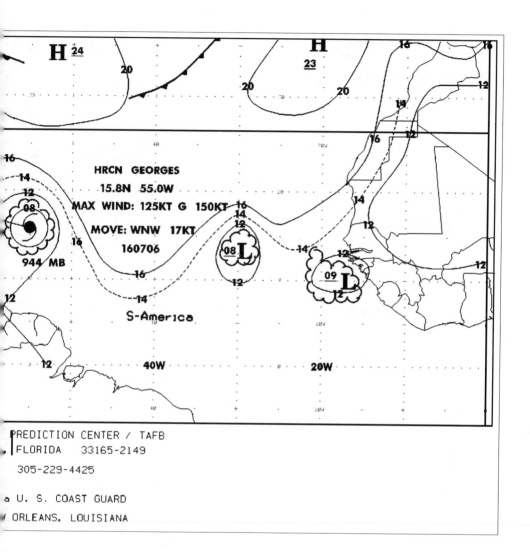

H $^+_{24}$ 20   +   20   H   23   20   16   12   14

HRCN GEORGES
15.8N 55.0W
MAX WIND: 125KT G 150KT
MOVE: WNW 17KT
160706
944 MB

16   14   12   08   16   14   16   14   08   L   14   09   L   12

S-America

40W   20W

PREDICTION CENTER / TAFB
FLORIDA   33165-2149

305-229-4425

U. S. COAST GUARD
ORLEANS, LOUISIANA

The two areas of low pressure shown in mid-Atlantic and further over to the east by the African coast will also need to be watched. Since it is late September, with warm sea temperatures and upper level conditions favorable for hurricane development, these two areas of thunderstorm activity could produce a hurricane. (They eventually turned into Fran and Jeanne).

The process of hurricane formation (called cyclogenisis) is discussed in detail in the following chapters. For now, we want you to be familiar with the look of these charts.

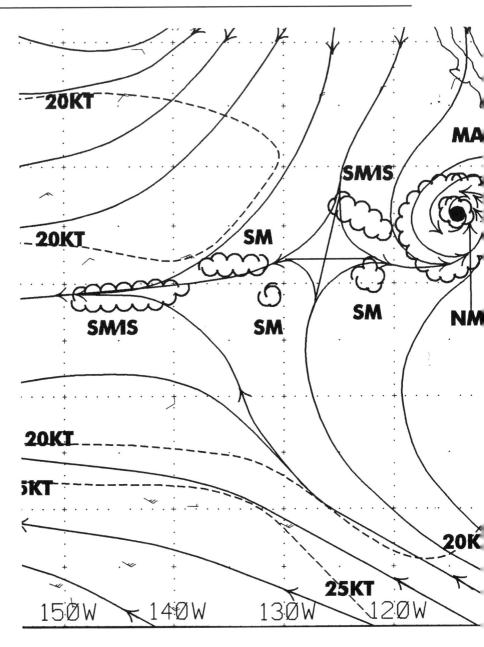

Another style of tropical chart. This type is quite common in many areas of the world. The solid lines represent the flow of the wind and are called streamlines. The dashed lines are areas of equal wind strength and are called isotachs. In this case, they are in five-knot gradients.

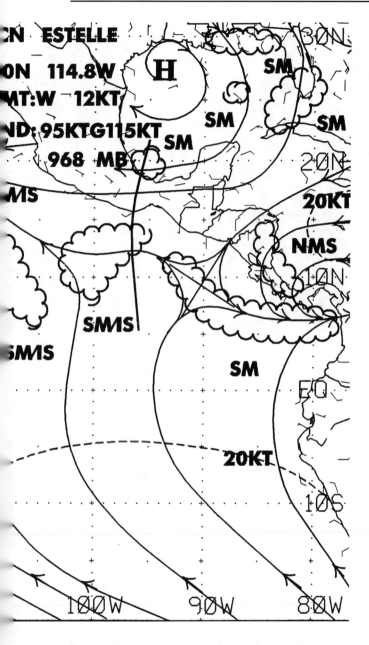

Chart labels: N ESTELLE, ON 114.8W, MT:W 12KT, ND:95KTG115KT, 968 MB, SM, SM, SM, SM, SM, NMS, SMMS, SMMS, SM, MS, H, 30N, 20N, 20KT, 10N, EQ, 20KT, 10S, 100W, 90W, 80W

The various cloud formations are indicated by abbreviations. These are standardized and you will find them the same on fax charts throughout the world.

- ❑ SM—scattered moderate convection.

- ❑ SM/IS—scattered, moderate isolated strong convection.

- ❑ SM/S—scattered moderate strong convection.

- ❑ NMS—numerous strong convection.

The scallops are areas of significant cloud development, as determined by satellite observation. The isotach (wind strength) lines are left off of the hurricane area as it would clutter the chart excessively.

327

The eye of the storm as seen from a hurricane hunter aircraft. (NOAA photo)

TROPICAL CYCLONES

Revolving or closed-system storms are, in essence, giant squalls. Hurricanes, cyclones and typhoons all operate on the same mechanisms—just the names are different.

Their genesis, maturation and decay mimic in many ways what we see in a squall—only on a large-scale basis.

To keep things simple, from here on out we will refer to these storms as hurricanes. However, what follows applies equally to cyclones and typhoons.

A tropical hurricane is a low pressure system that generates most of its energy from the evaporation and condensation process with convective clouds oriented around a central area of lowest pressure. These differ from extratropical lows that form above the tropics, in that hurricane systems generate their energy from a *horizontal* difference in temperature and moisture that exists in the atmosphere.

STORM GENESIS

We should start this topic with a somewhat unsettling caveat: Major debates persist among tropical storm forecasters about what ingredients are necessary to begin the process of building a tropical storm.

Most will tell you that the climatological models with which they work have a poor track record at predicting cyclogenesis (the birth of a tropical storm system).

Still, we can say a few basic, if simplistic things. To begin, hurricanes start life as minor tropical disturbances, often somewhere in the region of substantial convective (thunderstorm) activity occasionally a few degrees outside of the ITCZ (doldrums).

To begin, hurricanes start life as minor tropical disturbances, often somewhere in the region of substantial convective (thunderstorm) activity occasionally a few degrees outside of the ITCZ (doldrums).

TROPICAL WAVES

Tropical Waves—sometimes referred to as easterly or African waves—are a vaguely defined area that may have substantial convective (thunderstorm) activity, an upper-level low pressure, or a surface-level low— drifting on an east-to-west heading in the North Atlantic. These typically start off the coast of North Africa and are thought to be the result of a substantial imbalance between the temperatures of the Northern Sahara Desert and the cooler waters of the Gulf of Guinea.

Roughly 75 percent of all hurricanes originate from tropical waves, although only a small percentage of waves turn into hurricanes.

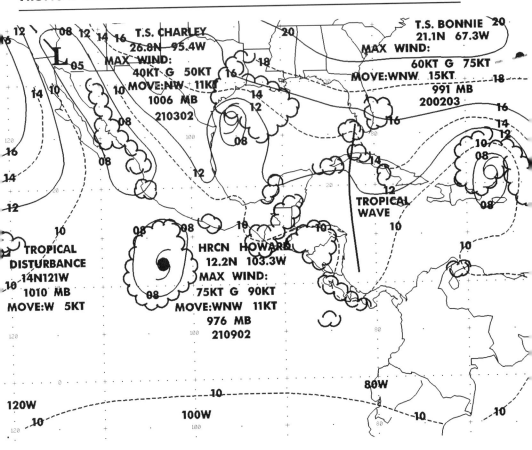

A typical midsummer tropical fax chart. Note the succession of tropical waves coming off the northwest coast of Africa. This particular set of waves spawned no less than five tropical storms and hurricanes including the infamous Bonnie.

These atmospheric waves typically have a period of three to four days between them, and cover a distance of 1000 to 1200 nautical miles. It is interesting to note that the hurricanes that form in the Eastern Pacific are thought to be the product of these waves which come all the way from North Africa.

If you see a wave called out on the fax and have access to satellite images, either on the Internet or

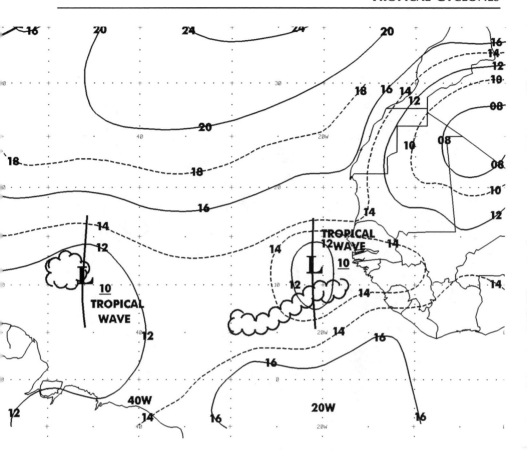

via weather fax, keep an eye out for the buildup of cloud mass that indicates thunderstorm activity. When you get this in a wave area, the odds improve for the formation of a tropical disturbance.

Surface pressures are slightly lower and at this point, the surface winds are light and pressures *almost* normal for the area and time of year.

If this confused area hangs on for a day or so, the weather services will define it as a tropical disturbance — and if you see information about a "tropical disturbance" on a fax, or hear about it on a weather broadcast, keep an eye on it.

If a tropical wave exists in conjunction with thunderstorm (convective) activity, watch for formation of tropical disturbances.

In the Eastern Pacific the Tropical Prediction Center refers to areas of potential trouble as a "tropical disturbance." In the Atlantic they call this a "low pressure system".

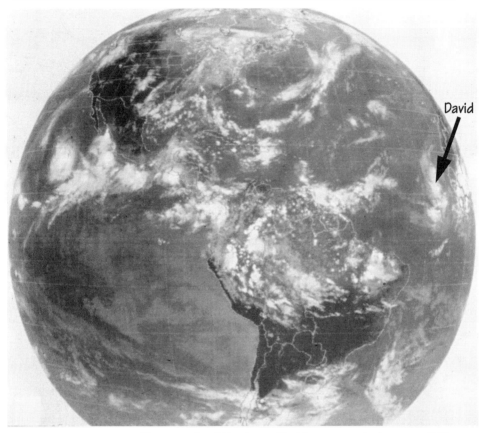

The genesis of Hurricane David as an easterly wave off the northwest coast of Africa.

ORGANIZED CIRCULATION

When winds reach 30 knots the area is called a tropical depression. When the winds reach 34 knots it graduates to tropical storm status. The winds themselves are not that strong at this stage. The concern is with what may be in the future.

The next stage is when the circulation begins to organize. One or two of the isobars will close, forming an area of low pressure, and the system slowly starts to rotate (counterclockwise in the Northern Hemisphere and clockwise in the Southern).

The winds pick up to 33 knots, and an area of several hundred square miles may be involved.

A key ingredient at this juncture, and from here on, is water surface temperature. It must be 80 degrees F (26 degrees C) or above. The higher the sea surface temperature, the more energy is available for the storm to grow.

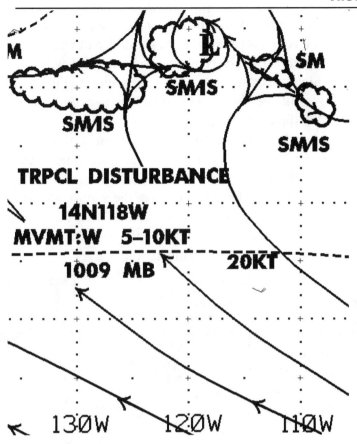

M

SM

SMMS

SMMS

SMMS

TRPCL DISTURBANCE

14N118W

MVMT:W 5–10KT

1009 MB   **20KT**

130W   120W   110W

A tropical disturbance has formed off an easterly wave that has traveled from northwest Africa to the west of Central America. The key factor now is how much energy is available from the surrounding thunderheads. If upper atmosphere conditions are right, these thunderheads will grow and add the spark to turn the tropical disturbance into a tropical storm and possibly a hurricane.

If the storm is brewing in tropical waters, and it is summer time, then all of the water is going to be at or above this temperature. However, if the storm starts to head beyond 20 degree latitude, where temperatures tend to be more varied and cooler, water temperature can play an important part in the direction, strengthening or more usually, weakening of the system.

You can track sea surface temperature on weather fax charts, and it is always a good idea to watch the convective activity above the warmest waters, which you can do to some degree with satellite photos available via weather fax or better yet with a satellite direct receiver.

At this stage, we have the beginnings of a giant squall. Warm, moist air is carried aloft, condenses, and releases energy.

However, if the upper levels of the atmosphere are benign, this tropical depression will fill from the pressure of winds rushing into the center from surrounding areas, and eventually die out.

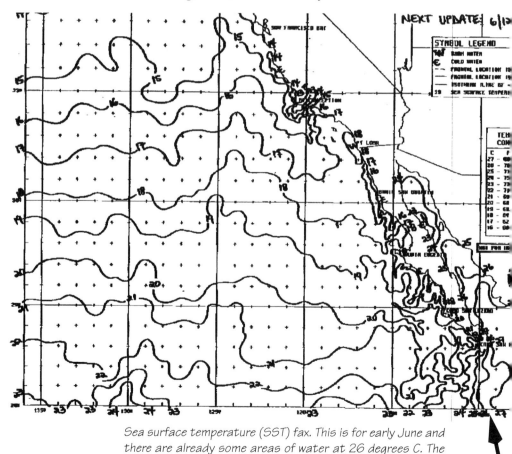

Sea surface temperature (SST) fax. This is for early June and there are already some areas of water at 26 degrees C. The adjacent cooler waters help convection by sending cooled surface winds over the nearby warmer water.

26C

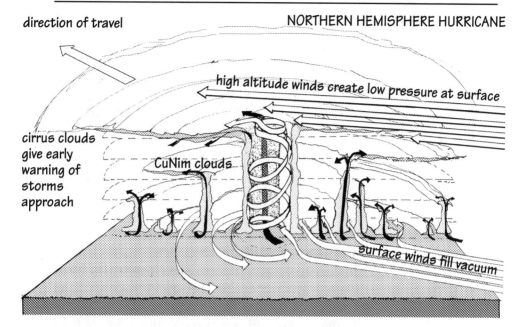

NORTHERN HEMISPHERE HURRICANE

direction of travel

high altitude winds create low pressure at surface

cirrus clouds give early warning of storms approach

CuNim clouds

surface winds fill vacuum

Putting it all together. Here's a cross-sectional view of a typical Northern Hemisphere hurricane structure. Note how the circulation inside the eye reverses at the top of the chimney.

MATURATION

For the storm to continue to grow, it needs a mechanism by which it can dissipate the in-rushing wind and heat energy.

This is provided by *upper-level* winds, blowing horizontally across the top of what is in effect a huge chimney.

These winds help to create a vacuum over the top of this central area pulling the uprising energy away, outside of the immediate region of the storm system.

It is, in effect, a pumping action, and the rapid vertical movement of air in the center of this system is probably what causes the low pressures at the sea surface.

This low pressure creates a partial vacuum, which is filled with accelerating winds drawn in from the outside, laden with moisture and heat, which are drawn ever faster up to the top of the chimney.

Conditions for a tropical depression to mature to hurricane status:

❑ Water temperature at or above 80 degrees F/26 degrees C.

❑ Sustained convective (thunderstorm) activity.

❑ Minimal wind shear between surface and upper atmosphere levels.

❑ High altitude winds rotating anticyclonically to create vacuum over top of chimney.

These condense, release their energy and create an even larger chimney.

As long as the upper-level winds are sufficient to continue the dissipation process, the storm continues to grow. If the upper-level winds become less favorable, or if the source of heat is lost because the storm moves over an area of cool water, the storm dies.

If the storm continues to grow, it is upgraded to tropical-storm status with winds in the 34-to 63-knot range. The next step, hurricane, brings winds of 65 knots and above.

Steering Currents

In the early stages of storm development, the hurricane system generally follows the flow of the weather systems in which it is embedded.

In many cases this starts out with a ridge of high pressure along which they travel, with slight poleward bias (from Coriolis forces). In the Eastern Pacific, for example, 90 percent of the time the storms follow a west northwest track, moving at 12 knots or so.

If the ridge of the surface-level high pressure is weak, or becomes weakened by upper-level conditions—sometimes the result of the jet stream dipping to the south—these storms can take off in a poleward direction. Then, if they come into contact with the pole side of the subtropical high pressure system, the easterly flow leads to a recurving of the hurricane to the east.

As the storms mature and grow, they will often have major impacts on the wind fields around them, bending both surface-level and high-altitude wind flows around their own circulation pattern.

Risk of Recurving

As long as the storm continues on a relatively steady track, with forecast speeds, you can plan tactics of how to deal with it.

Ideally, you will be behind the storm, and well away. However, there are varying risks of a given storm taking a jog this way or that, or even reversing its path.

During the normal summer season, within the tropics, the risk of a storm on an east to west track recurving or doing a loop is low. However, at the edges of the season, when the westerly wind flow reaches farther down towards the equator, there is more risk of erratic behavior.

As the storms move above 20 degrees latitude, into the subtropics, the risk of erratic behavior becomes much more acute. Storms have been known to stop, reverse course and do loops, and then continue on their original course.

SPEED OF MOVEMENT

These storms typically move at moderate rates, usually between five and 15 knots.

However, if they get connected to other, faster moving large-scale weather systems, they can accelerate beyond this range, although this is rare.

TROPICAL STORM GEOGRAPHY

Tropical storms and hurricanes are usually confined geographically to relatively distinct areas. They typically do not form closer than five degrees (300 miles) to the equator, and require the proper upper-level as well as sea-level conditions to start their process and then grow.

The following list is generally considered to be reliable. However, keep in mind that *these storms do not always follow the rules*!

❑ Atlantic Basin (including the North Atlantic Ocean, the Gulf of Mexico, and the Caribbean Sea).

❑ Northeast Pacific Basin (from Mexico to about the dateline) Northwest Pacific Basin (from the

dateline to Asia including the South China Sea)
- ❑ North Indian Basin (including the Bay of Bengal and the Arabian Sea)
- ❑ Southwest Indian Basin (from Africa to about 100 degrees E)
- ❑ Southeast Indian/Australian Basin (100 degrees E to 142 degrees E)
- ❑ Australian/Southwest Pacific Basin (142 degrees E to about 120 degrees W)

Having sailed between Cape Town, South Africa and the West Indies, I have tried to find out why the South Atlantic is not considered an area that has hurricanes. Several reasons are kicked around in the scientific community. First, there tends to be a lot of vertical shear in the wind strengths in this region; in other words, there's a lot more wind aloft than at the

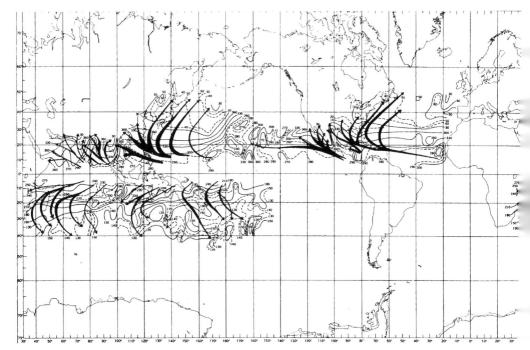

Typical storm tracks. Arrow thickness is an indicator of frequency.(Bowditch)

The Cape Nelson area of Papua New Guinea. Look at the trees in the forest behind Intermezzo. Two years before, in May, a category-five cyclone devastated this area, and it is theoretically outside of the tropical storm belt!

surface. As discussed previously, this prevents the "thermal" action at the core of the storm required to get started.

Second, the South Atlantic typically does not have a very strong ITCZ, with its associated thunderstorm activity, to kick off tropical storm development.

Now, having just given you the reasons, we also need to say that if these conditions change—i.e. the wind shear drops—and there is an area of convective activity, then you could have a tropical storm develop. Keep this in mind when you make that trip up the South Atlantic.

Here's proof you need to keep your eyes open. This tropical storm formed off the coast of Angola (West Africa) in April 1991—when and where it was not supposed to be!

Here's a geography test: the two images below are obviously of a tropical storm. The swirling cloud pattern and eye are clearly discernible. Take a close look now and see if you can figure out where this is. It took place in January. The answer is below the images.

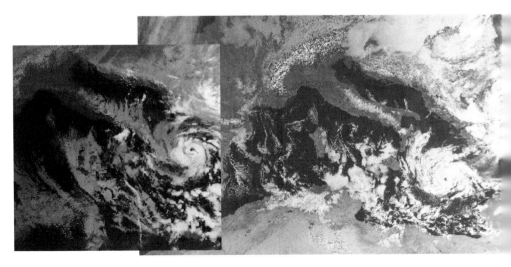

The eastern Mediterranean.

TROPICAL STORM FORECASTS

The quality of forecasting these storm systems varies considerably with the resources with which the forecasters have to work.

In the U.S., for example, especially along the Eastern Seaboard, there are hurricane hunter aircraft along with multiple satellite imaging systems at the forecasters disposal.

The forecasters use their satellites to watch cloudy areas of convective activity in the tropics. Then, they estimate what is happening based on the shapes and activity of the clouds. This process is based on what is called the Dvorak technique of cloud analysis. (For more on this, see page 366)

This analysis is quite difficult, and prone to error, as the forecasters are watching from 20,000 miles above the surface. Generally, if the area of cloudiness persists for several days, and no cold water or wind shear exists to stop the process, intensification will be forecast.

The use of aircraft allows the hurricane forecasters to obtain a detailed analysis of the wind field in which the storm is embedded. They get wind direction, velocity and barometric pressures at a variety of altitudes, and then feed these into their computer programs—plus use a lot of black art—to forecast the strength and potential movement of the storms.

Miles Lawrence, a forecaster with the Tropical Prediction Center in Miami, Florida told me that they do an analysis of their predictions of storm tracks to see how well their models are working. Over the last ten years in the Atlantic, the 72-hour forecasts of storm movement have been within 251 nautical miles. At 48 hours this figure is down to 169 miles, and at 24 hours it is usually within 71 miles.

In the Eastern Pacific things are a little easier to predict, and the figures are: 194 miles at 72 hours, 138 miles at 48 hours, and 71 miles at 24 hours.

Sitting on land, behind my comfortable desk, these seem like pretty good figures. But at sea, on a yacht moving at five to ten knots, and trying to figure what is the right direction to travel, they tell you that a large safety factor is required in your planning.

In other parts of the world, without the ability to sample the weather surrounding a storm, forecasters may go more by instinct, with satellite images to help out. However, the lack of wind-field data creates a major hole in the forecasting equation—one that instinct can fill only to a degree. As sailors, we must be aware of these limitations and keep our eyes open.

WHERE TO GET FORECASTS

If you have access to the Internet, a huge amount of data is available to you from all over the world. Satellite imagery, synoptic charts, results from aircraft and virtual real-time forecasting is there at the beck and call of your computer mouse.

Up to date broadcast schedules from most countries are posted on the Internet. For the URLs to these locations check http:// www.SetSail.com

For more prosaic analysis, you can turn to your single-sideband radio, Satellite receiver (Inmarsat A, B or C), WWV, or a telephone if one is handy. Here are is a breakdown of where to look for data as you move around the world.

The National Hurricane Center in Miami, Florida, has responsibilities for monitoring and forecasting tropical cyclones in the Atlantic and Northeast Pacific Basin east of 140W. Honolulu covers west of 140W to the dateline.

The Northwest Pacific Basin is shared in forecasting duties by China, Thailand, Korea, Japan, the Philippines, and Hong Kong.

The North Indian Basin tropical cyclones are fore-cast by India, Thailand, Pakistan, Bangladesh, Burma, and Sri Lanka.

Reunion Island, Madagascar, Mozambique, Mau-ritius, and Kenya provide forecasts for the South-west Indian Basin. Australia and Indonesia forecast tropical cyclone activity in the Southeast Indian/Australian Basin.

Lastly, for the Australian/Southwest Pacific Basin Australia, Papua New Guinea, Fiji, and New Zealand forecast tropical cyclones.

Note also that the U.S. Joint Typhoon Warning Center (JTWC) issues warnings for tropical cyclones in the Northwest Pacific, the North Indian, the Southwest Indian, the Southeast Indian/Australian, and the Australian/Southwest Pacific basins, though they are not specifically charged to do so by the World Meteorological Organization. The U.S. Naval Western Oceanography Center in Pearl Harbor, Honolulu does the same for the Pacific Ocean east of the dateline.

Here's a good reason to stay out of the tropical South Pacific during hurricane season. January 1998, with three nicely formed cyclones in a row.

SEASONS

Tropical storms usually (but not always) follow a seasonal pattern related to solar heating.

Theoretically, this would mean that at summer solstice (about June 21 in the Northern Hemisphere and about December 21 in the Southern) activity would be at its peak.

However, it takes a while for the energy from the sun to work its way into the system, so things normally begin to cook two to two and a half months later than this.

Following is a rough list of seasons courtesy of NOAA. However, once again, we want to caution you that strong tropical storms can occur two or

Super-typhoon Oliwa in September 1997. This is a huge, devastating storm, even for the Western Pacific. Note the cirrus clouds outflow radiating from the center.

three months late or early under some circumstances.

While the Atlantic hurricane season is "officially" from June 1 to November 30, the Atlantic basin shows a very peaked season with 78 percent of the tropical storm days, 87 percent of the minor hurricane days, and 96 percent of the intense categories 3, 4 and 5 hurricane days occurring in August through October.

Peak activity is in early to mid-September. Once in a few years a tropical cyclone may occur out of season — primarily in May or December.

The Northeast Pacific basin has a broader peak, with activity beginning in late May or early June and going until late October or early November with a peak in storminess in late August/early September.

The Northwest Pacific basin has tropical cyclones *occurring all year-round* regularly, though there is a distinct minimum in February and the first half of March. The main season goes from July to November, with a peak in late August/early September.

The North Indian basin has a double peak of activity in May and November, though tropical cyclones are seen from April to December. The severe cyclonic storms occur almost exclusively from April to June and late September to early December.

The Southwest Indian and Australian/Southeast Indian basins have very similar annual cycles, with tropical cyclones beginning in late October/early November, reaching a double peak in activity — one in mid-January and one in mid-February to early March, and then ending in May.

The Australian/Southeast Indian Basin's February lull in activity is a bit more pronounced than the Southwest Indian Basin's lull.

The Australian/Southwest Pacific Basin begins with tropical cyclone activity in late October/early November, reaches a single peak in late February/early March, and then fades out in early May.

Hurricane Fran —September 1996. Note the scale of the storm compared to the Bahamas outlined to the southwest of the eye. As large as this is, the eye and the area of hurricane strength winds is avoidable—if you act in time. Note how far ahead the cirrus clouds extend to the northwest and northeast.

MACRO FORECASTING FACTORS

There are a number of large-scale, long-term factors at work in the atmosphere that have substantial impacts on the number, severity and tracks of these storms.

Take for example the African West Sahara drought situation. When there is a drought, it substantially reduces the number and especially the intensity of Eastern Atlantic hurricanes.

We are all very familiar with El Nino/Southern Oscillation (ENSO). When the ENSO is in its warm phase, as it was during 1997/98, Atlantic hurricanes are reduced considerably due to the strong westerly winds aloft. At the same time, Eastern Pacific hurricane activity increases. In the tropical South Pacific, ENSO reduces activity in the west and increases it in the east. The Society and Tuamotu Islands of French Polynesia, which normally do not see hurricanes, will have a number of occurrences.

That these factors affect the hurricane season is pretty much accepted by most (but by no means all) forecasters.

Where the debate gets really intense is in the ability of forecasters to use this data to predict the quantity and intensity of storms in a given season.

Our own feeling is that from a cruising perspective you need to look at all the data. If some of it is being debated by the experts, talk to both sides and then keep an eye out so that you are aware of the factors from both sides of the argument which can affect your safety.

Understanding how these work will help you analyse your tropical cruising risks, and take proper, early action should a negative situation start to develop.

SAFFIR-SIMPSON HURRICANE SCALE

Most weather services use the Saffir-Simpson scale as an indicator of wind force and the damage (ashore) that the storm can potentially cause.

This is based on sustained wind speeds (keep in mind that gusts can be 20 to 30 percent higher):

Category 1 65—82 knots
Category 2 83—95 knots
Category 3 96—113 knots
Category 4 114—135 knots
Category 5 136 knots and above

RECAP

Let's recap the requirements for creating one of these storms.

First, water must be at least 80 degrees F (26 degrees C).

Second, the air aloft must cool fast enough with height to create an unstable situation conducive to convective (thunderstorm) activity.

Mid-level atmosphere (3 miles/5km) must be moist enough to keep the thunderstorms cooking.

Next, there must be at least five degrees of latitude (300 miles) of separation from the equator (to provide spinning energy from Coriolis effect).

There has to be a surface level disturbance with enough convective activity to provide the spark necessary to get everything going.

Next, the wind shear between the surface and upper altitudes (5 miles/8km) must be moderate — typically less than 20 knots of wind differential between the surface and the upper troposphere.

And finally, there must be upper-level winds present to remove the heat and rising air from the center of the system so it can continue to grow.

LIFE CYCLE OF A HURRICANE

In the early part of a hurricane, the winds will have just reached 64 knots over an area 30 to 60 miles or so in diameter. Gale-force winds will extend out another couple of hundred miles from the center.

Circular bands of rain clouds, with embedded thunderstorms will spiral out from the center. Heavy periods of rain will be interspersed with areas of light rain or dry conditions.

Requirements for a tropical cyclone:

☐ Warm water (80F or 26C).

☐ Cool enough air aloft to start convection.

☐ Light wind shear between surface and mid-latitudes.

☐ Upper level venting.

☐ Surface spark to get the brew cooking.

SOUTHERN HEMISPHERE HURRICANE

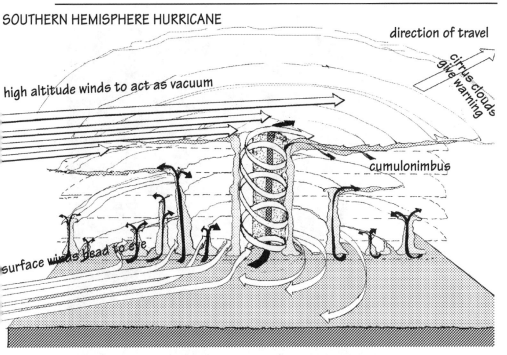

A typical structure for a Southern Hemisphere hurricane.

The bands of clouds rise up in huge decks of cumulus and cumulonimbus clouds. These ascend as far as the heat energy allows, and then the condensing water vapor is pulled away as ice crystals in fingers of cirrus clouds.

Areas of lightning discharges will usually be seen between the thunderheads.

In the first five thousand feet (1,500m) or so of the storm above sea level, the winds spiral inwards in a counterclockwise direction (in the Northern Hemisphere — and clockwise in the Southern) towards a center which acts like a giant thermal, drawing the wind upwards.

As the vortex spirals upward, it gradually expands, and the rotational speed decreases. Eventually, above 35,000 to 40,000 feet (10 to 12km) the circulation pattern is replaced by a clockwise air pattern (counterclockwise in the Southern Hemisphere), which is the exhaust system for the storm.

In the early part of a hurricane, the winds will have just reached 64 knots over an area 30 to 60 miles or so in diameter. Gale-force winds will extend out another couple of hundred miles from the center.

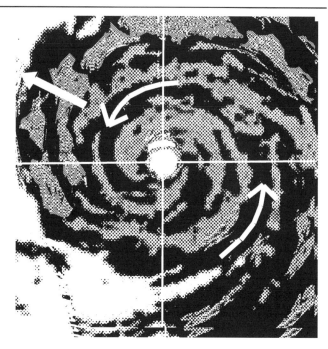

A cross-section of a typical hurricane (Northern Hemisphere on top, Southern Hemisphere on the bottom). Bands of rain clouds and cumulonimbus thunderheads surround the eye of the storm. The winds circulate about the core, increasing in speed as they get closer to the center.

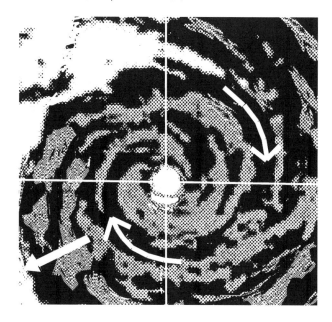

At lower levels, the wind follows a pattern much like a whirlpool. The farther you are from the center, the lower will be the wind force. The closer you get to the center, the higher the force.

At the outer edges of the storm system, winds may be only 20 to 25 knots. But as you draw close to the center they increase exponentially.

As the higher pressure air from the surrounding region rushes into the low pressure center of the storm, huge amounts of heat energy are released when the winds begin their vertical ascent.

A part of this process, as we've discussed before, is the condensation of humidity to cloud vapor. This reaches its most intense proportions at the center, forming an eye wall of very thick clouds around a clear central core.

The eye can be anywhere from five to 25 nautical miles in diameter. Once in the eye, winds diminish to almost calm. Then, as the opposite side of the eye is reached, the winds reverse direction and come back with full fury.

At the outer edges of the storm system, winds may be only 20 to 25 knots. But as you draw close to the center they increase exponentially.

The eye can be anywhere from five to 25 nautical miles in diameter. Once in the eye, winds diminish to almost calm.

DIURNAL FACTORS

Hurricane strength has a diurnal oscillation. During the day, solar radiation heating the cloud tops inhibits vertical air movement, the same way it does with squalls.

However, at night, the tops of the huge cloud mass cool rapidly increasing the temperature differential with the air below.

This change is easily detected with infrared satellite (temperature) sensors.

The *theoretical* result is a much faster vertical movement of air up the chimney or eye of the storm with more wind rushing in at the surface to fill the vacuum left behind. However, there seems to be little hard evidence of this from surface wind or pressure readings.

Still, it seems reasonable to assume that if your position relative to the storm center is the same at night as during the day, you should anticipate stronger winds during the late evening and early morning.

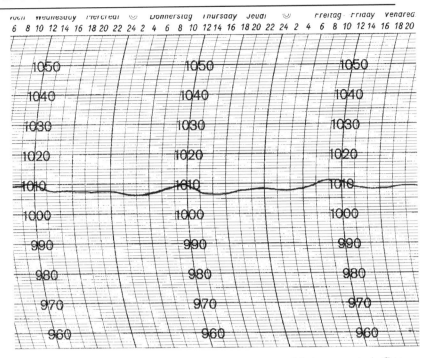

A typical tropical barometer trace over a 48-hour period. This particular trace was recorded in Cabo San Lucas, Mexico, on the edge of the tropics. It looks the same in Papeete in the South Pacific.

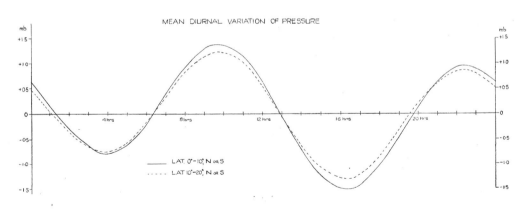

Here's the theoretical diurnal shift in barometric pressure in the tropics. You will see that it compares favorably with what is shown above. The amplified sine waves are helpful for picking off how big a shift in the barometer you should see at any given time. (Bowditch)

EARLY WARNING SIGNS

Let's assume for the moment that you've had an electrical problem and neither weatherfax nor SSB/ham rig is working.

There are still plenty of warning signs that trouble is brewing.

The first is the barometer. In the tropics the barometer almost always stays within a three-millibar range (plus or minus 1.5mb from the norm). Any deviation is cause for concern.

Even a three-millibar deviation, above or below the norm, signals the onset of a low pressure system, and this is one of the key ingredients for the birth of a cyclonic storm.

Even a three-millibar deviation in the barometer, above or below the norm, signals the onset of a low pressure system—one of the key ingredients for the birth of a cyclonic storm.

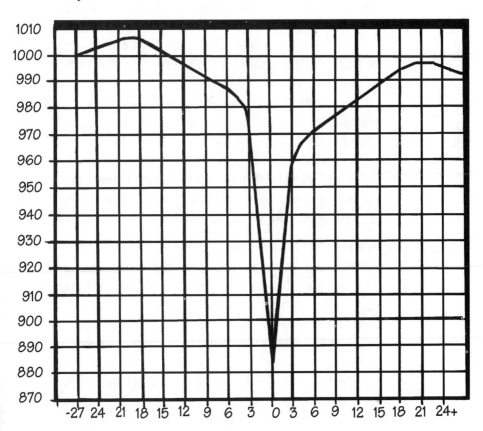

An approximation of the type of trace the barometer would make with the approach, and then passing, of the eye. The bottom line represents time in three-hour segments.

Early warning for
hurricanes in the
tropics:

❑ Long period swell.

❑ Cirrus clouds.

❑ Unstable barome-
   ter.

At sea, a long-period swell will be felt, emanating from the center of the storm. Crests may be as few as four a minute when first noticed.

The barometer may actually rise a hair when the storm is 500 to 1000 miles away, and skies will be quite clear. If fair weather cumulus clouds are present there will be fewer of them than is the norm, and they will not rise very high.

The barometer will appear jumpy, pumping up and down a millibar or two every couple of hours.

As the center of the storm approaches you will begin to see "mares' tails," (cirrus) clouds at a distance of 300 to 700 miles. These cirrus clouds are the ice crystals left over from the thunderstorms in the spiral bands nearer the center we discussed before.

The cirrus clouds typically look like they are pointing at the storm center. This is most pronounced at sunrise and sunset.

Concurrent with the appearance of the cirrus the barometer starts to fall (this can sometimes happen ahead of the cirrus as well).

The initial rate of descent will be quite gradual, and a recording barometer is most helpful in picking up this early record. As the storm center approaches the rate of descent will accelerate.

AS THE STORM APPROACHES

The mares' tails start to have a criss-cross pattern, and tend to look disorganized as the center approaches. These eventually give way to a thick film of cirrostratus.

Under this altostratus begin to form, then stratocumulus.

Cloud density builds up, the weather becomes unsettled, and a moderate rain begins to fall, while the wind starts to build, becoming quite gusty in the process. A little while later intermittent thundershowers begin to make themselves felt.

Up until this time the barometer probably has fallen between three and five millibars. From here on out, if the center is heading towards you, the fall will be more pronounced.

Lightning activity towards the center of a hurricane is reportedly rather subdued. However, studies suggest that a significant increase in lightning activity is sometimes a precursor to a storm rapidly intensifying.

THE BAR

The wind is now probably blowing 25 to 45 knots. On the horizon, in the direction of the storm center, you will see a black wall of mean looking cumulonimbus clouds.

This is called the bar of the storm, and signals that things are about to get serious. The barometer now begins to really take a tumble and the wind builds rapidly.

If you are offshore, the seas begin to break, becoming chaotic. Squall lines descend on you with strengthening gusts. Rain is probably continuous. The tops of the waves are blown off and combine with the driving rain. Visibility becomes almost nil.

The storm signals that things are about to get serious.

The barometer begins to really take a tumble and the wind builds rapidly.

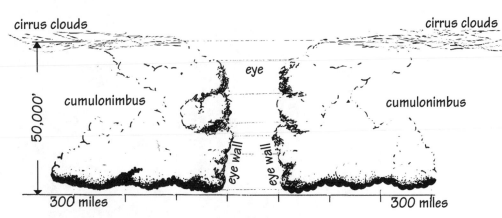

A typical cross-section through a hurricane. The cirrus clouds on top radiate out hundreds of miles to warn of the approach of the hurricane.

You will need to wear a diving mask to protect your eyes, and crawl on the deck against the force of the wind.

The eye of the storm at this point can be anywhere from a couple of hundred miles to 25 miles away.

When the eye passes over you, the winds go calm. Seas are confused, coming from all directions at once. The sky will clear, and blue sky (during the day) or stars will be clearly visible.

As you reach the other side of the eye wall, the direction of wind will reverse, and the wind force will come back with a vengeance. Obviously, it is better to avoid this process entirely!

Inside the eye of a hurricane. (NOAA photo)

WEATHER FAX DATA

A weather fax will help significantly, both in avoiding problems in the first place and in dealing with the storm once it has formed.

The surface forecasts will give you pointers to areas where there is a risk of storm formation.

You will see this in areas of convective activity, and any time a surface-level low pressure begins to form.

The forecasting service puts these in once a certain level of activity has been reached. However, before the annotation "tropical disturbance" has been earned, there will be signs which you can see on your own.

Equally important are the *500mb*, upper-level fax charts. These will sometimes show you upper level lows or troughs of low pressure which are sitting over a surface subtropical high pressure system.

Where this occurs, especially if there is warm sea surface temperatures, there is the risk of the upper-level low breaking through the surface high to start a tropical storm.

Upper-level charts are also helpful in estimating the risks of storm movement once it has matured.

If the high pressure system has vertical depth, the odds are that the storm will follow along with the high pressure circulation.

If you see upper-level high pressure over surface-level high pressure, this is a pretty good bet.

But, if the upper-level chart shows a low pressure system, it may very well act to reduce the steering influence of the surface high, in which case the storm may recurve to the north or east.

Miles Lawrence of the NOAA Hurricane Tracking Center puts it this way: "Almost every storm we look at puts us in the predicament at some point of not knowing which way it is going to head. Even with our sophisticated numerical models, when there is a clash between a ridge of high pressure and an upper-level cutoff low or shallow trough, it is anyone's guess what is going to happen."

"Almost every storm we look at puts us in the predicament at some point of not knowing which way it is going to head." Miles Lawrence, Hurricane Tracking Center

DANGEROUS SEMICIRCLE

Hurricanes act much the same as high latitude depressions when it comes to force of their winds, and the dangerous and navigable semicircles.

There are two reasons for this. First, on the dangerous side of the storm, to escape from the track of the storm and the dangerous center you must beat or power into the winds and seas. On the navigable side, the wind is at your back as you are running away from the storm center.

Then there are the winds. What you feel on the boat is a function of the wind that is circulating around the storm center and the increase or decrease due to the direction in which the storm is traveling.

On the dangerous side of the storm the winds are circulating at angles that are complemented, and reinforced by the speed of travel. On the navigable side of the storm, the speed of travel is opposite the circulating wind direction and so reduces the wind you feel.

In the Northern Hemisphere, if you face the storm center and the storm is coming right at you, the dangerous quadrant is to your left and the navigable quadrant is to your right. In the Southern Hemisphere, the dangerous quadrant is to your right when you face the storm, and the navigable quadrant is to your left.

Before we get carried away with terms like dangerous quadrant and navigable quadrant, keep in mind that these are relative terms. What is dangerous or navigable is very much a function of the storm structure and distribution of winds around its center. It is also a function of the seaworthiness of vessel and crew.

It is far better to take avoiding action early enough in the encounter so that the storm passes harmlessly far enough away so as to make this discussion academic.

Finding the navigable quadrant of a hurricane—face the storm center:

❑ In the Northern Hemisphere the navigable quadrant is to your right.

❑ In the Southern hemisphere the navigable quadrant is on your left.

What is dangerous or navigable is very much a function of the storm structure and distribution of winds around its center.

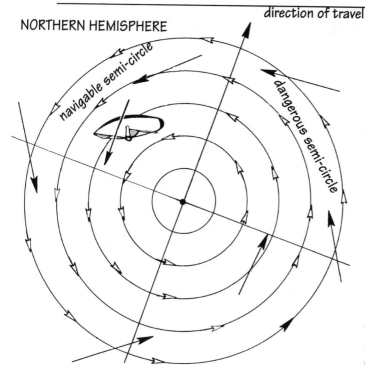

NORTHERN HEMISPHERE

direction of travel

navigable semi-circle

dangerous semi-circle

direction of travel

SOUTHERN HEMISPHERE

navigable semi-circle

dangerous semi-circle

In the Northern Hemisphere, hurricanes rotate counterclockwise around their centers. Looking at this top view of the storm, you can see that on the right-hand side of the storm, the wind is blowing in the same direction as the storm is traveling. When you feel this wind pressure on a boat you have the total of the circulation winds about the center plus the direction of travel speed.

If the wind were circulating at 100 knots, and the storm moving at 15 knots, you would feel 115 knots of wind force. On the left side you subtract motion speed from wind speed, so in this example you would feel 85 knots.

In the Southern Hemisphere, winds circulate clockwise around the low center (bottom drawing). In this case, the dangerous side is to the left when looking at the storm from the top. Here you add the speed of travel to the circulating wind speed on the left side and deduct it on the right-hand side.

EARLY WARNING WITH SATELLITES

The earlier we can detect the start of tropical cyclogenesis, the more time we have to take avoiding action.

As you know, the professionals rely on satellite imagery to keep tabs on this process. Often they see cloud formations which stand a chance of becoming a tropical hurricane, but since most of these won't mature, they don't mention this possibility in their forecasts.

From the mariner's standpoint, we want to know as early as possible that a potential risk exists. We need to be watching the same cloud patterns as the professionals, so we have as much data possible on the risks we are facing.

Watching cloud images on weather fax charts will help. But these are typically pretty difficult to work with until the tropical cyclone system is well established, and by then we'll know about it from the forecasters.

There are two alternatives. One is to get on the Internet and have a look directly at the satellite images for your area of the world. The other is to carry satellite direct receiving equipment.

On the chance that someday this data will come in handy we've included a series of satellite images of storms in formation—during the very earliest phase of cyclogenesis.

To be able to really detect what is going on you need quality images as well as experience. We're not advocating here that you replace the advice of the professionals. But understanding what to look for just might someday give you a head start that could prove extremely valuable.

Here are a series of satellite images in the visible range, taken at 24-hour intervals off the coast of Southern Mexico. The time frame is mid-July.

In these first two images we see a large mass of clouds which are starting to aggregate. This suggests the beginning of cyclogenesis.

Day three (above) and the clouds are beginning to rotate. In day four (below) you have a clearly defined tropical storm or, more likely, a hurricane eye, and the classical spiral bands of cirrus clouds.

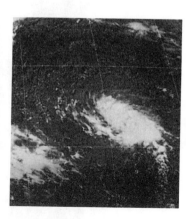

All three of these images (above) show the initial phase of cyclogenesis. This is what the Dvorak technique refers to as "T-1" cloud images.

In the image below the three individual masses of thunderstorms are a warning sign. If the open space between them starts to close, odds are something will brew up.

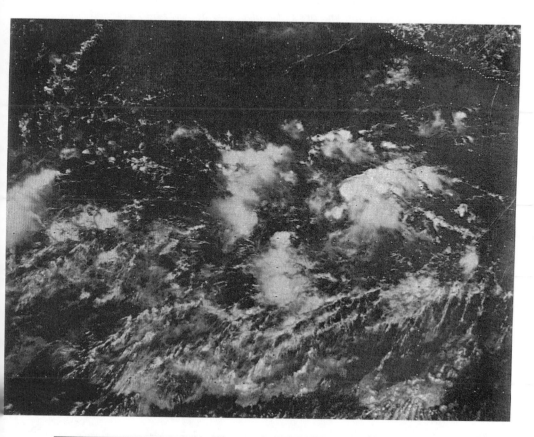

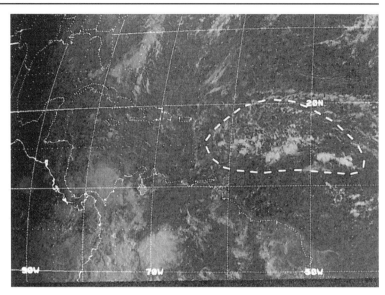

These two images are taken in the morning and afternoon of the same day. In the upper image you have a large area of isolated convective (thunderstorm) activity. By late in the afternoon the area of convective activity has widened considerably and filled in the gaps. With this rapid growth in cloud mass it would be wise to conclude something was brewing and remain upwind, to the east of the area. This way if the system matures rapidly you are not in its direct path.

The purpose of this exercise, and indeed of this entire section of the book, is to avoid a fully-developed tropical cyclone (in the case Hurricane Danielle). The key is to be aware, and not take anything for granted. There will always be warnings of these events well in advance. But you need to be in tune with your surroundings to feel, see, and hear the signs. Good facsimile receiving gear doesn't hurt either.

HOW EARLY DO YOU REACT?

The question of how early to begin taking defensive action when a tropical threat is not well defined is a tough one. So many of these alarms turn out to be false that at some point one is tempted to wait until the last minute before taking evasive action or finding a hurricane hole in which to anchor.

The problem comes when you guess wrong. That mistake can cost your vessel or your life.

Since most people don't take these risks seriously until the storm's impact is all but certain, you suddenly find yourself competing with a lot of other vessels for security. In even a small hurricane this can be a prescription for disaster. We feel it is better to take action early rather than later—and if it turns out to have been a false alarm, that is just part of the game of cruising in the hurricane belts out of season.

THE DVORAK TECHNIQUE

Before leaving the subject of hurricane forecasting we should come back to some of the techniques used in this process.

We've already discussed how important it is to have wind-field data and an understanding of the pressure distribution within and around one of these storms. When this data is available, from specialized aircraft, buoys, or vessels, the forecaster's job, although by no stretch of imagination easy, is based on some hard evidence.

Unfortunately, in most of the world where these storms occur, on-the-spot data is not available.

In this case forecasters use satellite images of the storms. These images are analyzed for cloud type and pattern, along with infrared data, which gives temperature information. This data is then compared to a set of standards.

With satellite image-based forecasting systems there exists a matrix from which reasonably reliable results can be obtained.

Over the years, as more and more satellites have been put into orbit, the database on tropical storms has grown. With research on using satellite imagery for storm forecasting and tracking going back to the 1960s, there exists a matrix within which reasonably reliable results for tropical-storm forecasting can be obtained

For several decades now, the guru of satellite forecast techniques has been Vernon F. Dvorak. An early pioneer in this field of research, he has developed a systemized approach to cloud-pattern recognition as an indicator of tropical cyclone development, tracking and intensity. This approach, referred to as the Dvorak technique, forms the basis of almost all tropical cyclone forecasting models.

The data that follows is an overview of this system, adapted from a workbook which Dr. Dvorak wrote for forecasters in remote parts of the world, and for use in training US Navy meteorologists. The workbook was sponsored under a NOAA/NESDIS/NWS contract.

The Dvorak technique allows you to make informed decisions with raw data available on weatherfax, from the Internet, and with direct satellite image receivers.

If you have access to the Internet, satellite imagery on a weather fax, or satellite direct reception equipment, Vernon Dvorak's technique will prove a valuable tool. It is not difficult to understand, and if you acquire a copy of his workbook, you will find yourself quickly being able to make informed judgements based on readily available satellite imagery.

INTRODUCTION

Hundreds of tropical cyclones have been observed from satellite platforms since the first meteorological satellite was launched in April 1960. The observations have provided meteorologists with a wealth of information concerning the relationship between a tropical cyclone's cloud pattern and its position, intensity and motion. Today, much of this knowledge is contained in operational-analysis techniques that use satellite images as their major data source.

Satellite imagery has been used as the primary observation tool for tropical cyclone surveillance over most tropical areas of the globe for more than 20 years.

Satellite imagery has been used as the primary observation tool for tropical cyclone surveillance over most tropical areas of the globe for more than 20 years. During that time, and especially in recent years, meteorologists have found that satellite data provides reasonable estimates of tropical cyclone position and intensity.

For strong tropical cyclones that are not distorted by the effects of wind shear, it is usually a simple matter to locate the storm center and make a reliable estimate of intensity. An example of this type of tropical cyclone is shown in Figure 1-1 on the next page. The vortex center is easily identifiable in a series of six hourly infrared images as the typhoon approached and struck the Philippines. The formation of an eye as the cloud pattern evolved was evidence enough for issuing typhoon warnings.

For strong tropical cyclones that are not distorted by the effects of wind shear, it is usually a simple matter to locate the storm center and make a reliable estimate of intensity.

(**Figure 1-1**) *GMS infrared satellite imagery taken at six-hour intervals as Typhoon Joe approached and struck the Philippines.*

Issues complicating satellite-based forecasting:

❑ The cloud pattern can take on a great variety of appearances.

❑ Cloud patterns can become severely distorted by interactions with adjacent weather systems.

❑ Central clouds that define the cyclone's surface location can be obscured by dense cirrus clouds.

❑ The cloud pattern can change more rapidly than the changes in wind and pressure.

Another example of a simple, straightforward analysis is shown in Figure 1-2. In this figure, Hurricane Hugo can be seen in enhanced infrared (EIR) imagery as it approached the coast of the United States in 1989. Shown in the image are some of the more than 100 satellite-derived eye positions spanning the 52-hour period from September 20 to September 22 The eye positions were obtained by tracing the inner contour of the enhanced infrared eye pattern onto an acetate overlay. The intensity, calculated from the temperature of the eye and the clouds surrounding it, was close to that determined from aircraft reconnaissance wind and pressure measurements.

Despite the apparent simplicity of tracking the storms in Figure 1-1 and 1-2, tropical cyclone analysis using satellite imagery is often much more complicated. Specifically:

The cloud pattern of a tropical cyclone can take on a great variety of appearances.

Cloud patterns can become severely distorted by interactions with environmental. winds and adjacent weather systems.

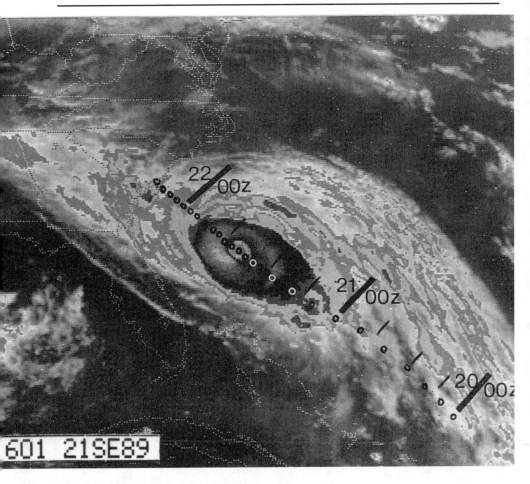

(Figure 1-2) *Enhanced infrared GOES satellite image of Hurricane Hugo in 1989 as it approached the U.S. coastline. Eye positions based on satellite imagery from September 20 through 22 are superimposed.*

The central features that define the cyclone's surface location can be obscured by dense cirrus clouds at any time. The cloud pattern, under certain conditions, changes more rapidly than the changes in wind and pressure. All these conditions require special knowledge and training to ensure accurate tropical cyclone analyses.

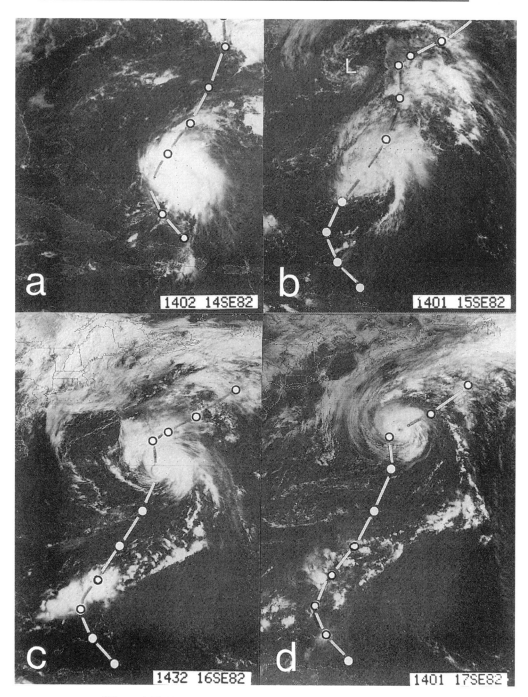

(Figure 1-3) *Hurricane Debbie, 1982. Visible images on four consecutive days in the western Atlantic with 12-hour track positions superimposed.*

An example of a complex analysis is shown in Figure 1-3. The visible images show Hurricane Debbie on four consecutive days in the western Atlantic Ocean. Debbie's track, shown at 12-hour intervals, has been superimposed on each image.

In image A, tropical storm Debbie is moving northward. Because of the strong upper-level westerlies at this time, Debbie's surface position (not highlighted) falls on the western edge of the cloud system.

The next day, image B, Debbie had reached hurricane intensity as she accelerates northeastward toward the upper-level cut-off low near the letter L.

In image C, Debbie had weakened, lost her eye, and begun moving northward under the influence of the weakening cut-off low (not visible in this image).

Once the effects of the interaction subsided in image D, Debbie intensified, regained an eye, and resumed a northeastward track.

Throughout this sequence of events, the analyst was faced with complex decisions regarding the tropical cyclone's surface center placement, changes in its intensity, and deviations in its track resulting from the interaction of the two circulation systems. These decisions are often made more complex during the nighttime hours when only lower-resolution infrared images are available.

Volume 2 of this workbook series was written to help meteorologists handle all aspects of tropical cyclone analysis using satellite imagery. This includes initial development and intensity analysis and forecasting under varying conditions of wind shear and diurnal influences. Techniques using visible, enhanced infrared and digital data are described. Methods for determining rainfall amounts from tropical cyclones, and for forecasting changes in cyclone motion, have also been included.

This workbook series was written to help meteorologists handle all aspects of tropical cyclone analysis using satellite imagery. This includes initial development and intensity analysis and forecasting under varying conditions of wind shear and diurnal influences.

SATELLITE OBSERVATIONS OF TROPICAL CYCLONES

Techniques that use satellite data to analyze tropical cyclones are based to a large extent on a conceptual model of tropical cyclone development and motion. The model is a representation of the typical life cycle of a tropical cyclone as it appears in satellite imagery. It was derived empirically from satellite observations and has been modified over the years as observations and understanding improved. This section contains descriptions and illustrations of the observations that were instrumental in the development of the model. The observations and the way in which they are used in analysis techniques are covered in detail in the section that follows.

DEVELOPMENT IN GENERAL

Tropical cyclone development as observed in satellite imagery is a process of cloud-pattern evolution that takes place under favorable environmental conditions. Observations have shown that the cloud patterns of tropical cyclones and their environments go through recognizable stages as the cyclones intensify and weaken.

In the early stages of a pattern evolution, convective clouds and upper-level cloud debris first become organized into a curved band pattern. This is shown in the pre-storm visible image in Figure 2-1a. As the disturbance continues to develop to tropical-storm stage (Figure 2-1b), the band gradually takes on more curvature around a cloud minimum area. During these early stages of development, the cloud patterns often show considerable variability over short periods of time. The variability appears in most cases to result from diurnal effects and from the influences of circulation systems in the vicinity of the tropical disturbance.

Early stages in cloud development patterns:

❑ Convective clouds and upper level cloud debris become organized into a curved band pattern.

❑ The cloud band gradually takes on more curvature around a cloud minimum area.

❑ Once the curved band coils around the storm center, the center then becomes embedded within the overcast clouds of the pattern at the hurricane stage.

Once the curved band coils around the storm center, the center then becomes embedded within the overcast clouds of the pattern at the hurricane stage (see Figure 2-1c). Further intensification is observed as the "eye" either becomes more distinct, or more deeply embedded in the overcast clouds surrounding it.

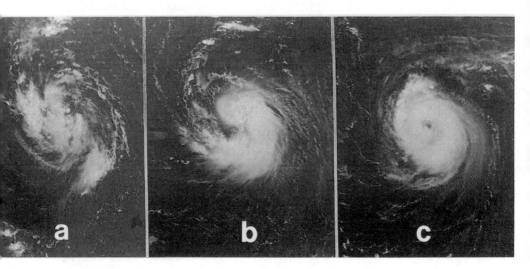

(**Figure 2-1**) *Cloud-pattern examples of (a) pre-storm; (b) tropical storm; and (c) the hurricane stage of tropical development.*

During the process of cloud-pattern evolution, it is the organization, not the amount of convective cells and upper-level clouds, that relates to the intensity of the tropical cyclone.

The cloud processes occurring in a tropical cyclone's broad-scale environment are also related to the developmental process. Disruptive influences, such as wind shear, land areas and cold water are known to arrest tropical cyclone development. The negative effects of land and cold water are obvious in satellite imagery; the effects of wind shear are often subtle and more difficult to understand.

Broad-scale processes affecting development are:

☐ Wind shear.

☐ Land areas.

☐ Cold water.

Some of the more commonly observed effects of wind shear are shown in Figure 2-2. These images were taken over the northwest Atlantic Ocean. In Figure 2-2a, a developing tropical storm is shown at A. Indications of a deepening trough at B to the northwest of A are apparent in the curvature of the cloud bands. The trough is already causing some cloud suppression on the west side of the storm.

In Figure 2-2b, 24 hours later, as the deepening trough approaches, storm A weakens and slows its westward motion. The weakening is indicated by the loss of deep-layer clouds near the center of the cloud system resulting in the exposure of the low-level circulation center. The disturbance continues to weaken during the next three days.

Four days later (Figure 2-2c), redevelopment of A is indicated by deep-layer convection building completely around the system center. Notice that all indications of trough B are absent and that the bands of clouds in the westerly stream to the north of the disturbance are bowing over the disturbance suggesting a broad-scale ridge at C to the northwest of A. Two days after Figure 2-2c, the system reached hurricane intensity.

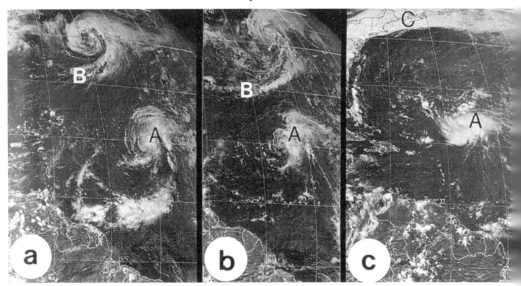

(Figure 2-2) Visible images show the weakening and slowing down of tropical storm A as trough B passes to its north. Four days later, in the right image, the disturbance begins to redevelop as ridge C builds in the westerlies to its north.

EARLY STAGES OF TROPICAL CYCLOGENISIS

One sequence of events which is often observed to precede tropical cyclogenisis appears two or three days before a disturbance reaches tropical storm intensity. A straightening of a boundary of a previously amorphous cloud cluster and a sudden increase of convective activity are commonly the earliest indications of initial tropical cyclone development.

It is usually apparent that the deformation of the cloud cluster is the result of an interaction with an upper-level trough or cut-off low in the westerlies. This is especially true when viewing animated satellite imagery. The interaction can be obvious, like the one shown in Figure 2-3. In this sequence of 12 hourly infrared (IR) images, a cloud cluster A in Figure 2-3a is deformed by a trough aloft that results in a straightening of the cloud boundary B on the north side of the system. Then in Figure 2-3b, the trough becomes cut-off with a center at C. In the next two panels (c and d), as C & A separate, A's cloud pattern begins to form curved cloud lines indicating tropical cyclogenisis.

Two common early signs of initial tropical cyclone development:

❑ Boundary of a previously amorphous cloud cluster straightens.

❑ Convective activity suddenly increases.

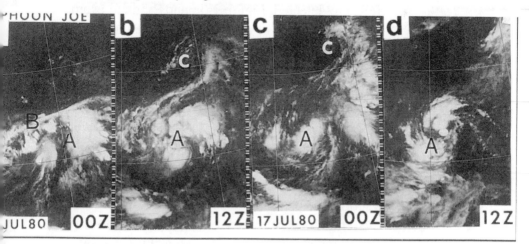

(**Figure 2-3**) *12-hour infrared imagery shows the interaction of A with a trough and cut-off low. The trough causes boundary B to form in the first panel. Then as cut-off low C forms and moves away, A takes on curvature indicating tropical cyclogenisis.*

Signs of a cloud cluster beginning cyclogenisis:

❑ A pattern of curved cloud lines appears.

❑ Or, a deep layer of convection appears in a previously observed pattern of curved low-level cloud lines.

Four common characteristics of cloud clusters which develop into tropical cyclones:

❑ Curved cloud lines or bands indicating a center of curvature within a small area.

❑ A center defined by or appearing near dense overcast clouds.

❑ A cloud system that has persisted for at least 12 hours.

❑ An environment favoring further intensification.

Although interactions like the one shown in Figure 2-3 are often observed, they are not observed in all cases and maybe only in one of several mechanisms involved in initiating tropical cyclogenisis.

The first reliable hint of cyclogenisis that has forecasting value occurs approximately one and one half days before tropical storm intensity (34 knots) is reached. At this time, either a pattern of curved cloud lines or bands appears in a previously observed convective cloud cluster, or a deep layer of convection appears in a previously observed pattern of curved low cloud lines.

Cloud clusters that develop into tropical cyclones are observed to have four characteristics in common. These are: 1) curved cloud lines or bands indicating a center of curvature within a small area; 2) a center that is defined by or appears near dense overcast clouds; 3) a cloud system that has persisted for at least 12 hours; and 4) an environment which favors further intensification.

This combination of characteristics is observed about 24 hours before significant surface pressure falls are detected. Figure 2-3c and 2-3d are examples of this stage of development. When low-level convective cloud lines are observed, they may show only merging during initial development. With increasing intensity, the lines become more curved.

Considerable variability in the cloud pattern is sometimes observed during initial stages of development. At times, tightly-curved upper-level cloud bands form patterns that appear very strong, but since the clouds are not associated with deep convection, the patterns are short-lived. There are also systems that eventually become powerful hurricanes, which in the beginning show little organization in the pattern, especially during the nighttime hours when it's usually less cloudy.

Even though the vast majority of tropical cyclones undergo their formative stages over warm tropical waters, a significant number of initial development cases have been detected in cloud patterns and also as low pressure areas over land.

During tropical cyclogenisis, especially in the initial stages, no indication of a deepening upper-level trough was present to the northwest of a westward moving disturbance. When a deepening trough was indicated, the cloud systems lost their organization and began weakening unless they recurved and started moving northeastward in advance of the trough.

A significant number of cases of cyclogenisis have been detected in cloud patterns over land.

CURVED BAND (COILING) STAGE

The cloud pattern of most tropical cyclones is observed as a band of convective clouds and upper level cloud debris that forms around a cloud minimum area. Occasionally, two interlocking curved bands are observed during early stages of development. The curved band usually takes shape on Day 1 as shown in Figure 2-4 about one to one and one half days before minimal tropical storm intensity (34 knots). After the curved band has formed, surface pressure falls are usually first detected. When indications of a cloud system center are observed in cloud lines, or when a reconnaissance aircraft locates a center, the center is most often found near the concave edge of the curved band. The curve of the band is normally observed to be open toward the upper level flow in the environment of the storm. The examples in Figure 2-4 on the following page are of westward moving cyclones developing under upper-level westerlies.

When the curved band is observed to curve at least one half the distance around the storm center, as on Day 2 of the figure, the cyclone has reached tropical storm intensity (34 knots of maximum sustained

When the curved band is observed to curve at least one-half the distance around the storm center, the cyclone has reached tropical-storm intensity.

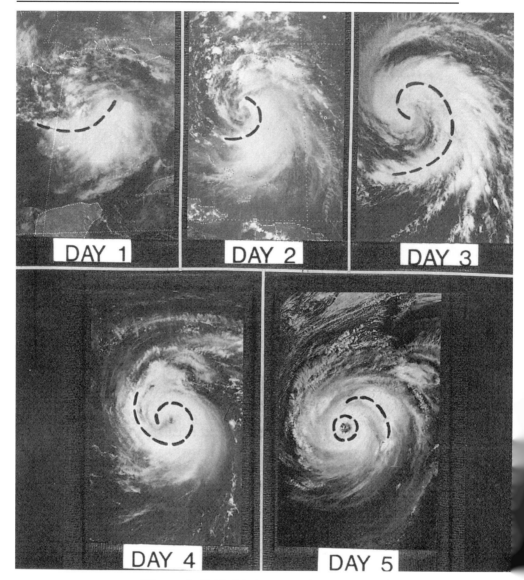

(Figure 2-4) *Visible imagery showing typical day-to-day tropical evolution of the curved band pattern.*

wind speed). At this stage, convective cells clustering within the curve of the band often form a tightly curved cloud line suggesting the formative stage of a wall cloud (see Day 2 image in Figure 2-4). Also, parallel curved low cloud lines are often visible near the cloud-system center at this stage.

When the band coils three-fourths of the distance around the center, as on Day 3, the strong tropical storm stage has been reached. And when the band coils completely around the center on Day 4, the cyclone has reached hurricane intensity (64 knots). The curved dashed lines were added to the images to highlight the coiling process.

During the process of curved-band evolution, the rate at which the pressure is falling increases as the storm center becomes more surrounded by dense overcast clouds. The rate at which the cloud pattern has evolved in Figure 2-4 is typical of most tropical cyclones worldwide. That is, there is an interval of about three days between the initial developmental pattern of Day 1 and the minimal hurricane pattern (64 knots) of Day 4. Rapidly developing tropical cyclones are observed to evolve to hurricane intensity in two days following curved band formation, whereas slow developments are observed to take four or more days.

EMBEDDED CENTER STAGE

The embedded center of the eye (Day 4 in Figure 2-4) is usually observed about 24 hours after the strong tropical storm stage on Day 3. The eye of tropical cyclone appears in the cloud pattern after the curved band has completely encircled the system center. After the initial eye formation, continued intensification of the cyclone is indicated in visible imagery by the eye becoming more distinct or more deeply embedded in the overcast clouds surrounding it. When the process is observed in enhanced infrared imagery, the eye becomes warmer and intensification and/or the clouds encircling the eye become colder. Both Dvorak (1985), working with Atlantic hurricanes, and Watanabe (1985), using regression techniques on Pacific typhoons, found that the eye temperature and the

When the cloud band coils three-fourths of the distance around the center, the strong tropical storm stage has been reached.

When the band coils completely around the center, the cyclone has reached hurricane intensity.

The eye of tropical cyclone appears in the cloud pattern after the curved band has completely encircled the system center.

temperature of the clouds surrounding the eye were highly correlated with the central pressure of the tropical cyclones.

An example of curved-band evolution resulting in eye formation is shown in Figure 2-5. The visible images across the top of the figure (Row A), were taken during the late afternoon of each day. The visible images across the bottom of the figure (Row E) were taken the next morning. The enhanced infrared images shown between the visible (VIS) ones were taken at approximately six-hour intervals throughout the nighttime hours. The enhancement of these infrared (EIR) images highlights the coldest, highest clouds as white and black. The lower, warmer, or thin clouds appear as shades of gray or off-white.

By studying the visible images in Figure 2-5, you can see once-a-day glimpses of cloud-pattern evolution from the pre-storm stage (Day 1) to the hurricane stage (Day 4). And by examining the daily columns from top to bottom, you can see short period variations in the appearance of the cloud pattern. The complexity of the patterns during the nighttime hours is due to diurnal and wind shear influences to be discussed later in the chapter.

The process of tropical cyclone intensification revealed in eye characteristics is shown on Day 4. In the top two images, the cloud-system center can only be inferred to be central to the curved cold (white) band in the enhanced infrared or as a shadow in the central dense overcast of the visible image. By the 9/01/09 GMT (Greenwich Mean Time) image, the center appears as a black (warm) spot surrounded by cold (white) clouds. In the next EIR image, a well defined (warm) eye is visible surrounded by dense (cold) overcast. In the VIS image below it, taken at the same time the eye shows up as a small dot.

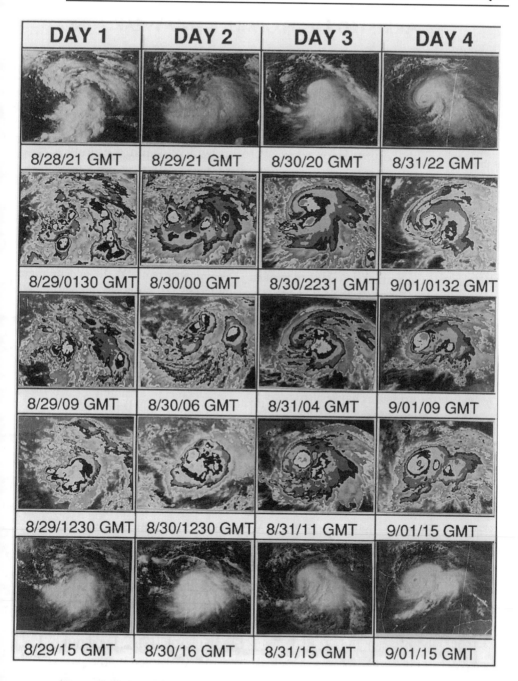

DAY 1	DAY 2	DAY 3	DAY 4
8/28/21 GMT	8/29/21 GMT	8/30/20 GMT	8/31/22 GMT
8/29/0130 GMT	8/30/00 GMT	8/30/2231 GMT	9/01/0132 GMT
8/29/09 GMT	8/30/06 GMT	8/31/04 GMT	9/01/09 GMT
8/29/1230 GMT	8/30/1230 GMT	8/31/11 GMT	9/01/15 GMT
8/29/15 GMT	8/30/16 GMT	8/31/15 GMT	9/01/15 GMT

(Figure 2-5) *Satellite images at approximately six-hour intervals throughout the life history of Hurricane Anita in 1977. The top and bottom rows are visible imagery. The middle rows are enhanced infrared images.*

ARRESTED DEVELOPMENT AND WEAKENING

The tendency for the cloud pattern change to precede the pressure change frequently shows up when a storm is developing, and is most apparent when storms are either weakening or developing rapidly.

Once the process of cloud-pattern evolution is initiated, it is observed to continue unless it is disrupted by an unfavorable environmental influence. When this occurs, the dense (cold) high clouds will begin separating from the low-level center, a non-diurnal lowering (warming) will appear in the cloud tops, or a persistent area of dense (cold) clouds will cover the storm center. As mentioned earlier, the unfavorable environmental influences that are associated with arrested development involve land, cold water, and regions of wind shear. An example of wind shear causing a tropical cyclone to weaken was shown in Figure 2-2 on page 374.

When a storm begins to lose strength, indications of weakening are observed from six to 12 hours before the central pressure of the storm begins to rise. The tendency for the change in cloud pattern to precede the pressure change also shows up when a storm is developing, and is most apparent when storms are either weakening or developing rapidly.

CLOUD-PATTERN VARIABILITY

The clouds making up the patterns observed by satellites are continually being affected by convective processes, diurnal effects, and the effects of adjacent circulations.

When viewing motion sequences of satellite imagery, the cloud pattern of a tropical cyclone is constantly changing. This is because the clouds that make up the pattern are constantly being affected by convective processes, diurnal effects, and the effects of adjacent circulations. These effects often give the observer the impression that cloud pattern evolution occurs in surges followed by lulls in development.

For instance, Figure 2-7 shows a four-hour period in the life of Tropical Storm Gert in 1981. In picture A, the storm's cloud pattern is disrupted by the passage of a short wave trough in the westerlies. Two hours later in B, the curved-band pattern begins to reappear. Then in C, two hours after B, we see the obvious pattern of a strong tropical storm similar to the Day 3 pattern in Figure 2-4 on page 378. This type of disruption is most apparent in weak pre-storm and tropical storm patterns. The same goes for diurnal fluctuations.

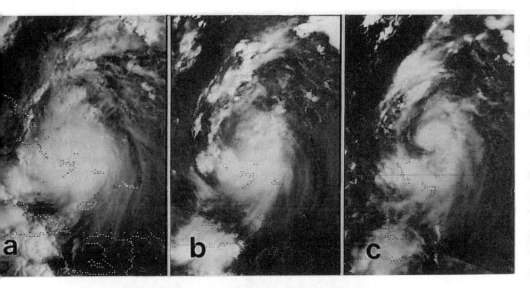

(Figure 2-7) *A four-hour period in the life of Tropical Storm Gert. Panel A shows a disruption of the cloud pattern as a trough in the westerlies passes to its north. Panels B and C show recovery of the curved-band pattern.*

Variations in the amount of convection and pattern organization observed in cloud patterns cause most of the problems an analyst encounters while interpreting satellite imagery. The technique described in the next section addresses these problems to achieve a high degree of reliability in tropical cyclone analysis under all circumstances.

Even though the curved-band pattern is the most frequently observed tropical cyclone cloud pattern, there are others. In addition to the curved-band pattern already described (Figure 2-4 on page 378), two other cloud patterns are observed with sufficient regularity to be mentioned here.

ADDITIONAL TROPICAL CYCLONE CLOUD PATTERNS

The "shear" pattern is also commonly observed. It occurs when the deep-layer convective clouds are kept from forming around the storm center in the pre-hurricane stage of development. This features an abrupt straight boundary on one side of the pattern. In the shear pattern shown in Figure 2-8, the low-level cloud lines are partially exposed and can be observed curving around the low level center of a tropical disturbance. As a disturbance intensifies, the lines become curved in a more circular fashion as well as more parallel and signal that the center is farther under the overcast. Weakening is taking place when the pattern indicates that the effects of shear are increasing with time, showing the center separating from the dense overcast.

(Figure 2-8) Visible image example of the shear cloud pattern type in the tropical storm stage.

Another pattern that we often see occurs when a central dense overcast (CDO) forms over the cloud lines which define the storm center. An example of a CDO pattern is shown in Figure 2-9 (see arrow). When the dense overcast is observed in visible imagery to be within the curve of the curved-band pattern, the size of the central overcast is related to the tropical cyclone's intensity. The CDO is roughly one degree latitude in diameter at the weak tropical storm stage, and about two degrees diameter at the weak hurricane stage.

When viewing tropical cyclone development in infrared imagery, especially in enhanced infrared, an expanding round mass of cold clouds may be observed near the cloud-system center. This central cold cover (CCC) pattern is usually observed in visible imagery as a thin cirrus overcast expanding outward from the system center. When the CCC pattern persists, development of the cyclone has been arrested.

Other common cloud patterns:

❑ Wind shear.

❑ Central dense overcast (CDO).

(**Figure 2-9**) *Visible image example of a central dense overcast (CDO) pattern in the tropical storm stage of development.*

DIURNAL EFFECTS

Diurnal influences also affect the appearance of the curved-band pattern, especially in the early stages of development. The cloud patterns of tropical cyclones generally appear weakest during the nighttime and early morning hours, when the upper-level cloud pattern contains the least clouds. Conversely the patterns appear most intense and well defined during the day-time hours. The amount of high clouds and the amount of convective activity are observed to be at a minimum near local midnight. Convection increases after midnight with the canopy clouds spreading out to a maximum during the afternoon hours.

CLOUD PATTERNS ASSOCIATED WITH TROPICAL CYCLONE MOTION

The cloud processes associated with the movement of tropical cyclones are most apparent when viewed in upper-level water-vapor (WV) imagery. In the 6.7 um infrared channel images, white shades are high clouds, often cirrus atop deep tropical convection. Lighter gray shades generally indicate the presence of moisture within the 300 to 600mb layer of the atmosphere. Dark areas are very dry aloft. The boundaries and shapes created by the moisture variations help describe upper-level flow patterns and system interactions.

Figure 2-10 compares WV imagery (shown across the top of the figure) with standard infrared imagery (across the bottom), taken at the same time. The images, taken at 24-hour intervals, show a cut-off low (C) and its associated trough approaching a large hurricane located off the west coast of Mexico. As the hurricane moves northwestward toward the approaching trough, the moisture envelope of the hurricane builds northward while the clouds and moisture to its west dissipate. The hurricane slows and begins to move northward. On the other hand, if there had been significant moisture dissipation (darkening) on the north side of the hurricane, then a turn westward would have been indicated. Interactions of this type are used by satellite analysts to forecast tropical cyclone motion.

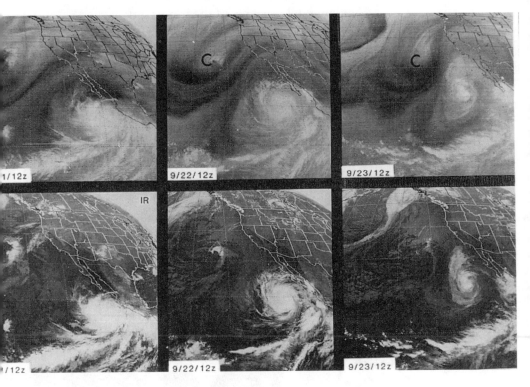

(Figure 2-10) Upper-level water-vapor imagery at 24-hour intervals (upper row) compared with simultaneous infrared imagery (bottom panel).

A Model of Tropical Cyclone Development

The Dvorak model contains descriptions of the tropical cyclone's cloud pattern on each successive day of typical development. The descriptions include both cloud feature measurements and drawings of the cloud patterns. Each day of evolution of the developing cloud pattern is defined as an increase in intensity of one T (for tropical) number.

On the first day, at the T1 stage, the cloud system is described as having curved convective cloud lines or bands that merge toward or curve around a cloud system center. Three of the more common initial cloud patterns are illustrated in Figure 3-1.

Fundamental precepts of the model are:

Once indications of initial development are observed, the disturbance is modeled (expected) to develop to maturity, unless it encounters a disruptive influence in its environment.

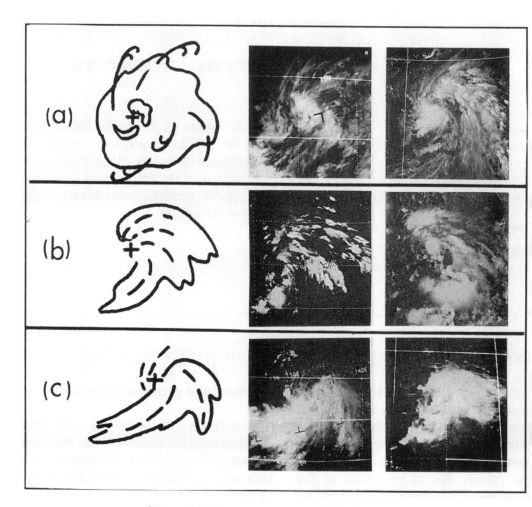

(Figure 3-1) *Three common types of cloud patterns associated with their initial stage of tropical cyclone development.*

Significant changes in tropical cyclone intensity will be preceded by a recognizable cloud pattern change.

When a tropical cyclone's cloud pattern indicates development or weakening, the change in the intensity of the cyclone follows after a time interval.

When a disrupted cloud pattern shows no sign of development or weakening, the cyclone is undergoing no significant change in intensity.

The primary pattern type defined in the model is the curved-band pattern illustrated in Figure 3-2. As shown in the figure, the typical curved-band pattern evolution begins as the band takes shape on the first day of development. As the system intensifies, the band forms or coils around the cloud system center at the daily rate of one T-number per day as shown in the figure. The curved-band pattern, like all the patterns in the model, represent an orientation that is commonly observed in the western Atlantic Ocean. It is often necessary to rotate the drawings to fit any particular cloud pattern observed in satellite imagery.

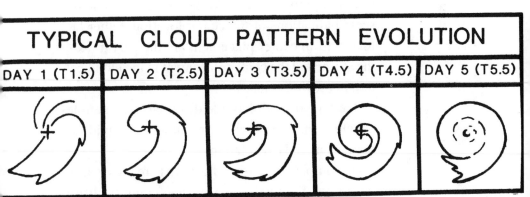

TYPICAL CLOUD PATTERN EVOLUTION

DAY 1 (T1.5)	DAY 2 (T2.5)	DAY 3 (T3.5)	DAY 4 (T4.5)	DAY 5 (T5.5)

(Figure 3-2) *Day-by-day changes in the curved-band pattern development. (See Figure 2-4 on page 378 for corresponding changes in satellite-visible imagery). Rotate the drawings as necessary to fit the cloud pattern being analyzed.*

The model depicts the tropical disturbance as reaching tropical storm intensity (labeled T2.5) 36 hours after the first classification (TI). At the T2.5 stage, the curved band is shown curved half the distance around the storm center (see Day 2 of Figure 3-2 on page 389). Once the curved band has coiled completely around the center, the minimal hurricane or T4 stage is reached.

As the cyclone continues to develop, the intensification is revealed by the eye becoming better defined (warmer in infrared), or by the clouds surrounding the eye increasing or becoming colder. The model also allows for rapid and slow rates of intensity change when the pattern evolution appears faster or slower than typical. The rapid rate is one and one half T-numbers per day, while the slow rate is half a number per day.

The modeled positions of the surface centers of disturbances are shown as plus symbols in Figure 3-2. These empirically derived locations are used in positioning a storm by directing the analyst's attention to a particular area for the more subtle small-scale indications of the center location. Other factors used in center placement are the past track of the storm and the center placement in the cloud pattern in previous pictures.

One type of high-latitude disturbance sometimes develops into a tropical storm at a more rapid rate than the model expectation.

The simple curved-band patterns are only part of the model. The model also includes common distortions to the curved-band pattern that result from a variety of atmospheric factors. Two additional pattern types contained in the model are shown in Figure 3-3. The central dense overcast (CDO) pattern

As the cyclone continues to develop, the intensification is revealed by the eye becoming better defined (warmer in infrared), or by the clouds surrounding the eye increasing or becoming colder.

There is a type of high-latitude disturbance that sometimes develops into a tropical storm at a more rapid rate than the model expectation.

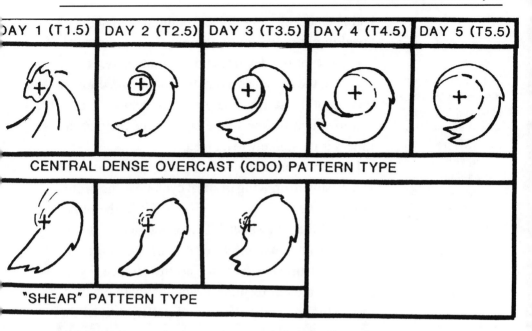

| DAY 1 (T1.5) | DAY 2 (T2.5) | DAY 3 (T3.5) | DAY 4 (T4.5) | DAY 5 (T5.5) |

CENTRAL DENSE OVERCAST (CDO) PATTERN TYPE

"SHEAR" PATTERN TYPE

(**Figure 3-3**) *Additional cloud pattern types used in the Dvorak model. The modeled positions of the surface centers are shown as crosses.*

(top row) is used when the central features of the pattern are covered by dense overcast clouds. The shear-type patterns (bottom row) are used when wind shear distorts the curved-band pattern in the manner shown the drawings. The modeled surface center positions are indicated as pluses in the figure.

To account for more complex patterns, the model also contains a general description of development. It defines development as either convective clouds building farther around the system center, or as an improvement in center definition without a significant loss of central overcast.

The model is also used to forecast intensity changes in tropical cyclones. The forecast is made by simple extrapolation along the modeled (expected) intensity curve at the rate the cyclone

The most common disruptive influence observed in a westward-moving tropical cyclone is the occurrence of increasingly westerly winds in the upper levels of the atmosphere.

had been developing or weakening unless signs of "peaking" or a disruptive influence are observed. The peak, or the day of maximum intensity, is predicted in the model as a function of the direction of motion of the storm. The prediction alerts the analyst to watch for the subtle signs of peaking at the time it is most likely to happen.

The most common disruptive influence observed in a westward-moving tropical cyclone is the occurrence of increasingly westerly winds in the upper levels of the atmosphere. The phenomenon is usually associated with a curved cloud band approaching the disturbance from the northwest (see Figure 3-4a), or a band forming in its upstream environment (Figure 3-4b). The cloud pattern (A) of the cyclone shows the interaction by a straightening of its northwest boundary.

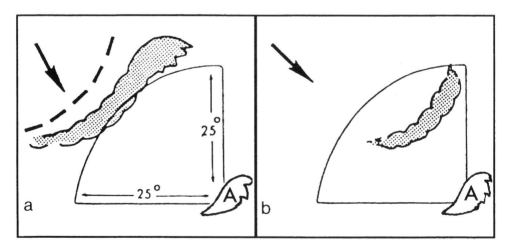

(**Figure 3-4**) *Commonly observed disruptive influences on tropical cyclone development. Either a curved band (trough of westerlies) approaches a westward-moving tropical disturbance as in the left panel, or a band forms in the storm's upstream environment as in the right panel.*

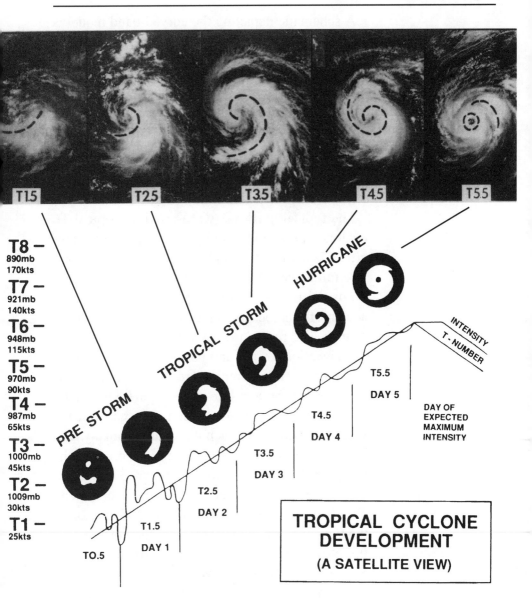

(Figure 3-5) A modeled depiction of tropical cyclone development with corresponding satellite imagery. The straight-line intensity change represents the typical growth rate. The superimposed wavy curve reflects variability in cloud feature indications of intensity. Conventional wind and pressure measurements of intensity for the Atlantic Ocean accompany the T-values on the left side of the figure.

A schematic depicting the curved-band model is shown in figure 3-5 on the preceding page. The drawings represent "typical" development as a straight line increasing at the rate of one T-number per day. The uneven curve superimposed on the straight line represents the expected variability of cloud-feature parameters with time. The variability is shown to be greatest during the early stages of development and decreases as the cyclone intensifies. Diurnal variability is also suggested.

The typical northwestward-moving tropical T6 cyclone in the model is expected to peak five days after T1 classification (unless it encounters a disruptive influence). As the storm weakens, the model holds the intensity higher than the T-numbers to account for an observed lag between cloud pattern changes and central pressure changes.

Conventional wind and pressure values of intensity for the Atlantic region are shown under the T-numbers on the left side of the figure. The model also contains an approximate long-range forecast of when the storm will reach its "peak" intensity. The forecast is based on the direction of motion of the storm. In the model as shown in Figure 3-6, the typical storm "peaks" on the fifth day of development. This is based on the normal direction of motion of the typical storm, which is toward the northwest in the Northern Hemisphere and southwest in the Southern Hemisphere. Westward-moving storms are expected to take slightly longer to "peak" (around six days), while northward-moving storms should peak sooner, on about the fourth day. These empirically derived expectations of when a storm will reach its maximum intensity are only rough approximations. They are intended primarily to alert you to be on the lookout for the subtle signs of "peaking" in the storm's cloud pattern.

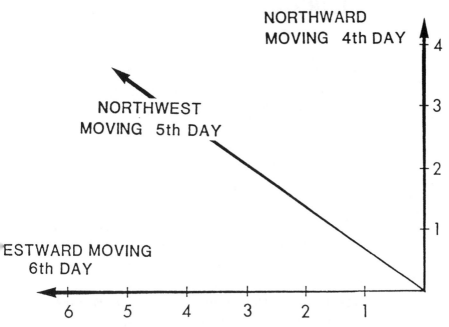

DAY OF EXPECTED MAXIMUM INTENSITY

(Figure 3-6) A "first-guess" long-range intensity forecast of the day of maximum intensity based on the direction of motion of the tropical cyclone.

CI Number	MWS (Knots)	MSLP (Atlantic)	MSLP (NW Pacific)
1	25 K		
1.5	25 K		
2	30 K	1009 mb	1000 mb
2.5	35 K	1005 mb	997 mb
3	45 K	1000 mb	991 mb
3.5	55 K	994 mb	984 mb
4	65 K	987 mb	976 mb
4.5	77 K	979 mb	966 mb
5	90 K	970 mb	954 mb
5.5	102 K	960 mb	941 mb
6	115 K	948 mb	927 mb
6.5	127 K	935 mb	914 mb
7	140 K	921 mb	898 mb
7.5	155 K	906 mb	879 mb
8	170 K	890 mb	858 mb

(Figure 3-7) The empirical relationship between the current intensity (similar to the T-number in figure 3-5), mean wind speed, and minimum seas level pressure is shown beside.

Hurricane Avoidance Tactics

Fortunately, most hurricanes have areas of severe winds that are *relatively* small in diameter.

If you are offshore, with plenty of sea room, it is not usually that difficult to stay away from the dangerous parts of the storm.

The logic and tactics to be employed are, in fact, the same as when dealing with a low pressure system in higher latitudes.

The fact that the high wind centers of these storm systems are so tight makes them easier to deal with, in most cases, than large, well organized depressions in the higher latitudes.

Having said that, a mistake with hurricane strength winds is going to be a lot more painful than with one with a high-latitude gale.

Most (but by no means all) hurricanes have relatively small areas of strong winds. Avoiding this region is best accomplished by taking early action.

Boat and Crew Factors

As in so many other areas, the right tactics to use depend on the capability of vessel and crew.

All of the factors discussed so far now begin to rely on the preparation of your vessel and crew.

If you have a sound rig, are confident in your structure, have a variety of storm canvas at your disposal and know how to deploy it, you have the greatest array of options.

A key factor is how well you know your boat and its handling characteristics in heavy weather.

Crew experience is another major issue.

Remember that in port your vessel may be in danger but you have the option of getting ashore and finding a secure place in which to ride out the storm.

Sea Room

The first decision that needs to be made is whether or not to close with shore and seek shelter. While this may seem, at first thought, to be the safest approach in many cases, given adequate sea room, just the opposite may be true.

It is critical, however, to have the sea room necessary to maneuver away from the storm center, being able to run off so that the navigable, lowest wind quadrant of the storm passes over you—if you cannot avoid the storm entirely.

The worst possible scenario is to be caught without adequate sea room, and forced to close reach or beat due to local obstructions, while headwinds try and draw you into the storm's eye.

SHELTERED CONDITIONS

If you are at sea, looking to the land for shelter is subject to all of the vagaries of closing with land under inclement conditions. What will the weather be like when you arrive? Will visibility be good enough to allow you a safe entry?

Another factor when dealing with severe storms is the type of bottom for your anchor to dig into. Even more important are the neighbors you are likely to have and how well *they* are secured.

It is often ill-prepared, unattended commercial and pleasure vessels that drag, causing all sorts of problems to vessels that were doing just fine on their own.

FINDING THE STORM CENTER

Whether you are anchored or at sea, knowing where the storm center is relative to your position, and how the storm is tracking, will be of vital importance. At anchor, this data allows you to prepare for a possible wind shift.

Offshore, the primary objective will be to avoid the storm-force winds entirely. And if this is not possible, then to minimize the wind and sea state to which you are exposed.

Fortunately, there is a relatively simple method of finding the center of any depression. This is the same system we discussed in the section on Low Pressure Tactics (See page 193).

Issues to consider in finding shelter:

❑ Protection from wind and seas for a variety of wind directions.

❑ Room to swing on the hook.

❑ Bottom condition—is the holding good?

❑ How close are your anchored neighbors and what are the risks from them?

❑ If you are blown ashore, what will the grounding be like? Some areas will do little damage. Others will puncture your hull.

If you stand with your back to the wind (in other words at right angles to it) the storm center will be on your left in the Northern Hemisphere and on your right in the Southern Hemisphere.

Take a look at the drawing below, and imagine yourself with the appropriate arm pointed at right angles (or more accurately 100 to 110 degrees) to the wind. That shows you the bearing to the low center.

We need to finesse this a little bit. Nowadays most yachts have wind speed and direction indicators aboard. Some of these are pretty accurate. So, rather than standing on deck and getting wet, we can sit in the cockpit, look at the instruments, and work out the same data with a bit more accuracy than standing with your back to the wind.

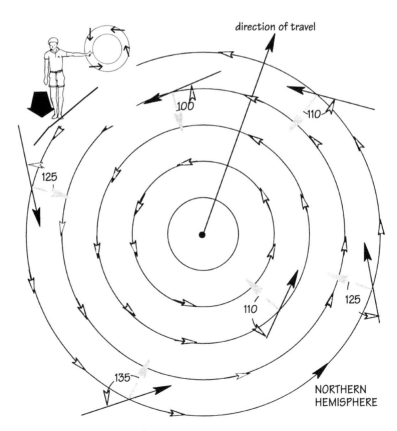

direction of travel

100

110

125

110

125

135

NORTHERN
HEMISPHERE

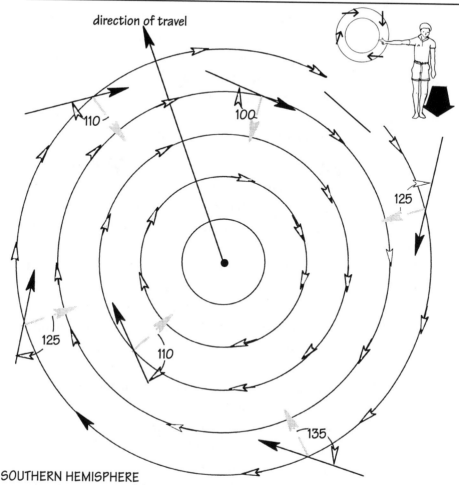

direction of travel

SOUTHERN HEMISPHERE

Use the drawing above in the Southern Hemisphere to find the storm center. First, determine the true wind angle. Next, depending on where you think you are relative to the storm center, the angles shown will indicate the difference between true wind direction and the center of the storm. It is easier, although not as accurate, to point across with the wind at your back. The drawing on the opposite page is for the Northern Hemisphere.

Along the outer edges of the storm, the wind is veered towards the center, rather than pointing directly along the isobars. The amount of the veering depends on where you are relative to the center.

You have the smallest amount of veering ahead of the storm, and the greatest amount behind the center. This angle ranges from 20 degrees or so of veering towards the center from ahead to as much as 30 to 40 degrees from behind the low center.

As the storm center approaches the winds blow more nearly along the isobar lines.

ESTABLISHING THE STORM TRACK

Early on in the approach of the storm system, you can use the swell direction and the point of convergence of the cirrus clouds to indicate where the center is located.

If the swell and/or cirrus convergence maintains a constant heading, then the storm track is directly toward you. If the storm is to pass to one side or the other, the bearing to the point of convergence and the swell angle shifts in the direction of storm movement.

As the wind begins to increase, using the system just discussed you can track the storm's progress. Once again, if the wind direction remains the same, and the barometer is falling steadily, then you are directly in the path of the storm.

When the rain bar of the storm becomes visible, the darkest portion of the bar indicates where the center of the storm is located.

When you begin to be encompassed by dense clouds their movement should be noted carefully. Because they are not subjected to surface friction, their track is usually directly in line with the isobars surrounding the storm center.

If you draw an arrow on your chart representing cloud direction, and then take a bearing at right angles (to the right in the Northern Hemisphere and to the left in the Southern Hemisphere) this will be pointing right at the storm center.

Finding the storm track:

❑ Cirrus clouds converge at a point on the horizon, indicating storm center.

❑ Long-period swells radiate out from storm center—back bearing indicates storm center.

❑ If barometer drops and wind direction remains the same, storm center is headed directly for your position.

❑ When rain bar is visible, if it maintains same bearing as it moves towards you, you are in the path of the eye.

If it appears stationary, then the center is probably heading toward you. If the bar drifts slowly to one side, then that is the direction in which the storm center is moving, hopefully away from you.

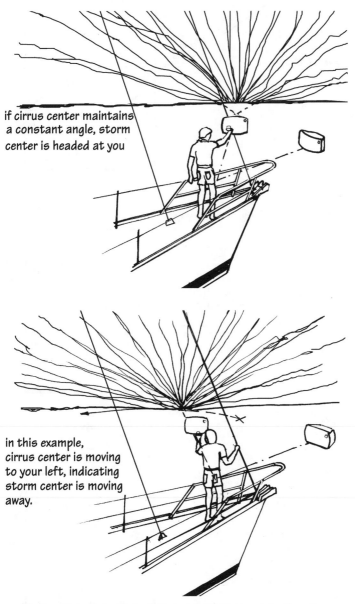

if cirrus center maintains a constant angle, storm center is headed at you

in this example, cirrus center is moving to your left, indicating storm center is moving away.

During the early part of the storm's approach, the cirrus clouds will come to a point on the horizon. This indicates the direction of the storm center.

NORTHERN HEMISPHERE

The clouds you see aloft as the storm approaches are traveling in line with the isobars rather than at a toed-in angle as you see with the surface wind.

By noting the direction of travel of the clouds, you can then draw a 90-degree bearing on a chart to the cloud movement. This will point to the center of the depression.

In this example the bearing to the storm center is moving aft, so the storm center is going to cross behind the boat.

These hurricanes are shown for Northern Hemisphere circulation (i.e., counterclockwise wind circulation around the center). This means the boat is heading towards the navigable side of the storm.

With the first bearing in this drawing, the boat is running. As soon as the location of the storm center is determined, the wind should be brought more on the bow. In this way, a course at right angles to the storm track can be maintained to keep as much distance as possible between yourself and the storm center.

track of storm

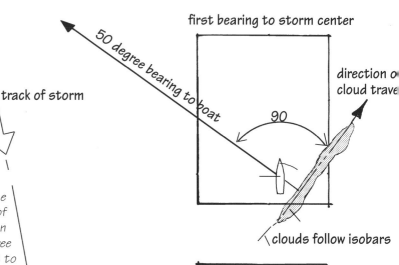

first bearing to storm center

50 degree bearing to boat

direction of cloud travel

90

clouds follow isobars

second bearing to storm center

90 degree bearing to boat

90

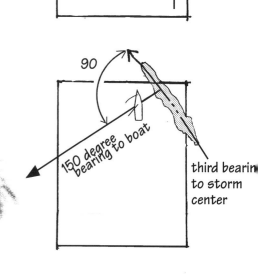

90

150 degree bearing to boat

third bearing to storm center

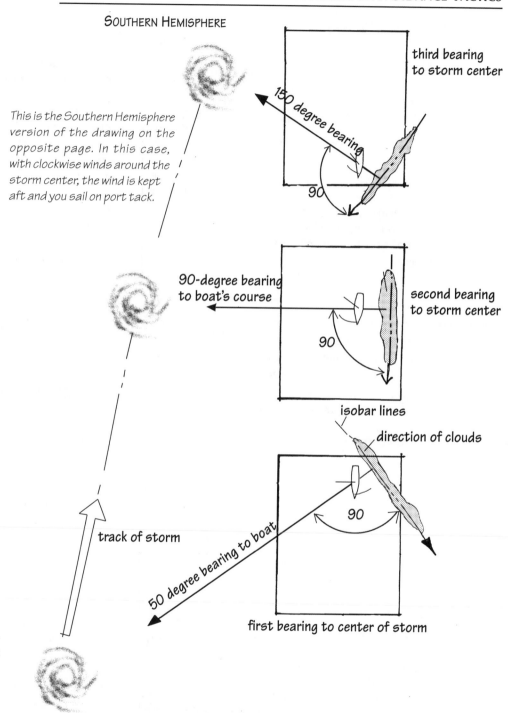

SOUTHERN HEMISPHERE

This is the Southern Hemisphere version of the drawing on the opposite page. In this case, with clockwise winds around the storm center, the wind is kept aft and you sail on port tack.

third bearing to storm center

150 degree bearing

90

90-degree bearing to boat's course

second bearing to storm center

90

isobar lines

direction of clouds

90

track of storm

50 degree bearing to boat

first bearing to center of storm

NORTHERN HEMISPHERE

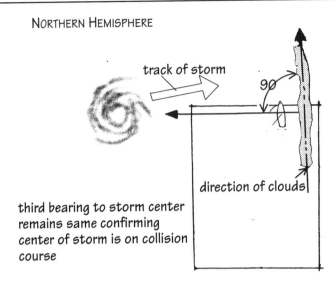

track of storm

90

direction of clouds

third bearing to storm center remains same confirming center of storm is on collision course

If the bearing with the clouds remains the same, as in this series of sketches, then you know that the storm center is closing with you and some form of avoiding action needs to be taken. Note that the wind direction will also remain constant if the storm center is heading right at you.

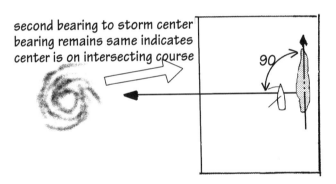

second bearing to storm center bearing remains same indicates center is on intersecting course

90

As this drawing is of a Northern Hemisphere hurricane, if there is sufficient time and boat speed available, the objective should be to try to cross to the navigable side of the storm (as drawn here, continue towards the North).

However, if you can stay out of the storm or hurricane force winds by reversing your course and avoiding the storm track rather than crossing, this would be the better tactic.

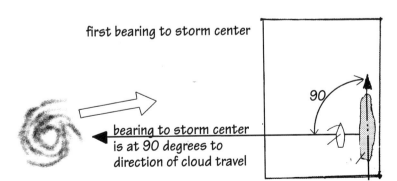

first bearing to storm center

90

bearing to storm center is at 90 degrees to direction of cloud travel

The decision in this case is a tough one—based on what you or the forecasters think the storm may do as it approaches, and the speed of your vessel.

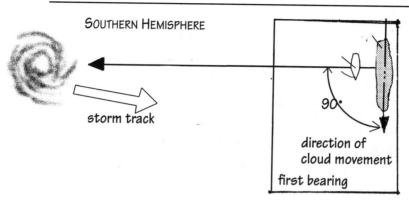

SOUTHERN HEMISPHERE

storm track

90°

direction of
cloud movement

first bearing

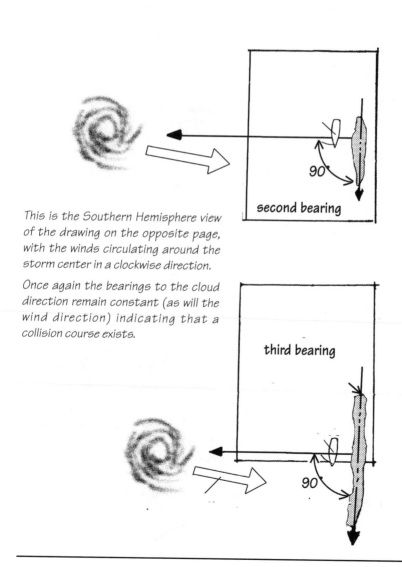

90°

second bearing

This is the Southern Hemisphere view of the drawing on the opposite page, with the winds circulating around the storm center in a clockwise direction.

Once again the bearings to the cloud direction remain constant (as will the wind direction) indicating that a collision course exists.

third bearing

90°

Once you can see the storm bar—a mass of dense, black clouds, heavy with rain—you know that the region of hurricane strength winds is approaching.

Early in the approach, while you still have visibility, if you take periodic bearings on the bar and write them down, you will be able to tell if the storm center is heading directly for you, or to one side or the other.

In this example the bar is coming straight at the yacht in the foreground, as the bearing on the bar remains the same as it draws closer.

If this were taking place in the Northern Hemisphere, with counterclockwise winds, this vessel would be headed into the dangerous (left when facing the storm center) quadrant. In the Southern Hemisphere, the boat would be headed correctly to the navigable quadrant.

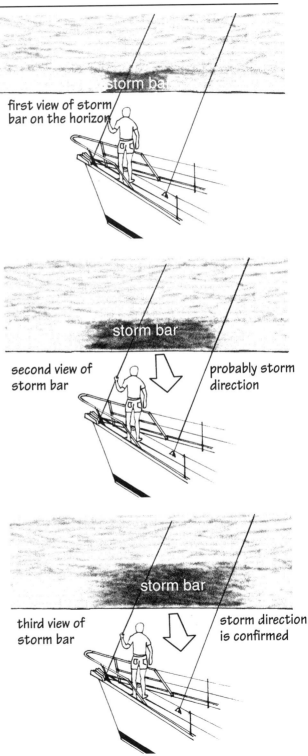

first view of storm bar on the horizon

second view of storm bar

probably storm direction

third view of storm bar

storm direction is confirmed

This would be the correct course of action in the Northern Hemisphere if you were at sea and saw the storm center bearing down on you. In this case, the vessel is headed to the right of the storm center (when facing into it) towards the sector of the storm with less winds, and where the direction of wind makes it easier to escape the storm center.

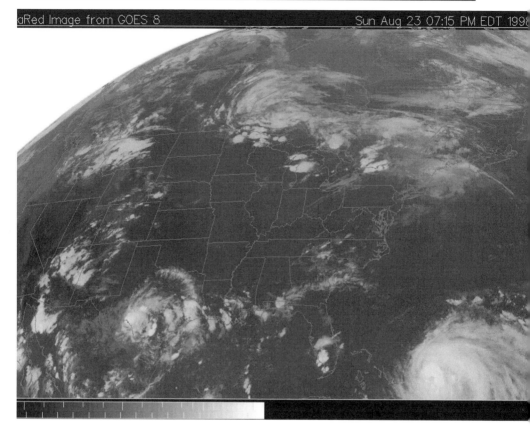

Sun Aug 23 07:15 PM EDT 1998

aRed Image from GOES 8

It is never certain what a tropical storm is going to do. However, if you have access to the Internet, or can contact someone with access to the net there is a huge amount of data available.

Here is a satellite image of Hurricane Bonnie together with a wind speed vs. time probability chart. If you are sitting in an anchorage, wondering if it is worth the risk of moving, this type of data from the Tropical Prediction center can be very helpful.

WIND SPEED FORECAST FOR BONNIE
EXPRESSED AS PROBABILITY
FROM NHC ADVISORY 024
8:00 AM EDT AUG 25 1998

TIME	WIND SPEED INTERVAL IN MPH							
HOURS	DISSIPATED	TROPICAL DEPRESSION <39	TROPICAL STORM 39-73	HURRICANE >=74	HURRICANE CAT.1 74-95	CAT.2 96-110	CAT.3 111-130	CAT.4- >=131
12	<2%	<2%	<2%	>98%	15%	25%	50%	10%
24	<2%	<2%	5%	95%	15%	30%	35%	15%
36	<2%	<2%	<2%	>98%	30%	25%	30%	15%
48	<2%	<2%	3%	95%	35%	20%	20%	20%
72	<2%	3%	25%	75%	35%	15%	15%	10%

NAVIGABLE SEMICIRCLE

If you are facing *into* the direction of the storm track, the safest part of the storm is to the right in the Northern Hemisphere and to the left of the track south of the equator.

These are the sides of the storms where their forward velocity is *subtracted* from wind speed. On the other hand, the opposite, dangerous sides of the storms is where their relative motion is *added* to the wind speed.

If you do not know the storm track, or in which part of the storm you are located, a written record of the wind direction can be of some assistance.

In the Northern Hemisphere, a wind which is shifting to the *right* (clockwise) indicates you are in

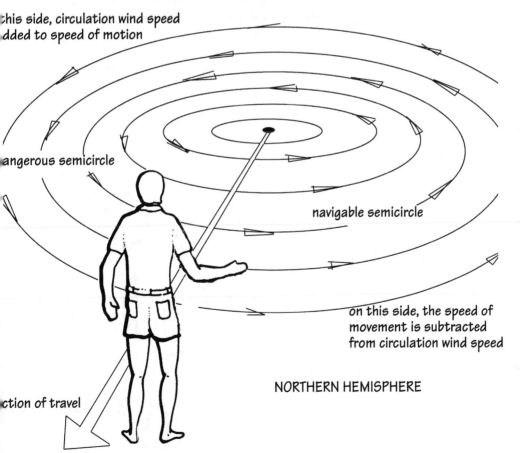

this side, circulation wind speed
added to speed of motion

dangerous semicircle

navigable semicircle

on this side, the speed of movement is subtracted from circulation wind speed

NORTHERN HEMISPHERE

direction of travel

N. Hemisphere wind-shift summary:

☐ If the wind is shifting clock-wise you are in the dangerous semi-circle of the storm.

☐ If the wind is shifting counter-clockwise you are in the navigable quadrant.

S. Hemisphere wind-shift summary:

☐ If the wind is shifting counter-clockwise you are in the dangerous.

☐ If the wind shifts clockwise you are in the navigable quadrant.

the dangerous semi-circle of the storm. In the Southern Hemisphere a wind which is shifting to the left (counterclockwise) gives the same prognosis.

Left hand (counterclockwise) shifts north of the equator indicate you are in the safer side of the storm (right hand shifts—clockwise— indicate the safer side of the storm south of the equator).

Lets recap some of the external signs you can use for establishing the bearing to the storm center. The first is the point on the horizon where the cirrus clouds converge. Another is tracking cloud move-ment and drawing a right angle bearing (keep in mind that at some point cloud movement may be obscured by night, rain, or a thick deck of low clouds. Keeping track of the direction of the long period swells is another, means, and finally, watch-ing the direction that the wind shifts as detailed in the beginning of this section.

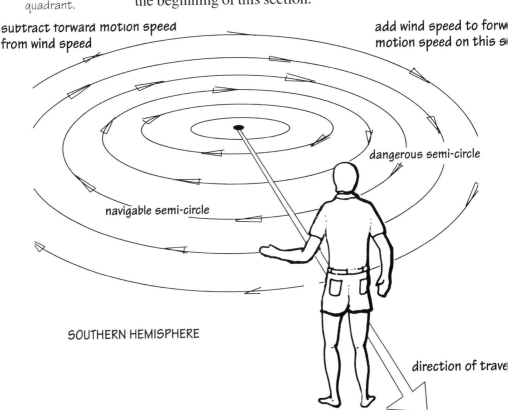

subtract forward motion speed from wind speed

add wind speed to forw motion speed on this s

dangerous semi-circle

navigable semi-circle

SOUTHERN HEMISPHERE

direction of trave

NORTHERN HEMISPHERE

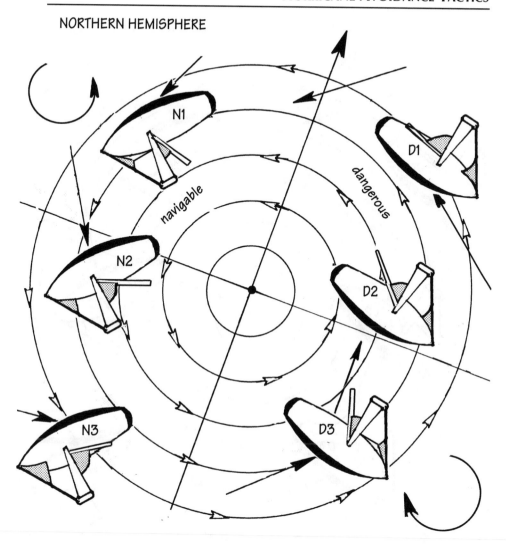

By watching the manner in which the wind shifts, you can tell if you are in the navigable or dangerous part of the storm. In the Northern Hemisphere the wind will back; that is, shift counterclockwise if you are in the navigable quadrant. N1 is on a starboard tack broad reach to a run. N2 is on a reach as the wind backs, and N3 is on a close reach to a beat.

On the dangerous side of the storm, the wind veers; that is, it shifts in a clockwise fashion. D1 is on a starboard tack beat, D2 on a reach, and D3 on a broad reach as the center moves past.

SOUTHERN HEMISPHERE

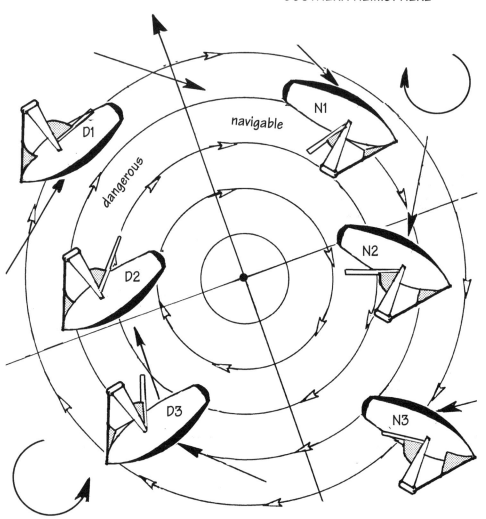

In the Southern Hemisphere the wind veers—changes direction clockwise—when you are in the navigable quadrant of the storm. N1 has the wind on the port quarter. N2 is reaching, and N3 is beating.

In the dangerous quadrant the wind backs—goes counterclockwise—as the storm advances. D1 is beating on port, D2 is reaching, and D3 is broad-reaching.

COURSES OF ACTION

The earlier you take avoiding action, the easier the job will be. Usually just 50 or 100 miles make the difference between a modest gale and a full-fledged hurricane.

Even if the action takes you away from your intended destination, by far the safest thing to do is to take avoiding action sooner rather than later. Once you begin to be influenced by the wind and sea of the stronger parts of the storm, your options becomes much more limited.

Within the context of being able to make progress, here are some general rules for the *Northern Hemisphere*:

If the storm is tracking directly towards you, bring the wind on the starboard quarter (about 150 to 160 degrees) and move as fast as possible. This will take you at right angles to the course of the storm.

If you are behind a storm center, slow down and watch carefully for anything that would indicate the storm was reversing.

If you are in the lefthand side of the storm, in the navigable semicircle, keep the wind just aft of the beam (starboard tack) and move as fast as possible away from the storm center.

If you are caught in the dangerous, right hand side of the storm, bring the wind as close on the bow as possible and do everything possible to gain distance, even motorsailing if that helps you make progress to windward.

In the *Southern Hemisphere* the actions are just the opposite:

On the dangerous lefthand side of the storm, stay on port tack and make as much progress to weather as possible.

If you are in the safer side of the storm, to the right- hand side of the track, keep the wind just aft of the beam on port tack.

If the storm is heading towards you, and you are on its track, keep the wind on the port quarter, at a broad-reaching angle (150 to 160 degrees true) and move as fast as possible.

N. Hemisphere tactics:

❑ If storm is heading for you, bring wind on starboard quarter.

❑ Behind the system, slow down and/or head away from center on tack that is closest to equator.

❑ In navigable quadrant, keep wind on starboard quarter or beam.

❑ In dangerous quadrant sail as close to wind on starboard as possible.

S. Hemisphere tactics:

❑ If storm is headed for you, bring wind on port quarter.

❑ If behind center slow down and/or take action that brings you closest to equator.

❑ In navigable quadrant keep wind on port quarter or beam.

❑ In dangerous quarters, beat on port tack.

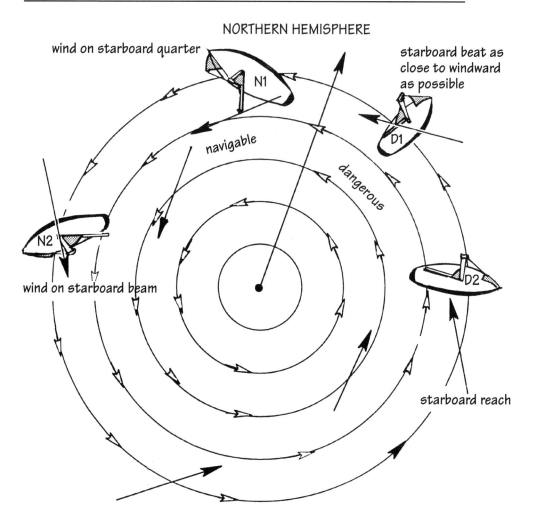

NORTHERN HEMISPHERE

wind on starboard quarter

starboard beat as close to windward as possible

navigable

dangerous

N1

D1

N2

D2

wind on starboard beam

starboard reach

In the Northern Hemisphere, on the navigable side of the storm, bring the wind on the starboard quarter as the storm approaches (N1). As the center of the storm draws abeam the, wind should be on the starboard beam (N2).

In the dangerous side of the storm, start out on starboard tack (D1) sailing or motorsailing as close to the wind as possible. As the storm center draws abeam (D2), the wind will be on a forward starboard quarter.

To the extent possible, keep moving away from the storm center as quickly as is feasible. Sometimes a matter of 50 miles will make a huge difference in sea and wind conditions.

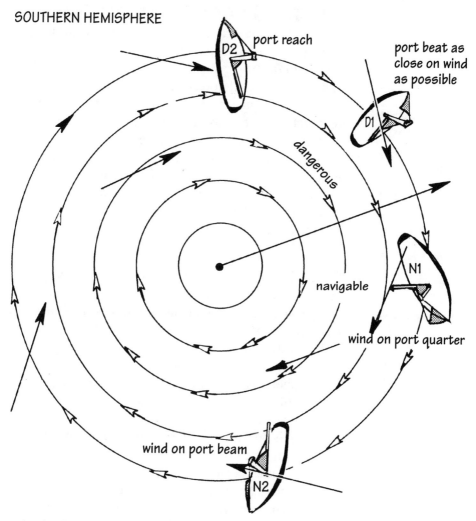

SOUTHERN HEMISPHERE

port reach

port beat as close on wind as possible

dangerous

navigable

wind on port quarter

wind on port beam

In the Southern Hemisphere, on the navigable side of the storm center as the storm approaches, bring the wind on the port quarter (N1). As the center of the storm draws abeam the wind should go onto the port beam (N2).

In the dangerous side of the storm, as the center approaches, sail as close on the wind on port tack as possible. Motorsail, if you have that capability (D1). As the center comes abeam, the wind will back so that you are close-reaching.

Keep a log of barometric pressure and wind direction, so you can tell if the storm changes direction of travel, in which case different tactics might be required.

EQUATOR SIDE OF THE STORM TRACK

Most hurricanes track parallel with the equator or have a poleward bias in their course—at least while they are in the tropics.

This means that if you ensure that your position is closer to the equator than that of the hurricane you are watching, the odds of coming into contact with it are much reduced by this course of action.

You can use this technique when at sea of course. But it also makes sense if you find yourself at risk from a tropical storm system while at anchor. The key is to know where the storm center is located, and then make sure your latitude is less than that of the storm.

PASSAGING IN HURRICANE SEASON

Sometimes an external situation forces you to make a passage during the hurricane season. Where these are short hops, the risks are moderate, and with a judicious review of the weather and the avoidance options, it may be feasible.

On longer passages, the risks escalate as the predictable time horizon is much shorter relative to the time you are at sea.

Often it is possible to have a fallback scenario that would minimize your exposure—a "plan B" should something unexpected brew up.

One approach is to stay within range of the region near the equator where hurricanes rarely form or track. Storms normally need at least five degrees of latitude (300 nautical miles) of separation from the equator.

So, if you are on a north-to-south, or south-to-north passage, you can wait in the region around the equator for a clear shot to cross the active hurricane area. If you see something to the east that makes you nervous, you can always head back towards the equator until you have a sufficient period of time to make the crossing of the active tropical-risk area.

Passaging during hurricane season:

❑ Watch sky, swells, barometer and forecasts for danger signs.

❑ If worrying signs detected but no confirming forecast, believe the worst.

❑ Maintain a constantly updated fallback/avoidance plan.

❑ If close enough, use equator/ ITCZ as safety zone.

❑ Possibly run for high latitudes and cooler water.

❑ Keep an eye on steering currents aloft.

❑ Stay below the latitude of any storm you are watching.

USING A WEATHER ROUTER

For many years now commercial shipping companies have used the services of weather routers to pick the most efficient course for their vessels.

Fifteen or so years ago racers started to employ these shore based gurus as well.

As communications have become more reliable and less costly, these services have come to be used by cruising sailors as well.

Although we have suggested that a number of our clients used weather routing for initial passages, it wasn't until the Northern Hemisphere summer of 1995 that Linda and I had our first taste of this service.

We were taking *Beowulf* down to New Zealand to have her interior fitted, and would be crossing the region to the west of Southern Mexico and Central America where hurricanes could be a problem.

It was the end of July, and so far the year had been quiet.

We had the ability to receive weather faxes, SSB and Sat C weather broadcasts, but I wanted someone with whom I could discuss strategy, should the need occur.

Most on my mind was being able to toss avoidance strategies around, and get a handle on steering currents—information which was not readily available to us aboard.

I had been chatting with Bob Rice at Weather Window who was pushing us to leave as soon as possible as things had been quiet for a long time, and he felt we were in for some storm formation.

The day arrived when we were ready to go. I checked in with Bob to get the latest, to find an area of convective activity off of an easterly wave.

With *Beowulf's* speed we felt we could probably make it safely across the region before anything drifted out and across our course. In reserve we had the option of heading back to higher latitudes should we find our way blocked by active tropical storms.

As we worked our way southwest towards the Marquesas we communicated with Bob each day in the morning about his latest thoughts on our Sat C modem (e-mail). I would then compare his information with what we were seeing on the fax charts, and then sometimes e-mail back a question or two along with our local conditions.

As it turned out, the disturbance we were watching formed into a tropical depression, and then went to storm strength.

At this point we had two choices: one was to keep to the west, using the counterclockwise wind to reinforce the tradewind flow in which we were sailing. This promised a very fast, and comfortable trip to the equator.

However, there was a major risk factor. If the storm quickly matured and accelerated its movement and we had some form of a mechanical problem, we'd be right in the path of the hurricane. This did not seem like a prudent option in light of the fact that *Beowulf* had only been in the water two months before our departure (although she did have a thousand miles on the log).

The alternative, more conservative approach, was to go behind the storm, to the east of it. This meant that the storm would be moving away from us as it tracked in the normal west to northwest direction.

The only problem with this approach, of course, was wind direction. Behind the storm we had southerly quadrant winds, turning what should have been a nice broad reach into a dead beat—with steep, uncomfortable seas.

While Bob and I discussed the options, and then Linda and I discussed them further, there really was only one choice—go behind the storm.

To be realistic about this whole scenario, and how it turned out, we had all of the data we needed from our fax and high seas forecast, along with what we could see in the sky and read on the barometer.

However, having someone with whom we could discuss our tactics was a distinct comfort factor, and the $400 or so in costs for Bob Rice's services, was inexpensive insurance, just in case the computer models at the Tropical Prediction Center were off a bit.

COMMUNICATIONS

To use a router effectively you need to have the ability to communicate efficiently. One method is via single side band radio and the high seas operator. However, this leaves you at the mercy of band conditions and the $3.00 or more per minute charges make this a rather expensive option.

E-mail, either via ham, a commercial station (like Globe Wireless or Pin Oak Digital) is a more efficient way to get your data. Not only do you end up with a written summary of comments, but e-mail can get through on SSB when voice could not be heard.

The other approach is with some form of satellite direct e-mail, like the Trimble Sat C modem we carried aboard *Beowulf*. This is fully automatic and not subject to the vagaries of the sun spot cycle and band conditions. You also get weather forecasts updated four times a day for your location.

COSTS

You have two categories of costs. One is for the router and the other for communicating back and forth.

Routers work in different ways. Some charge a relatively large initial forecast and route planning fee, and then a fixed amount for each day's communications.

The other cost is for transmission of this data to you, and your queries back. If you are using SSB e-mail these costs will be negligible. We found that our bills with our Sat C Service provider (Stratos) were about $125 for the trip down to the Marquesas and about $160 for the trip back a couple of years later.

The fees we paid to Weather Window were in the order of $300 to $400.

Taken together this seems like a lot of money. However, we were passaging out of season, with a hurricane threat always present. Without the ability to double check our weather data and plans with a professional onshore, with all of the tools available from the Internet, we probably would have waited for the correct voyaging season.

DISCUSSING YOUR NEEDS

If you use a router, you will want to discuss in detail, *before you leave*, what sort of data you want and how you want it sent to you.

For example, there is really no need for salutations and general information otherwise available. If they are sending you an e-mail, and you are paying for each character, you may want to have the router only send you the guts of their message, leaving off anything at all extraneous.

You will want to be clear on timing. I like to get my data first thing in the morning, preferably as the sun is coming up. Then I can compare it to the late evening fax charts and our barometric, cloud and wind conditions.

If there are any questions, I can e-mail them back to the router's office before he leaves for the day.

An alternate plan is to have an agreed upon time each day when you transmit your current conditions to the router, after which he can put together his data for you, taking into account your on the spot information.

You will want to establish how far out you want the router to look at the prospective weather patterns, and how many potential scenarios he should discuss.

When we are passaging in hurricane season one of the things I like to hear about are areas of convective activity which could eventually lead to tropical storm formation. These areas will often exist for several days before the weather service places them on a synoptic chart or voice forecast. The weather router can give you a heads up on the prospects — good or bad in their earliest stages.

Issues to discuss establish with your weather router:

❑ Boat sailing capability.

❑ Range and speed under power.

❑ Alternate destinations.

❑ Type of information desired.

❑ Information not required.

❑ Primary and secondary means of communication.

❑ Communication schedule.

❑ Time frame in which to ask questions so timely answers are received.

TRADE-OFFS

Throughout this weather routing process there are many trade-offs to consider. You have the skill and stamina of the crew on one hand. On the other are performance factors for the vessel.

Sometimes there will be a route which, if everything works out just right, will get you to port much earlier. However, there may be risks associated—weather or otherwise—with this plan. Someone has to make those types of decisions.

When you are discussing various scenarios with the router you will want to be clear about the trade-offs, making sure you know the potential up and downside of each course of action.

I find it helpful to keep notes in the log about each scenario, and what factors have to occur, and in what time frame for the good or bad results to affect us. This way, we have a form of quality control over the decision making process and it is much faster to see how things are working out.

And, if they are going wrong, to adjust our strategy accordingly.

PERFORMANCE FACTORS

A very big part of any routing decisions will be realistic assumptions about how fast you can sail, motor, or motorsail at given wind angles and velocities, and in different sea states.

Another factor is range under power.

This data is necessary for any route planning you do, not just working with an outside professional.

If you don't have a good feel for this data from experience, it is worth spending some time putting together performance tables for the boat before you head offshore.

It works best if this data is realistic in the context of how the boat is being sailed. Don't use racing type numbers, which are based on a full crew, if you are cruising with just two people aboard.

NUKA HIVA TO SAN DIEGO

Following is an account from a passage Linda and I recently made between the Marquesas Islands and San Diego.

It is an interesting challenge weatherwise at any time of year, but especially in September, as we are crossing the tropical North Pacific during hurricane season.

To give you a feel for the decision-making process on a passage like this, we are including all of the weather faxes used for the trip, along with the e-mail messages between ourselves and Bob Rice's Weather Window, whose services we used for this voyage. The e-mails were sent via Satcom C terminal.

There is quite a lot of data to go through. You may find it easiest to read the basic text of the story first, and then come back and study the weather faxes and e-mail dialog later.

NUKA HIVA

Nuka Hiva in the Marquesas Islands is rapidly fading astern. Ahead of us lies 3,600 miles of passage to California. The wind is blowing a steady18 knots from the east-southeast and *Beowulf* is beam-reaching at a comfortable14 knots. Linda and I are alone aboard, which is the way we prefer to sail.

It is September, hurricane season in the North Pacific. This is also an El Nino year that so far has made it an easy trip against the trades from New Zealand (just wait for the fronts every week to ten days and then make easting with westerly-quadrant winds). A clear weather fax and the re-emergence of the easterly trade winds has tempted us from our anchorage.

This is the first in a series of messages between us and the team at Weather Window. Note that our messages are in upper and lower case, while the Weather Window replies are in caps.

Since we are paying by the character for the transmissions, a lot of abreviations are used.

The ***MSG: heading is the way these look when they come in on the sat C modem. From here on out we'll remove the message headers to save you reading time.

We should be ready to go Tue.Keep in mind we motorsail very efficiently to weather.If true wind angle 30 degrees in trades of 17 or less can maintain 9/10 knots with mainsail and engine (speed depends on seas/comfort-can do 11 if seas moderate)-if expect stronger NE winds will be better to keep close reaching on strbd tack until close enuf to center of high for winds/seas to drop off, and then turn right and motor towards N/NW flow along coast-this is mch longer route but if seas are slowing us down on direct route it wll be same elapsed time and more comfortable.How far N do you think we can carry E/SE trades?Steve

*** MSG: 436320 1997/09/06 13:29:57 ROU-TINE *** // TELSTRA SATCOM-C SERVICE 97-09-06/13-28 UTC MSG REF: 436320 FROM:30207810100517 via X.25 LES ID:PERTH (222) // From: COM-PUSERVE:102535,1331 (BOB RICE) Subject: Weather
WE ASSUME DEPARTURE TUES. DOMINANT LARGE-SCALE WEATHER FEATURE IS MASSIVE HI PRESS RID NOW NR 40S 110W, THAT IS SPREADING A RDG LOBE NWRD TO MARQUESAS. THUS, A BRISK (11-17 KT) ERLY TO E-SERLY WIND REGIME HAS SET UP BETWEEN YOU AND EQ. BETWEEN THE EQ AND 10N LAT, THERE IS A DEAD REGION OF BROAD LO PRESS WHOSE AXIS RUNS ALONG 5N LAT FROM NEAR COAST OF COLUMBIA WESTWARD TO THE CENTRAL PACIFIC. SOME LO PRESS IS ALSO LOCATED OFF THE CENTRAL AMERICAN COAST, TO 130W LONG. EMBEDDED WITHIN THIS TROUGHING, IS THE REMAINS OF TS KEVIN (NOW NEAR 20.7N 125.8N). HES DOWN TO 30 KTS AND IS MOVING WESTRD OVER COOLER WATER. KEVIN EXPECTED TO BE DISSIPATED WITHIN 36 HOURS, AND SHOULD NOT BE A FACTOR FOR YOU. THERE ARE CURRENTLY NO OTHER SUSPECT AREAS IN THE EASTERN PACIFIC. HOWEVER, THE REGION HAS BEEN VERY ACTIVE THIS YEAR SO FAR, AND

SHOULD REMAIN SO. THUS, THERE IS A FAIR
CHANCE THAT A TS OR H WILL BE FACTOR AT
SOME POINT AS YOU TRACK NORTH. UNFORTU-
NATELY, THE PERIOD THAT YOU COULD BE
THREATENED IS TOO FAR IN FUTURE FOR US TO
RECOMMEND ANY POSSIBLE STRATEGY NOW.
WELL HAVE TO PLAY IT BY EAR, WITH THE
GOAL OF GIVING YOU ABOUT A 72 HOUR HEADS-
UP, WHICH SHOULD BE ENOUGH TIME TO TAKE
EVASIVE ACTION, GIVEN YOUR OVERALL
SPEED. ELSEWHERE, THERE IS A MASSIVE NE
PACIFIC HI PRESS RID, WHOSE AXIS IS
LINED-UP EAST-WEST OFF SOUTHERN-CENTRAL
CALIFORNIA. YOU ARE QUITE RIGHT IN YOUR
OBSERVATION THAT THE CENTER OF THE RIDGE
IS FARTHER S THAN TYPICAL. IT IS GENERAT-
ING MOD TO STG NEERIES TO EERLIES.ON TUES
VERY LITTLE CHANGE IN THE OVERALL LARGE-
SCALE PRESS PATTERN IS ANTICIPATE.
EXCEPT, THE RID TO YUR S MAY WEAKEN A
TAD, WHICH WOULD RESULT IN A SLGT
DECREASE IN THE EERLY QUAD WINDS NEAR
YOU. ALSO, THE LIGHTER WIND ZONE NEAR THE
EQ (BETWEEN THE NERN AND SERN RID OVER
THE EASTERN PACIFIC, WILL EXPAND, WITH
SOME LG/VBRL ZONES POSSIBLE BETWEEN 0-N
AND 8-N LAT. UNDERSTAND YOU DO WELL TO
WEATHER, BUT THINK THAT HEADING TO 10N
130W MAY BE TOO FAR EAST. CONDITIONS TO
THAT POINT MAY BE OK, BUT FROM THERE TO
LAX WOULD PUT SOME INCREASING WINDS ON
THE NOSE. IF YOU WANT TO GET INTO THE
CENTER OF RIDGE, YOULL HAVE TO GET N OF
30N SO. TOO EARLY TO FIGURE WHERE RIDGE
WILL BE IN 10 DAYS, BUT SUGGEST YOU HEAD
ALMOST DUE NORTH, TO 20N 138W, THEN WELL
REEVALUATE LATER. THIS MORE N ROUTE WOULD
KEEP YOU IN GOOD WIND ANGLE, AND ALSO
HELP TO GET YOU OUT OF THE TROPICS
QUICKLY, AND FARTHER WEST, WHERE TROPI-
CALS TEND TO BE WEAKENED. EXPECT WINDS
090-110/12-17 KTS ON TUES, THEN BECOMING
MORE SOUTH AND FALLING NEAR THE EQ (120-
140/8-13). NORTH OF THE EQ, LOOK FOR
LIGHT TENDING SE WINDS, WITH HI CHANCE

This first long message is a general heads-up on how the guys at Weather Window see the year shaping up.

Most of the trade wind-related data we already know from firsthand experience and the weather fax charts. What we are really interested in is how things are looking off the coast of Central America and Mexico—and so far they are quiet.

FOR PERIODS OF VAR (TEMP GALE POSSIBLE IN
THUNDERSTORMS). NEAR 10N YOULL CATCH
SOME BUILDING NELIES (050-070/8-13KTS).
THEN STRONGER NELIES KICK-IN AROUND 20N
(060-080/13-18). WELL SEND QUICK, SHORT
UPDATES THROUGH DEPARTURE, AND AS REQD
UNDERWAY.

TACTICS

Tactic for crossing an active hurricane belt:

❑ Stop at ITCZ and analyze situation.

❑ Head across dangerous area as fast as possible.

❑ Always keep an alternate escape scenario in mind, in case the first course of action does not work out.

Tactics for this passage are straightforward. Sail quickly out of the tropical South Pacific toward the center of the North Pacific high to reduce the risk of a hurricane. As we get into the ITCZ (just north of the equator) we'll reassess the situation. If it looks like the run from seven degrees North latitude (where one starts to encounter hurricanes) onwards is dicey, we'll heave-to, awaiting a clear shot towards the high. Once we're in the high, we can put *Beowulf's* powering capabilities to work in the light airs and head east till we contact the northwesterly circulation along the Pacific Coast (we have a range under power of 2,000 miles at 12 knots).

FROM WEATHER WINDOW: NO REAL CHANGE IN THE PATTERN NEAR YOU. DOMINANT LARGE-SCALE WEATHER FEATURE IS STILL THE MASSIVE HI PRESS RID NR 40S 110W, THAT IS SPREADING A RDG LOBE NWRD TO MARQUESAS. FORECAST WIND EVOLUTION (AS YOU TRACK NORTH) REMAINS AS FORECAST IN LAST MESSAGE. CONTINUE TO RECOMMEND A MORE NORTHWARD, VS NORTHEASTWARD, INITIAL ROUTE.

This is the first indication we've had that conditions are ripe for a hurricane to brew up.

SOME SUGGESTION OF TROPICAL CYCLONE GENESIS OCCURRING NEAR 15N 100W (SOME ADDITIONAL, SMALLER, AREAS TO THE WEST), BUT ITS STILL TOO EARLY TO RECOMMEND THAT YOU ADJUST TRACK. REGARDS, GEORGE

To Weather Window: If the TD matures it has to move 2100NM to intercept us-if it goes WNW at 250/day thats about 8days-At normal speed We'll probably be 20N/140W in 7/8 days-so if things go this way we'd

have to slow down and wait-also, we don't
want to deal with headwinds if it is E of
our position! Much rather have following
winds to E of center! My feeling is to
push fast to 6/7N-watch and if need be,
heave too for a few days.Does this make
sense to you? What we don't want is to
have this CHASING us from behind.Steve

FROM WEATHER WINDOW:YR PLAN SOUNDS
FINE.CYCLONE NOW NAMED: TROPICAL STORM
LINDA. STILL EARLY FOR FORECAST TRACK.
ONE MODEL SAYS NW, ONE SAYS WNW. PLENTY
OF TIME TO PLAN FOR HER. LATEST DATA
SHOWS 10N AS LAT FOR FIRST NE TRADES,
WITH ACTIVE TSTMS 15SEP ON ITCZ 10-15N,
120-135W, BUT MIN ACTIVITY ON 140W.
REGARDS, LEE

One of the advantages of working with a router is the resources they have at their command—like alternate computer models.

Night falls and Linda goes to the freezer for the first of her pre-prepared dinners. Into the microwave goes the stuffed cabbage, while she makes a fresh salad. Sitting in the pilothouse, listening to the BBC on shortwave, we eat slowly, savoring the dinner and the comfortable reaching conditions. We both know that before long we'll be punching our way uphill against the Northeast Trades. Hot apple pie provides the *denouement*.

It is my turn to clean up the galley while Linda keeps watch. She has the first trick tonight; we'll start out with three hours on and three hours off. Our routine is to keep the radar going at night while we step out of the pilothouse every ten to 15 minutes to visually check the horizon for traffic.

I go forward to take a shower and slip into my nightshirt. My preferred bunk at sea is the leeward pilothouse seat, where I am close if Linda needs me.

Midnight: The aroma of hot chocolate mingles with the pleasure of a soft backrub. "Your watch, dear," Linda whispers in my ear. Weather conditions come hazily into focus as I fumble with my glasses. The wind is starting to veer more into the southeast.

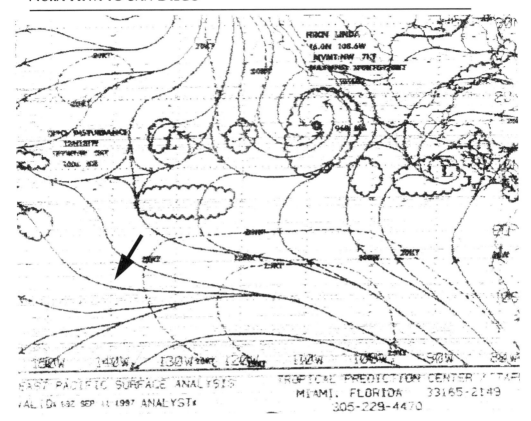

This is a typical fax chart when reception conditions are less than ideal. You can see Hurricane Linda starting to mature off the coast of Mexico, and directly to our north is a disturbed area which we'll have to watch carefully. Our position is noted by the heavy arrow just to the east of the 140 degree longitude line.

HURRICANE LINDA

Linda slides off below to prepare herself for sleep while I check the log, look at the latest weather fax charts, and see if any e-mail has been received Satcom C modem. A message from Bob Rice at Weather Window gets my immediate attention.

FROM WEATHER WINDOW: WIND DROPS SOON. SSE 10KTS AT EQ. 5KT BY 5N LAT. LINDA STRENGTHENING. NOW CAT 3 HURRICANE. POS 11/15Z: 16N 108.5W, 100KTGUST120. FCST 13/12Z: 19.5N 114.5W, 110KTGUST135. FCST

14/12Z: 21.5N 118.5W, 110KTGUST135. PSBL
MORE WNW TRACK AFT 48HRS; WILL MONITOR.
SECOND AREA OF CONCERN: DISTURBED AREA
THAT MAY BECOME OFFICIAL TROPICAL
DEPRESSION W/IN 24HRS: 15N 131W, WITH
MAIN THUNDERSTORM CLUSTER 100NM RADIUS
FROM CENTER. BEST REGARDS. LEE

This disturbed area would be visible on satellite photos—if we were receiving them. However, band conditions have been poor and the satellite fax images unreadable.

The hurricane is too far to the east to affect us for at least a week, but that area at 15 degrees N will bear watching.

Without the capability of maintaining fast daily averages that *Beowulf* provides we would not be attempting this passage. Instead, we'd wait till November, reducing the hurricane threat. However, with the ability to average 280 or more miles a day, we have the speed to stay out of harm's way, with the potential of using the odd tropical storm to our advantage. With plenty of sea room in all directions we can always run from bad weather should it become necessary.

Morning brings with it a glorious sunrise, showing us lengthening swells and 20 knots of breeze veered to the quarter. We could easily carry more sail, but with 329 miles on the log in the first 24 hours, we figure why bother.

The sun is almost directly overhead at local apparent noon and it is getting warmer, although with our three sailing awnings and 14 dorade vents, we are quite comfortable. However, the real secret is taking refreshing showers during the afternoon. We run our DC genset for an hour each day when passaging (half of this when we're at anchor), making upwards of 50 gallons (200 liters) of fresh water in the process. This is hard to get used to when you consider that we and our two children used to think we were living high using a tenth of this.

Day two ends with 300 miles on the log, and we have an interesting message from Weather Window.

One of the options we've discussed is heading for Hawaii, if hurricane and or tradewind conditions are really unfavorable. The negative is that this is quite far out of our way to the east.

This plan, keeping on the 140 degrees W longitude line, leaves us at risk from the TD (tropical disturbance) immediately to the west.

Even with professional weather routers it pays to question their suggestions—in fact, the ability to kick things back and forth is one of the biggest advantages to using them. In this case, we do not want to have the TD to our immediate west.

FROM WEATHER WINDOW: YOU HAVE DISTINCTION OF SAILING IN SAME OCEAN WITH STRONGEST EAST PACIFIC HURR ON RECORD. LINDA NOW CAT 5 WITH SUST WINDS 160KT, GUSTS TO 190KT. GOOD NEWS IS LIKELY TRACK IS NW AND WEAKENING OVER COOLER WATER (BUT STILL WARM ENUF FOR CONT HURR STATUS). CURR POS: 12/09Z, 17.5N 110.1W. FCST 15/06Z: 25N 119W, 85KTGUST105. SOME CHANCE FOR WNW TRACK, WHICH WOULD MAINTAIN STRENGTH. BUT UPPER-LEVEL TROF SHUD TURN HER ALONG FCST TRACK. SECOND AREA OF PSBL TROPICAL CYCLONE NEARLY STATIONARY AT 130W AND SMALL. LONG PERIOD SWELLS TO 8-10FT BY 10N W/O HURR INFLUENCE. BEST PLAN SEEMS TO BE CONT ON 140W, WHICH KEEPS YOU CLOSE ENUF TO HI FOR DIVERT. ALSO, SOME DRIFT WEST OF 140W MAY BE NECESSARY NORTH OF 12N IN 20+KT WIND FROM NNE (030), SO CRACKING OFF FOR HAWAII RELATIVELY EASY MOVE AFT 15N. BUT SHUD NOT BE RQRD IF LINDA MOVES NW. LINDA SOUTH RECURVE NOT LIKELY. BEST REGARDS, LEE

To Weather Window: I am not getting the feedback from WW I need-have all the usual data (fax/Email) and can read the synoptic charts, so I don't really need a re-hash of this data from you.What I need most is current answers to my questions, so I can make timely decisions for fastest/safest passage.Right now I have a question about sailing N on 139/140-I have several concerns-first, the wind angle is then very deep and slow (wind mostly SSE now).Second,if we end up on W side of TD at 15N/133W we have very poor wind angle (N to NNE) and the rsk of the TD rolling over us since we are in its path.Is it not better right now to head so we come in E of TD in an assumed position for it in 4 to 5days?This way we have lighter winds with more favorable angle.We will average at 250/day without difficulty motorsailing-if you concur a

waypoint to head towards is needed-
Finally, since we have the ability to
motorsail from here all the way to CA
(lots of fuel aboard) and would rather
have light winds (or none) than fight a
NNE angle, does it make any sense to work
to the E when wind permits perhaps up
UNDER Linda assuming trades will be
lighter or non-existent in her wake? This
assumes nothing to the E to cause us
problems-it will take us about 6 days to
get from here to 25N-aside from TD and
Linda, does it look clear in this period
to the E?-Does this make any sense? Or
are we better heading N on this more E
track? RIght now we can make efficient
Easting so a quick response is
needed.Steve

This is the first point
at which we began to
think about our ulti-
mate scenario—
sailing under Hurri-
cane Linda and using
her to block the
trades.

FROM WEATHER WINDOW: RECEIVED YOUR LAST
MESSAGE WITH QUESTIONS...HOPE THIS GETS
THROUGH TO YOU.... FIRST. FOLLOWING IS
INFO ON NEW TD 15-E: CURRENT LOCATION:
14.3N- 133.7W - 30 KT MAX WINDS; FORECAST
POSITIONS: 13/1200Z 14.4N-134.5W 30 KTS;
14/00Z 14.4N-135.7W 35 KTS; 14/1200Z
14.4N-137.4W 35 KTS; 15/00Z 14.4N-
139.1W-139.1W 50 KTS; 16/00Z 14.5N
142.5W 50 KTS. LINDA IS SLIDING NORTH-
WESTWARD ALONG BAJA COAST AND WILL NOT BE
A NEGATIVE FACTOR FOR YOU. YOU SHOULD NOW
BE NORTH OF EQUATOR, AND BEGINNING TO
FEEL LIGHT SOUTHERLIES AS INFLUENCED BY
TD 15-E. GIVEN PROJECTED TD TRACK, A WAY-
POINT OF 15N 133W MAY BE A LITTLE TOO FAR
WEST...THUS, SUGGEST ALTERNATE WAYPOINT
OF 10N 129W. IF TD MOVES OUT FASTER THAN
EXPECTED, YOU MAY BE ABLE TO ADJUST A
LITTLE FARTHER TO THE WEST (RADIUS OF
GALE FORCE WINDS IS ESTIMATED AT LESS
THAN 100 NM). FROM THAT POINT, AS YOU
SUGGESTED, LINDA SHOULD BEAT DOWN THE
TRADES FOR AT LEAST A FEW DAYS, AND YOU
MAY BE ABLE TO GET SOME LIGHTER WINDS BY
ATTEMPTING TO WORK UP UNDER LINDA, I.E.,
AFTER 10N-129W, HEAD TOWARDS 20N-120W.
LINDA MAY MOVE INTO SOUTHERN CALIFORNIA

Weather Window is
confirming our
strategy. The light
southerlies we were
to feel at this point
failed to materialize
and we continued to
have favorable sail-
ing conditions.

At this stage nei-
ther of us had any
idea that we'd be
able to use more
than a day of favor-
able conditions from
the backside of 15E.

BY EARLY NEXT WEEK, SO A RETURN TO NORTH-
EASTERLIES IS LIKELY BY MID-WEEK. AT THIS
POINT, HOWEVER, PRIMARY CONCERN IS TO GET
AROUND TD 15-E. NORTHEASTERLIES WILL
BUILD BACK IN EVENTUALLY, PRIOR TO YOUR
ARRIVAL IN LA ANYWAY, SO BEST BET MIGHT
BE TO JUST TAKE ADVANTAGE OF THE WIND
DECREASE DO TO LINDA, FOR AS LONG AS POS-
SIBLE, THEN ADJUST COURSE AS NECESSARY AT
MID-WEEK. WITH RESPECT TO ADDITIONAL
TD'S.BEST,GEORGE

DEPRESSION 15E

Of immediate interest to us is the tropical depression to the northeast now called 15E. If we can get

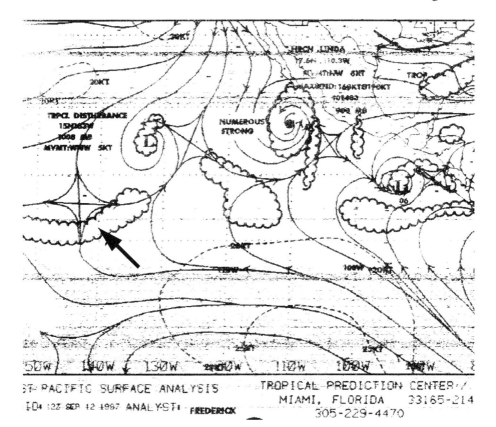

*We are nearing the equator now and the tropical disturbance
to the north-northeast is going to have a big influence on our
plans. Hurricane Linda is still well to the northeast, and too
far away to impact what we are doing—for now.*

around to the east of the center the Northeast Trades will be blocked and we will have southwesterly-quadrant winds. We are going to play this by ear, and can always heave-to waiting for it to pass. But with the prospect of fair winds instead of a beat, if we can get to the right place at the right time, we dig out the asymmetric spinnaker.

Nothing better illustrates the progress in cruising yacht design than this sail. It is tacked off an articulating bowsprit, so at deep sailing angles we can move the luff six feet (1.8 meters) to weather. It keeps us moving at 300 miles a day in Force 4 to 5 winds. The two of us can jibe main and mizzen spinnakers in less than seven minutes. With true wind angles around 150 degrees, apparent wind is just aft of the beam. This steadies the boat down so tradewind roll is nonexistent, and air flow is enhanced with hatches and vents working much more effectively.

All of this transpires with the WH Autopilot driving. This fast-acting and reliable piece of machinery is coupled to a large, balanced rudder. Our hull lifts its bow at any sort of speed, so that steering loads at deep sailing angles are very light. At rest, *Beowulf's* bow is immersed nine inches (225mm), softening her ride upwind—but at speed it is not unusual to have the speedo, which is located 12 feet (4 meters) aft of the bow, clear of the water. This combination has proven itself in Force 10 conditions, with boat speed averaging 20 knots. We have never found it necessary to hand-steer.

The breeze has dropped to 11 knots, so we set the mizzen jib, and begin to pay closer attention to trim and sailing angles. Speed is down to ten knots, and we are pushing to eke out a 240-mile run. Now that we are getting close to the ITCZ, squall activity is picking up. We track these at night on radar. When we see a big one, we drop the forward spinnaker.

To Weather Window: Do you agree with latest NOAA Frcst.on TD 15E (12z/14-14.4N-137.4W)?Where do you expect it to be in four days (17th)?We've been forced to sail 030T by wind from 160/170T-10/12kts-so we are somewhat E (just E of 138).We assuming once in trades to close reach as fast as possible N.It will take til 18/19 to get to 25N-are there any NEW potential problems in that time period that you foresee? Do you agree to go behind TD? Suggested way point? Re Linda, where do you expect her to be on 18th?It would be helpful if I can ask questions after your report and get immediate reply-how do we arrange this? Steve

FROM WEATHER WINDOW: IN ANSWER TO QUESTION: 1. YES, I AGREE WITH LATEST FORECAST FOR TD 15-E. 2. I EXPECT TD 15-E TO BE SOMEWHERE NEAR 14.2N 142.0W 40 KTS. 3. NO NEW TROPICAL CYCLONES ON THE HORIZON, HOWEVER, AS INDICATED IN PREVIOUS MESSAGE, A CLUSTER OF THUNDERSTORMS CAN REACH TS STRENGTH IN 3 DAYS. 4. STILL RECOMMEND WAYPOINTS INDICATED IN MESSAGE SENT A FEW HOURS AGO. 5. LINDA COULD BE OVER ARIZONA BY 18 SEP. 6. OUR HOURS OF OPERATION ARE 0400 TO 1600 EDT DAILY. WE CAN ONLY AFFORD TIME TO CHECK EMAIL EVERY 2 TO THREE HOURS, DEPENDING ON THE WORK LOAD. BEST, GEORGE

Because it is hard to tell the quality of the broadcast weather forecasts (both voice and fax charts) we like to get a quality check from the routers.

In this case, they are confirming what the NOAA meteorologists are saying.

Day three finds us motoring at 11 knots in overcast, drizzly conditions. We are in the ITCZ and the weather has cooled down. We are reading, munching, listening to story tapes, and catching up with the news on the BBC and VOA. *Beowulf* has just passed her 15,000th mile since launching and we feel a party is in order. Pizza and chocolate-chip cookies sound just right.

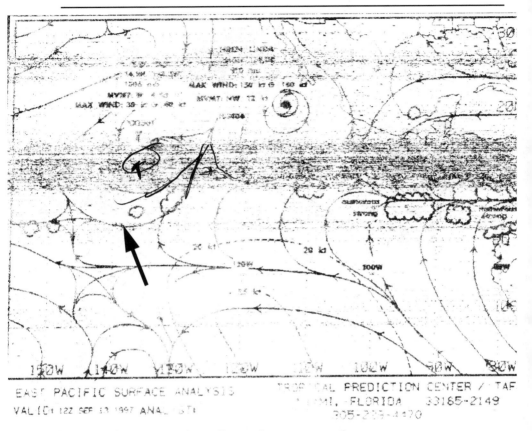

EAST PACIFIC SURFACE ANALYSIS
VALID: 12Z SEP 13 1997 ANAL &T:

TROPICAL PREDICTION CENTER / TAF
MI, FLORIDA   33165-2149
305-229-4470

Reception conditions are still poor, but we can make out enough on this chart to get a feel for the placement of the weather systems. We are closing with the disturbed area to our north, which has been moving slowly to the west for the last couple of days.

TROPICAL STORM MARTY

Sunday, day four, is not a day of rest. Off with the motor and up with the spinnakers. Then back on with the motor. We want to maintain a fast average, but not burn too much diesel fuel this early in the game. Depression 15E has become a tropical storm Marty and it is slightly to the west of our track, which is now headed northeast. Hurricane Linda is moving up the Baja California coast. The two systems have established a circulation pattern between them, and we want to ride the southwesterly winds

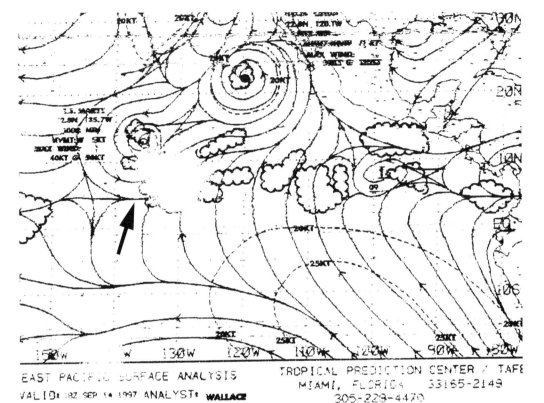

EAST PACIFIC SURFACE ANALYSIS
TROPICAL PREDICTION CENTER / TAFB
MIAMI, FLORIDA   33165-2149
305-229-4470
VALID: 18Z SEP 14 1997 ANALYST: WALLACE

September 14, our fourth day at sea and a very unusual and beneficial weather pattern has established itself. There is a coupling of circulation between the two depressions—Linda to the east and Marty to our north. And we are riding the southwesterly flow on the south side, right towards San Diego.

as long as possible. Right now we are sailing directly towards San Diego on port tack.

There are two questions: What will Hurricane Linda do, and when will the Pacific High return and force us to beat?

To Weather Window: Local winds past 18 hrs SSW6/14-isolated TShwrs-100% Ocast-looks like ITCZ-Have no data here on steering currents for Linda-is it jet stream/and or is she still headed inland before we get into that part of the world? Anything new cooking to the E? We've got 20kts from WSW-adjusting course to 030T whle this lasts-may take us few degrees west of 10/129-sky is clearing-bar.averaging 1005 with normal diurnal shift-do you see any problems with this for now? What are the risk factors now in Linda? We are concerned with two possibilities:1)that she will become stationary, or slow down her WNW movement;2)that she could recurve in a S direction. What are the probabilities of either happening? Until we are well past risk of Linda would like to get two updates/day from you-how about one in AM first thing and second at end of day-unless you feel you need to contact us sooner.Steve

In the absence of upper-level steering data for Hurricane Linda, we are nervous about the projected track to the northeast. Ninety percent of East Pacific storms head northwest, and if Linda goes in this direction, we want as much advance warning as possible.

From Weather Window: WITH RESPECT TO THE CHOICE OF WAYPOINT OF 10N-129W....DONT SEE MUCH CHANCE OF TD RECURVING BACK TO THE EAST, BUT THERE IS ALWAYS THE CHANCE FOR IT SLOWING DOWN OR STALLING....WE LIKE TO RECOMMEND THAT ANY TROPICAL CYCLONE BE GIVEN A WIDE BERTH. IN ADDITION, STRONG RAIN BANDS, WITH LOCALLY HIGH WINDS/SEAS AND HEAVY PRECIP CAN EXTEND MANY HUNDREDS OF MILES FROM THE RELATIVELY COMPACT CENTER. THUS, WE WOULD WANT TO KEEP YOU OUT OF THAT STUFF ALSO. FINALLY, GETTING SOME EASTING IN WOULD BE ADVANTAGEOUS, SINCE THE GOOD WINDS ASSOCIATED WITH LINDA WILL BE RETREATING TO THE EAST, AND THE NORTH-EASTERLIES, WHEN THEY EVENTUALLY RETURN, WILL BE MOVING IN FROM THE WEST. BEST, GEORGE

To Weather Window: We are currently at 08.5N/132.5W-heading between 025/040T-this is best wind angle for sailing or motorsailing, but takes us N of your suggested way point-how about if we hang onto this for the day and then as we get

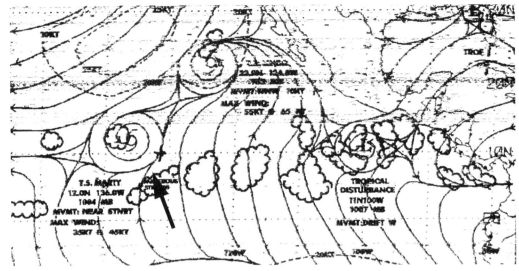

You can tell from the cloud symbols that we are almost through the ITCZ. We now have Marty to our north-northwest, a much more comfortable location. Note the new tropical disturbance directly to the east, off central America. This is not currently a threat, but if it matures, and then accelerates up the coast, it could be a problem for us.

Linda and I are starting to see the possibility of a very fast trip. Between the fax chart (above) and onboard conditions, it now looks like we can use the flow under Hurricane Linda for a much larger bit of the passage than we previously thought possible.

The Weather Window reply indicates they feel that we may get away with our optimum scenario.

to 10/11N go E if required? With Linda weakening and potential problems to E (and I assume a N wind component of trades flowing into new TS) are we better to head N as soon as Linda's center is safely to our W? Lets stay with twice daily reports until we are more comfortable with situation-Steve

FROM WEATHER WINDOW: MARTY IS NEAR 12N 136W AT 35 KTS AND WEAKENING....HE'S BEING SHEARED APART BY THE LOW-LEVEL FLOW FROM THE NE (ON SOUTH SIDE OF RIDGE) AND UPR-LEVEL SW'RLIES. HE'S EXPECTED TO REMAIN NEARLY -STATIONARY OVER NEXT SEVERAL DAYS AND JUST SPIN DOWN...HE MAY BE BELOW TS STRENGTH ALREADY. THE STRONG WINDS YOU'RE EXPERIENCING ARE THE RESULT OF YOUR PROXIMITY TO THE SOUTHERN EXTENSION OF HIS BROAD CIRCULATION PATTERN. SIMILAR FATE FOR LINDA. SHE'S NEAR 22.9 122.8W, AND HAS LOST MOST OF HER STRONG THUNDERSTORMS.STEADY WEAKENING EXPECTED

TO CONTINUE, AND SHE IS FORECAST TO BE NEAR 25N 131W BY THE 18TH. REASONABLY FAIR POTENTIAL FOR HER TO BECOME STATION- ARY OR MOVE SLIGHTLY SOUTHWARD. A SOUTH- WARD MOVEMENT WOULD BE A GOOD SIGN, HOWEVER, SINCE IT WOULD BE THE RESULT OF HER BEING SHEARED APART, WITH A RAPIDLY WEAKENING LOW-LEVEL CENTER BECOMING DETACHED FROM UPPER-LEVEL CENTER. A TS DOES NOT LAST TOO LONG AFTER THIS BEGINS TO HAPPEN. STILL REASONABLY GOOD POTEN- TIAL FOR SOMETHING TO SPIN-UP TO THE SOUTH OF THE GULF OF TPECK-IT'S THE RIGHT TIME OF YEAR AND THE TROPICS SHOULD NOT WAIT TOO LONG TO FILL THE GAP LEFT BY MARTY AND LINDA. INDEED, A FLAIR-UP IN THUNDERSTORM ACTIVITY HAS ALREADY OCCURRED ALONG A LINE FROM ABOUT 5N 130W TO 10N 110W TO 9N 100W. REALISTICALLY, THE NEXT TROPICAL LOW WILL MOST LIKELY DEVELOP WITH 24 TO 48 HOURS ALMOST ANY- WHERE ALONG THIS LINE, WITH MOST PROBABLE LOCATION (I.E., VERY GOOD POTENTIAL AT THIS POINT) BEING NEAR 10N 100W, WITH OTHER POTENTIAL GENERATION AREAS BEING 11N 115W AND (TO A LESSER EXTENT) 7N 125W. AS A ROUGH ESTIMATE, ASSUME THAT THE TYPICAL TS IN THE EAST PAC WOULD WANT MOVE ABOUT 280 DEG AT 10-12 KTS. YOU SHOULD NOT THINK OF EITHER MARTY OR LINDA AS A PRIMARY THREAT RIGHT NOW....IT'S WHAT'S COMING UP IN THE NEXT DAY OR TWO THAT NEEDS TO BE MONITORED. UNFORTU- NATELY, YOU'RE NOW TRACKING ACROSS THE HEART OF THE SECOND MOST ACTIVE TROPICAL CYCLONE REGION IN THE WORLD, AND AT THE HEIGHT OF THE SEASON. BEST BET IN THE NEAR-TERM IS TO HEAD TOWARDS A WAYPOINT OF, SAY, 11N 120W, BOTH TO USE THE FAVOR- ABLE FLOW AROUND THE MARTY-LINDA COUPLET AS LONG AS POSSIBLE, AND GAIN AS MUCH LAT AS POSSIBLE, WITHOUT GETTING TOO CLOSE TO THE CENTER OF THESE DISSIPATING SYSTEMS OR THE NEW POTENTIAL ONES. ONCE NEAR 120W, OR MAYBE BEFORE IF THE CURRENT CYCLONES TOTALLY FALL APART, YOU CAN THEN HEAD STRAIGHT NORTH, TO GET OUT OF THE

This "early warning" about thunder- storm activity is exactly the kind of thing that makes a shore-based router so valuable for an out-of-season pas- sage like this.

Note the threat warning here. This a realistic assess- ment of the situa- tion. We would not be in this part of the world at this time of year without the ability to maintain a 280-mile-a-day clip under sail or power, regardless of wind and sea state.

TROPICS AS QUICKLY AS POSSIBLE. THIS ROUTE IS A MATTER OF THREADING THE NEEDLE BETWEEN THE KNOWN CYCLONES AND THE UNKNOWN (BUT EXPECTED) CYCLONE(S). THIS ISN'T THE MOST COMFORTABLE SITUATION, BUT YOU'LL JUST HAVE TO WAIT UNTIL THE NEXT CYCLONE SHOWS ITSELF BEFORE WE CAN RECOMMEND JUST HOW TO PLAY IT.   WE CAN PROVIDE TWICE DAILY UPDATES (AM AND AFTERNOON) FROM NOW ON. SUGGEST YOU UPDATE US ON YOUR POSITION TWICE DAILY. BEST, GEORGE

To Weather Window: Wind down 215T/7-12kts-BAR maybe up 1mb, sky clearing to N, light squall activity. Would like to use as much of Linda's circulation as possible to work our way N before she dies out and is replaced by NE trades.We are now averaging 10kts against current-how about sailing due N for a while until we feel the W flow (or NW) and the turning under the bottom to E if required? 35/45kts of wind is not a big deal for us as long as we are not beating into it-and are not being sucked into the eye.Steve

FROM WEATHER WINDOW: BEING NORTH OF SUGGESTED WAYPOINT IS OK, SINCE BIGGEST THREAT AT THIS POINT IS WHAT MAY BE BREWING TO EAST, IT WILL BE IMPORTANT TO GET OUT OF TROPICS AS QUICKLY AS POSSIBLE, WITHOUT GETTING TOO TO CLOSE TO WHAT'S LEFT OF MARTY/LINDA. IF TREND CONTINUES AND MARTY/LINDA ARE REALLY DROPPING OFF IN INTENSITY, WE MAY SUGGEST PUTTING EVEN MORE NORTH IN YOUR COURSE. WILL BEGIN TWICE DAILY UPDATES. BEST REGARDS, GEORGE

The course of action proposed here, heading north to get closer to the remnants of Linda, is designed to keep us within her favorable wind pattern as long as possible. When we talk about waiting until we feel the west or northwest flow, we are assuming that we are headed almost right for the center of the low pressure system.

Weather Window answers in the affirmative.

We reel off 252 miles on day four and then 256 miles on day five. Not much to brag about except for the fact that we are headed in *exactly* the right direction. We pass the halfway point, always a cause for celebration. In light of our progress the crew votes for an apple pie dessert.

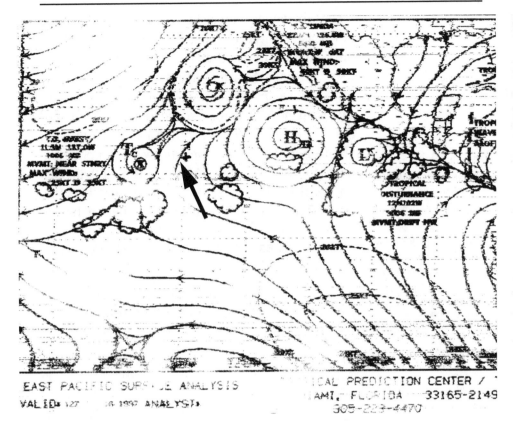

EAST PACIFIC SURFACE ANALYSIS
VALID: 12Z   6 1997 ANALYST

TROPICAL PREDICTION CENTER /
MIAMI, FLORIDA   33165-2149
305-223-4470

Day six comes with a bit of a shock on the fax machine. That high located between Linda and the developing hurricane should not be there. We have never seen anything like this before and it makes us very nervous. Even though the pressure of the high is pretty low, it still gives us cause for alarm. Twelve hours later (below) and the high has disappeared. In reality this is worse looking than it really is—and our alarm was needless.

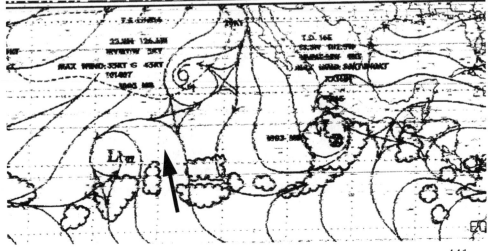

Day six dawns with a short period swell from the northeast, right on the nose. Is this coming from the hurricane or the Pacific High trying to reestablish itself? Tropical Storm Marty is now to our west and moving away poses no threat. Hurricane Linda continues up the Mexican coast and looks likely to head out over cooler water rather than ashore in Southern California. We are watching a new area of potential development off Central America. Rather than push on, we slow down a bit to get a better handle on the weather. Day six ends with just 235 miles on the log.

We are now at a critical juncture in the passage. There is the strong possibility of using what is left of Linda to our advantage. However, this is about as far north as we can go and still turn around and escape to the ITCZ if anything comes at us from the east.

Beyond this point, we'll have to race any new threats to the cooler waters north of us.

Our main focus in the questions to Weather Window is our approach to the North Pacific High, so as to minimize expected headwinds and have the most favorable angle.

FROM WEATHER WINDOW: TS LINDA WKNG AND SLOWING DOWN. FCST 17/18Z: 23.5N 130.5W, 30KTG40KT. MARTY STNRY AND WKNG. NEXT LIKELY TS DVLPMNT AT 10N, S OF ACAPULCO. SO GAP AVAILBL FOR YOU. BY WKND, 10-15KT N WINDS IN PLACE FROM 27-40N, 125W-135W, WITH LEAST BEAT WEST OF 125W. BUT IN BTWN, PERIOD OF LIGHT AIR INDICATED WED/ THU. FOR NOW, N IS BEST, ADJUSTNG FOR SEAS AND WIND, AND GIVING LINDA SOME SPACE. SUGGEST PLAN WPS OF 20N 128W, THEN 30N 130W, THEN DIAL IN LA IF N WINDS STILL IN FCST. BEST REGARDS, LEE

To Weather Window: Last 8hrs to now S.wind-5/7-Bar/1005-Iso squalls with lite rain-aside from Linda & anything new, main concern now is what is going to happen with SE corner of high and how to approach coast.If wide spacing/lite winds towards coast and/or of Baja and no TD's is it better to head that way (i.e. E)?If the corner is going to push down and the isobars flatten, then we may be better heading N and approach through the center-we have 1400NM to go direct-probably more like 17/1800 by the time we allow for some tacking-this is probably 7/8 days-Steve

FROM WEATHER WINDOW: WITH LINDA AND MARTY WEAKNG AND TD16E STRENGTHENING SOUTH-EAST OF BAJA, I'M UNCOMFORTABLE WITH A ROUTE THAT HAS MUCH EAST IN IT. TROP CYCLONE RISK TOO HIGH ON E OR NE COURSE, FOR NOW. CONTG NNE AS LONG AS WIND IS NOT A TOUGH BEAT WILL HELP GET YOU OUT OF THE RISK AREA AND SET UP FOR EVENTUAL NE WIND. SOME WESTING NEEDED STARTG ARND 20N, WHEN STRONGER NE WINDS FILL IN, BUT A TURN TOWARD LA SHUD BE PSBL AT 30N (AXIS OF THE HIGH PRESSURE RIDGE). SEAS PRBLY STILL 8-10FT IN THE NE WINDS, BUT DOWN FROM 12-14FT NOW IN THAT AREA. REC-OMMEND ROUGH WPS OF 20N 127W OR UNTIL NE WIND/SEA IS TOO STRONG, THEN TO STARBOARD IN THE NE WIND UNTIL SHIFT TO NNW (ABOUT 30N). LA DIRECT THEREAFTER. MORE EAST IN ROUTE MAY BE PSBL AS WE GET FEEL FOR MOVMNT OF TD16E AND SEE DVLPMNT OF NES, SO I'LL LOOK AT AGAIN TOMORROW. BEST REGARDS, LEE

The strategy suggested vis-a-vis the high assumes a classical circulation scenario.

To Weather Window: We want to use Linda's winds if possible-now have W/8-9.But prefer not to have the breeze up our tail-does the rhumb line take us close enough (we want some, but not too many of her leftovers!) All afternoon N wind 5/10.By 2200 sun time backed to NW/5.Bar. cycling around 1004-but diurnal shift very weak. See that Nora is getting act together.What are the steering currents like? I assume will track NW at 10 or so.What are chances for her to accelerate and pull N winds out of hi next 3 to 4 days? We are 3.5 days from 30N if present progress continues.How about the SE corner of the high-will it bulge down behind Linda and create some E/ENE winds? Or do you figure NE? We need to start thinking about fuel management vs. boat speed.Now doing about 230/day over bottom (loosing almost knot to current)-If Nora is not a problem we'd like to sag off to a rhum-

From the data Weather Window has this approach makes sense. But from our perspective there is still some advantage to be gained from Hurricane Linda. The difference in outlook is based on the actual conditions we are finding as opposed to the theoretical data the routers are watching.

The most important data for a router to have is your projected locations as you move down your course in time. In this case we know we can maintain these positions with sail— or power if the winds go light.

This news on Nora is excellent as it means the chance of her intersecting our course is now of low probability.

Once again, Weather Window is suggesting a classical approach to the coast through the Pacific high. We have to see what happens.

bline course which would be a bit faster with current W quadrant wind and shorter.Our positions would be roughly as follows: 18th-19.5/126;19th-23/123;20th-27/122.7;21st-30/120.Last couple of days might have to take the trades on a more N heading if they are blowing.This only works if Nora isn't a problem and we can continue to motorsail 030T if winds are light and/or not closer than 20 degrees to bow.

FROM WEATHER WINDOW: DWNLD'D YR. SCND MSG WHILE PREPRNG TO SEND RSPNS TO FIRST, BUT ANSWER SHD BE HERE. DBTFL THAT YOU CAN MAINTAIN YR SUGGESTED CRS ALL THE TIME DUE TO STRNGTH AND/OR ANGLE OF WIND, BUT OVERALL PLAN SHD BE TO DO IT AS YOU CAN, AND CRACK OFF ON STARBOARD AS NEEDED FOR FUEL SAVINGS. LINDA CONTS WKNG AND MOVG SLWLY W. TROF EXTENDS TO HER SSE, SO YR WIND SHD BACK AS YOU MOVE THRU TROF ON YR CURR HDNG. AS SHE WKNS, NE WINDS FILL IN, BUT PRBLY NOT'TIL FRI FOR YOU. NORA MOVG SLWLY NW AND EXPCTED TO STRNGTHN; STEER-ING NOT WELL-ORGANIZED. COULD STAY ALONG MEX COAST FOR NEXT FEW DAYS OR SLIP NW, TO POSTN W OF S BAJA. EITHER WAY, PAC HI NOT WELL-FORMED, AND N WIND SPREADS WWARD WITH TIME. BY SAT, N WIND (340-020DEG) 15-20KT FM BAJA TO 125W, THEN WKNG TO N 10-15KT BY SUN BUT SPRDNG FM BAJA TO 132W. RECOMMEND HDG AT LA ADJSTD FOR BEST SPEED, THEN TAKE STARBOARD AS WIND BACKS INTO E AND NE QUAD, WITH IDEA OF NORTH-ING'TIL LA LAT, THEN TO PORT FOR BEAM REACH FINISH. PSBL PROBLM WUD BE MORE NE DVLPG, WHICH MAY RQR MOVG A BIT N OF LA LAT TO ENSURE REACH TO LA TO SAVE FUEL. SVRL DAYS DOWN ROAD, BUT WORTH THINKING ABOUT. WITH NORA AND N WINDS IN PLACE TWRD BAJA, LTL ROOM FOR ALTRNT STRATEGY. BEST REGARDS, LEE

NORA MATURES

Nora is now a hurricane and on our latitude 1,000 miles to the east. She is probably not a threat, but we are going to watch her very carefully. Hurricane Linda is dissipating, and while still powerful, has lost much of her punch, with little risk of reforming due to cooler water temperatures. If everything were to go against us (Linda reforms and Nora accelerates) we'd have to reverse course and dive towards the ITCZ. We are hoarding diesel fuel (by cruising this slowly when under power) in case such an occurs.

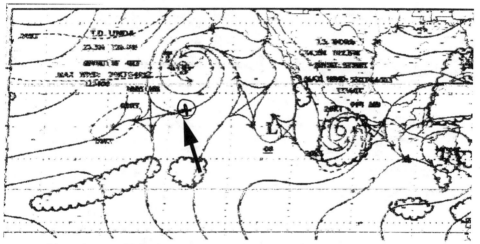

Marty is now off the fax chart to the west while Linda continues to weaken. Nora is still well to the east, and unless something really unusual happens (always a possibility) she poses little threat to us.

The big news is that it is getting cold at night. The northeast swell is gone and we've put 254 miles on the log for day seven.

Clothes are no longer optional. We still have a light west wind from the remnants of Hurricane Linda, now shown as a low pressure cell on the weather fax. There is a large front coming down from Alaska and if we can get north quickly enough to hook onto it we might be able to ride it all the way to the coast.

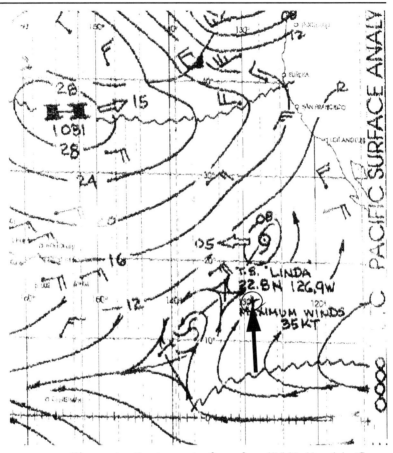

We are starting to receive faxes from KVM in Honolulu. These are helpful in that they show the Pacific High, which we will probably have to play with next. Note that Marty is still shown organized on this fax, while the Tropical Prediction Center has pretty well written it off.

We've just broken through the 1,000 mile to go barrier, and tonight we'll pass the three-quarter mark. So a party is in order. However, we have a major dilemma: We don't know whether to consummate the party with the last two pieces of apple pie, banana cake, or fruit cobbler. After considerable debate, the crew vote for the latter.

We've been fighting adverse currents of 15/24 miles a day, but these have eased up a bit and we've added another 250 miles for our eighth day at sea.

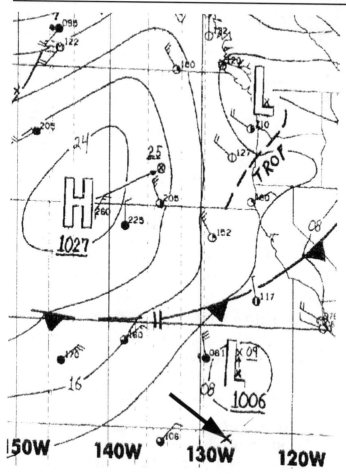

This section of fax chart is from Point Reyes, California. It still has a remnant of Linda shown, which is why we have favorable winds at this point. A key feature on this chart is the front dropping down from the north. This has the potential to bring the wind more to the northwest as we approach the coast.

To Weather Window: Last 12hrs wind 290/ 320T@5/10-Bar.oscillating around 1005-mainly Q's with occasional cirrus-want to take advantage of Linda as long as possible-is rhumbline still best for next few days (current KVM fax shows this taking us right up backside until 25N)?SOG about 220/day against current-should only need daily update from now on unless you see shift in situation which we can use to advantage. Steve

FROM WEATHER WINDOW: NE OR E WIND GRDLY
FILLS IN ALONG RHUMB. LINDA WKNS AND
MOVES W, AND E AND NE WIND MOVES IN
BEHIND, SO NO BENEFIT TO MOVE OFF RHUMB
TO CATCH HER. ON RHUMB, YOU SHD BE HEADED
BY FRI, SO SHD PLAN FOR EVENTUAL STAR-
BOARD TACK. RECOMMEND SAILING FOR BEST
CONDITIONS WITHIN RANGE OF 125-128W,
BECAUSE NEAR 30N YOU MAY BE ABLE TO TAKE
PORT IN A NNW WIND FOR FINISH TO LA. SHD
SEE INCRS IN CLDS SOON, BUT NO SIG WX
WITH THEM. NORA NOW MIN HURR, POS 18/09Z:
14.5N 103.7W 65KTS, FCST NW TO 21/06Z:
19.5N 110.5W AND INCRS TO 100KTS SUS-
TAINED.LEE

September 19, 1900GMT, and we are officially out of the tropics. The deck is cold underfoot, and we are sitting under a blanket during evening watches. The low is still organized to our north and we've had a lovely beam reach with working sails the last few hours. Hurricane Nora is well to the southeast and in no position to threaten.

APPROACHING THE COAST

The major question now is our approach to the coast: Do we get a lift from the cold front headed our way, or do we end up beating? We've set the mizzen jib, and have been thinking about the spinnaker, but the breeze is fitful.

The water-ballast system is getting a workout as we try to optimize our performance. All of this effort has resulted in 259 miles for the ninth day at sea.

The low pressure cell has disappeared from the fax. Normally at this juncture we'd head due north to gain some ground to weather in anticipation of the coming northwest windshift, but with our motoring ability we keep heading northeast, right on the rhumb line.

A decade ago, we would have had to choose between an upwind hull shape and one that was at its best downwind. Upwind was the usual way to go, but this presented steering control problems when pushing hard downwind. The norm was a half-entry angle of between 19 and 26 degrees. But as waterlines have lengthened, and displacement lightened, it has become possible to draw hulls that knife through the seas to windward while providing excellent buoyancy off the wind. *Beowulf* has a half entry angle of under 11 degrees, and right now we are slicing through the waves at 10 1/2 knots with main bladed out, motorsailing at 1,900 RPM.

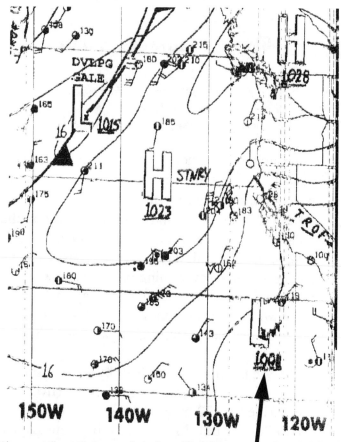

We are still getting some help from Linda's remnants barely to our north. All of the isobars in our area are indicating northeast winds to come, so our sleigh ride may be just about over.

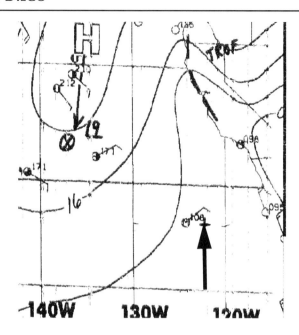

Our tenth day at sea and we are now closing in on the coast. The wind is right on the nose for now, but there's a chance the isobars will bend a bit as they hit the coastal influence, lifting us on the last day or two.

We are losing a knot and a half to current, so we manage just 238 miles and then 225 miles — slow, but comfortable, considering the sea state.

Day 12. San Diego and Point Lama are on the radar. A lovely reach for the past 24 hours has us looking at a 280-mile day. The crew is busy cleaning and polishing so everything is tidy when we clear customs. In spite of the tension of being on the same ocean with *three* hurricanes at once, this has turned out to be our most comfortable passage in the past 23 years.

The San Diego sea buoy slides by our port side 12 days and three hours after leaving Nuka Hiva. Distance sailed: 3,122 miles. Average for the passage, 257 miles per day. Maintenance list: replace one worn clew strap (mainsail) and four sail slides. So ends this voyage.

Beowulf at speed during her sea trials in New Zealand. Her ability to maintain 280 to 300 miles per day was the key to our strategy in this out-of-season passage.

Two interesting views of Linda on September 12, 1997. This is at the point of maximum power for the storm, with sustained winds of 160 knots.

An upper-level trough of low pressure was in the area, and at this point in the storm's life cycle, there was a good chance it would follow that upper-level circulation into Southern California. Now that would have been interesting! However, she didn't "bite" on the trough and continued to the northwest on the normal track for these storms.

HURRICANE NORA

At the same time Linda and I were heading up from the Marquesas, Dennis Choate was sitting aboard his 60-foot (18.4m) *Gitana*, anchored behind Punta Pequenaa on the West Coast of Baja California. Dennis and a couple of cohorts had sailed south looking for surf, and things were definitely looking up in the bay at San Juanico.

SAN JUANICO

Dennis calls the anchorage behind Punta Pequena the most protected spot on Baja's West Coast. With good coverage from north to west, the only exposure is to the south and east. When the hurricanes are pumping to the south, this makes for wonderful surf, if a somewhat rolly anchorage.

Dennis has been building custom yachts for 30 years now. And with almost 400 boats through his shop doors (ranging in size from 20 to 80 feet), you would expect his own vessel to be special.

Gitana is a Dick Carter design from the 1970s, an early ULDB with a displacement of just 44,000 pounds, contained in an aluminum hull.

Gitana at anchor in more peaceful times. (Dennis Choate photo)

Dennis Choate at Gitana's helm.

Over the years she's been modified and re-built by Dennis, and most would consider her an excellent candidate for heading offshore, which is a good thing considering what is about to happen.

Aboard with Dennis are two of the fellows from his shop, Uriel Guererro and Duane Richardson. Both Uriel and Duane were old hands at racing and deliveries, plus boat building.

I'll let Dennis fill you in on the details. "I was looking forward to surfing when I got a call on the single-sideband from Heather Clute. They were tracking Hurricane Nora as it came ashore at Cabo (on the Southern tip of Baja) and she wanted to make sure we knew about the storm.

"There was this little restaurant on the beach, and the guy had a satellite dish so he could get the weather channel. I went ashore to check it out and the track showed that Nora had gone up the Baja coast, nailed La Paz, and was now heading up the coast towards Magdalena Bay.

The anchorage behind Punta Pequena as Hurricane Nora approaches. Good for surfing, but a little tough for getting the dinghy ashore with its occupants dry. This is before any impact from the wind. Imagine what it must have been like as the hurricane drew nearer. (Dennis Choate photo)

"There was a bumpy swell coming in from the South, and the breeze was southerly. By the time I got back out to the boat the wind was blowing 20 knots from the south, so we hurried to get out of there.

It is always better to leave an exposed anchorage early, than wait until it is too late.

HEADING NORTH

"I figured we would run up the coast a ways until it was safe to turn back to do some surfing. Hurricanes almost never come north of Magdalena Bay, and we weren't finished with our trip yet.

"We got out of there early, about 0900. We were broad-reaching up the coast in 20 to 25 knots of breeze, with the wind on the starboard quarter. We had a wonderful sail up to Abreojos, then the breeze quit and it was the hottest and muggiest I have ever seen it in Baja.

"About this time we got another call from Heather telling us the storm was still coming up the coast. We powered in the flat conditions, taking it easy as we didn't want to get too far north so we'd have an easy trip back down to Punta Pequena. We motored all night at about seven knots.

"In Mexico the barometer is usually so steady that it is hard to tell if it is moving at all. We were watching it and nothing much was happening. It was still calm, and the sky was clear. And then suddenly there was this thick, gray overcast. There were no cirrus clouds—just the overcast. We could see these big thunderheads about twenty to thirty miles inland."

"The next day we were off Turtle Bay, still powering along, and we started to see these clouds coming in (see the photo below). We were talking to the Klutes in the morning, getting the latest on the storm track.

"By now we'd stowed all the loose gear from on deck below. About three in the afternoon we were at the point where you have to decide to go inside or outside of Cedros Island. The wind started coming

"In Mexico the barometer is usually so steady that it is hard to tell if it is moving at all. We were watching it and nothing much was happening. It was still calm, and the sky was clear. And then suddenly there was this thick, gray overcast. There were no cirrus clouds—just the overcast."

Twelve hours before the breeze reached storm strength this impressive mass of clouds rolled over Dennis and his crew aboard Gitana. Note how calm the sea was at this point.

Within a few hours large, almost breaking swells had caught up with the boat. (Dennis Choate photo)

in from the northeast, and I decided to go outside so we would have plenty of sea room.

"There were more dolphin and fish around than I have ever seen before. The fishing was phenomenal too. The water was just jumping with marine life as far as I could see. As we cleared the north end of Cedros the breeze came up to twenty knots, still out of the northeast.

"The breeze quit, so we went back to motoring up the back side of Cedros. Then the swells started to arrive from the south. They were huge, at least 25 feet (eight meters), almost breaking, and very close together—the swell period was between three and five seconds. These were not in sets of three or four and then a calm spot, but continuous, swell after swell.

"...the swell period was between three and five seconds. These were not in sets of three or four and then a calm spot, but continuous, swell after swell."

THE BAROMETER PLUMMETS

"The barometer took a sudden dive, dropping maybe 15 to 20 mb in what seemed like a matter of hours. At this point we knew we were in for it so I took the roller-furling jib down and triple reefed the mainsail. Forty miles north of Cedros the wind came back suddenly from the northeast at about 25 knots—we could see it moving across the water towards us. The whitecaps looked like a school of porpoise. We were keeping the wind on the starboard bow, at an apparent wind angle of about 30 degrees, heading offshore.

"At this point we knew we were in for it so I took the roller-furling jib down and triple reefed the mainsail."

"Just about sunset the wind went up suddenly—to 55 to 60 knots—and changed direction more to the north.

"Then the shit really hit the fan. Our wind speed meter pegged out at 60 and it was blowing so hard we could not stand up against the wind. The swells began to come from an easterly direction, and you could almost see them bending from the previous direction.

REACHING ON STARBOARD TACK

"We eased the main off about 30 degrees from center, and kept the apparent wind at 60 to 80 degrees — still on starboard tack. The seas were unbelievable. It was totally white — not patches, but totally white everywhere you looked. The water felt like it was coming from a fire hose or that you were in a breaking wave.

"We kept the boat in a slot between the swells. It was like being in a record groove, and we were able to stay in the trough, sheltered from the full force of the wind. The swells were really strange, almost like standing waves in a river rapids that we were traveling between. We had continuous foam blowing over the starboard side of the boat as we broad-reached. We were able to steer with the Robertson Autopilot, adjusting the course continually to keep the boat in this easy groove she'd found."

When I asked Dennis how hard he thought it was blowing, he hesitated a moment. "I've raced in 60 knots and been in 80 to 85 knots on land. I would say it was blowing at least a steady 80 knots, maybe more."

"As the wind backed we followed it around (counterclockwise), until we were finally heading back towards Cabo, on a southeasterly heading at the end of the storm. There didn't seem to be a problem with cross seas as the wind shifted, probably because the wind was coming pretty much offshore. At night, and in the early morning hours, we could see patches of blue overhead and stars. The clouds were in bands, like a pinwheel. Around 0400 all of a sudden the wind dropped to 40 to 50 knots — this felt like nothing after being in the stronger winds for six or seven hours.

"By mid morning the wind was gone and the sea was almost like glass. The coast guard flew over us and we told them we were OK. The sun was shining, there were no clouds, and no wind — and the sea was like glass."

"The swells were really strange, almost like standing waves in a river rapids that we were traveling between."

"As the wind backed we followed it around (counterclockwise), until we were finally heading back towards Cabo, on a southeasterly heading at the end of the storm."

IN HINDSIGHT

This is a story in which the right decisions were made at the correct time as *Gitana* moved up the coast.

The first and perhaps most critical decision was getting the anchor aboard and heading north, away from the storm center.

Given the track of Nora, it is easy to see that, as Dennis says, "If we had been ten hours later leaving we'd be dead." *Gitana* would have been caught on the dangerous side of Nora's center rather than the safe side with its *relatively* light winds.

The next key decision point was at the bottom of Cedros. Heading offshore took them to the west of the storm's track, and not only gained sea room in which to maneuver, but kept them on the safe side of the storm center.

Had anything gone wrong with *Gitana's* systems—maybe a mechanical problem with the engine, drive line, or steering—she'd have been caught in the full fury of the storm's center. So maintenance—or preparedness—played a key role.

The fact that Dennis and crew stripped the deck and removed the roller-furling jib early paid dividends too. Once the wind came on suddenly, there would have been no way to take down the jib, and if they'd had the extra windage aloft of the roller furled jib during the seven hours of 80-knot winds, the outcome of the story might have been different.

Finally, Dennis's tactic of keeping the wind on his starboard beam and then quarter, kept him moving as fast as possible away from the storm center and, in this case, towards the open sea. Any other course of action would have taken him towards the storm center.

"If we had been ten hours later leaving we'd be dead."

OUTSIDE INFORMATION

Now let's take a look at Nora from the standpoint of the forecast, warning, fax and satellite data that was available on both the Internet and from the high seas radio

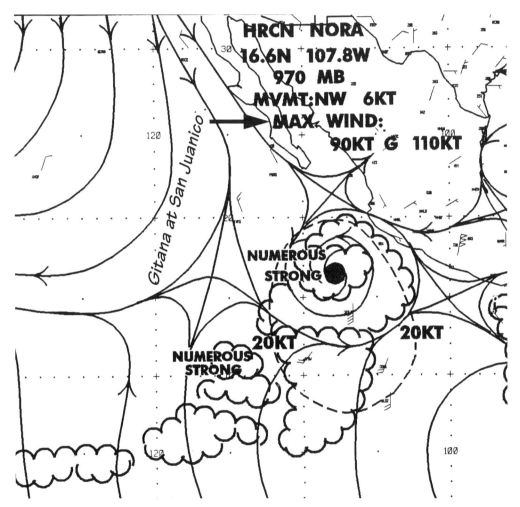

September 21, 1997. Nora is 400 miles southwest of the tip of Baja California (Cabo San Lucas) and heading north. She is a full-fledged hurricane with substantial convective activity around a rather small core.

At this stage she is a threat to the peninsula, but if you were well to the north, where Dennis was anchored, you'd probably feel safe enough.

HURRICANE NORA ADVISORY NUMBER 26
NATIONAL WEATHER SERVICE MIAMI FL 8 PM
PDT **MON SEP 22 1997**
...HURRICANE WATCH ISSUED FOR PORTIONS
OF BAJA CALIFORNIA... A HURRICANE WARN-
ING REMAINS IN EFFECT FOR SOCORRO ISLAND
AND THE NEARBY REVILLAGIGEDO ISLANDS.
THE GOVERNMENT OF MEXICO HAS ISSUED A
TROPICAL STORM WARNING FOR THE BAJA CAL-
IFORNIA PENINSULA SOUTH OF LATITUDE 25N
AND A HURRICANE WATCH FOR THE BAJA CALI-
FORNIA PENINSULA NORTH OF LATITUDE 25N TO
PUNTA EUGENIA. THE GOVERNMENT OF MEXICO
HAS ISSUED A COASTAL FLOOD WARNING FROM
PUNTA ESTRECHO TO MAZATLAN FOR THE WAVES
AND SWELLS GENERATED BY HURRICANE NORA.
AT 8 PM PDT...0300Z...THE LARGE EYE OF
HURRICANE NORA WAS CENTERED NEAR LATI-
TUDE 19.6 NORTH...LONGITUDE 112.5 WEST
OR ABOUT 285 MILES...455 KM...SOUTH-
SOUTHWEST OF THE SOUTHERN TIP OF BAJA
CALIFORNIA. NORA IS MOVING TOWARD THE
NORTHWEST NEAR 8 MPH...13 KM/HR...AND A
GRADUAL TURN TOWARD THE NORTH IS EXPECTED
DURING THE NEXT 12 TO 24 HOURS.
MAXIMUM SUSTAINED WINDS ARE NEAR 115
MPH...185 KM/HR...WITH HIGHER GUSTS.
LITTLE SIGNIFICANT CHANGE IN STRENGTH IS
FORECAST DURING THE NEXT 24 HOURS. HURRI-
CANE FORCE WINDS EXTEND OUTWARD UP TO 85
MILES...140 KM... FROM THE CENTER...AND
TROPICAL STORM FORCE WINDS EXTEND OUT-
WARD UP TO 200 MILES...325 KM. CONDITIONS
OVER SOCORRO ISLAND AND THE NEIGHBORING
ISLANDS SHOULD GRADUALLY IMPROVE
TONIGHT. ESTIMATED MINIMUM CENTRAL PRES-
SURE IS 960 MB...28.35 INCHES. THE OUTER
RAINBANDS OF NORA ARE CURRENTLY MOVING
OVER PORTIONS OF THE SOUTHERN BAJA CALI-
FORNIA PENINSULA...PRODUCING GUSTY WINDS
AND LOCALLY HEAVY RAINS. REPEATING THE 8
PM PDT POSITION...19.6 N...112.5 W.
MOVEMENT TOWARD...NORTHWEST NEAR 8 MPH.
MAXIMUM SUSTAINED WINDS...115 MPH. MINI-
MUM CENTRAL PRESSURE... 960 MB. HURRI-
CANE NORA FORECAST/ADVISORY NUMBER 26
NATIONAL WEATHER SERVICE MIAMI FL

The Tropical Prediction Center has Nora pegged just about right at this time.

Note the change in direction forecast from northwest to north. This will send the storm right up the Baja Peninsula, if it pans out.

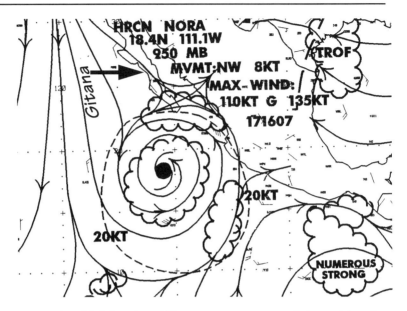

September 22 (above) and Nora is now impacting Cabo and heading north. Based on this fax chart rain bands (and probably swells) have not yet reached Dennis's anchorage.

September 23 (below) and the wind has just reached San Juanico. By this time you would expect the swells to be sending a message, and they were. Note that the cloud cover/rain bands are not as yet shown at San Juanico—this was the latest one could head north to escape the full fury of the storm.

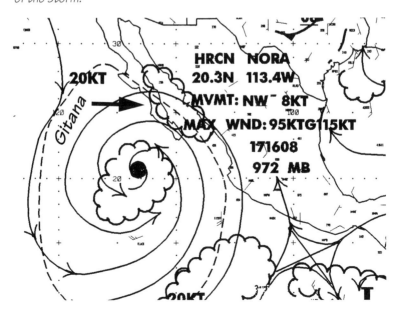

WARNING REMAINS IN EFFECT FOR SOCORRO ISLAND AND THE NEARBY REVILLAGIGEDO ISLANDS. THE GOVERNMENT OF MEXICO HAS ISSUED A TROPICAL STORM WARNING FOR THE BAJA CALIFORNIA PENINSULA SOUTH OF LATI- TUDE 25N AND A HURRICANE WATCH FOR THE BAJA CALIFORNIA PENINSULA NORTH OF LATI- TUDE 25N TO PUNTA EUGENIA. THE GOVERNMENT OF MEXICO HAS ISSUED A COASTAL FLOOD WARNING FROM PUNTA ESTRECHO TO MAZATLAN FOR THE WAVES AND SWELLS GENERATED BY HURRICANE NORA. HURRICANE CENTER LOCATED NEAR 19.6N 112.5W AT 23/0300Z POSITION ACCURATE WITHIN 30 NM PRESENT MOVEMENT TOWARD THE NORTHWEST OR 310 DEGREES AT 7 KT ESTIMATED MINIMUM CENTRAL PRESSURE 960 MB EYE DIAMETER 50 NM MAX SUSTAINED WINDS 100 KT WITH GUSTS TO 120 KT 64 KT....... 75NE 75SE 50SW 50NW 50 KT.......100NE 100SE 75SW 75NW 34 KT.......175NE 175SE 125SW 125NW 12 FT SEAS.400NE 500SE 300SW 350NW ALL QUAD- RANT RADII IN NAUTICAL MILES REPEAT...CENTER LOCATED NEAR 19.6N 112.5W AT 23/0300Z AT 23/0000Z CENTER WAS LOCATED NEAR 19.3N 112.3W FORECAST VALID 23/1200Z 20.5N 113.0W MAX WIND 100 KT...GUSTS 120 KT 64 KT... 75NE 75SE 50SW 50NW 50 KT...100NE 100SE 75SW 75NW 34 KT...175NE 175SE 125SW 125NW FORECAST VALID 24/0000Z 22.0N 113.2W MAX WIND 100 KT...GUSTS 120 KT 64 KT... 75NE 75SE 50SW 50NW 50 KT...100NE 100SE 75SW 75NW 34 KT...175NE 175SE 125SW 125NW FORECAST VALID 24/1200Z 24.0N 113.3W MAX WIND 95 KT...GUSTS 115 KT 64 KT... 75NE 75SE 50SW 50NW 50 KT...100NE 100SE 75SW 75NW 34 KT...175NE 175SE 125SW 125NW REQUEST FOR 3 HOURLY SHIP REPORTS WITHIN 300 MILES OF 19.6N 112.5W EXTENDED OUTLOOK...USE FOR GUIDANCE ONLY...ERRORS MAY BE LARGE OUT-

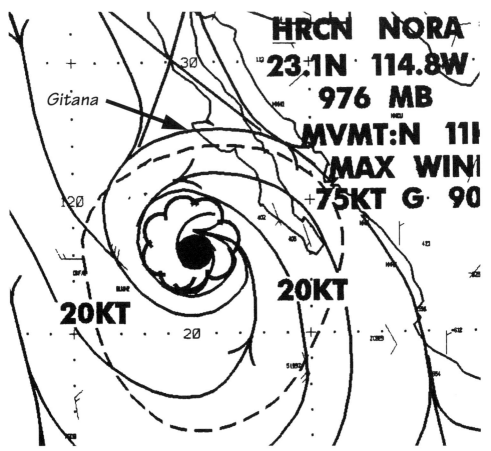

LOOK VALID 25/0000Z 27.0N 113.3W MAX WIND
80 KT...GUSTS 95 KT 50 KT... 75NE 75SE
50SW 50NW OUTLOOK VALID 26/0000Z 33.0N
113.0W...INLAND MAX WIND 45 KT...GUSTS
55 KT NEXT ADVISORY AT 23/0900Z PASCH
HURRICANE NORA ADVISORY NUMBER 35
NATIONAL WEATHER SERVICE MIAMI FL **8 PM**

June 24 and the race is on. This fax is valid for about the time frame when Dennis and his crew are heading towards Turtle Bay, about half-way up the peninsula. The prediction indicates a seven-knot movement for the storm center, the same speed as Gitana is traveling under power. The fax seems to be accurate given this was about the time they started to pick up cloud cover. You will recall that the wind came in initially from the northeast when they were farther north late in the afternoon. This ties with the storm moving towards land while they were moving offshore.

WED SEP 24 1997

...NORA HEADING FOR BAJA CALIFOR-
NIA...AND THE SOUTHWESTERN UNITED
STATES... THE GOVERNMENT OF MEXICO HAS
POSTED THE FOLLOWING WATCHES AND WARN-
INGS... BAJA CALIFORNIA PACIFIC
COAST...HURRICANE WARNING FROM BAHIA
BALLENAS TO PUNTA SANTO TOMAS...AND
TROPICAL STORM WARNING FROM BAHIA BALLE-
NAS SOUTHWARD TO LATITUDE 24N...AND
TROPICAL STORM WATCH FROM PUNTA SANTO
TOMAS NORTHWARD TO TIJUANA. BAJA CALI-
FORNIA GULF OF CALIFORNIA COAST...HURRI-
CANE WARNING NORTHWARD FROM SANTA
ROSALIA...AND TROPICAL STORM WARNING
SOUTHWARD OF SANTA ROSALIA TO LATITUDE
24N. NORTHWESTERN MAINLAND MEXICO GULF
OF CALIFORNIA COAST...TROPICAL STORM
WARNING AND A HURRICANE WATCH NORTHWARD
FROM BAHIA KINO. THE COASTAL FLOOD WARN-
ING FROM PUNTA ESTRECHO TO MAZATLAN HAS
BEEN DISCONTINUED. AT 8 PM
PDT...0300Z...THE CENTER OF HURRICANE
NORA WAS LOCATED NEAR LATITUDE 26.5
NORTH...LONGITUDE 114.8 WEST OR ABOUT 90
MILES...140 KM...SOUTH OF PUNTA EUGENIA
ON THE WEST COAST OF BAJA CALIFORNIA.
NORA IS MOVING TOWARD THE NORTH NEAR 17
MPH...28 KM/HR...AND THIS GENERAL MOTION
IS EXPECTED TO CONTINUE INTO THURSDAY. ON
THIS TRACK THE CENTER OF NORA IS EXPECTED
TO MAKE LANDFALL OVER THE NORTHERN BAJA
CALIFORNIA PENINSULA WITHIN THE NEXT 12
HOURS. PREPARATIONS IN THE HURRICANE
WARNING AREA SHOULD BE RUSHED TO COMPLE-
TION. MAXIMUM SUSTAINED WINDS ARE NEAR 85
MPH...140 KM/HR...WITH HIGHER GUSTS.
ESPECIALLY STRONG GUSTS ARE LIKELY OVER
HIGH TERRAIN. WEAKENING IS LIKELY DURING
THE NEXT 24 HOURS. HURRICANE FORCE WINDS
EXTEND OUTWARD UP TO 85 MILES...140 KM...
FROM THE CENTER...AND TROPICAL STORM
FORCE WINDS EXTEND OUTWARD UP TO 200
MILES...325 KM. ESTIMATED MINIMUM CEN-
TRAL PRESSURE IS 976 MB...28.82 INCHES. A
STORM SURGE OF 3 TO 5 FEET ABOVE NORMAL
TIDE LEVELS CAN BE EXPECTED IN THE WARNED
AREA...AND IN THE NORTHERN GULF OF CALI-
FORNIA...ACCOMPANIED BY LARGE AND DAN-
GEROUS BATTERING WAVES. RAINFALL TOTALS

OF 2 TO 5 INCHES...WITH ISOLATED AMOUNTS NEAR 10 INCHES ARE POSSIBLE IN ASSOCIA-TION WITH NORA. THE RAINBANDS OF NORA ARE MOVING OVER PORTIONS OF BAJA CALIFOR-NIA...THE GULF OF CALIFORNIA...AND NORTHWEST MEXICO...PRODUCING GUSTY WINDS AND LOCALLY HEAVY RAINS. RAIN IS ALSO SPREADING WELL AHEAD OF NORA INTO SOUTH-ERN ARIZONA AND SOUTHERN CALIFORNIA. THIS ACTIVITY WILL CONTINUE TO SPREAD NORTHWARD OVER THE NEXT DAY OR TWO...AND COULD CAUSE LIFE-THREATENING FLASH FLOODS AND MUD SLIDES.
REPEATING THE 8 PM PDT POSITION...26.5 N...114.8 W. MOVEMENT TOWARD...NORTH NEAR 17 MPH. MAXIMUM SUSTAINED WINDS... 85 MPH. MINIMUM CENTRAL PRESSURE... 976 MB. HURRICANE CENTER LOCATED NEAR 26.5N 114.8W AT 25/0300Z POSITION ACCURATE WITHIN 30 NM PRESENT MOVEMENT TOWARD THE NORTH OR 360 DEGREES AT 15 KT ESTIMATED MINIMUM CENTRAL PRESSURE 976 MB MAX SUS-TAINED WINDS 75 KT WITH GUSTS TO 90 KT 64 KT....... 75NE 75SE 50SW 50NW 50 KT.......100NE 100SE 75SW 75NW 34 KT.......175NE 175SE 125SW 125NW 12 FT SEAS.175NE 175SE 300SW 350NW ALL QUAD-RANT RADII IN NAUTICAL MILES REPEAT...CENTER LOCATED NEAR 26.5N 114.8W AT 25/0300Z AT 25/0000Z CENTER WAS LOCATED NEAR 25.8N 114.8W FORECAST VALID 25/1200Z 29.0N 114.8W MAX WIND 65 KT...GUSTS 80 KT 64 KT... 50NE 50SE 40SW 40NW 50 KT... 75NE 75SE 50SW 50NW 34 KT...150NE 175SE 150SW 125NW FORECAST VALID 26/0000Z 32.2N 114.5W...INLAND MAX WIND 50 KT...GUSTS 60 KT 50 KT... 60NE 60SE 40SW 40NW 34 KT...100NE 125SE 125SW 75NW FORECAST VALID 26/1200Z 35.0N 113.0W...INLAND MAX WIND 30 KT...GUSTS 40 KT REQUEST FOR 3 HOURLY SHIP REPORTS WITHIN 300 MILES OF 26.5N 114.8W EXTENDED OUTLOOK...USE FOR GUIDANCE ONLY...ERRORS MAY BE LARGE OUTLOOK VALID 27/0000Z 37.0N 110.0W...INLAND MAX WIND 20 KT...GUSTS 30 KT FORECAST VALID 28/0000Z...INLAND NEXT ADVISORY AT 25/0900Z PASCH

GOES-9 INFRARED 4 25 SEP 97 AT 06:30 UTC

The infrared image (above) was taken about 2300 local time, at the height of the storm for Gitana and her crew. The arrow above indicates both the location of the boat, and their direction of travel at this time. This ties in with the tactic of keeping the wind on the starboard quarter, so that they were reaching away from the storm center.

Another infrared image, this one from about six hours before. The eye is just east of Cedros Island. If the storm had taken a more northerly track, this story might have had a different ending.

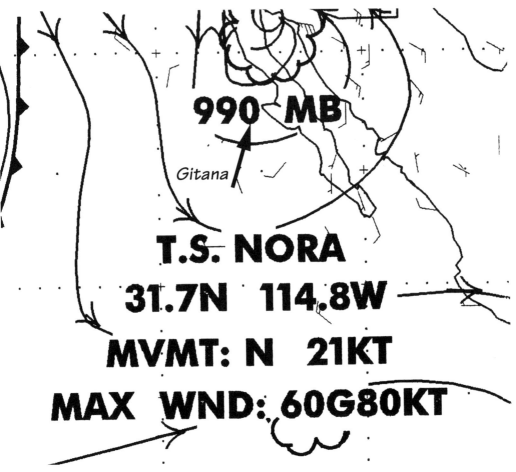

990 MB

Gitana

T.S. NORA
31.7N 114.8W
MVMT: N 21KT
MAX WND: 60G80KT

Fax for September 25—during the night of the 24th Gitana ran off, heading first west, then southwest, and finally south-southeast—away from the center of the storm. The next day (the 25th shown here) Dennis reports that the wind was calm and the sea smooth, like glass. Once again the fax chart seems to be accurate.

The fax data and voice forecasts for this storm were unusually accurate for a West Coast hurricane. It would not be a good idea to assume that these forecasts are always this reliable. It would be more conservative to allow for a much wider margin of error.

The difference between surviving with a harrowing tale to tell and losing one's life in this case was a matter of perhaps six hours and 50 miles—a bit on the close side!

At 0130 local time (above) you can see the storm is now moving to the northwest. Below, an hour and a half later (0300), the storm is moving well inshore.

If you had been spending the summer in the Sea of Cortez you would have been keeping a close eye on Nora. Once she crossed the Baja Peninsula she regained strength over the warm waters of the Gulf for 24 hours. This was enough to bring hurricane force winds and torrential rains in her path.

At 0500 local time (above) only remnants are bothering anyone offshore. But those in the Gulf of California are still seeing hurricane-force winds and torrential rain. 0700 (below) and you can see why things are so calm south of Cedros Island.

TROPICAL TO EXTRATROPICAL TRANSITION OF HURRICANES

Hurricanes in the high latitudes? Yes, we are sorry to report that from time to time a tropical hurricane finds its way into the higher latitudes, sometimes with a new lease on life—with as much power as the tropical counterpart.

These situations occur with some frequency along the Eastern Seaboard of the U.S., in the Western Pacific, and in the tropical South Pacific.

This means that leaving the tropics for the temperate latitudes during hurricane season does not guarantee you 100% security. You still need to keep an eye on the weather.

TRANSITION MECHANICS

The mechanics of these transitions appears to be fairly straightforward most of the time.

The first stage is for the circulation around the depression center to become embedded in the flow around the subtropical high pressure as the storm edges its way out of the tropics. This westerly flow is made up from a surface high pressure system which has vertical depth, with augmentation from higher altitude wind flow.

In order for the storm to continue it must maintain the ability to vent out the top at higher altitudes.

Initially, this venting is typically disrupted as the storm transitions out of the tropics (you will recall that in the tropics this venting mechanism is provided by a weak high pressure dome at upper levels—around 37,000 feet/11,000 meters).

In order for the storm to continue it must find a new way to vent. Out of the tropics this venting process is provided by an upper level low pressure trough. This is the same mechanism discussed in the 500mb section, which makes surface low development so dangerous.

The storm is looking for a divergence (an area where it can spread out) aloft which the surface low pressure can rise into and deepen.

The tropical hurricane has a vertical structure; in the higher latitudes this becomes the normal tilt back structure that we are familiar with for extratropical lows.

With venting established you now have all of the ingredients for a powerful storm, loaded with energy and moisture. This is an explosive combination, and can grow rapidly.

WARNING SIGNS

The best place to look for warning signs is on the 500mb charts.

The favorite place for the tropical storm to hook up to the subtropical high pressure flow is ahead of an upper altitude short wave trough (see page 140).

When you are watching a tropical storm and are keeping an eye on the 500mb charts, you will want to watch these short wave features closely.

Next, in order for venting to work, the storm requires the same tilt back structure as the 500mb low pressure we've discussed previously. So you keep an eye out for troughing at the 500mb level, to the west of the storm center.

SPEED OF MOVEMENT

In the tropics storms move at a leisurely pace, typically at seven to 15 knots. But when they hook up onto the upper level flow in the mid latitudes they can begin to move very rapidly.

Examples of storms moving at 50 to 60 knots are not uncommon.

Obviously this reduces the time in which you have to act, and places a premium on situational awareness — watch those 500mb fax charts!

TACTICS

Because of the potential for rapid movement, the wind speed differential around these storms can be significantly more substantial than with other tropical systems.

If you have a surface movement of ten knots, and a central wind speed of 100 knots, you will have a maximum of 110 knots on the dangerous side and a minimum of 90 knots on the navigable side.

If the storm system is moving at 50 knots, with circulation winds of 60 knots, the dangerous side of the storm will be at 110 knots while moderate breezes will prevail in the navigable side.

This large disparity in the surface wind field maxima means that a much greater (and earlier) effort must be made to avoid the dangerous quadrant of the storm.

Tactically, if you are voyaging at the time of year where these risks exist, you should shoot for a three to five day weather window in which to complete your voyage.

SEASONAL ISSUES

Seasonal issues vary with locale. On a historical basis, the East Coast of the U.S. is typically at greatest risk for tropical to extratropical transition during late summer and early fall — August through October.

In the Western Pacific the range is much greater — typically August through December.

When a tropical weather system moves into the higher latitudes, it generally heralds its approach first with cirrus clouds and then with typical warm front cloud progression. The main difference compared to the tropics is the speed at which things move. In the tropics most storms advance at a clip of 8 to 15 knots. Once in higher latitudes, hooked onto upper level high speed features, the speed of advance can be anywhere from 25 to 50 or even 60 knots.

HURRICANE DANIELLE

Every year, a number of transitions from tropical hurricanes to extratropical storm take place. In the Northern Hemisphere fall of 1998, two interesting examples of this phenomenon occurred, as we were putting this book to bed.

The first took place in early September, along the Eastern Seaboard of the U.S. The second was in mid-September, half way across the world, starting off the coast of Japan.

In both cases dangerous, although relatively small, hurricanes became much larger and even more dangerous extratropical depressions.

Bear in mind that while the tropical hurricane phase of these storm systems gets the publicity, it is their rebirth as an extratropical storm that should be of the most concern to mariners.

A brief study of the faxes that follow will illuminate the reasons quickly enough—in the tropical phase the area of hurricane and storm-force winds is modest. In the case of Hurricane Danielle, this is less than 100 miles across, and the system is moving at ten knots. Yet when this storm is a fully-developed extratropical, the area of storm-force winds covers more than 500 miles of open ocean while the storm moves at a speed of 600 miles a day.

It is quite obvious that the extratropical phase of this storm is more difficult to avoid, and has the potential to generate larger seas than the hurricane phase due to the extra fetch of the storm system.

On the following pages are a series of surface and 500mb charts kindly gathered for us by Lee Chesneau and Joe Sienkiewicz at the Marine Prediction Center. These charts show the development of two storm systems and their relationship between the surface and 500mb levels.

Extratropical depressions can be more dangerous and difficult to avoid than tropical storms.

This is because of their much larger size and faster speed of travel.

Keep in mind that, if you were just looking at the surface charts, you would have little inkling of the risks involved in the early phases of these scenarios.

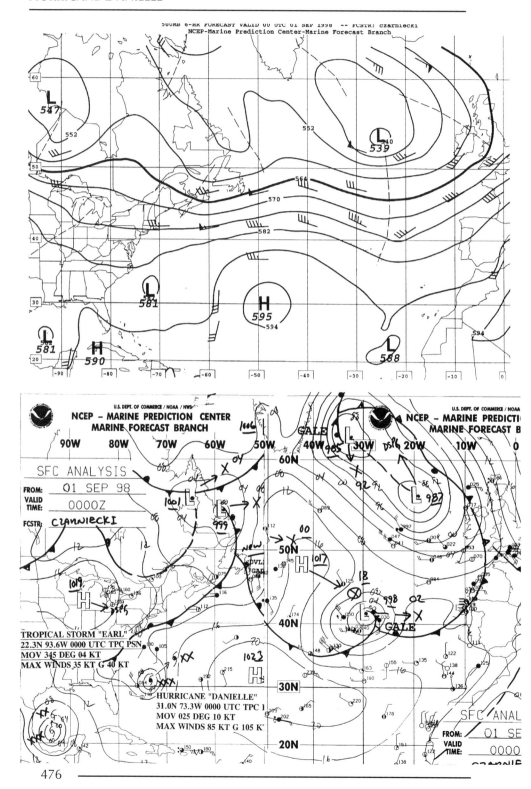

SEPTEMBER 1, 1998

Danielle is at 31 degrees N, 73 degrees W, moving north northeast at ten knots. The 500mb chart shows a 5810 meter (581) low over the top of the hurricane. The normal venting action for the hurricane structure is taking place at higher altitudes (250mb levels and above) with a weak high (not shown at this level on the chart). Note that 500mb winds in the region of Danielle are light—another necessary feature to keep the tropical structure intact.

If you were at sea in the mid-latitudes of the Atlantic and looking at these two charts, you would see little to indicate that Danielle could become an extratropical transition risk. Instead, the inference would be that this hurricane would wind down and die quickly as it moves over cooler waters.

There is a short wave trough well to the northwest, above 50 degrees N around 92 degrees W. However, it is questionable if this will come into play.

The two high pressure ridges on the 500mb charts on either side of the 5810 meter (581) closed low are well separated from Danielle, suggesting that weak steering is available and Danielle will continue on its northeasterly course.

Move now to the east to the surface gale shown at 40 degrees N 30 degrees W. If you look at the 500mb chart you will not see any troughs associated with the surface feature. Obviously, this does not appear to be an accurate portrayal of the 500mb situation. However, this is an early output from the computer. Subsequent charts will show a trough. We point this out as an indicator of the computer anomalies that can creep in—you need to keep an eye on these and watch the subsequent charts for the correction.

In mid-latitude extratropical systems there is almost always a direct correlation of a 500mb short wave trough and synoptic scale surface lows (although that is not the case here).

Without a shortwave trough near enough to hook onto, and no immediately apparent source of polar air to mix with the warm, moist air from the tropics, one would think there is nothing on these charts to keep Danielle going.

A detail of Danielle on September 1—at this point she is quite small and ordinary looking.

In the fall there is always the risk of things developing in an unusual manner—so a very close eye needs to be kept on this storm and similar storm systems as they exit from the tropics.

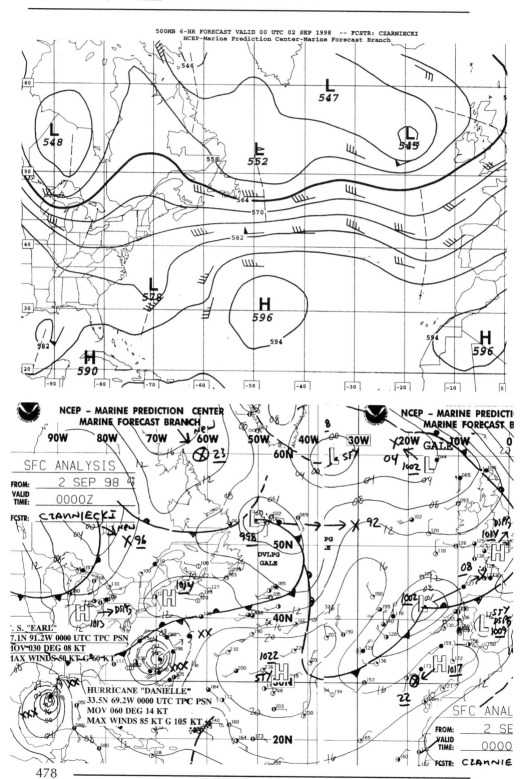

500MB 6-HR FORECAST VALID 00 UTC 02 SEP 1998 -- FCSTR: CZARNIECKI
NCEP-Marine Prediction Center-Marine Forecast Branch

SEPTEMBER 2

Danielle is still maintaining its tropical nature. There is no indication of cold air coming in from the poles to create a bomb.

There is a weak trough over Danielle on the 500mb chart starting at 32 degrees N 70 degrees W and angled south-southwest. The surface forecast indicates Danielle's speed is now 14 knots, and the course has moved to a bit more of an easterly direction (060 as compared 025 on the first of September). This is an indicator that the computer models are showing a strengthening of the steering currents.

The short wave trough just above the Great Lakes on the 500mb charts does not appear to be moving fast enough to catch up with Danielle. All indications are still that Danielle will wind down shortly and dissipate.

Take a look now at the short wave trough on the 500mb chart running north-south at 46 degrees N 48 degrees W. On the surface fax a developing gale is called out. The winds aloft indicate up to 50 knots around 40 degrees N, and there is a good sized 5596-meter high to the south that will help keep the upper-level wind flow at speed.

Further to the east, centered on 40 degrees N 16 degrees W, is the missing trough from yesterday's 500mb chart. The associated surface low appears to be opening up and weakening. The relatively weak winds aloft, in this case 30 knots, usually indicate that the surface low will not develop rapidly.

What could change this, however, would be a push down from the north (a dig) of the cold polar air indicated to the north of the trough, or a blocking ridge developing over Africa (which might then force more curvature into the wind flow around the trough). However, the weak winds aloft make this unlikely.

Wind speeds at the 500mb level are usually a good indicator of what is going to happen on the surface.

HURRICANE "DANIELLE"
33.5N 69.2W 0000 UTC TPC PSN
MOV 060 DEG 14 KT
MAX WINDS 85 KT G 105 KT

Higher winds indicate surface activity will strengthen. Lower wind speeds are usually taken to mean benign surface conditions—or a transition to lower winds or the winding down of a depression.

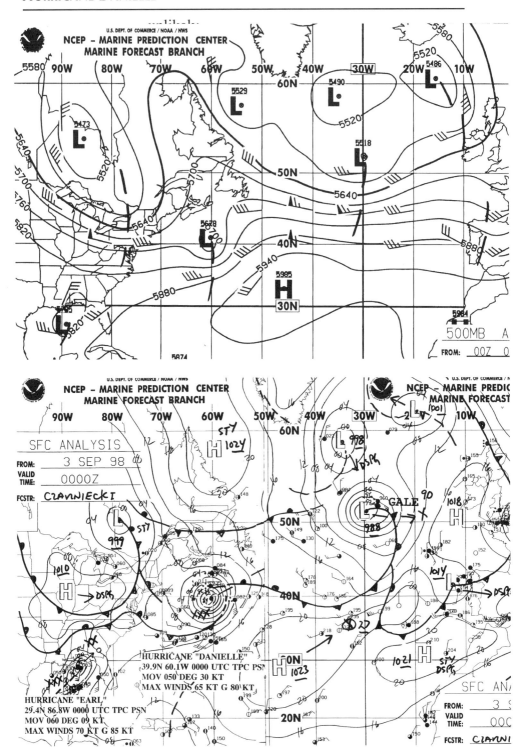

SEPTEMBER 3

Danielle still has her tropical status, and is now moving at 30 knots to the northeast. The area of gale force winds has expanded to the south with the increase speed of movement.

There is no question now that Danielle is caught up in the westerly flow aloft, as indicated by her predicted speed of movement. With 500mb wind speeds showing in the 40-to 50-knot range, it is impossible to maintain the tropical structure.

However, there is still no sign of a source of cold air to aid in the transition to an extratropical storm. Yet for Danielle to be this size, moving at 30 knots while at 40 degrees North latitude, something other than a pure tropical structure must be involved.

We know that the energy is there by the surface wind field that has been reported by ships in the vicinity — and confirmed with satellite imaging.

When I asked Lee Chesneau about this, he indicated that the storm must have created its own environment, rather than relying on external assistance.

Our gale at 52 degrees N 30 degrees W is now well developed, if small in area. The 500mb trough structure slightly to the west with its 65 knot winds hints that a strengthening of the gale is possible. The 500mb short wave trough is not of particularly significant amplitude. The gale farther south which we looked at yesterday has now weakened significantly which shows a lack of support at 500mb.

The 500mb trough now associated with Danielle has strengthened (i.e., deepened).

This deepening of the upper-level trough indicates that the tropical storm structure is breaking down.

It is also a warning signal that Danielle could develop into an extratropical system.

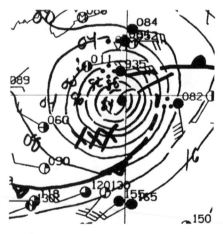

It is always helpful to look at the reports from shipping and buoys when analyzing these charts. This is the real world—not computer-based. As such, it gives you a reality check on the theoretical.

In this case, without ship reports of the surface wind field, you and the forecasters would not have precise knowledge of Danielle's intensity.

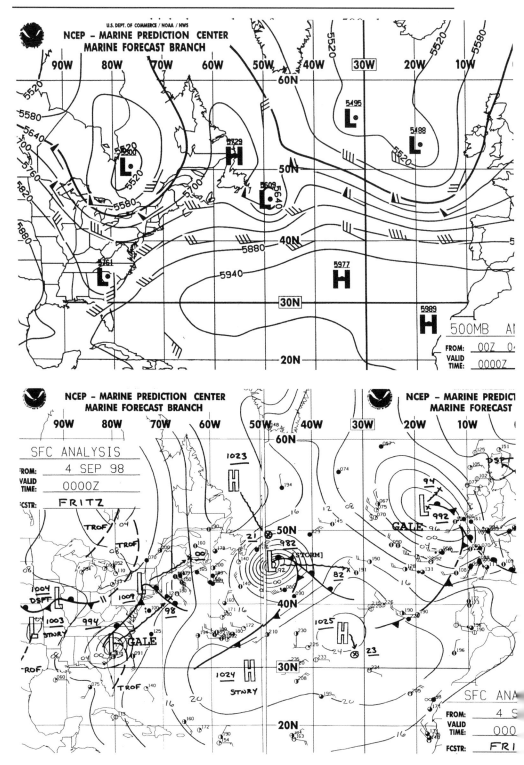

SEPTEMBER 4

Take a look at the region to the south of Greenland on the 500mb chart (60 degrees N, between 50W and 40W). Notice the northerly flow coming down the 5640 meter height contour (heavy line).This is now feeding cold, dry polar air south towards what was Danielle—but is now classified as an extratropical low with storm-force winds.

This polar flow provides the ingredients for a successful transition to extratropical structure.

Upper-level winds have accelerated, and a closed 5640-meter low has now formed over the surface low.

The forecast position 24 hours from now for this fast moving low is 600 miles to the east, with the central pressure remaining the same.

You would normally infer from the closing of the 500mb circulation, and from the fact that the forecast central pressure will remain the same, that this storm would not grow in intensity.

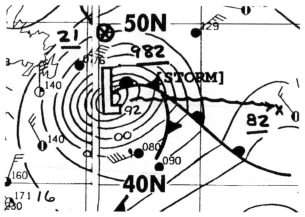

This detail of the storm and its projected track over the next 24 hours (to the "x" at the east side of the image) gives you an idea of how much more power this structure holds.

The total area of storm force winds is many times that of the hurricane which preceded it— and it is moving a lot faster than the tropical structure as well!

The other gale we were watching farther to the north has developed a 992mb center. It is shown with modest movement for the next 24 hours, without much change in central pressure. However, the shape of the upper level trough indicates that further deepening is possible.

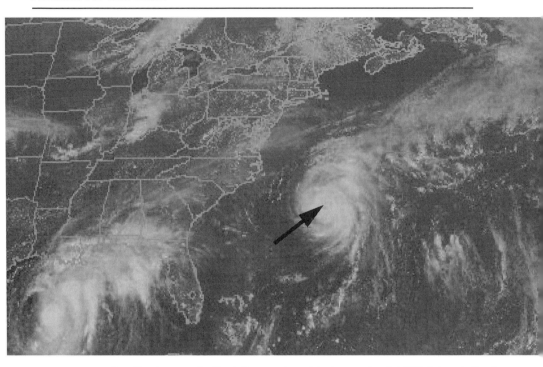

Satellite images for Danielle starting with September 1, 1998 (above). The first image clearly shows the tropical signature. On September 2 (below) the tropical cloud signature is still well defined, although less so than a day earlier.

September 3 (above) and the cloud images still have that tropical look, but are now spread out over a much larger area. The final image is from the fourth (below) where this is now an extremely large extratropical cyclone. Notice how far to the east the storm has moved in the previous 24 hours.

TACTICS

This series of charts makes for interesting conjecture because of their somewhat abnormal nature. They provide us with a reminder about weather of which we need to be constantly aware — keep your eyes open for anomalies.

And there are several anomalies present here. The first is the continued movement and strength of Hurricane Danielle, in the absence of any apparent help from an upper-level polar wind component.

It is not until the fourth day of this series of charts that we see the ingredients for a tropical to extratropical transition. Yet Danielle obviously has found (or created) an environment in which she can prosper.

The other anomaly is the lack of 500mb trough associated with the surface gale on September 1. This is obviously a computer glitch which was not picked up by the forecaster for this initial analysis.

You need to be aware that oversights happen, and that the next chart, which comes out after more computer analysis has been done, will usually show the missing feature. Continuity and consistency are key to forecast accuracy.

This is one of the reasons why you should never rely on any single chart or bit of data. If you were looking at these charts on a six-hour basis, the problem would quickly be resolved. And if it isn't, the ship reports from the area obviously indicate that the gale is for real.

What are the tactics to employ with this situation? That's a tough call. Ideally, you would not be on the ocean at this time of year when the risk of hurricanes marching in with the semi-permanent Atlantic High are greatest. It is better to do the westbound trip

Always be alert to anomalies in the weather.

The first fax charts broadcast from a computer run sometimes have features that are missing or wrong. These are often corrected in the chart broadcast at the next point in the schedule.

Never rely on any single bit of information. Always check your assumptions, and those of the forecasters.

much earlier in the year, or wait until later after hurricane season, and head south of the winter storm track before turning north to follow the winter trade wind circulation (or better yet spending the winter in the tropics).

Sometimes you do not have this luxury. If you are sitting in Europe or the U.K., getting ready to head west, what can you do?

First, be aware that the high latitude risks of these storms is significant. Next, have the ability to receive satellite images so you can track the cloud structure and temperature—both good signs of what is happening with the tropical and extratropical systems.

Next, keep careful track of not only the current analysis, but also the 24-, 48- and 96-hour forecasts for both 500mb and surface conditions. Run the fax continuously so that you have the six hourly surface reports as well as the twice daily prognosis.

Keep in mind the very high potential speed of closure should the tropical storm hook up on a substantial westerly flow aloft.

You then have two choices. Get well above the potential storm track, or below it. The polar-oriented course digression will be the shorter of the two options—albeit a lot colder.

By keeping a careful watch on the upper-level charts and the likely direction of upper-level wind flow, you will have a pretty good idea if there is any tendency for the storm to jog north. As the normal track is east or east northeast, by mid-Atlantic the odds of a jog north happening are usually low.

Being on the poleward side of the storm keeps you in the navigable quadrant, with following winds and seas as opposed to head seas and headwinds.

Considerations for late season subtropical and extratropical passages:

- Avoid the weather risks by choosing another time of year.

- Make sure you have good weather analysis tools aboard and know how to use them.

- Keep careful track of all tropical storms even when they do not look like they can make the transition to extratropical structures.

- If a storm scenario risk arises, take early action to avoid the system.

SURFACE PROG CHARTS

We've mentioned the forward-looking prognosis briefly several times. These computer projections of what is likely to happen in the future are typically issued for 24, 48, and sometimes 72 and 96 hours in the future.

The various computer models in use (for example the MRF at the Marine Prediction Center) are getting better at giving the mariner a feel for what the future holds.

The key with these charts is to watch the flow, get used to them over time, and compare the results of the progs to the surface charts several days hence.

As some computer models do a better job in one area than another, and vary to some degree with season, by watching and evaluating you will get to know the strengths and weaknesses.

NORTH PACIFIC

The following three progs are for a period in mid-September, 1998. To keep things simple we will show just the 96-hour forecasts, and then in the next section about Hurricane Stella becoming an extra-tropical storm, we'll see how these turned out (see page 491).

The North Pacific is one of the more active weather areas on the oceans. A combination of cold dry polar air to the north, and warmer, moist, sub-tropical air to the south (brought towards the pole by an active sub tropical high) provides lots of potential energy. When these get mixed up at the frontal boundary, all sorts of exciting things happen.

This is true for any time of year, but particularly so during the spring and fall when temperature differences are at their greatest. The norm is to see a succession of large depressions forming, and then marching across the ocean basin from west to east.

The key with prog charts is to watch the flow, get used to them over time, and compare the results of the progs to the surface charts several days hence.

In the North Pacific a combination of cold dry polar air to the north, and warmer, moist, subtropical air to the south (brought towards the pole by an active subtropical high) provides lots of potential energy.

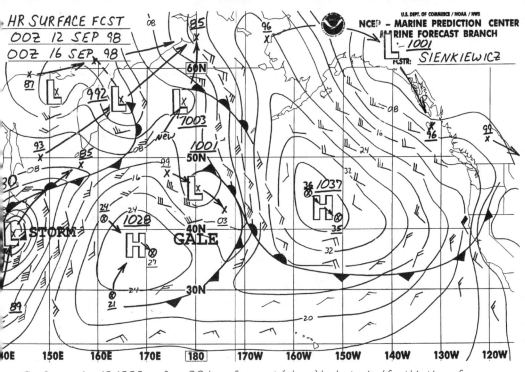

The September 12, 1998 surface 96-hour forecast (above) looks typical for this time of year. The subtropical high is broken into two large segments, and there's an active storm system to the west shown at 40 degrees N 140 degrees E. The following day's 96-hour prog (below) indicates that this storm system is expected to rapidly intensify. It is following the upper-level and surface wind flow clockwise around the high pressure system to the immediate east. A couple of gales are in the Gulf of Alaska, again normal for this time of year.

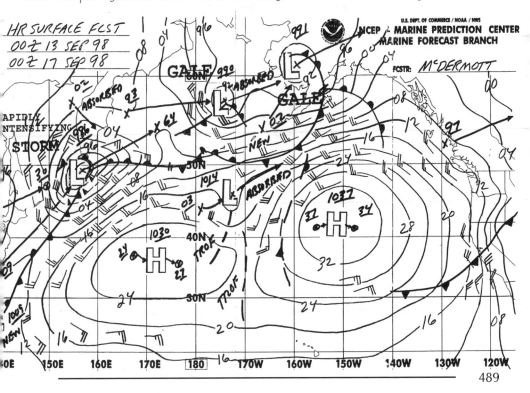

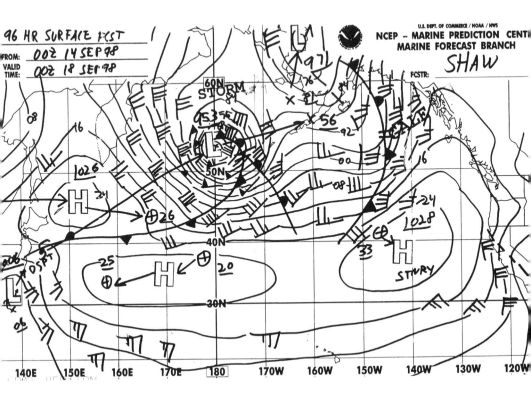

The 96-hour surface prog issued on the 14th shows that yesterday's rapidly intensifying storm (bomb) is expected to become a major storm, covering a huge amount of distance (900 miles) in the 24-hour period. Obviously, the 500mb charts show substantial upper-level winds to move the storm this fast.

Based on the September 12 and 13 96-hour progs, if you were on a west-to-east voyage, perhaps from Japan back to the States or from Hawaii back to the mainland, the temptation would be to stay in the westerly flow around the high centers, with wind and seas aft of the beam. By staying within one or two isobars of the high center winds would be strong enough for good progress, but it appears—at least through these first two progs—that you would be far enough south of the storm track to be in good shape.

But then comes the prog on the 14th. This indicates the likelihood of storm-force winds in place of the high-pressure westerly "trades".

The issue here is that these are forecasts four days in the future. That gives you four day's warning.

If you need to take evasive action, the only option given this scenario is a turn southward closer to the center of the highs and well away from the forecasted storm track.

TYPHOON STELLA

From the projected presence of that large storm in the Gulf of Alaska, it is obvious that the forecasters have something interesting going on both at the surface and in the upper levels. In this case we are discussing Typhoon Stella as she works her way up the coast of Japan.

The 96-hour forecasts we've looked at are for this storm to transition from a tropical structure to an extratropical system, being picked up by the upper level westerly winds in the process.

If you were sitting in Hawaii, Japan, Alaska or even the Pacific Northwest with an offshore passage in mind, you would be watching not only the prog charts, but the current surface and 500mb charts as well. Even if you were just cruising the backside of Vancouver Island for a couple of weeks, keeping a wary eye on the weather to your west and north would be prudent.

The events developing to the west would be arrayed on your chart table, and you would have a feel for the flow of the upper-level short wave troughs as well as the surface features.

With all of the surface and 500mb charts broadcast during the day, both current and future prognosis, this adds up to a lot of paper. Yet in the trends you see, the rhythms of the weather will be evident.

You want to make sure that you have feel for these rhythms, and understand how they may affect your plans today and in the future.

Given the very large scale of these extratropical weather features, you need as much time as possible to take prudent action.

SEPTEMBER 16, 1998

Lets go back now to current data—surface and 500mb analysis for the North Pacific Ocean. We pick up the paper chase on September 16.

Stella is over in the west at 34 degrees N 145 degrees E. She has been downgraded to a tropical storm, and it is obvious by her speed of movement—48 knots to the north-northeast—that she has hooked onto some upper level flow.

A glance at the 500mb chart indicates a 60-knot flow along the 5582-meter contour height (582). This means that the surface storm is moving at 80 percent of the 500mb wind speed.

Nothing is showing on the 500mb chart to indicate a flow of polar air into this system, something required for a transition to extratropical status. The clockwise high pressure circulation will, in fact, do just the opposite—continue to feed warm moist air from the tropics into the system.

Farther to the east on the 500mb chart, at 55 degrees N 175 degrees E, there is a well-defined trough with significant winds above and below the 6540-meter contour (heavy line). You would expect this to be associated with a surface depression, one that was probably going to deepen—in fact, you can see this feature on the surface chart.

Another upper-level low is off the Pacific Northwest coastline at 45 degrees N 135 degrees W. There is a closed 5553 (553) height contour above the surface low that would usually indicate that the surface feature has developed about as deep a central pressure as it can, and will shortly begin to dissipate.

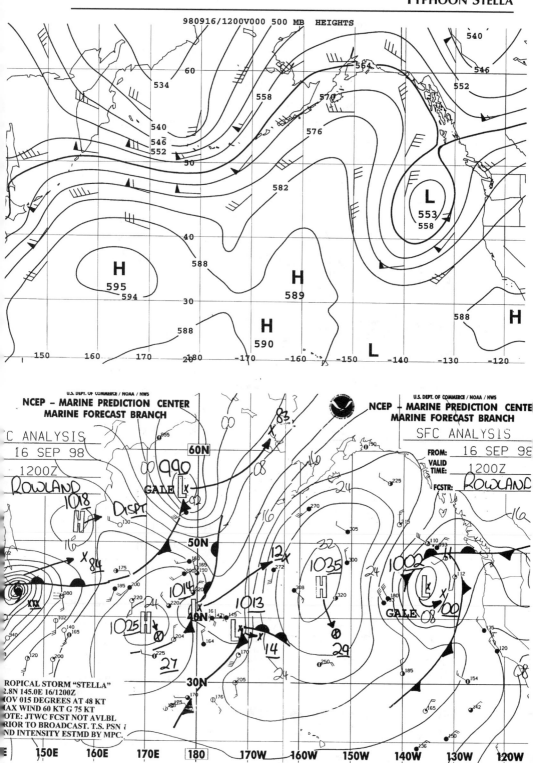

980916/1200V000 500 MB HEIGHTS

SEPTEMBER 17

The two factors now present—polar air and good venting—are the ingredients necessary for the storm to grow, rapidly in many cases.

Let's look at the surface chart first. Stella has changed to an extratropical, in honor of which her name has been dropped from the fax. There is a 976mb low, and she is projected to move over a thousand miles to the east in the next 24 hours.

A look now at the 500mb chart gives us some clues as to why this is happening. First, a nice trough has formed with an associated short wave, just to the west of the surface low. Strong winds are associated with this 500mb trough, up to 95 knots on and just below the 5640 (564) meter height contour.

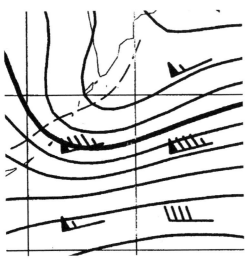

The north-south orientation of the height contours to the west will bring down the cool, dry air from the pole needed to energize the storm.

At the same time the east-northeast angle of the height contours to the east of the trough indicate efficient venting can occur of the surface low.

The 500mb detail (above) and surface detail (below) clearly show the "tilt-back" relationship discussed earlier in the section on upper-level charts. From this feature alone you would expect the surface storm to strengthen in the future.

In the meantime, the other two lows we discussed on the previous day's chart both look to be on the wane based on the closed nature of the lows on the 500mb chart.

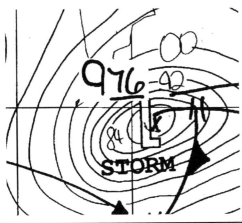

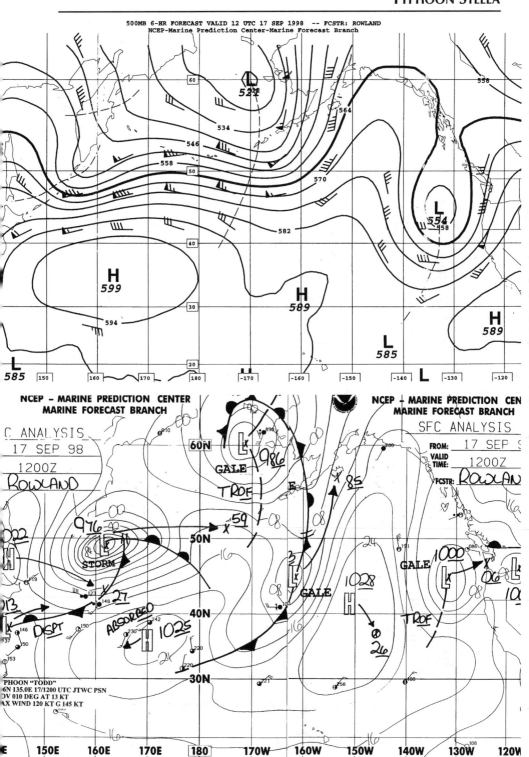

500MB 6-HR FORECAST VALID 12 UTC 17 SEP 1998 -- FCSTR: ROWLAND
NCEP-Marine Prediction Center-Marine Forecast Branch

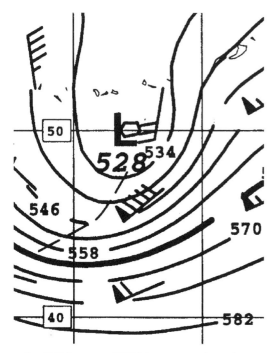

The 5528-meter (528) low is now directly over the 961mb low on the surface. The upper-level structure is closing, which lessens venting of the surface low. You would normally infer from this that the surface feature would begin to fill in the near future.

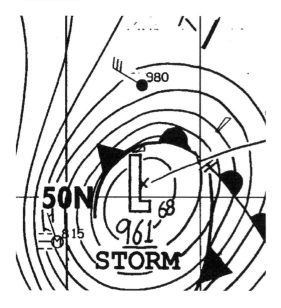

SEPTEMBER 18

Our extratropical depression has indeed grown substantially in the past 24 hours. The central pressure at the surface has dropped to 961mb from 976, a change of 15mb in 24 hours. The Marine Prediction Center has been right on with their forecast position, and is saying the storm will move another 400 miles to the east, indicating that its movement is expected to slow down.

Since the winds at the 500mb level are essentially the same as yesterday, it is expected that the upper-level trough will be overtaking the surface low, reducing the offset. This, in turn, will probably reduce the upper-level venting for the surface low, so you would reasonably expect that the surface low will begin to fill and eventually die down over the next couple of days.

Now take a look at the two storms that were present yesterday. Both have dissipated, something inferred from the closed upper-level lows on yesterday's 500mb chart.

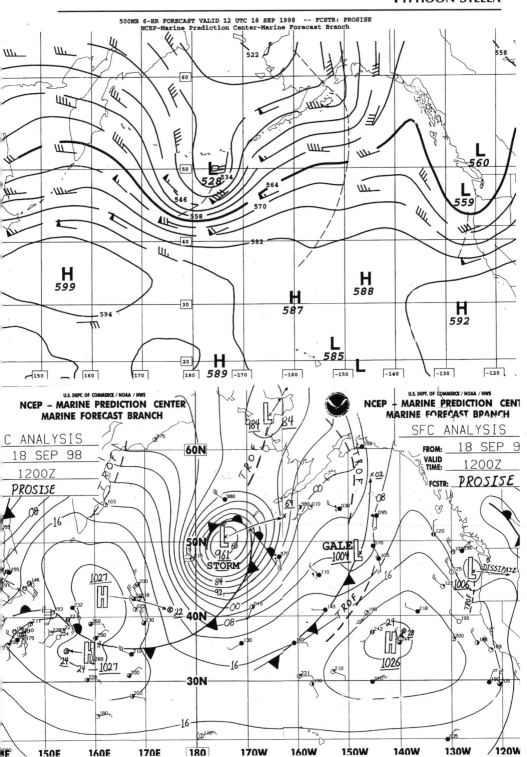

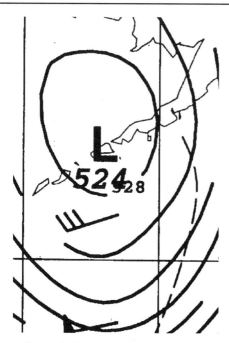

The end of the line for this surface depression. The closed circulation of the 5524-meter height contour (above) is directly over the 971mb surface low (below). The ability of the surface system to vent is now lost, and the system will fill and dissipate.

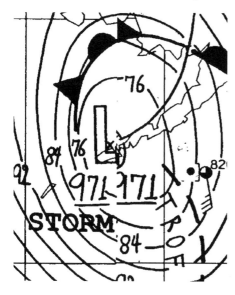

SEPTEMBER 19

The storm has definitely begun to wind down. Central pressure on the surface is up 10mb in the past 24 hours to 971mb.

The 500mb chart now shows a closed 5524 meter height contour (524) directly over the surface low.

While this storm still covers a very substantial area, it is on its last legs.

If you were in Hawaii, waiting for a shot to head back to the mainland, yesterday would probably have been an ideal time to begin the passage.

With today's confirmation of the storm system dissipating, you could continue making your northeasterly course.

The shape of the eastern section of the Pacific High, and the very long front coming off the 971mb low, indicate lovely south to southwest breezes for several days to come.

If the storm system somehow became reenergized, you could heave-to or head south, to get out of its area of influence, until the situation stabilized.

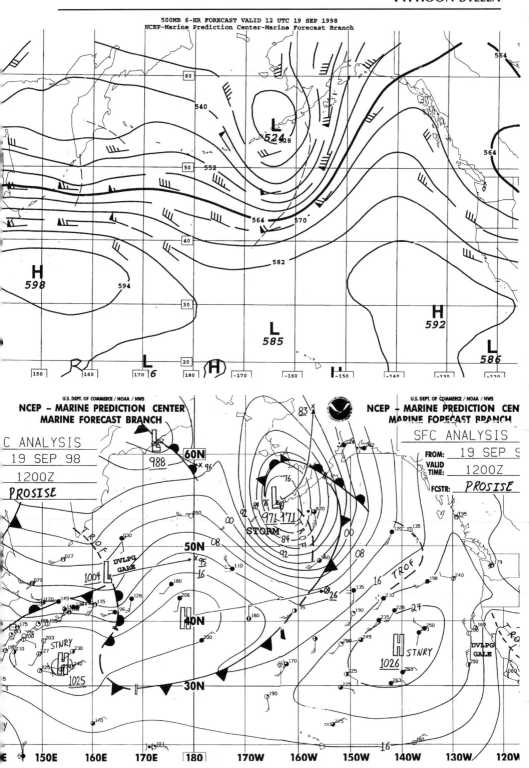

500MB 6-HR FORECAST VALID 12 UTC 19 SEP 1998
NCEP-Marine Prediction Center-Marine Forecast Branch

499

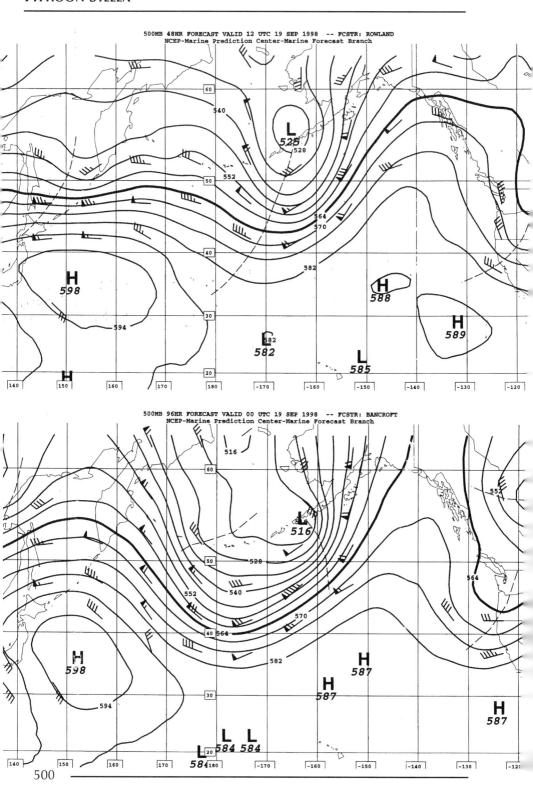

500MB 48HR FORECAST VALID 12 UTC 19 SEP 1998 -- FCSTR: ROWLAND
NCEP-Marine Prediction Center-Marine Forecast Branch

500MB 96HR FORECAST VALID 00 UTC 19 SEP 1998 -- FCSTR: BANCROFT
NCEP-Marine Prediction Center-Marine Forecast Branch

500MB PROG CHARTS

Forecasts of the 500mb level are in some ways more valuable than those for the surface.

These charts give you a feel for the risks inherent in a given scenario, from your own perspective.

Both of the examples alongside are for September 19, the same day as the current analysis on the previous pages.

The upper chart is for a 48-hour period while the lower is the forecast for 96 hours hence. These days they are reasonably accurate and provide useful data when looking for a weather window, but still have to be taken with a grain of salt. Let's check the 48-hour prog first.

Two short wave troughs are shown. The first, at 55 degrees N165 degrees W over the Aleutian Islands indicates continued filling and dissipation of the surface low. That storm will gradually wind down based on this projection. Note: 48 hours from now it is still going to be kicking up seas and wind on the surface, but at least we can infer that in all likelihood it will not strengthen.

Another short wave trough is farther to the west, with an axis running through 50 degrees N 150 degrees E. The zonal flow (west to east) indicated over the Western Pacific will probably not remain stable, and when it breaks down, we can expect something to start to cook on the surface.

Now switch to the 96-hour forecast. The short wave trough from two days ago has moved to the east and is now associated with an open 5516-meter (516) height low. Given the tight spacing of the height contours, and significant winds on and to the north of the 5640 height contour line, it is reasonable to expect rapid surface development. Note that the zonal flow shown two days ago in the west is now meridional.

The 500mb charts (opposite page) are for 48 and 96 hours in the future. They show a significant rotation of the trough axis, which would indicate vigorous surface low pressure.

Return from Hawaii

No sooner had we finished the preceding sections on North Pacific weather, than the phone rang. On the other end of the line was Warwick "Commodore" Tompkins, a professional seaman who learned forecasting the old-fashioned way — by looking at the sea, sky, wind and barometer (today he compares what this tells him to fax charts).

Commodore had just finished sailing a Saga 43 back from Lahaina in the Hawaiian Islands for her San Francisco Bay owner.

By chance, he had put to sea on the evening of September 11, right at the beginning of the period we've just been discussing. In light of what was transpiring to the west with Stella (and eventually in the Gulf of Alaska as Stella went extratropical) Commodore's notes on his passage provide an interesting frame of reference.

First, some data on vessel and crew. The Saga 43 is a relatively new design from Bob Perry. She has a masthead rig with dual headsails in the forward triangle — a reaching jib on a short bowsprit and working jib set on the main headstay at the stem head.

With a passage back from Hawaii, range under power is an important consideration. This is what dictates how close you can cut the windless center of the high. In this case they were able to get about 100 U.S. Gallons into the tanks. As close as Commodore could figure, this gave them a range of around 400 miles at five knots in smooth water — although he prefers to sail.

Andrew Minkwitz, crew for the passage, was an experienced dinghy sailor, and this was to be his first offshore passage.

The faxes that follow were all recorded aboard with a Furuno weather fax (model #207). The quality varies — and will give you a realistic feel for what

"My primary focus at sea is being aware of the weather. Once I have a feel for what our local conditions indicate, and what the sky, sea and wind foretell about the future, I try to relate it to the weather fax." Commodore Tompkins

you can expect. They were tuned to station NMC in Point Reyes, California. Faxes were received aboard two to three times per day. Only surface analysis faxes were recorded.

LEAVING PORT

With the tanks topped off and supplies stowed, they departed Lahaina on the island of Maui on Friday evening, September 11.

Conditions were moderate. Winds were 15 to 20 knots from the east, gusting 25. They carried a full working jib, staysail, and triple reefed main (to ease steering and keep the boat on her feet).

By 0930 on the 12th, conditions had lightened to where they had just one reef in them main. During the day a squall was encountered with winds to 30

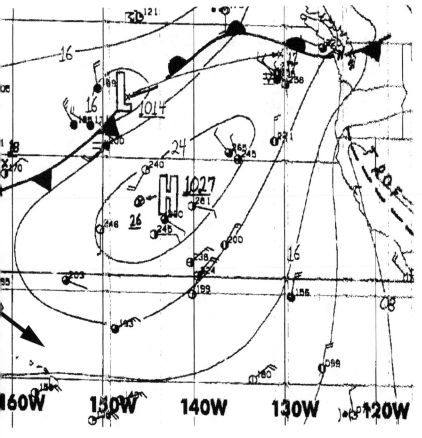

September 12— This is an ideal scenario for returning to the coast over the top of the high. The center axis is oriented northeast-southwest and winds are apt to be moderate. The front pushing down will probably squash the high center south.

knots. They dropped the main and then reset it in the light airs after the squall. This routine was followed for the next few days.

Close-reaching they were making good a course of 27 degrees true, with 129 miles in the bag for the first complete day at sea

MAKING NORTHING

Days two through six were more of the same— 130 to 140 miles a day on a course of north by northeast. Moderate tradewind conditions prevailed, about what you expect from the Pacific High at this time of year.

The only unusual pattern was the center of the high. Normally this moves south with the sun in early fall. This year the center was still quite far north for mid-to late September.

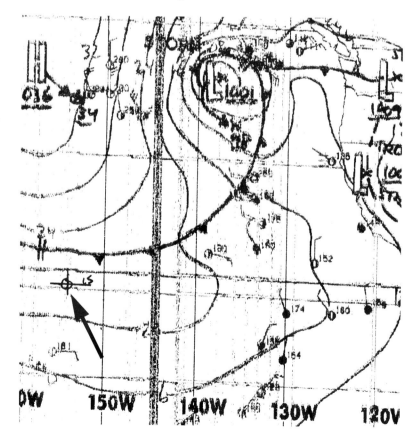

September 15— The high has fragmented with a weak front pushing down from the north. From the isobars you would expect to have east winds, allowing good progress to the northeast.

CUTTING ACROSS THE HIGH

By the end of the sixth day, they were within 200 miles of the latitude of San Francisco Bay. On the afternoon of the 17th, as Commodore puts it, "We had a big-time lift. The wind backed and allowed us to head almost on the rhumb line."

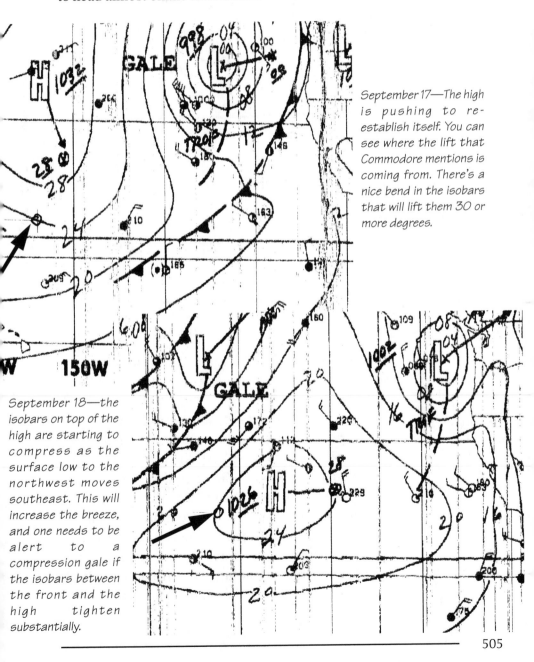

September 17—The high is pushing to re-establish itself. You can see where the lift that Commodore mentions is coming from. There's a nice bend in the isobars that will lift them 30 or more degrees.

September 18—the isobars on top of the high are starting to compress as the surface low to the northwest moves southeast. This will increase the breeze, and one needs to be alert to a compression gale if the isobars between the front and the high tighten substantially.

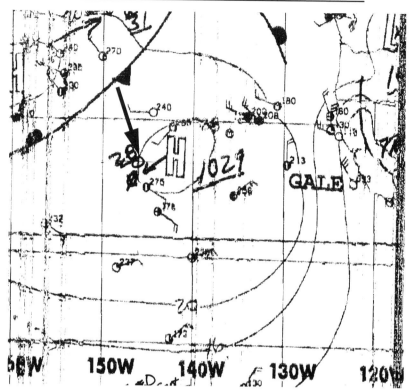

September 20—Rather than a squash zone gale from the southwest, the high has expanded overnight, pushing the center well to the south. Commodore and crew are caught up in the windless center and need to fire up the engine for the first time. There is a silver lining in this—they know that they will shortly be through the center and into the north quadrant winds on the east side of the high pressure center.

Go back and look at the September 18th surface chart on page 496. Seeing that huge extratropical depression to your northwest, without any idea of steering currents, would make you very nervous. On the other hand, if you had been watching the 500mb charts you would know that the surface low was about to fill, and in any event, upper-level steering currents would keep it well to your north.

On the ninth day at sea, September 20, they were motoring, finally caught up in the center of the high. The following day, the 21st, the breeze started to come in from the north. Just catspaws at first, then a nice steady close reach with 25 knots of wind.

This was very much a gift from the remnants of Stella, a fact confirmed by the contemporaneous arrival of a large set of swells from the northwest. The cold front extending down from the Gulf of Alaska was pushing the high center southwards,

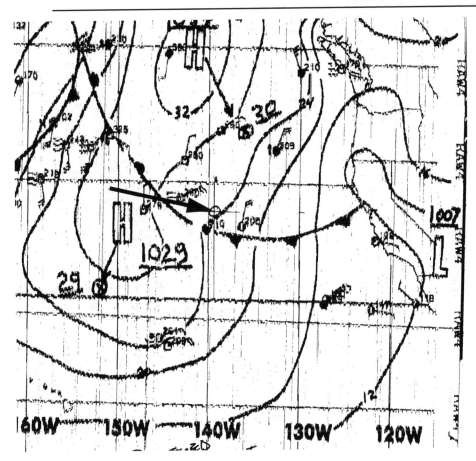

September 22—The high is well on its way to strengthening now with well established northerly flow. From here to the coast it is a nice reach. As the northern high center pushes down, there's a chance of a moderate gale near the coast as it comes into contact with the coastal low and mountains.

tightening the isobars in the process to create a more favorable wind slant with better velocity.

Using WWV, Commodore had been tracking Stella's progress. He always had the option of heading south in case the storm began to track southeast.

Sixteen days after leaving Lahaina, Commodore was on the marina phone to his client informing him of their safe arrival after an uneventful passage.

"During the middle part of the trip I was watching that big depression in the Gulf of Alaska. There was a chance we'd feel some effect, but the odds were the high would block it."
Warwick Tompkins

September 24—
Most good things in
life have to do with
timing, and weather
is no exception.
Look at the shape
of the high now. This
is what you would
expect at the
height of summer.
The center is well to
the north. The trip
back from Hawaii
would be long and
arduous with lots of
beating if this is
what you had to
deal with in the
beginning.
Commodore is on
the backside, so he
has favorable winds.

A track of their
course is below.
They sailed just
300 miles more
than the rhumb line.

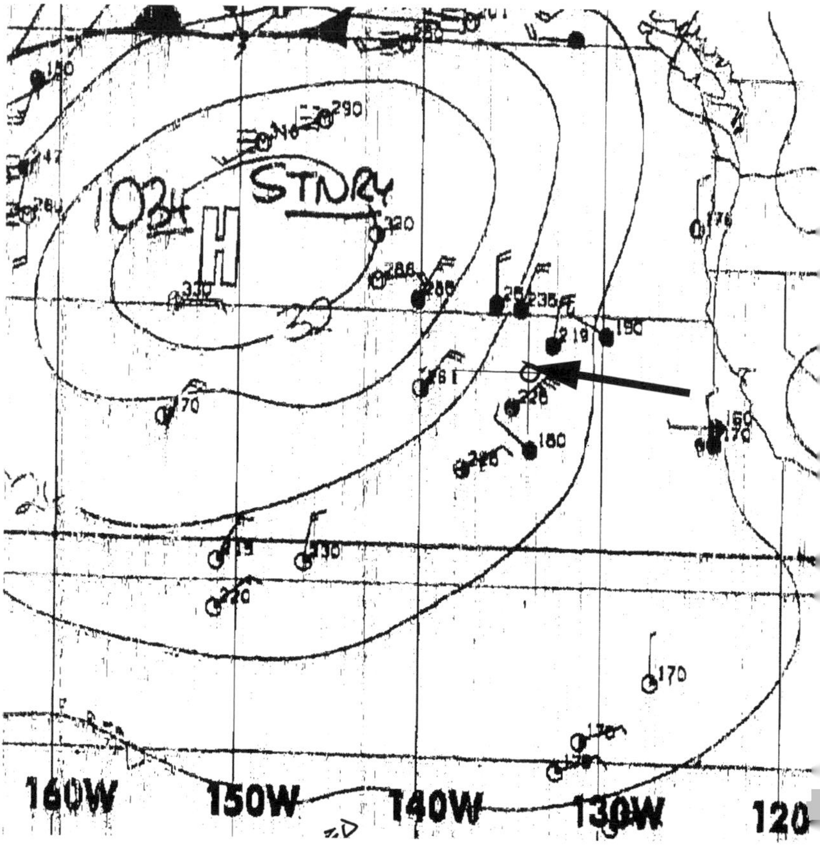

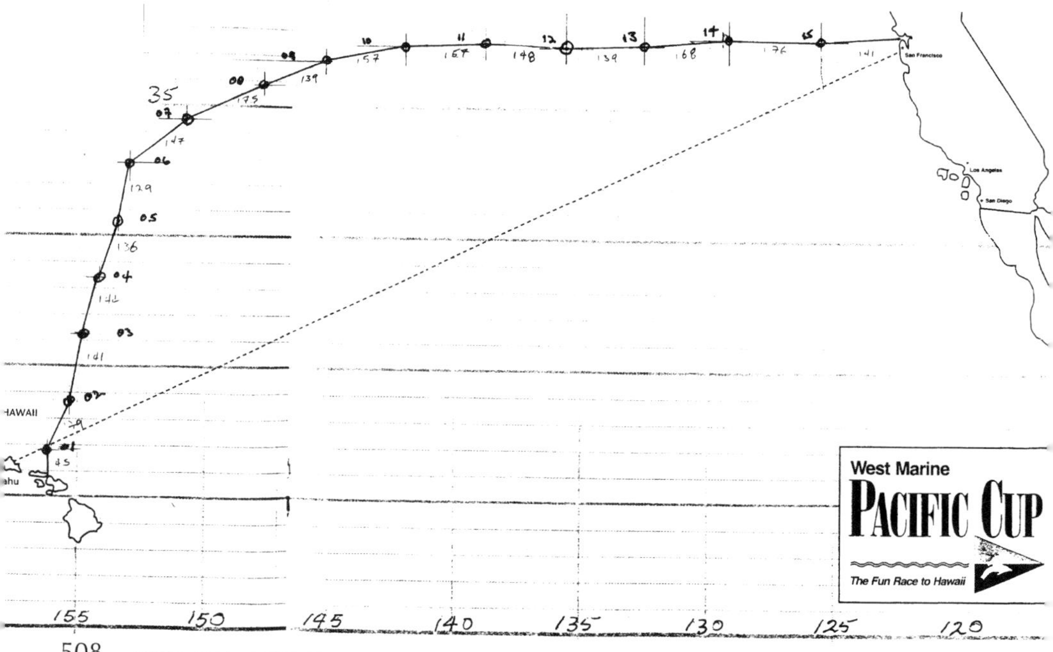

West Marine
PACIFIC CUP
The Fun Race to Hawaii

Some areas of the world have semi-permanent fog conditions due to water that is colder than the surrounding air. This one is off the coast of Cambria in Central California.

FOG

Depending on where you cruise, fog may or may not be an issue. In our experience, we've probably spent less than half a dozen mornings in foggy surroundings—all of these in San Diego, California. But then, we have not spent much time on the northeast coast of the U.S.

Fog is actually a low lying cloud. It is formed by the same condensation process that creates higher clouds.

ADVECTION/SEA FOG

Advection or sea fog is the result of a layer of warm, moist air moving in over cooler water. The water cools down the air until it reaches the dew point, and the humidity condenses into water droplets forming a low-level cloud. This is a fairly common situation when you have a warm front (with warm, humid air) moving in over an area of cool water.

If, after the fog forms, a measure of vertical instability is introduced (perhaps by solar heating), the mixing process will cause the surface-level fog to lift off the water and form a layer of low-lying stratus clouds.

Advection fog can persist for days or weeks on end, and will be found with surface level winds as well.

WHERE DO YOU FIND SEA FOG?

Sea fog is typically found in areas of cool currents, and is particularly prevalent in late spring and early summer when air temperatures are beginning to warm, but the sea surface has yet to follow suit.

Where you have cold currents—Labrador on the northeast coast of Canada, for example—you can have fog for 30 percent to as much as 50 percent of the year.

FORECASTING SEA FOG

If you are sailing in a cold water area, the fog-making process is started by either a warm land breeze blowing out over the cooler water, or an equator-quadrant wind (from the south in the Northern Hemisphere—or the north in the Southern Hemisphere) bringing warm, moist air up from the subtropics.

This means that there will usually be a bit of breeze associated with sea fog (as opposed to radiation fog which requires still conditions to form).

Sea fog can last a few hours or for days on end if conditions are right.

Radiation Fog

This is caused by the land cooling rapidly at night, faster than the air above it is giving off its heat. This cools the air closest to the ground while the air above is still warm. This inversion layer keeps the air quite still, which promotes more cooling.

An example of radiation fog, in this case in the early morning hours. Once the sun has had a chance to warm things up a bit, this fog will probably dissipate.

When the air temperature close to the ground has reached its dew point, fog forms.

Radiation fog is sometimes enhanced by cooler air dropping down through mountain valleys.

While this is primarily a land-based phenomenon, radiation fog does spread offshore a ways, typically not more than eight to ten miles.

Radiation fog tends to form just before dawn, when the night air is at its coolest point. It will then persist until early afternoon when the warming process has reached its maximum, at which time the warmer air prevents condensation from taking place.

During the winter, in settled high pressure conditions, radiation fog will persist in some areas for days on end.

USING A SLING PSYCHROMETER

A sling psychrometer is a handy device for determining the dew point of the surrounding air, from which you then interpret how close you are to having fog.

This device has two thermometers, one for measuring dry air and another for measuring wet.

The mounting board for the twin thermometers is attached to a string, which ends in a handle. Holding the handle you then whip the sling psychrometer, accelerating the evaporation process on the wet thermometer.

When the wet bulb readings reach a stable point— i.e., stop dropping—you make note of the difference between the two temperatures.

Enter the temperatures in a table in order to find the air temperature at which fog will form.

NEAR LAND

As we close with the land, we need to consider other factors that affect the weather. These can either augment or reduce the pressure gradient winds we've been discussing.

LAND MASS COMPRESSION

Any time you have a land mass that reaches high enough to interfere with the winds aloft, a chance for compression and acceleration of the wind exists.

A classic example is found between the North and South islands of New Zealand.

The South Island is high, precipitious on its west coast, and lies directly in the path of weather systems tracking up the Tasman Sea from the underside of Australia.

The North Island, while less rugged, nevertheless blocks an easy escape for these weather systems.

The only relief the low-level pressure can find is a narrow opening between the islands called Cook's Strait. And boy can it blow there! Weather systems that might produce 30 knots of fresh breeze in the open ocean will accelerate to 50 or 60 knots as the isobars stack up against the mountains.

Another example of this is found off the Big Sur coastline, just south of Monterey, California.

For 35 miles, high cliffs at the water's edge are backed up inland a couple of miles by mountains. When the Pacific High is pumping 25 knots well off-shore, you can expect 35 to 45 knots along this stretch of coast. And if a front is working its way down from Alaska, with significant wind shear (where the wind is much stronger aloft), the increase between the offshore winds and those along the coast will be even more pronounced.

Most areas where this type of phenomenon occurs are well known. If you are new to an area, the coast pilots will probably have warnings. But even if they don't, keep an eye on the topography shown on your

Land mass compression is an issue when:

❑ The wind blows parallel to the mountains, in which case wind from aloft may be brought down to the surface.

❑ The wind blows at right angles and an opening exists through which it can funnel.

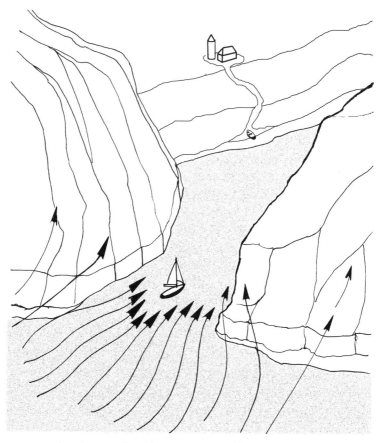

Anytime you have large masses of land with small openings, the wind will tend to accelerate through the openings if it is blowing towards the opening. When the wind is parallel with the coast, the acceleration effect is minimized.

charts and a good lookout on deck. When you see precipitous mountains in your area, be extra watchful with the weather.

THE SEA BREEZE

Most of us spend a good bit of our sailing lives with a local sea breeze providing the motive power. It is a circumstance with which we are all familiar.

The morning dawns clear, the land starts to heat up, a few puffy cumulus clouds form over the beach

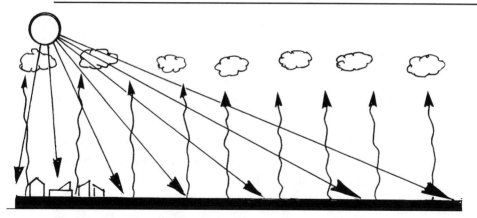

The sea breeze starts out with the sun warming the land surface, which heats up faster than the surrounding air. The land, in turn, heats the layer of air closest to it. The warm air rises, frequently forming small cumulus clouds.

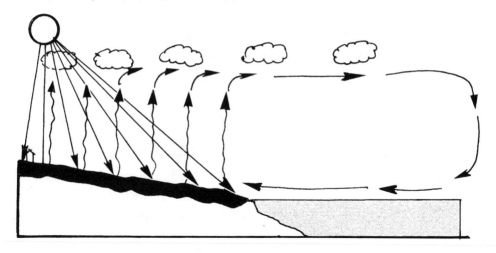

In the next phase cool air is drawn in from over the adjacent water. This air is heated in turn by the warm land and rises. It is this inward flow from the sea which causes the sea breeze. Meanwhile, the warmed air aloft, at and above the cloud base, is moving out over the ocean (opposite to the direction of the sea breeze). This is why you sometimes see the cumulus clouds formed by the sea breeze moving offshore (while the sea breeze is moving onshore).

or perhaps a mile inland.

About ten o'clock, an onshore wind starts to blow fitfully. As the afternoon progresses and it gets hot-

Sea breeze:

- Cold water and warm land create a local thermal wind.

- Wind starts out offshore, and moves in towards land as land heats up.

- Is typically strongest in late afternoon.

- Dies down in early to mid-evening.

- If there is an offshore flow present during the night this may delay onset of sea breeze.

ter inland, the breeze increases. The clouds that formed initially over the beach become higher, somewhat larger, and begin to move offshore — opposite the surface wind direction. Late in the afternoon or early evening, as the sun heads for the horizon, the breeze begins to taper off a bit.

What causes this mechanism is the same thing that drives the worldwide weather patterns, a difference in temperature. The water is usually cool. The sun hits the land, warming it faster than the water. The warmed air rises, and the cool air over the ocean rushes in to fill the void over the hot land.

In areas where there is a hot desert environment inland, fronted by cool water, the sea breeze can be very strong.

This is the case on San Francisco Bay and off Freemantle, Australia. Water temperature is cool, yet a few miles inland it can easily reach temperatures almost double the sea surface. The result is a very dependable and boisterous afternoon sea breeze.

The sea breeze normally starts to flow at right angles to the coastline, so that it is heading directly inland. However, it is the norm for the breeze to begin to veer (turn clockwise) in the Northern Hemisphere as the afternoon wears on, due to Coriolis effect (it backs — turns left — below the equator).

Generally speaking, sea breezes are benign. However, when their flow coincides with a larger pressure gradient wind, the two can reinforce each other with a much stronger combined wind result.

On the other hand, the sea breeze and gradient breeze may oppose each other, in which case the end product is less wind.

DOWN-SLOPE (KATABATIC) WINDS

The sea breeze dies off as temperatures even out at night. When there are mountains and valleys around you, they have the potential for a different phenomenon to take place.

The air at the top of the mountain is quite cool. It begins to sink, and flows down the valleys or down the flanks of the mountain and offshore. At first it may conflict with sea breeze, and a zone of calm air results. Once it takes over, it may blow miles out to sea, sometimes with surprising force.

As with the sea breeze, any gradient winds may reinforce this katabatic wind flow or oppose it.

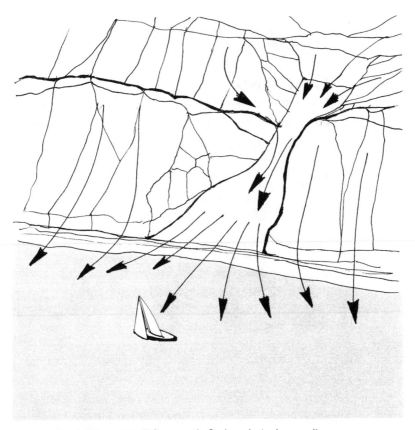

During the evening you will frequently find cool air descending down canyons and mountain slopes and spreading out to sea. This process typically starts between 2200 and 2400.

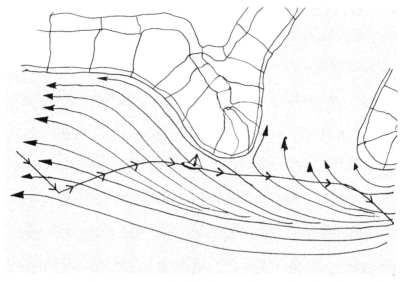

Large topographical features close to the shoreline tend to bend the wind parallel to their contours.

HEADLANDS

When you have a long coastline fronted by mountains, the mountains will tend to turn any breeze so that it runs more or less parallel with the coast.

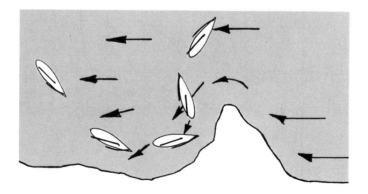

When the wind is blowing along the coast, headlands will usually provide a nice lift when you are sailing to windward. The best tactic is usually to head into the shore so that you have to tack out just where the shore starts to curve out towards the headland.

When you are traveling against this breeze, usually dead upwind, headlands can provide an excellent lift (favorable wind shift).

It is often possible to make good progress by planning an inshore tack so that it brings you into the beach below the headland. The wind will sometimes bend around the headland, giving you a lift as you travel up the coast.

It is not unusual to find increased winds at headlands, and sometimes a countercurrent. The combination of the increased wind and countercurrent can combine to make for a nasty chop. When this occurs, it is better to head on an offshore tack before you get to the headland to avoid the increased winds and confused seas.

Headland tactics when beating:

❑ Approach shore to leeward of the headland.

❑ Stay on inshore tack until lift dies and you sail into a header.

❑ Tack out to sea in the header and tack back as soon as lifted back on the favored tack.

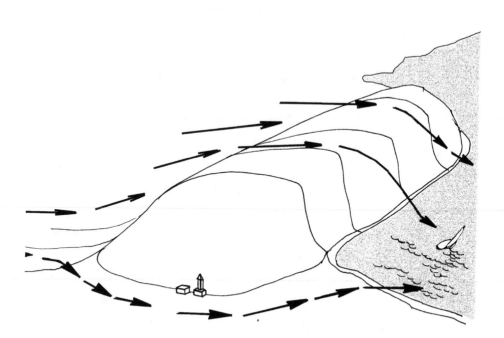

Acceleration situations are quite common where you have a hill or mountain shaped like the cross-section of a wing, at right angles to the wind flow. This can increase wind velocity from 30 percent to as much as 100 percent, depending on the height and shape of the topographic feature.

SPECIAL ACCELERATION SITUATIONS

There are times when the shape of the hills or mountains influencing your wind are like an airplane wing.

The breeze is forced to lift over it, and then accelerate over the top until it comes back to sea level, and meets with the rest of the wind. This acceleration phenomenon can be quite strong and create what the locals will probably call "Hurricane Gulch" or "Windy Lane."

Under normal situations, this will provide a bit of fun on an afternoon sail. However, if a gradient wind is present, the acceleration can be quite extreme and sometimes dangerous.

LONG NARROW BAYS

In some parts of the world you can cruise in long, narrow, fjord-like bays. When this occurs, the wind direction will invariably blow up or down the channel. Gustiness will typically be more severe in these situations than offshore, as the surrounding mountains trip the wind aloft and bring it down to sea level.

COASTAL TACTICS

The time may come when you are forced to play the sea breeze during the day and downslope winds at night. Perhaps your engine has quit, or you don't have enough fuel to make it to the next anchorage.

Here are a few tips for playing this game. First, determine how and where the sea breeze starts, and be as close to where it begins to flow by mid-morning. In many cases, the sea breeze begins a couple of miles offshore, then flows ashore as the land heats up after an hour or two.

During the day, as the breeze builds, whether you sail along the shore or further offshore is usually a function of wind angle and current. If there is an adverse current (and you are beating into it), it sometimes pays to sail close to shore and stay out of the current's influence.

A key question is where do you position yourself for the evening? If a gradient wind is blowing, try moving offshore where the gradient wind may be blowing stronger. On the other hand, if there's a good chance for an offshore downslope mountain wind to begin to blow, you will want to be as close to the beach as possible by the time it is ready to start flowing.

If you spend much time going up and down the west coast of Mexico and the U.S., even when powering, you are faced with some of the same issues.

If heading north against the prevailing winds (unless you are lucky enough to have a front blowing that gives southerly quadrant winds), the best policy is to leave in the late evening, after the sea breeze has died down. Then power while it is calm, and begin to sail on a nice reach as the downslope offshore breeze fills in.

In the early morning hours, when this breeze quits, back on comes the engine. You'll power again, usually through the first few hours of the sea breeze. Once it gets uncomfortable, or to the point that you are paying some real penalties for your progress uphill, find an anchorage, set the hook until the sea breeze dies down, and then start the process all over again.

Heading upwind along a mountainous coast:

- In early morning hours motor as far as possible until sea breeze begins to blow.

- Continue sailing until early afternoon, then anchor until the sea breeze dies down around midnight.

- Resume journey under power, then sail as offshore night breeze begins to blow.

- In early morning when night breeze dies, continue on under power.

HOLES IN THE WIND

For every mountain or headland that accelerates the wind, there is another situation where the local topography blocks the wind.

This is generally the case where the local mountains are at right angles to the wind flow. In this case, the breeze will frequently lift off above sea level. You may see nice movement in the clouds aloft, but nothing on the surface.

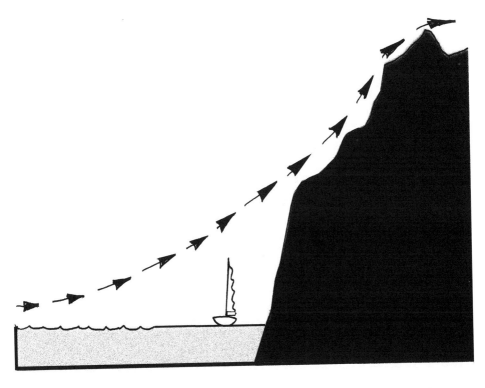

When there is a relatively abrupt feature along the shoreline— a mountain, series of buildings, or even a large ship—if the wind is blowing at right angles to this it will lift, leaving a windless vacuum for some distance out from the feature. In the case of a building or ship the wind hole might be a few boat lengths, but with mountains, the effect can extend many miles out to sea. This is also true in the lee of tall features.

SPECIAL SITUATIONS

Around the world you will find localized conditions that bear special watching. The rules by which the weather works in these areas may be different from what you are used to seeing, or from what we've covered in this text.

SOUTH AFRICA

One of these areas we've already mentioned briefly—the coast of South Africa (see page 57).

This is indeed one of the more challenging coastlines along which to passage. The distances are far between ports of refuge, there is the Aghulas current to contend with—both fast moving so that it creates huge seas when opposed by the wind, and warm so that it tends to intensify low pressure systems when they start to feel its surface.

Still, this is an interesting part of the world in which to voyage. If you are westbound sailing across the Indian Ocean and looking for a fast trip back to Western Europe or the States, you will find the route around the bottom of Africa faster than the alternate through the Red Sea and Mediterranean.

Let's start this discussion with some comments on a local phenomenon known as a coastal low—a semi-permanent feature along this coastline.

The example shown is from April 12, 1976—late summer in the Southern Hemisphere

Ian Hunter, Director of Marine Forecasting and Analysis for South Africa has been kind enough to share his thoughts on voyaging down their very interesting coastline.

"This first example sounds a warning to yachtsmen that the Southern Hemisphere is nowhere near as seasonal as the Northern Hemisphere. Certainly in terms of heavy swell from the Southern Ocean, it could occur at any time. And in this case, major cyclogenesis not far from the summer solstice."

Why is the South African coast so challenging?

❑ Harbors of refuge are few and far between.

❑ The warm Aghulas current flows southbound at up to seven knots in places opposing southerly quadrant gales.

❑ Weather systems move and develop quickly, especially when exposed to the warm influence of the Aghulas current.

"You cannot simply translate a system eastwards on the synoptic chart. A deep low at Gough Island quite often weakens by the time it is south of us. Furthermore, most frontal troughs are heading southeast as they pass South Africa." Ian Hunter, Deputy Director, Marine Forecast, South African Met. Bureau

"Mariners should take particular note of the *coastal low* on the east coast. This is a regular feature on the South African coast which is linked to the following frontal trough. Between Port Elizabeth and Richards Bay, the costal low passage may be associated with a so-called 'Buster' — a gust front which can raise the wind from near-calm to gale force in less than 5 minutes."

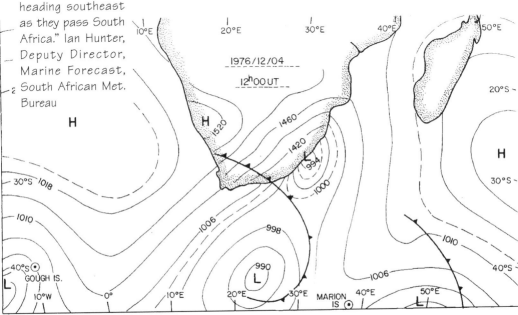

In the late 1970s, when we were voyaging down the coastline aboard Intermezzo, we would frequently see charts like this in the newspapers and on the evening TV news. For someone planning a passage, there are three lows with which you need to be concerned. The first is the one right in your face, just along the coast. There is another off the bottom of the continent, and a third out to the west. Given the speed these systems move all three could affect a single three- or four-day span.

The key is that big high pressure system to the west. It promises stable weather for a few days—if it doesn't get pushed too far north.

If you were coming down the coast and got caught in a system like this, you would have two choices. One would be to seek shelter as quickly as possible, or at least get into shallow water along the coast and out of the current. The other would be to head offshore to gain sea room and possibly reduce the speed of the current.

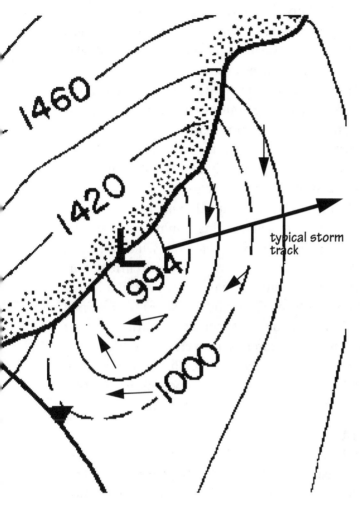

As a storm system like this approaches, the initial winds are from the north quadrant, giving you a fast ride along with the current. As the center of the system passes out to sea, the circulation on the backside brings southerly winds which oppose the Aghulas current and turn your run into a beat. Sometimes there isn't much wind with the leading edge of the system, and then when the backside hits—wham! It is blowing like stink in only a few minutes.

"This particular system caused havoc amongst a fleet of sailing dinghies competing off East London—many had to be abandoned. In Algoa Bay waves of up to 10m (33 feet) were reported and several ships estimated winds at over 50 knots. Coastal lows sometimes propagate at over 100 km/hour (60 knots!).

"The second example on May 10, 1998 depicts a cut-off low/blocking high combination which, depending on its exact location, is responsible for the 'Black Southeaster'. In this case the pattern

"Mariners who are tempted to hitch a ride on the Aghulas current when sailing southwards down the east coast must be aware that both wind and wave conditions are enhanced over the warm current. Furthermore, the current may interact with a heavy southwesterly swell to produce waves of abnormal height.

"The eastward ridging of the South Atlantic High is one of the most important features of our weather. On average it takes place after every second to third frontal passage but two 'bud-off' highs can come around in less than two days.

"The 'stable' weather associated with the 'bud-off' high is very transitory off the southern and eastern coasts (~1 day). Ahead of it generally fresh southwesters with some rain—behind it freshening east-north-east winds with fine weather and choppy seas. If the peak pressure passes through overnight an enhanced land breeze may occur (over 10 knots in winter)." Ian Hunter

remains relatively stationary as the low is blocked by an intense high. In many cases the low originates overland and may cause onshore southeasterly gales on its western flank as it exits seaward.

South African ports are designed for protection from the prevailing southwesterly swell and this system may thus disrupt port operations with its easterly components. In this particular case Durban harbor was closed for 48 hours. Winds of up to 50 knots occurred in coastal waters."

"Mariners who are tempted to hitch a ride on the Aghulas current when sailing southwards down the east coast must be aware that both wind and wave conditions are enhanced over the warm current. Furthermore, the current may interact with a heavy southwesterly swell to produce waves of abnormal height. During a yacht race from Durban to East London in 1984 three boats were lost, one of these without trace of yacht or crew. This was also a case of rapid intensification of a low pressure system close to the coast (explosive cyclogenesis)."

COASTAL TACTICS

In the late 1970s, when we were voyaging down this coastline aboard Intermezzo, we would frequently see charts like the ones on the preceding pages in the newspapers and on the evening TV news. Given the speed these systems move all three could affect a single three- or four-day span.

The key is that big high pressure system to the west. It promises stable weather for a few days—if it doesn't get pushed too far north.

If you were coming down the coast, and got caught in a system like this, you would have two choices. One would be to seek shelter as quickly as possible, or at least get into shallow water along the coast and out of the current. The other would be to head offshore to gain sea room and possibly reduce the speed of the current.

We asked Ian Hunter if he had some forecasting rules that might be of value. His reply is worth noting if you are sailing in this part of the world.

"If you are close inshore on the east coast with a rapidly-falling pressure, a slackening northeast wind, and a worsening haze, you can normally expect a 180-degree wind switch in the next few hours. It may come as a marked gust front (or "Buster") if the pressure is very low (about 1000 mb).

"If you are experiencing steady, heavy rain off the east coast with a southeast to northeasterly wind, a cut-off low could well be moving offshore."

When we asked Ian about early warning from the barometer his comment was, "Roughly speaking a sustained fall of 1mb per hour for more than 6 hours should be regarded as a danger sign. But heavy long-period swell generated at a distance may often arrive with no local "weather" as such. The thing to keep an eye on is the surface analysis. Sudden development of a deep low at about 55 degrees S and the dateline will usually be linked to the arrival of moderate to heavy swell two to three days later."

And cloud signs which seemed to be missing in our voyages in that part of the world? "We do not see the normal sequence of frontal clouds as we are too far north. Warm fronts pass to the south of South Africa and even cold fronts may not have much of a signature (except in the southwest where thickening stratus starts coming in roughly 6-12 hours ahead of the front.) The exception is when a secondary low pressure system forms on the passing cold front bringing far more cloud cover and precipitation — and, of course, wind."

We asked Ian about the signs from 500mb charts in his part of the world. "The 500mb prognosis goes

"Along the west coast in summer the Atlantic High is responsible for the persistent southeasters and fine weather—southeasterly winds frequently reaching gale force, especially where channelled through the mountains of the Cape Peninsula."

Passaging along the South African coast:

- ❑ Always watch the fax charts and barometer closely.

- ❑ Have a fall-back plan if caught unexpectedly by a south quadrant gale.

- ❑ Get out of the current as fast as possible in southerly conditions.

- ❑ A 1 mb/hour fall in the barometer for more than six hours (even with a clear sky) is a danger signal.

- ❑ Normal 500mb trough axis rules apply (i.e. westward tilt on trough axis indicates deepening surface low.

out at 0630 UTC on the radiofax. You find a westerly slant to the trough axis with a developing system and straight up and down trough axis when the system is weakening. Unfortunately, our upper air analysis does not go very far south."

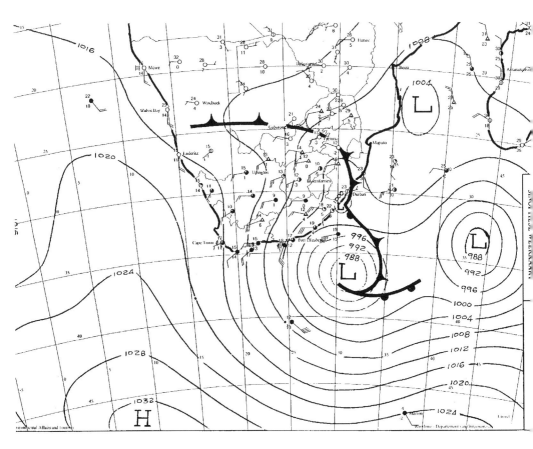

This scenario is very much like the one we encountered on our passage from Mauritius to Durban. We met a series of fast-moving southerly gales—typically lasting less than 12 hours. Then, just as we entered the Aghulas current a final gale came into play. This one hung on for a couple of days, with the barometer barely moving during the time in question.

The lack of change on the barometer indicates a stable low pressure system, which in turn means there is a high downwind blocking the low's progress—as we have here. In this case the blocking high is to the south and east, off the chart.

THE GULF STREAM

The Gulf Stream represents one of the most dangerous bodies of water on earth. A combination of factors creates an environment which is ripe for exciting weather and uncomfortable (or worse) seas.

On one hand you have a large land mass, typically quite cool, to windward. On the other you have the warm and fast-flowing Gulf Stream just offshore.

Take a moderate continental low or high pressure system and move it over warm water in the winter and you have an explosive mixture.

THERMAL-BASED WEATHER

You know by now that all inclement weather is based on differences in temperature and moisture content. The greater the difference, the more vigorous the weather.

Recall that it only takes a few degrees F, sometimes as little as one or one and half degrees C to start a giant thunderstorm rolling—and that thunderstorm can eventually turn into a hurricane.

Major storm systems can start to explosively deepen under some circumstances with as little as four degrees F (two degrees C) difference in temperature between sectors.

And then consider the Gulf Stream in fall and winter. The temperature gradient can easily be as great as 30 degrees F (18 degrees C) between air and water.

Add to this dry, cold air sweeping over the warm, moist water and you have what is truly an explosive mixture.

CURRENT

As if the atmospheric conditions weren't bad enough, you then have to factor in the Gulf Stream current and its impact on waves.

This is a complex issue, one which requires more space than we can devote in this text on weather.

Keep in mind, however, several factors: First,

The comments which follow on the Gulf Stream apply to all of the great ocean currents of the world. In each case these exhibit similar characteristics which can substantially affect weather and sea state.

- Rapid changes over water temperature relative to air.

- Fast-flowing currents opposing wind direction.

- Steep current speed gradients that cause ducting of seas.

Gustiness plays a big part in sea state. With the passage of a cold front, and an increase in gusts from the vertical turbulence behind the front, sea state can grow as much as 30% from what would have otherwise been the case with more stable winds in the warm sector.

Waves which run into a current wall, like the North Wall of the Gulf Stream, will sometimes act as if they have hit the entrance to an inlet, rapidly steepening and then breaking.

A northeaster off Nova Scotia may generate steep seas thousands of miles away off the coast of Florida, days later, due to Gulf Stream interference.

when winds are turbulent or gusty, the wind creates larger seas than with steady wind conditions. And the warm water situation creates far gustier conditions than is normal for the type of weather scenario you are likely to see at this latitude and time of year.

Next, there are a whole series of interactions between a current and waves, especially a current which is tightly channeled with large variations in water flow.

Wind blowing at right angles to dead against a current raises a much steeper sea which breaks earlier.

As little as one knot against a large open ocean wave can cause what would be an otherwise stable shape to steepen and break. The Gulf Stream runs at speeds of one knot on the low end to five knots at the top end.

Shorter period waves, i.e. waves which are newly generated, are more impacted by current than longer period open ocean seas.

Winds which quickly build tend to raise a steep, short period sea.

Finally, a variety of *ducting* situations can take place within a tightly channelled current, especially one with steep speed gradients.

This ducting can trap wave energy within a given area, bouncing it back and forth, or accelerate its movement to a distant location.

With any of the great ocean currents these problems exist. Be it Gulf Stream, Aghulas, or Kyushu, all of these can exacerbate the wind state with warm water, and create breaking seas in a very short time frame.

CAPE HATTERAS WEATHER

Cape Hatteras is infamous for its weather and rightly so. However, with today's ability to forecast upper level conditions using both direct soundings and water vapor imaging from satellites, the risk of making a wrong guess is diminishing.

There are several likely scenarios for unpleasantness in this part of the world. The first starts with a 500mb trough over the central United States. If the tilt axis is positive, i.e. the equator (bottom) end of the trough axis is to the west, then you have the first ingredient in place for a vigorous surface low on the Eastern Seaboard. The offset of the trough provides the venting mechanism required by the surface low.

Now, consider the equator side of this upper level trough. It is bringing warm, moist air from the Gulf of Mexico into the equation. This will mix with the cold air being brought down from the pole with the upwind side of the trough.

As this volatile brew moves over the Atlantic from the continental United States more heat/moisture energy is obtained from the ocean and the Gulf Stream.

The other scenario involves a vigorous high pressure system over New England or even further north. The clockwise circulation of these highs bring dry, cold air down from the arctic. This cold air interacts with the Gulf Stream and everything begins to hit the fan.

GULF STREAM CROSSING TACTICS

While all of this sounds scary, and there is no avoiding the fact that it can be dangerous, there are still plenty of safeguards to help you get to your destination safely.

The most important of these is patience, as well as the time horizon to wait for the right conditions before departing.

It is important to keep in mind that progress in moderate weather can be much slower due to sea state than you might otherwise imagine.

There might be periods of the year where conditions just never seem right. If that's the case, rather than taking a chance it is better to make alternate plans, or wait for another season.

Tactics for dealing with major ocean currents:

- Allow the weather to dictate the schedule.

- Make sure there is plenty of margin of error in your weather window.

- If the right conditions do not materialize, put the trip off and wait for another season.

- When at sea be prepared for sudden, potentially dangerous changes in wind and sea state.

- Avoid equinoctal periods when possible.

- Do everything possible to maintain speed, keeping passage time to a minimum.

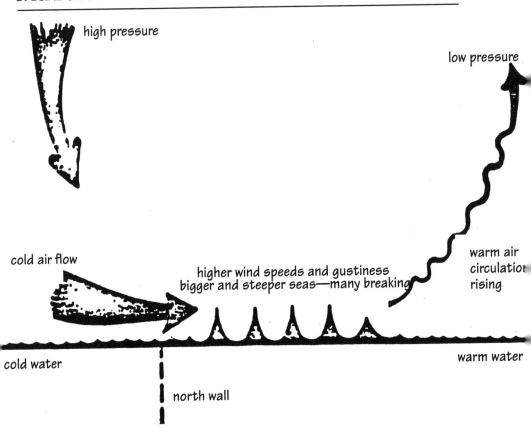

high pressure

low pressure

cold air flow

warm air circulation rising

higher wind speeds and gustiness
bigger and steeper seas—many breaking

cold water

warm water

north wall

The Gulf Stream scenario: Cool, relatively dry air from a low or high flows over the warm water. The air becomes heated, instability increases, and wind speed goes up dramatically.

At the same time sea state is growing rapidly from the base wind speed, with an added factor for gustiness (the gustiness coming from instability caused by the warm environment).

If the wind is at right angles or opposing the current, the current is then interacting with new, short period waves, where it has the most impact.

The result is a chaotic sea state, with far more breaking seas than would be the case in the open ocean with similar levels of wind.

Areas of confused seas will be found within the current, sometimes well after the storm has passed. These can be dangerous for a couple of days after the wind has died down.

'ere is a typical
cenarios you
hould try to avoid.
this case a weak
rontal system is
st to the east of
he main stream
xis.

high pressure is
ushing out from
anada (1045mb!).
hese highs
ometimes are
table, circulating
old air down from
ne arctic over this
rea of warm water
r days on end.

he wind flow is
irectly opposing
ost of the
tream flow.

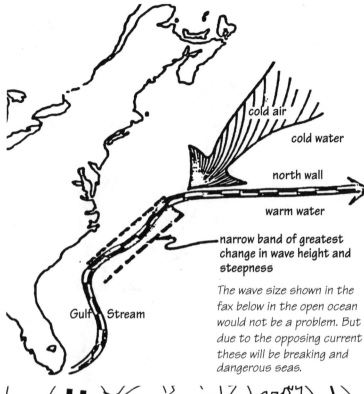

narrow band of greatest
change in wave height and
steepness

The wave size shown in the
fax below in the open ocean
would not be a problem. But
due to the opposing current
these will be breaking and
dangerous seas.

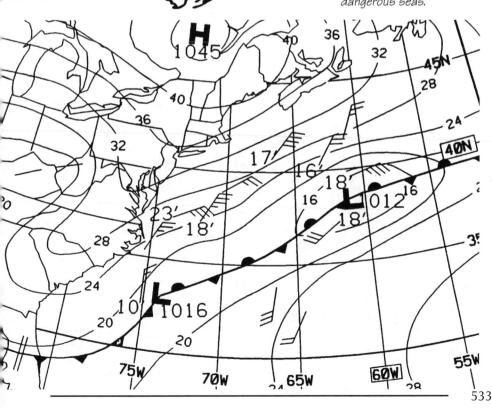

In a situation where the wind is blowing at right angles to the stream, sea state may not be quite as chaotic from current/wave interaction, but the area of higher winds and gustiness due to temperature differential can be greater than shown in the previous panel.

In the synoptic chart (below) we have a squash zone set up between the moderate low pressure system and high following from the west. Note the sea state indicated—up to 35 feet (11m)—which means occasional waves of even greater size.

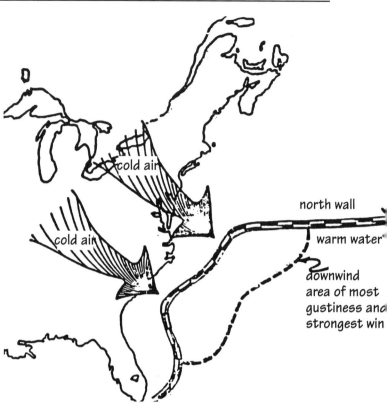

north wall

warm water

downwind area of most gustiness and strongest win

cold air

cold air

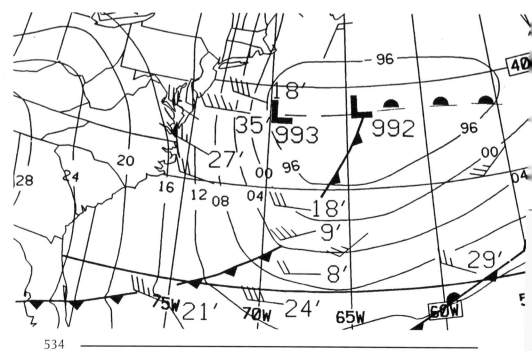

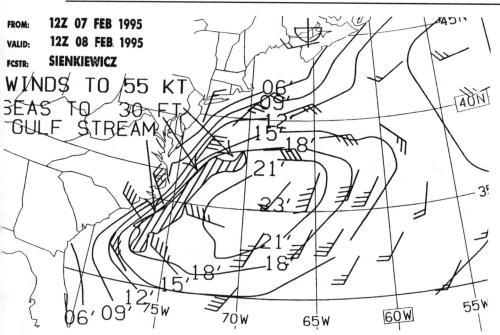

FROM: **12Z 07 FEB 1995**
VALID: **12Z 08 FEB 1995**
FCSTR: **SIENKIEWICZ**

WINDS TO 55 KT
SEAS TO 30 FT
GULF STREAM

Here are a couple of (unfortunately) typical equinoctal and winter scenarios for the Gulf Stream. Note that in both cases maximum winds are called for on the east side of the stream (due to the warm water). Gustiness will further enhance the force in the wind. The biggest seas are shown right in the stream itself, to the west of the wind maxima.

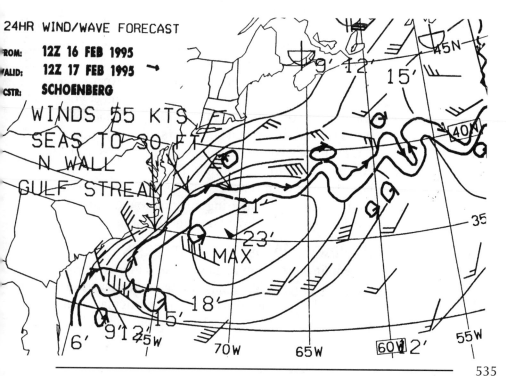

24HR WIND/WAVE FORECAST

FROM: **12Z 16 FEB 1995**
VALID: **12Z 17 FEB 1995**
CSTR: **SCHOENBERG**

WINDS 55 KTS
SEAS TO 30 FT
N WALL
GULF STREAM

CRUISE PLANNING

When the time comes to plan your next cruise many factors are to be considered.

Plans are best prepared with a series of options based on what you find as the departure date comes closer.

Some of them are personal, like when you can get away. Others are related to the skill level you and your crew have at your disposal. You also have to consider how your boat is designed, its structure, and what it is capable of withstanding.

Into this mix — indeed into every decision that has to do with the sea — comes weather.

Weather is the great arbiter of what is possible and what gets you into trouble. It is the key factor in comfort, enjoyment and safety.

PHILOSOPHY

Try to avoid passages that must conform to a schedule.

It is worth remembering that long-term cruise planning is something of an oxymoron, and the comments that follow must be considered academic, for they are based on what is "normal," and the weather is rarely normal.

Plans are best prepared with a series of options based on what you find as the departure date comes closer. It rarely makes sense to try to force a passage into what looks like less than ideal conditions. This is typically a prescription for trouble.

Try to avoid passages that must conform to a schedule. If you have people expecting to meet you, leave plenty of leeway — and advise them that nothing is for certain when it comes to sailing schedules.

Remain alert for atypical weather patterns.

Use all the weather resources at your disposal, and compare them to one another. There will frequently be differing data on the same subject, but if you wait, continually gathering information, eventually the correct approach will become apparent.

ATYPICAL WEATHER PATTERNS

Remain alert for atypical weather patterns. It may be that a major volcano has erupted in the past year, spewing huge quantities of ash and particulate matter into the air. This will affect temperatures, rainfall, and storm formation, and will throw off all of the seasonal issues we've discussed in the preceding sections.

Or there may be an El Nino or La Nina event taking place, in which case there will be major disruptions from what may be considered the norm. You may not know about these issues when you make your initial plans, but the question should be asked before departure.

And if conditions are changed, you may want to consider an alternate plan.

Take, for example, the situation many cruisers in Mexico faced in the 1997 cruising season. With a major El Nino event occurring did they want to chance a hurricane season on the Eastern or Central South Pacific?

While these areas are relatively free from cyclones during their summer months in normal years, with El Nino kicking in they would be seeing a lot more action. Do you head down to the South Pacific anyway and then make sure you are out of the area when summer arrives, or do you spend another year in Mexico and then head to Polynesia the following year?

Both options work—the main thing is to be aware of the issues involved, discuss them, and come to an informed decision.

PILOT CHARTS

Linda and I used to spend hours pouring over pilot charts, planning our passages to miss the squares indicating lots of gales or more than normal calms. However, with the exception of the southern Indian Ocean tradewinds, we've never seen much correlation between the pilot charts and the real world.

Why? Because the charts represent statistical samplings of data accumulated over many years. As such, they are averages. The high and low figures tend to even out.

The results are worth studying, but only in a generic context. You can, for example, use the pilot charts for a long-term plan, with the understanding

Pilot charts rarely relate to the real world you find on the ocean.

that, as the date for departure approaches, it is important to study the existing weather conditions and how the season is shaping up.

SAILING DIRECTIONS

Sailing directions, both those issued by the British Admiralty and U.S. Government, are a step up from the pilot charts.

Here you will find a discussion of the typical weather patterns throughout the year. This data is certainly worth studying for an understanding of what the normal patterns look like. However, don't expect to see many matches to what you read.

The best way to use this data is in conjunction with current synoptic charts, so that you see what is actually happening in comparison to what the books say. Between the two—current fax and historical sailing directions—you will be able to formulate a realistic plan for the passage intended.

The best way to use sailing directions is in conjunction with current synoptic charts—so you can compare theory to reality.

EQUINOCTIAL GALE SEASON

We've discussed in some detail the fact that solar heating—or the differences therein—accounts for our weather. Seasons when the temperature is at its greatest variation are the early spring and late fall. Because the atmosphere warms and cools faster than the surface of the ocean, at these times of year you have the greatest divergence in air mass temperatures.

In fall, for example, polar winds which are very cold collide with air masses from the tropics or extratropical regions where the sea surface still retains much of its summer heat.

Fall and spring gales tend to be more severe than those taking place in winter and summer.

The resulting temperature gradient, greater than either in deep summer or the dead of winter, creates more instability and wind force.

In many cases—for example, heading to the tropics for the winter—you have no choice but to voyage during the equinoctial gale season. Linda and I have done this dozens of times ourselves. The key is to remember that the weather risks are greater at this time of year, and then plan and prepare accordingly.

If your passages are of short duration, the risks are obviously of a lesser magnitude.

TROPICAL VS. MID-LATITUDE STORMS

Traveling between the temperate latitudes and the tropics (or vice versa) involves a trade-off in risks.

When you head towards the tropics in the fall, the earlier you leave, the greater the risk of a late season hurricane. On the other hand, the later you leave, the bigger the threat from a major equinoctial depression.

There seems to be a tendency to regard the hurricane threat as greater than the equinoctial gale. However, our own feelings are that this is not necessarily the case.

Yes, hurricanes tend to have much stronger surface wind fields than depressions. However, these wind fields are relatively small in area (most of the time) compared to the much larger size of the equinoctal and winter depressions.

It is easy to see scenarios where the much larger equinoctial storms, which have so many miles of fetch in which to build waves, are actually more of a threat than the smaller hurricane that does not blow over enough of an area to create really huge seas.

Another factor is the speed at which these systems move and your ability to dodge them. Mid-and high-latitude storms move much faster than do tropical hurricanes. In addition, their very size makes them harder to dodge.

Our own preference is to go a little earlier, when the risks of a fall storm are at a minimum, and to stay a little longer until the risk from spring storms has subsided. (For an interesting comparison between a hurricane and an extratropical storm, see page 547.)

TROPICS

Passage planning from within the tropics is usually much simpler than in other areas. Of course, you need to be aware of the hurricane season and the risk of out-of-season storms.

Traveling between the tropics and temperate climate you are faced with a trade-off. Do you worry more about late season hurricanes, or early equinoctial gales?

Hurricanes have stronger winds, but cover much smaller areas and move more slowly, so are easier to dodge than larger fast moving extratropical storms.

This is done by evaluating the season-long charac-teristics (like El Nino) and then watching the local weather signs (sky, barometer, wind and sea).

If those signs turn negative, and if it is during the winter when theoretically there should be no hurri-canes, you will want to assume the worst, until the situation proves otherwise.

During many seasons the trades are anything but steady. They may blow hard, die down, have fronts interspersed with periods of high pressure stable weather.

The tradewind direction can vary from northeast to southeast and back. If there are fronts around, the winds may reverse.

When you are looking at a given passage keep these wind-shift cycles in mind. Often there is a pat-tern to them, and you can use the pattern—time per-mitting—to have the optimum wind direction and speed for the intended voyage.

When you are look-ing at a given pas-sage keep these wind-shift cycles in mind. Often there is a pattern to them, and you can use the pattern.

AGAINST THE TRADES

Sometimes, you may have a destination that is in theory upwind, against the tradewinds. You can beat or motorsail your way to weather. Or, you can wait for a frontal passage, light period, or major shift to help you on your way.

This is the situation Linda and I found ourselves in during the South Pacific winter of 1997. We were bringing *Beowulf* back to California and our trip from the Australs to the Marquesas was in theory dead to weather.

However, in the 1600 or so miles of sailing we had less than a day and a half of beating. We accom-plished this by waiting until a convergence zone would approach blocking the easterly tradewinds, and then heading to the next island or group along the way. We frequently had westerly-quadrant winds or calms (in the latter case we motored).

When your destina-tion is against the tradewinds by wait-ing for the north-east/southeast oscillations and/or for frontal pas-sages, you can fre-quently avoid beating.

During the winter of 1997 you could count on a shift every ten days or so. On several occasions, when we were headed northeast, we waited for the trades to shift to the southeast, almost a beam reach.

HIGH LATITUDES

Sailing in the high latitudes brings some interesting weather trade-offs. In the summer, when temperatures are apt to be cruiser-friendly, a lot more solar energy is available to create temperature and pressure gradients. So summer blows can actually be stronger than what you find in winter. They also can develop and move very quickly.

The windy periods are apt to be interspersed with periods of flat calm as high centers move over you. It frequently makes sense to motor during the calms and hide out in a snug anchorage when it is blowing.

MID-LATITUDE CONSIDERATIONS

Planning for mid-latitude weather can sometimes be the most difficult of all.

This is due to the nature of the frontal systems — typically a combination of cold, dry polar air masses interacting with warm, moist subtropical or tropical air masses.

The variations from year to year in how these two air masses form and move are substantial. Even within a given year, major changes take place from week to week.

You can form a generic plan, but then you need to watch the weather developments closely as passage time approaches. Since most mid-latitude cruising tends to take place in areas with lots of weather resources, you have more tools with which to work than is usually the case in high latitudes or the tropics.

EXTREME TEMPERATURE GRADIENTS

Any time there is an extreme temperature gradient, you are going to have extreme winds. So we must be constantly aware of conditions that can cause these temperature differentials.

The collision of cool and warm air masses is one that we've discussed in detail throughout the book. Another is what happens when a given weather system encounters a new large source of heat energy.

Any time there is an extreme temperature gradient, you are going to have extreme winds.

This is the case with cold fronts moving from the East Coast of the U.S. out into the Atlantic where they encounter the warm temperatures of the Gulf Stream.

Anytime this occurs there is a risk of a major increase in wind strength. This risk is particularly acute in the colder months as the continental air masses are quite cool while the Gulf Stream remains almost constant in temperature — so the temperature gradient becomes even greater in colder months.

HURRICANE SEASONS

The hurricane season is always a major cruising weather consideration. The primary question is how close do you cut the season? The later in the year you head into the tropics, the lower the hurricane risks.

However, the longer you wait, the colder it gets in the mid-latitudes from which you are escaping.

At the end of the winter cruising season, the issues are a little different. Here you have a more difficult risk assessment. In most areas, the early part of summer sees little or no hurricane activity. In the Caribbean, for example, things are usually quiet until the end of July or August. But there have been storms in May, so there are some risks involved.

How you deal with this question has a lot to do with your abilities, those of your crew, vessel preparation, and the availability of hurricane holes in which you can seek shelter.

Then there is the question of spending the hurricane season in the tropics, with a close eye on the weather. Obviously, having somewhere to shelter is a major consideration in this strategy. Along with the shelter is the quality and quantity of neighbors; odds are, your neighbors will pose the biggest risk to your vessel during a major storm.

THE HERD MENTALITY

Most of us who cruise seem to make friends more quickly on the water than on land. Friendships tend to be stronger because of a common interest. There are always lots of discussions about systems, rigs, the ultimate boat, where to go next and, of course, the weather.

Cruising with a group of boats can be great fun, and you can learn a lot. But it is important to think for yourself when it comes to weather risks and what to do about them.

If a potentially dangerous situation exists—a given passage can pose more obstacles at certain times than at others—it is always best to go with your own conservative approach and forget what the others are doing.

PLAYING THE ODDS

Everything we do in life has risks. When you get out of bed in the morning, you take a risk of breaking your leg. When you drive home from a movie on Saturday night you risk a run-in with a drunk driver. And when you make a passage, there is always some degree of risk from the weather.

However, just as you drive more carefully in the evenings and on weekends because of the risk of drunk drivers, you can plan your passages to have a majority of the odds in your favor.

And once you are committed, by keeping an eye on how the weather is developing and taking appropriate, conservative action in line with the risks that exist, passages can be made with maximum safety.

Cruisers get into trouble when they ignore the odds starting out, or don't pay attention to the signs once they are at sea.

LONG-TERM CRUISING

As your cruising plans stretch out, you begin to work within the confines of the seasons. In the winter months you cruise in the tropics. Then, during the summer, you head for the temperate zones where a different diet, clothing and culture await your arrival.

Passaging to and from the tropics means voyaging during the equinoctial seasons. However, the period of exposure is typically moderate, usually about a

1,000 miles or so and a week to ten days in time. Picking the right time to make the passage is a function of watching the weather at both ends of the trip.

Passages to the tropics are usually somewhat easier than passages from the tropics to the higher latitudes.

The ITCZ (Doldrums)

If you are headed to or from the South Pacific, or finishing a circumnavigation via the Red Sea or South Africa, you will be dealing with the doldrums, or what is more properly called the Intertropical Convergence Zone (ITCZ).

This is the region between the tradewind belts, roughly just north of the equator. Here the air flow tends to rise and, once at altitude, flow out towards the poles.

Because of the heat and moisture available there can be quite a lot of convective (thunderstorm) activity in the doldrums.

Crossing Tactics

The Pacific and Atlantic doldrum belts have a tendency to be widest at their eastern edges and by mid-ocean are usually fairly thin.

When you are deciding where to cross there is frequently a trade-off. The most direct course may take you through the thickest part of the doldrums. Frequently, by moving to the west a few hundred miles, you will have more wind and an easier passage through. Of course if you have good powering range, this is less of a factor.

What to Expect

The ITCZ is typically squally, with lots of rain, wind shifts and changes in velocity. One moment you may have 30 knots of wind from the southeast, the next it will be blowing from the southwest, and a few minutes later it will be flat calm. Squalls can be quite intense, especially in the evening, but most of the time they are moderate in velocity.

If this sounds like you have to be ready for just about anything—you're right. Back in the 1980s, Linda, the kids and I were bringing *Intermezzo* up from South Africa towards the Caribbean for the first time. We were in contact with our friends the Naranjos aboard *Windshadow* a few hundred miles ahead of us.

One evening on our schedule Ralph Naranjo indicated they had experienced storm-force winds for a number of hours as they entered the ITCZ.

The next day, as the sky became leaden and very ominous, we started to reduce sail. By nightfall we had *Intermezzo* shortened down to her third reef in the main and heavy staysail. We ended up motoring the entire night and the next day emerged on the northern side of the ITCZ into the Northeast Trades and a clear, blue sky filled with puffy cumulus with virtually calm conditions.

If we had pressed on with full canvas that night, we would have been nailed for sure.

Today, with weather fax capabilities on hand, it is easier to pick a narrow spot at which to cross. Not only can you check the tropical streamlines, but the satellite images give a good indication of where the ITCZ is thin and thick.

We've crossed the ITCZ three times with a fax aboard and have been able to pick the best route quite easily. Total time spent in the ITCZ in these three trips is probably less than half a day.

USING RADAR

When you are working your way through the thunder squalls that are a part of the ITCZ process, radar will give you an indication of where the rain is, and therefore where the wind may (or may not) be. It is especially helpful at night.

If you are trying to get a nice deck wash, and top off the water tanks, radar really helps.

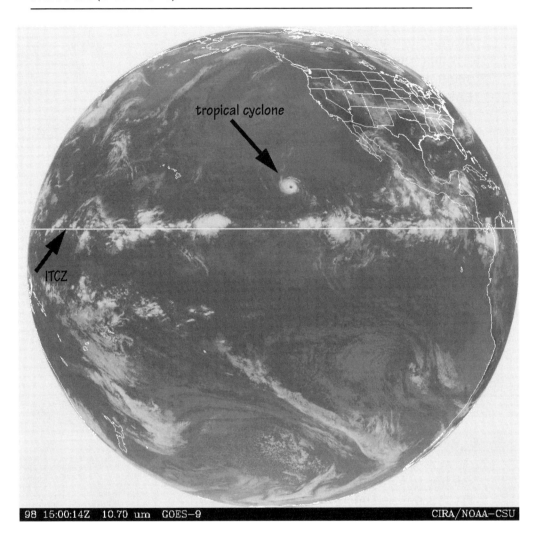

The best way to visualize the ITCZ is with full disc satellite images. This view is for the 27h of July, 1998. The white line running horizontally is the ITCZ. Note the cloud mass built up to the east, coming from South America. There's a clear spot, and then another mass of clouds. If you were headed across the equator there are two areas of clear air which, if they were on your course, you could use.

There is also a well developed hurricane shown about 15 degrees North (with a black arrow pointing it out). This is, of course, the issue with summertime passages. You would want to keep a close eye on the tropical fax charts for tropical waves, and watch the satellite images for convective activity.

We've made hurricane season passages across the ITCZ three times. Each time, however, was in a boat fast enough to use any tropical storms encountered to our advantage, or to get out of the way if necessary.

TROPICAL AND EXTRATROPICAL STORM SIZE COMPARISON

As we were finishing off the last details in this book we received an e-mail from Lee Chesneau at the Marine Prediction Center. "Check out the North Pacific system we are working right now, and compare it to Mitch. Both are really interesting systems. They will give your readers a sense of scale."

For a late season (October 27, 1998) Caribbean hurricane, Mitch is a record breaker. With a central pressure of just 902mb and sustained winds of 155 with gusts to 180 at its peak, you would think this is a big storm.

Yet the region of hurricane strength winds—64 knots and above—cover a radius of just 100 miles from the storm center.

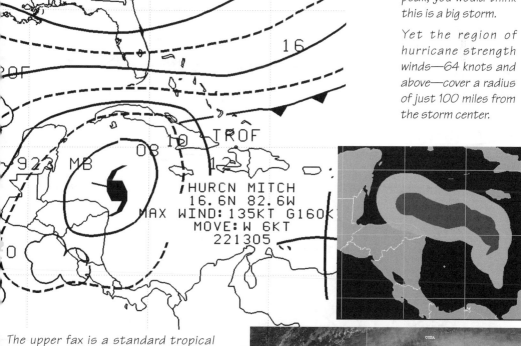

HURCN MITCH
16.6N 82.6W
MAX WIND: 135KT G160K
MOVE: W 6KT
221305

The upper fax is a standard tropical chart. The high pressure system to the north will keep Mitch tracking west. The upper right image is area of hurricane and storm strength winds for the track of the storm. The dark areas are hurricane strength while the lighter area is storm strength wind. The satellite image (lower right) looks huge, but the area of hurricane strength winds are relatively confined.

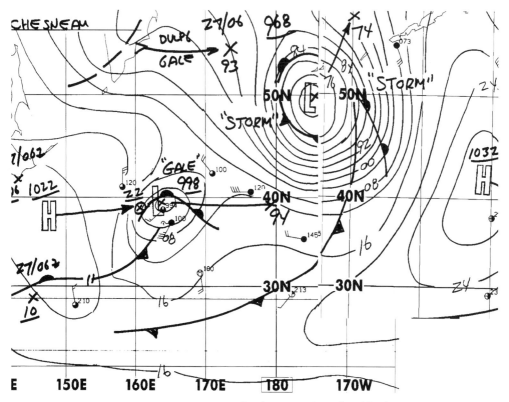

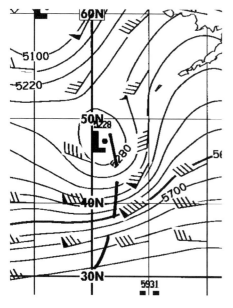

At the same time that Mitch was grabbing the headlines, this huge storm was creating highly unpleasant conditions in the North Pacific.

From the 500mb chart to the left you will note that the upper level low has closed off and that this signals the dissipation of the surface storm system. On the previous day, winds to 80 knots were experienced and storm force winds covered an area of close to 1000 miles. Significant seas were 50 feet (15 meters) with maximum wave heights even taller than this.

For October 27th, shown here, things are winding down a bit with winds in the 45- to 60-knot range forecast within 360 nautical miles of the center.

While this system's top winds are not even near those of Hurricane Mitch, this storm is harder to get away from and will create much larger seas.

WEATHER WINDOWS

At the beginning of every passage a window of opportunity presents itself, during which you have a pretty good idea of what the weather conditions will be for that period of time. Many factors affect how long this window is open.

BOAT SPEED

A primary factor is how fast your boat can travel under a variety of conditions. Obviously, the faster you can move, the more control you have over the weather environment you find yourself in.

This is not only important when the breeze is blowing, but when it is light as well. Often by motoring in calm, or motorsailing in light airs, you can substantially reduce passage time and/or increase your weather window.

A corrolary of the boat speed under power is range.

KNOW YOUR CAPABILITIES

Racing boats put together performance tables known as *polars*. These show the speed the boat should be making in any given wind strength and direction. For cruising this makes sense too. This is a significant aid in planning your passages and evaluating weather windows.

Ideally, you will have boat speed in a variety of wind and sea conditions, as well as performance under power and when motorsailing.

It will take time to accumulate the information, but you will eventually find it extremely valuable, especially when it comes to planning your tactics once you are at sea.

WEATHER SYSTEM SPEED

In establishing how long your weather window will be open, speed of movement of weather systems is the major factor.

Weather window issues:

❑ Boat speed under sail in adverse as well as nice conditions.

❑ Range under power.

❑ Weather system speed and direction of movement.

As you know, highs move rather slowly compared to low pressure systems. And the speed of both are affected by other major weather systems.

At times, a given high or low will be stationary. This can provide extra time for you to make tracks, but you always have to be mindful that whatever slowed or stopped the system can allow it to begin moving at any time.

Conversely, you must keep an eye on acceleration of systems. This applies more to lows than to highs.

RELATIVE DIRECTION

If you are moving in the same relative direction as the weather, then you have two or three times the window you have when you are moving towards the weather systems.

Keep your eye out for upper level conditions which could accelerate speed of surface weather systems.

Heading across the Atlantic towards Europe the weather is going the same way, so you will see fewer systems. Coming back from Europe to the States, you are headed towards the weather on the northern route.

DEFINING A GOOD WINDOW

What makes a good weather window is often subject to debate. Obviously, you look at your own skills, the boat, your crew, and how much discomfort you are prepared to endure.

As your experience grows, what once seemed like stormy weather may begin to look like an opportunity to get the passage over with quickly.

A key ingredient in this definition is the advantage (or disadvantage) of waiting.

At times you will have reinforced tradewinds, a steady 25 to 30 knots, making for a boisterous sail. If you wait for milder weather, you may be faced with a total calm. On the other hand, there are areas where the calm is welcome if you have long-range motoring capability.

U.S. EAST COAST DEPARTURE

Leaving the East Coast of the U.S. for Bermuda or the West Indies calls for careful analysis of the weather patterns. As we have discussed in some detail, you do not want to be caught anywhere near the Gulf Stream with its wave building currents and wind enhancing warmth, if there is unsettled weather about.

The key is to be patient, watch the patterns, and wait until you see a calm period, typically dominated by high pressure, about to unfold.

The series of fax charts which follow are for a period which appears settled in the fall of 1998, mid-October to be exact. The key is how quickly you can get away from the coast and well south — before problems erupt.

This first chart is the current 500mb evaluation. A benign upper level high is shown sitting over the midwest of the U.S. Note the trough axis southeast of Greenland with a positive tilt on the axis (to the west). You would expect vigorous surface development to the east of this trough, but that is well out of the area of our concern for this voyage.

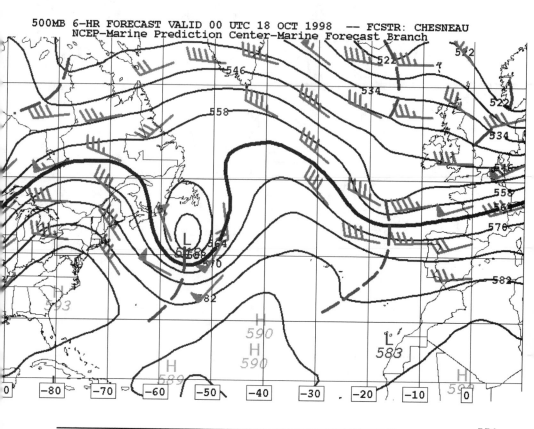

500MB 6-HR FORECAST VALID 00 UTC 18 OCT 1998 -- FCSTR: CHESNEAU
NCEP-Marine Prediction Center-Marine Forecast Branch

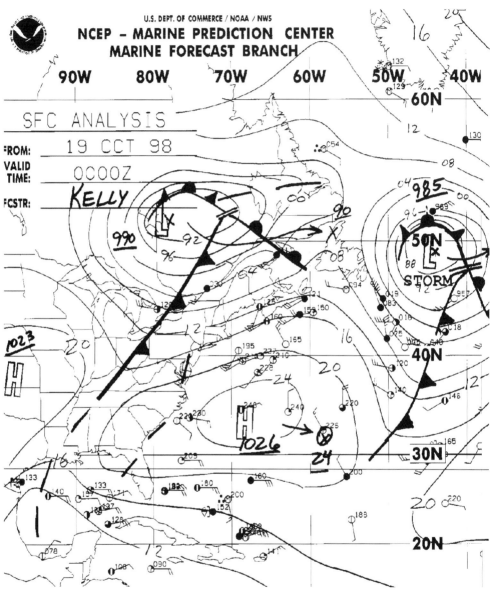

The surface forecast shows the high to be slow moving, with the central pressure expected to drop from 1026 to 1024mb in the next 24 hours. You can tell by the arrow and "x" just east of the "H" that this system isn't going anywhere fast. Heading offshore winds will be light, and unfortunately on the nose. It is probably better to wait for the leading edge of the high to the west to bring fair winds. Note the storm system south of Greenland which ties to the 500mb trough on the preceding page.

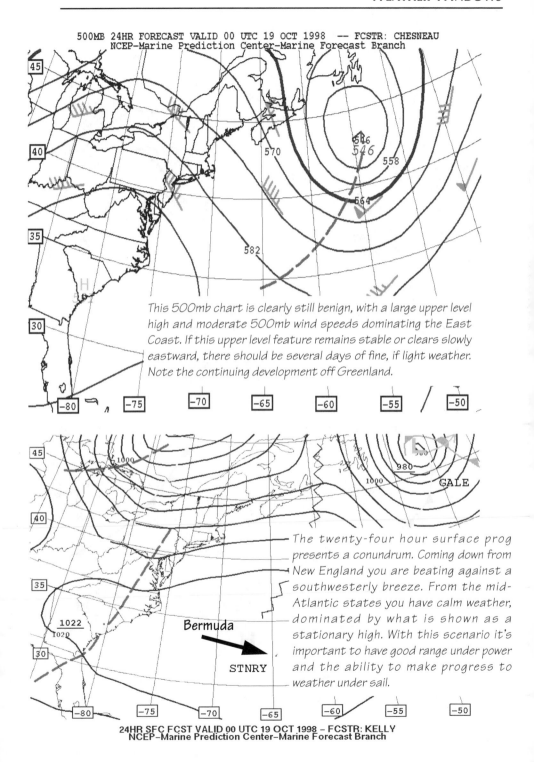

500MB 24HR FORECAST VALID 00 UTC 19 OCT 1998 -- FCSTR: CHESNEAU
NCEP-Marine Prediction Center-Marine Forecast Branch

This 500mb chart is clearly still benign, with a large upper level high and moderate 500mb wind speeds dominating the East Coast. If this upper level feature remains stable or clears slowly eastward, there should be several days of fine, if light weather. Note the continuing development off Greenland.

The twenty-four hour surface prog presents a conundrum. Coming down from New England you are beating against a southwesterly breeze. From the mid-Atlantic states you have calm weather, dominated by what is shown as a stationary high. With this scenario it's important to have good range under power and the ability to make progress to weather under sail.

24HR SFC FCST VALID 00 UTC 19 OCT 1998 – FCSTR: KELLY
NCEP-Marine Prediction Center–Marine Forecast Branch

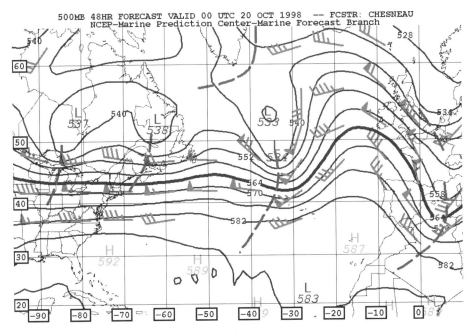

500MB 48HR FORECAST VALID 00 UTC 20 OCT 1998 -- FCSTR: CHESNEAU
NCEP-Marine Prediction Center-Marine Forecast Branch

The 48-hour prognosis shows zonal flow at the 500mb level and favorable wind angles at the surface as the surface front passes over the coast bringing northwest winds behind it. In a powerful sailing vessel you might be tempted to head offshore. But look at the two short wave trough axes in the zonal flow, one over the Great Lakes and the other just off the coast of Nova Scotia. You will need to be well south of this area before this zonal flow turns meridional. At that point there will probably be a vigorous low on the surface.

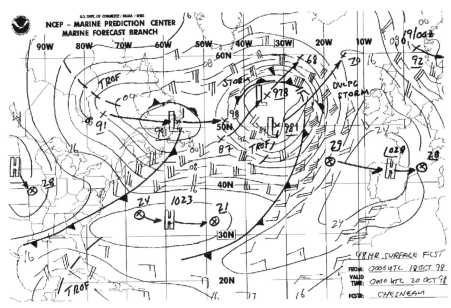

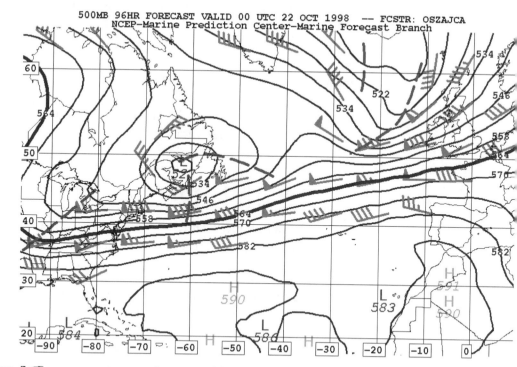

500MB 96HR FORECAST VALID 00 UTC 22 OCT 1998 — FCSTR: OSZAJCA
NCEP-Marine Prediction Center-Marine Forecast Branch

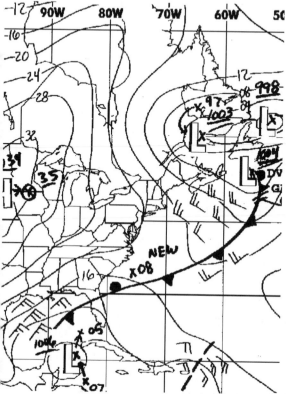

Here is where the go/no go decision becomes difficult. The surface forecast at 96 hours (lower left) actually looks pretty good. As the front and then high moves offshore there will be favorable winds for heading to warmer climates.

But then look at that heavily tilted 500mb trough over the Great Lakes. If this computer projection is correct, there will be a very significant surface depression associated with that trough axis— especially as the surface low moves out over the Gulf Stream.

This is where a call to a professional forecaster—someone who can give you a heads up on the believability of the computer model—would be a good idea.

If you have lots of reliable boat speed at your disposal, you might be disposed to chance it. After all, if you could maintain 200 miles a day on average you would be 800 miles south by the time the potential surface low impacts the coast. But, the conservative thing to do would probably be to wait for another window, or head down the Intercoastal Waterway.

WORKING WITH LOCAL FORECASTERS

Before departing on a passage, regardless of how many forecasting tools you have aboard, it always makes sense to check in at the local meteorological office and chat with a forecaster.

This gives you a chance to pick their brains, find out about their biases, and analyze how the local forecast process will affect you.

You will usually find the forecaster on duty is happy to chat about the weather, how it cycles over time, and how they put together their forecasts.

Check with the local forecasters well before departure to get a feel for their prediction process and biases.

Ask about:

❏ How accurate computer models are in predicting the 500mb level.

❏ How they confirm computer models.

❏ When they deem a potential risk serious enough to broadcast warning data.

RISK ASSESSMENT

When we go through this process we want to know first about how the forecasters treat the potential of developing threats.

This is usually best addressed with a discussion of how the atmosphere behaves in this region, during the current season, and within the weather pattern for this season as it is unfolding.

The 500mb level, of course, usually holds the keys to this process.

We like to get a feel for how accurate the computer models are, and what other tools (such as water vapor satellite images) are used to confirm or refute the computer modeling.

In this same context, we like to have a feel for when a risk is deemed great enough to get mentioned in the written, voice and fax chart broadcasts.

Most met services have policies in this regard. You will probably find that you want to know before the data is broadcast that a potential threat exists.

Since this data is probably not going to be made public, the only way to get your hand on it is to talk to the folks making the forecasts, to find out what is going on upstream at the 500mb level.

WEATHER CYCLES

Weather patterns tend to go in cycles. Sometimes these cycles are just a few days, other times they may be on a weekly or biweekly basis. If you are new to an area, or have not been watching the fax charts, you will probably not be aware of the cycles.

The local forecaster can give you a "heads up" on this issue, both in general terms as well as where the weather specifically sits right now.

UNUSUAL LOCAL CONDITIONS

Almost all areas of the world have unique weather situations which you may not have experienced before. It is a good idea to ask about these, and make some notes about special warning signs (barometer, wind direction, cloud progression, etc.).

These special situations may have to do with local upwellings of warm water; they might be topographic in nature; they may involve the formation of secondary lows; or might be related to compression zones between highs and lows under certain conditions.

The forecasters live with these occurrences on a daily basis and to them they are not unique — so you need to ask detailed questions.

Direct weather issues to discuss:

- ❏ Local weather cycles, and how you tell what phase you are in.

- ❏ Unique weather and its warning signs.

- ❏ Action of 500mb troughs and ridges and how it affects surface conditions.

- ❏ Potential for explosive storm generation and conditions required.

DISCUSSING WEATHER WINDOWS

In the end, all of this dialog comes down to the time duration of the weather window you are seeking. This time issue is a function of how fast you can travel in various conditions and range under power.

The odds are the capabilities of your vessel and crew will be different than those of other vessels with whom the forecasters have spoken. It is important that if time-specific questions are addressed, they are done so in such a way that you are sure the replies apply to your performance capabilities.

The objective of this book is to prevent this from happening to you! This photo was taken from the bridge of the 700-foot (215-meter) bulk cargo carrier MV Selkirk Carrier. The crew estimated waves at 70 to 80 feet (21 to 25 meters). (Photo courtesy of Captain George Ianiev)

SEVERE WEATHER REVIEW

You have been through almost 600 pages of data for the most part devoted to the avoidance of severe weather.

Some of these systems develop with incredible speed. Others take their time. Fortunately, the occurrence of truly severe weather is a relatively rare phenomenon, usually (but not always) confined to certain definable seasons. The length of these seasons does vary from year to year, but these trends are typically discernible and allowances can be made to take the current situation into account.

As long as you watch the sky; keep an eye on upper level charts; and monitor the sea state, wind, and barometer, the odds of being caught unawares are minimal.

TROPICAL REVIEW

Tropical cyclogenesis is well defined phenomenon. The seasons are pretty straightforward, and the warning signs unmistakable. Amongst the warning signs are: long period swell, cirrus cloud bands, and a barometer which behaves abnormally for the tropics.

With satellite direct gear aboard you will want to watch for any sort of activity in the visible or infrared ranges signaling that convection (thunderstorms) is accelerating. The initial cloud signatures usually fall into defined categories. If you don't have the speed to outrun these systems, then the best thing is always assume the worst.

Any sort of activity at the jet stream or 500mb level which drops below 25 degrees latitude is cause for extra vigilance.

EXTRATROPICAL REVIEW

Cyclogenesis out of the tropics is somewhat easier to define. With 500mb charts you will want to watch for strong zonal (westerly) flow with the wind maxima to the equator side of the 5640mb isoheight. As troughs form if the tilt axis is positive (to the west) surface development is likely to be significant. Wind maxima to the west of the trough axis also indicates surface development on a significant scale.

Short wave troughs which get into phase with each other or with a long wave will also give rise to more severe weather.

Always keep an eye out for the comma-shaped cloud signature on satellite images which is indicative of the bent-back warm fronts.

Remember that when the isoheights are confluent (close together) on the downwind side of a trough axis this is a favorable condition for bent back warm front development. When they are diffluent (spreading) a Norwegian model front is probable.

WEATHER FORECASTING TOOLS

When we started cruising 25 years ago, only a couple of options in forecasting tools were available. One was a barometer and the other was a short-wave receiver. Today, however, we have choices in weather facsimile receivers, satellite direct-imaging systems, not to mention wind instruments of varying quality and complexity.

None of these tools is worth having unless you understand their operation and are familiar with interpreting the output. But on the assumption that, by now, you have a feel for the forecasting process, we thought we'd take a few minutes and discuss what to take from a budget standpoint.

PRIORITIES

There are always priorities and trade-offs with yachts. Budget and space are almost always in conflict. So many demands are on the bank account that at some point one needs to say, "enough already!"

Still there are some items we feel should be at the top of the list, especially if you sail in areas with inclement or rapidly changing weather, or are headed offshore.

Heavy ground tackle, storm canvas, and a secure, well constructed vessel are right at the top of the list. The very best tools you can acquire for weather forecasting should be next on the list. Linda and I look at these tools this way: If we can avoid just one blow, or position ourselves on the correct side of just one storm, the investment will have paid for itself.

We'll proceed in order of priority—at least as we see things.

In terms of budget and cash flow, think of the cost of replacing a heavily damaged sail. On many yachts, this will equal the entire budget for the very best forecasting tools you can acquire. So, good forecasting tools should come before gensets, fancy dinghies, and a lot of the other equipment of marginal use that modern yachts frequently carry.

BAROMETER

A good quality barometer is an absolute must. You can purchase these units for around one hundred dollars, and this is not an area in which to skimp. If budget is available, you will find a recording unit a boon to forecasting.

Several electric barometers (some with delta alarms) are now on the market. We have no experience with these, so it is hard to give a recommendation.

However, if budget is an issue, we'd go with a simple non-recording conventional barometer, and put the balance of the budget into a good weather fax.

FACSIMILE RECEIVERS

It is worth repeating that a dedicated unit, with all of the stations and frequencies in memory, is going to be easier to use and give you better results than a computer-based system.

The Furuno #208 is what we've used for the past decade, and with excellent results. You can typically buy these for around $1,500 at discount outlets. Installation is simple and you do this yourself.

WIND INSTRUMENTS

In general we consider wind instruments—or performance instrument systems—to be a luxury. It is not that difficult to look at the masthead fly or a bit of wool in the rigging to determine the apparent wind.

With a little practice you can predict true wind speed by looking at the water better than most instrument systems.

So, we'd put this gear at the bottom of the list—with one exception. If you have a system that gives you true wind direction—the magnetic heading of the wind—we have found this extremely valuable in tracking the trend in wind direction. As you know now, the trend in direction is a key indicator of where you are relative to a storm center.

WEATHER RADAR

Radar is an extremely useful weather forecasting tool. It can warn you about the approach of squalls and fronts and give you an idea how to avoid or use these phenomena to advantage. And while radar has many other uses, Linda and I feel that weather forecasting is its most important function.

An early model Raytheon 41X radar with enclosed radome. This photo was taken coming up through the tropics in a moderate squall (you can see here about six miles in length). About 25 knots of breeze and strong rain occurred for about 20 minutes.

RANGE AND POWER

Range and power are important considerations. The longer the range and/or the more powerful the set, the better job the radar will do of warning you about what is out there.

On modern radars, 24-mile range—with the ability to offset the image so you can see in one direction 50 percent or so farther—is a minimum for effective use with weather.

Power is important as well. A 3-KW set will provide good squall images when rain is light, or just falling partway to the surface of the ocean.

Ideally, you would have a 36-or 48-mile range which, with offset, will allow you to see a substantial squall line or rain bar at 50 or more miles.

If clouds are dense with rain, radar will pick them up out to the edge of its capabilities.

Key factors in using radar for weather:

- *Transmitter power and range.*
- *Antenna size (bigger is better).*
- *Manual controls.*

ANTENNA SIZE

Antenna size is vital in target definition—pulling out the return of a small vessel in sea clutter for example. However, when you are using radar for weather analysis, the targets are large and definition is not as critical.

So, for the best results at minimum cost, go for a more powerful, longer-range set with a smaller, perhaps enclosed antenna. (An open array is better for all-around use but is more costly.)

CONTROL SETTINGS

You will want to be familiar with gain, rain and sea clutter, as well as tuning functions on your radar. These will probably have automatic modes as well as manual (stay away from radars that are totally automatic).

Whenever you see rain squalls about, experiment with the various settings. Adjust tuning up and down and play with the gain. You will generally find a combination of settings which yields the best long-range results with tuning and gain set a little higher than would be the norm if you are just looking for shipping.

Weather signs to look for on radar:

❑ Size and shape of rain band can be an indicator of wind strength.

❑ Elongated and/or U-shaped rain bands typically have the most wind.

❑ Round and smaller rain bands seem to have lighter winds.

❑ Rain bars ahead of fronts can be seen at 50 or more miles, if the radar has enough range.

USE WITH SQUALLS

A good-sized squall will show up 20 or more miles away. Smaller squalls will begin to appear at five to eight miles. The shape, size, and change you see on the radar will give you some clues as to the strength of wind to be found inside the squall system.

Our own anecdotal experience is that round squalls do not have as intense a wind field as squalls that are stretched out or shaped like a horseshoe.

Larger squalls that show four to six or more miles across tend to have significantly more rain than the smaller squalls.

Obviously this is a help at night, but it also works well during the day in gauging just how much activity you are likely to find in a given system.

FRONTAL SYSTEMS

Radar will also show you the approach of weather fronts when they have rain bands associated with them. This is particularly useful with fast-moving weather systems.

We've seen approaching fronts at 50 or more miles, giving us several hour's warning to get set up. When you have a radar with the ability to offset the image, so that you see farther in one direction (extending range) than in the other, you can offset the range so that you have the longest warning in the direction of expected weather.

WEATHER ALARM

Most modern radars come with some form of alarm zone. This can be used either on a sector basis, or to put a guard zone all the way around the boat. Normally used for collision avoidance, this is also quite helpful when watching for squalls.

The problem comes in how the alarm is tuned. If the tuning is set too tight, (too small a target sets off the alarm), you will be besieged by false alarms. If this is a problem, the target-density setting on the alarm is increased, requiring a larger target to initiate the alarm signal.

The only problem with this approach is that you will then lose your small yacht and fishing vessel targets—so you must be judicious in its use.

ON WATCH

Linda and I tend to run the radar at night, primarily as a squall watch. Depending on what sail we are carrying, we will set size and relative bearing parameters. If we have a spinnaker up, these parameters are tighter than with just plain sail.

Usually we try to intersect the squalls to get some push from them. But if conditions are highly unstable—perhaps we are crossing the ITCZ with big thunderstorms about—we'll adjust course away from the larger radar targets.

SATELLITE DIRECT RECEIVERS

Your standard fax receiver will generate several images a day of the cloud cover in your part of the ocean. In the subtropics and higher latitudes, these are of some interest, but not critical.

What they do is confirm what you are seeing on the weather fax synoptic charts—in some cases, telling you that what is on the synoptic chart is wrong.

Here are two sample screens from the OCENS satellite direct system.

The upper view is for infrared, with cloud temperature indicated by color gradiation. The color scale is indicated to the left of the image. In black and white you cannot really get a feel for what this looks like, but once you get a feel for cloud temperature you can then use this to indicate the height of the cloud systems. From this you can infer the level of convectivity.

The bottom image is visible light and will give you an idea of the detail in cloud shape that you can pick out—it is really quite remarkable.

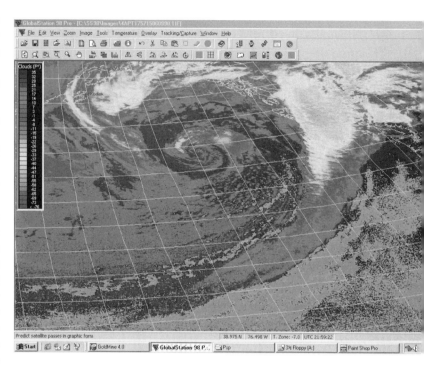

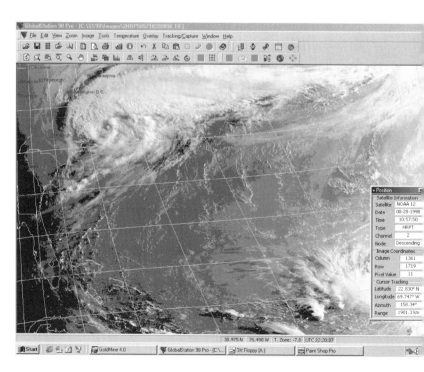

As you start to sail more aggressively, perhaps using hurricanes to advantage, or cutting close to them on your way across the ocean, this data becomes more valuable. And when you sail closer to the equator, cloud images start to become important, especially when you are watching for the start of a hurricane—or keeping an eye on the track of a hurricane.

These images are also of value when picking out how to cross the doldrums.

The images that these receivers pick up are broadcast by polar orbiting satellites. There are three of these, and they circle the earth every 104 minutes. This means that on average, in the middle latitudes, you can pick up 12 satellite passes per day—and six on the equator.

There are a number of companies offering satellite direct equipment. These systems vary in their software and hardware approach, as well as in the cost. All offer web sites with demonstrations of how their software works.

Our suggestion is that you check this out on the web, and then meet the supplier or their dealers at a boat show and get a real hands-on demonstration.

All of the systems work on the same principles. They start with a helix antennae for receiving the satellite signal. This is connected via a coaxial antenna cable to a receiver. The receiver turns the signal into a form that your computer can understand, and then exports this data to the computer via a PCMIA card which plugs into your PC.

In order for the system to work at its optimum, you should have a GPS connected to the computer. This helps position your boat relative to the image received, and gives the software the time and position data required to know which are the best satellite images to download.

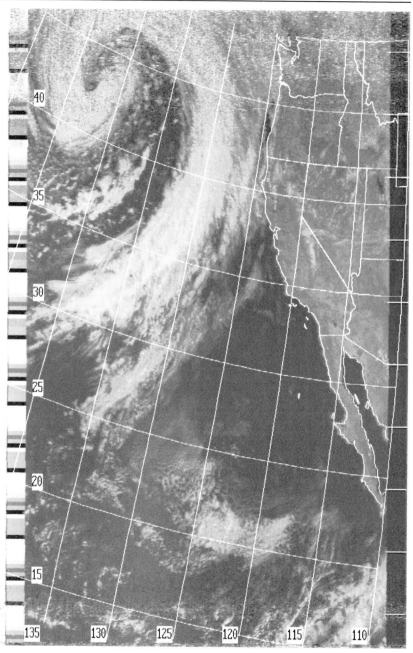

Here's an image from Software Systems Consulting. All of these software packages give you the ability to put reference grids and coastal outlines on the images to help identify where the weather is relative to your own position. It is important that there is a piece of land to use to orient the grid as without it there can be large errors of positioning. The storm system off the Pacific Northwest will by now be familiar to you as a bent back warm front.

All of the systems also will work with an audio system from an all-band receiver to interpret weather fax broadcasts.

Once in the PC you then go to work on the data with the software.

This allows you to check both visible cloud images and infrared images. The latter are important as they can be interpreted for temperature which in turn tells you about the heights of the clouds—a particularly important feature when studying tropical storm development.

All of this gear can be run at home using the receivers, or by plugging into the Internet and downloading satellite images.

All serious ocean-racing yachts and many commercial fishing vessels carry this gear. With some systems available for under $600 and really fancy systems now under $3000, it can make sense for those who earn their living from the sea or journey upon it for pleasure.

However, if you go in this direction, remember the key to using it successfully is getting familiar with it on a leisurely basis before heading offshore.

SATELLITE DIRECT SUPPLIERS

Here are some of the vendors of this equipment:

Software Systems Consulting. 615 S. El Camino Real, San Clemente, California 92672 USA. Phone 949 498 5784; fax 949 498 0568; e-mail support@ssccorp.com; website http://www.ssc-corp.com.

OCENS. 19655 1st Avenue South, Suite 202, Seattle, Washington 98148 USA. Phone 206 878 8270; fax 206 878 8314; e-mail freeberg@ocens.com; website http://www.ocens.com.

WEATHER ROUTING SOFTWARE

The Kiwitech weather routing image below can be seen in animated form on your computer (for a demonstration, visit their website).

This gives you a better feel for planing weather tactics than you can get with inanimate fax charts.

This software package uses GRIB files which are sent out by shoreside routers (usually using Sat C) which you load into the software. The software then allows you to see and manipulate the wind data, including seeing how things are projected to change with time.

If you load the performance polars for your vessel the software will even suggest the fastest route based on what the weather is expected to do. One of the pioneers in this field is a New Zealand firm, Kiwitech (P.O. Box 5909 Wellesley St., Auckland, New Zealand—http://www.kiwitech.com). Their software suite includes charting and vessel management modules as well as weather.

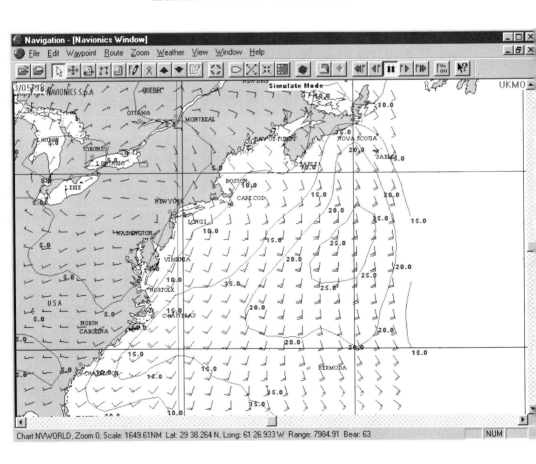

THE INTERNET

Of all the uses for the Internet the one we like best is weather research. There are literally thousands of sites. In fact, the problem is too much data rather than too little.

At the end of this section you will find several of our favorite locations. You will find a much more detailed list of weather-related sights on the CD-Rom version of this book, as well as on our Web site (www.SetSail.com).

AS A TEACHING TOOL

We hope that by now you will be wanting to practice your forecasting skills, to pit your growing expertise against the professionals.

There is no better way to do this than by visiting the Internet and downloading pertinent weather fax charts.

You can download exactly the same fax charts that you would receive on a weather fax receiver, but these are much easier to read and you do not have to worry about band conditions.

PRACTICE!

Get in the habit of downloading the surface forecasts for the area in which you are interested, along with the 48- and 96-hour prognosis. Then do the same for the 500mb charts.

If you do this for a couple of weeks, checking perhaps every evening, you will begin to get a feel for how the weather systems are working. Remember it is the pattern which is the key, and this varies from season to season and from year to year.

The more you watch, think, make your own forecasts, then compare these to the surface analysis a few days hence, the better you will become at this forecasting business.

Then, when you are offshore, perhaps a little short of sleep, and busy with all the details of running your vessel, the facsimile interpretation will be second nature.

Few preparations offshore will yield as great a benefit in peace of mind, comfort, safety and the cost of cruising as practicing your weather analysis on the World Wide Web.

SUGGESTED WEB SITES

http://www.SetSail.com. (A good selection of weather-related links.)

http://www.ncep.noaa.gov/mpc/Frames.html. (Home page for the Marine Prediction Center in the U.S. Links to all fax and text forecasts as well as links to text forecast messages overseas.)

http://weather.noaa.gov/fax/marine.shtml. (Extratropical forecasts for East and West Coasts of U.S. along with the products of the Tropical Prediction Center.)

http://taiga.geog.niu.edu/nwslot/marine.html. (Great lakes marine weather.)

http://www.nhc.noaa.gov/. (National Hurricane Center Tropical Prediction Center. Latest faxes, hurricane advisories and satellite images.)

http://www.saa.noaa.gov/index3.html. (Home page for NOAA satellite images.)

http://www.MET.CO.NZ/. (Met Service New Zealand. Latest text-based marine forecasts along with local weather data.)

http://www.meto.gov.uk/sec1/sec1.html. (United Kingdom Met. Office Web site. Some fax charts, text forecasts, miscellaneous meteorology.)

http://www.bom.gov.au/bmrc/meso/New/ wmocas_pubs/global_guide/ globa_guide_intro.htm. (A global guide to cyclone forecasting put together by experts around the world. Interesting facts, charts, images.)

http://www.bom.gov.au/. (Australian Met Service—along with usual local weather high seas forecasts and region specific satellite images.)

http://www.rdc.uscg.mil/iippages/home.html. (United States Coast Guard Ice Patrol. Data on ice location, forecasts, fax charts of same and satellite images.)

http://www.wmo.ch/. (World Meteorological Organization home page. Links to other Met groups around the world.)

http://lumahai.soest.hawaii.edu/ Tropical_Weather/tropical.shtml. (University of Hawaii tropical ocean/cyclone home page. Forecast data, tracks, and satellite images for Pacific and Indian Oceans Note that this includes links to the Navy in Guam, Fiji, and Australia.)

http://www.noaa.gov/. (Home page of NOAA with links to different departments.)

http://www.nws.fsu.edu/. (National Weather Service in Tallahassee, Florida. Local and regional weather with interesting links.)

http://www.ems.psu.edu/cgi-bin/wx/offshore.cgi. (Penn State Offshore Weather Data home page. U.S. and international links including data on offshore reports of actual conditions.)

http://taiga.geog.niu.edu/nwslot/ other.html#noaa. (NOAA-maintained sights with links to universities, various governmental sights in the U.S. and internationally.)

http://www.ncdc.noaa.gov/ol/satellite/satellite-data.html. (Home page for satellite images in the US. Current and historical data.)

GRIB FILES

GRIB files define the world's weather based on the output of a number of different weather models (many of which are available free on the Internet).

These are based on a World Meteorological Organization standard format, and once you have software to read one computer output, you can read them all.

With this data you can, for example, compare the U.K, European, and U.S. medium-range forecast models.

A variety of free software decoding packages are available, along with several commercial packages.

Dr. Jordan Alpert, Chief, Systems Development Branch, NCEP/Environmental Modeling Center, has been kind enough to share the following data with us for obtaining and using GRIB files.

"For decoding digital data (numbers) from a GRIB file, so you can make inventories, tables or further customized data, you need a grib decoder. I suggest Wesley's (an NCEP employee) GRIB decoder. It is the grib decoder I use and is available and described at http://wesley.wwb.noaa.gov/wgrib.html. Page down about a page to get to "Documentation". Wgrib has versions that will work with DOS PC's, Macs and windows in addition to Unix platforms.

"To make Vis5D files from GRIB, see the "GEM-PAK to Vis5D program GEMVIS" on the homepage http://sgi62.wwb.noaa.gov:8080. A link to explain GEMPAK and Unidata is present on this home page (click "GEMPAK") as well as the GEMVIS program. As far as I know, Vis5D, GEMPAK and GEM-VIS run only on Unix platforms.

"Grib files can be obtained from our homepage (http://sgi62.wwb.noaa.gov:8080) under the "reanalysis home page" (http://wesley.wwb.noaa.gov/reanalysis.html), which also links to the wgrib page mentioned above. Click on "Plots and Data." This page contains ftp (file transfer protocol) capabilities through the web. Data as well as Plots can be made of past and present data/

Observations from NCEP models.

"Our homepage is not official and is not operationally supported (which means it may not be up all the time) and except for the above does not have ftp capability. An unsupported (means it could stop working) public ftp area has an address: nic.fb4.noaa.gov. One can use anonymous ftp to get files under the directory pub/avn for the aviation model. For the aviation model one would cd pub/avn/avn.00z (00 can be 12 too) and then list the files. The GRIB files have names like gblav.T00Z.PGrbF33 for the 33rd hour forecast past the initial condition (Today's date at 00Z) and forecasts are given on 3-hour intervals.

"The operational server for a lot of data and observations is the Office of System Operations. Its ftp server is 140.90.4.103 and information about this anonymous ftp server is on a homepage at http://www.nws.noaa.gov/oso/ftpgate.shtml. I have found this official ftp site harder to negotiate then most."

Vis5D

If you are really into computers, the Internet, and weather (a powerful combination!) and were able to follow Dr. Alpert's comments, there is an incredible free program called Vis5D.

Go to the URL http://www.ssec.wisc.edu/~billh/vis5d.html. You will find instructions on how to download and use this program. It runs on UNIX, and there are versions of this operating system which can be run on Windows computers.

You can slice and dice the world's atmosphere in any number of ways, showing synoptic charts in movie loops with 500mb overlays, for example. Vorticity, wind field data, and everything else imaginable is available once you have this system up and running.

The photos on the next page show just a small part of what Vis5D will do. The Eastern U.S. is displayed, including mountain ranges, with a surface level synoptic chart and 500mb charts overlaid. The strange looking shapes are of vorticity—a key indicator of surface level development. All of these elements run as a loop, showing you how things are expected to progress over the next few days (you select the time frame). The bottom image has wind speed in the vertical displayed as well.

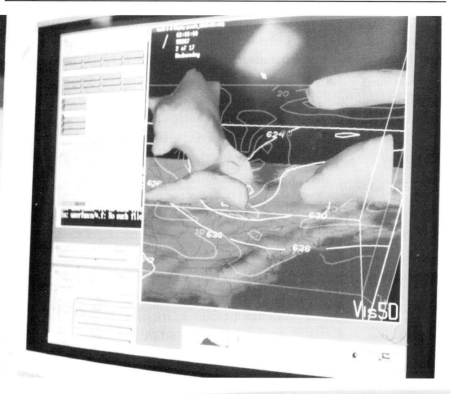

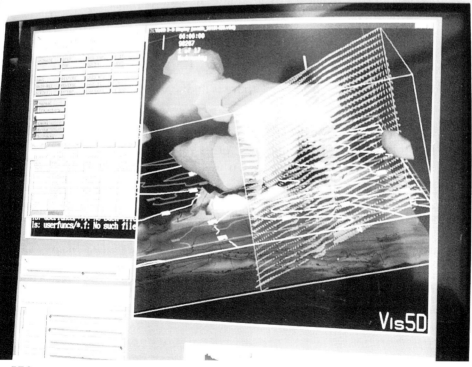

AFTERWORD

We want to close *Mariner's Weather Handbook* with a couple of final comments on the concept of weather at sea.

With so much of this book focused on interpreting and avoiding severe weather, it bears repeating that in several hundred thousand miles of sailing, we have spent less than 48 hours in truly dangerous conditions.

When you consider that the bulk of our passaging around dangerous weather areas has taken place without benefit of weather fax or in many cases even single-sideband radio, you begin to see that severe weather is not the norm. So the odds are very much in your favor.

And the most important rule—pick your seasons correctly. If you take care with this issue, the odds of encountering serious conditions are substantially reduced.

Next, never let schedule force you into a decision. The weather does not respect our time frame. It is imperative that you allow weather rather than your own requirements dictate when to leave.

Another issue we feel strongly about is doing *your* thing, as opposed to what everyone else is doing. All too often, when there have been problems with large groups of boats, many of the yachts have gotten into trouble by going with the herd—even though the herd was demonstrably wrong.

Finally, remember that for most ocean areas the forecasters work with a paucity of data, and it is impossible for them to accurately predict on a micro basis what will happen in your own patch of water.

Be constantly aware of the weather—even when it appears benign, and during the fair seasons—as things can change rapidly.

If the conditions you are experiencing, or the longer-range signs, point to a different scenario than that which is being broadcast, go with what you are experiencing.

Weather analysis, forecasting, and tactics are not the easiest subjects in the world to master. However, the basics—the 90 percent that will keep you out of trouble most of the time—are not difficult to grasp.

It may take a few cycles of reading through this book and some of the others we have recommended. If you add a formal course to all this, you will be far better prepared than the two of us were when we first headed offshore.

And then practice. When you are shorebound, keep a barometer handy, check it and the sky on a daily basis, and make a few notes. Get on the Internet and download the fax charts for your part of the world. Pay particular attention to the 500mb data, and watch the rhythms of the long and short waves and how they interact with the surface lows.

You will quickly find yourself making excellent analyses, and when the time comes to head offshore, you will do so with far more confidence than before. Your passages will be more comfortable, faster, and a lot safer.

See you out there!

ADDITIONAL REFERENCES

Following are a list of publications which you may find of interest on the subject of weather.

BOOKS

The 1994 Pacific Storm Survey. Kim Taylor. Captain Teach Press and Quarry Publishing. (Order from Boat Books, Ltd., 23b Westthaven Drive, Auckland, New Zealand). *An excellent review of the Queen's Birthday Storm, with discussion of tactics, boat design, and how these all worked out.*

The American Practical Navigator. Nathaniel Bowditch. Defense Mapping Agency Hydrographic/Topographic Center. *One of the best values in marine literature. Chock-full of weather, oceanography, and navigation data.*

The Annapolis Book of Seamanship. John Rousmaniere. Simon & Schuster. *A good all-around reference with an excellent section on weather.*

Guide to Facsimile Stations, 10th Edition. Klingenfuss Publications. Hagenloher Str. 14, D-7400 Tuebingen, Germany. *A list of all the fax stationas around the world with sample charts, schedules, and frequencies.*

Heavy Weather Sailing, 4th Edition. K. Adlard Coles (revised by Peter Bruce). International Marine. *Weather analysis for each of the storms discussed which, while strictly surface-based, is still informative.*

Instant Weather Forecasting. Alan Watts. Sheridan House. *A cloud-based forecasting system that will give you another way of checking the forecasts. Well organized with nice color photos.*

Met Service Yacht Pack. Bob McDavitt. New Zealand Met Service. (Order from Boat Books, Ltd., 23b Westthaven Drive, Auckland, New Zealand). *A good general reference and a must if you are sailing in the South Pacific.*

The Royal Ocean Racing Club Manual of Weather at Sea. Dag Pike. David & Charles (Great-Britain). *One of the better Northern Hemisphere oriented manuals.*

The Sailor's Weather Guide. Jeff Markell. Sheridan House.

The Weather Book. Jack Williams. USA Today. *A non-marine general weather book, richly illustrated with lots of interesting data for sailors and land-based weather nuts.*

Weather for the Mariner, 3rd Edition. William J. Kotsch, Rear Admiral, U.S. Navy, Retired. Naval Institute Press. *For years one of the basic texts everyone carried aboard. A little out of date, but lots of interesting data nonetheless.*

The Weather Handbook. Alan Watts. Sheridan House. *Another book by Alan Watts, this one also written for the land-bound with excellent art work.*

The Weather Wizard's Cloud Book. Louis D. Rubin Sr. & Jim Duncan. Algonquin Books (Chapel Hill, NC). *A small but interesting work on clouds. A good bet to carry aboard along with Watt's work on cloud forecasting.*

Weather Trainer. Starpath School of Navigation. 311 Fulton St., Seattle, WA 98109-1740, USA. info@starpath.com. *Software to help you learn the weather forecasting process.*

INDEX

Numerics

Offshore Cruising Encyclopedia

The decision to buy a yacht and head out over the horizon is easy. What's hard is knowing the right kind of boat, gear, and personal skills necessary to turn your dream into reality...confidently, in the shortest time for the smallest budget.

That's where the second edition of Linda and Steve Dashews' *Offshore Cruising Encyclopedia* comes in. With over 2500 photos and drawings packed into 1232 pages, it will dramatically increase your knowledge of yacht design; construction; rigging; systems; and the cruising lifestyle. Rather than being at the mercy of dockside "experts," you'll learn how to make the right decisions for your own cruising plans and budget.

Listen to three of today's top naval architects. "If you are equipping, buying, or building a boat the Dashews' reference work will prove invaluable. Every serious sailor ought to have this book." Chuck Paine. "The Dashews' book is indispensable..." Robert Perry. "The most comprehensive and sound cruising reference yet produced." Angelo Lavranos

Real World Know-How

Steve and Linda Dashew are lifelong sailors who write in a conversational, inviting style. Their information is laced with personal anecdotes and the stories of hundreds of other cruisers, making *Offshore Cruising Encyclopedia* an enjoyable as well as informative read. They have sailed over 200,000 miles, owned two boatyards, and designed and built more than 47 cruising yachts. Their books and videos are considered to be top resources for sailors.

Reviewers are Unanimous

"The single most useful text available anywhere for sailors who are outfitting a boat for voyaging—full of good ideas, educated opinions, ingenious solutions, useful charts and tables, and world cruising savvy." *Blue Water Sailing* (USA)

"Comprehensive cruising advice...an absolute compendium of concise, definitive information for cruising sailors. The second edition, refined and updated from the first, contains so much information it defies a quick description. For thoroughness...the *Offshore Cruising Encyclopedia* is unparalleled. For those who cruise there is not another book on the market as comprehensive as this one." *Practical Sailor* (USA)

"Cruising bible...indispensable." *Boat International* (United Kingdom)

"Two kilos of pure knowledge from the experts will expand your know-how on countless subjects such as yacht design, finishing and interiors both above and below deck, construction, sails and towing, motortechnics, electronics, modern communications, safety, life on board, sailing locations, and still much more." *Zeilen* (Netherlands)

"This is surely the finest, most complete, authoritative and, above all, most human among the guides to the serious side of ocean voyaging and local cruising. The Dashews share knowledge they have collected over years of sailing and designing their own yachts, and every bit of it will enhance our safety and enjoyment aboard." *Yachting* (USA)

"Comprehensive and utterly fascinating... now in its second edition, would be a superb reference book for anyone planning a long cruise...If you've ever wanted to consult the views of an expert, a yacht designer with real hands-on experience at the sharp end, this book is a sort of detailed consultation. A whacking 1,200 pages are filled with information on everything from choosing the right propeller, davits, or charging system to sea berths and upholstery. And every conceivable subject in between." *Yachting World* (United Kingdom)

"Vital for anybody planning to take up ocean voyaging as a lifestyle...Encapsulates a lifetime of cruising experience...*Cruising Helmsman* (Australia)

"Everything you'll ever need to know about offshore cruising from people who have been there. A true encyclopedia built on first-hand knowledge." *Motor Boating and Sailing* (USA)

"If you're new to sailing or are interested in increasing both your theoretical and practical knowledge of all aspects of cruising, we can't imagine why you wouldn't purchase the *Offshore Cruising Encyclopedia*. We at *Latitude* rarely endorse anything but going sailing, but we think the *Offshore Encyclopedia* is extraordinary. And we're not even getting paid to say so." *Latitude 38* (USA)

"This is a book of superlatives...It will likely replace four books in your library...obviously of great value for any owner who wants to upgrade any system...Recommendations are extremely complete." *Sailing Canada*

"Encyclopedia is the right word for this huge reference book, which for years will be a standard guide for sailors preparing to go cruising. The Dashews are vastly experienced...They know what it takes to live comfortably and safely aboard a yacht, both at sea and in the marina. Steve is a skilled engineer, rigger, and boatbuilder who has borrowed from the best of traditional and modern yacht design to produce some excellent seagoing boats. Linda has studied all the possibilities of cabin arrangements and designed handsome, functional interiors. Together they have sailed thousands of miles, lived aboard for years at a time, created many wonderful yachts, and written this important book." John Rousmaniere, author of *The Annapolis Book of Seamanship; Fastnet, Force 10;* and other books.

"This is a time of great change in sailing design and technology, yet the most important elements of the sport remain the same — seaworthy design, sound construction, and good seamanship. *Offshore Cruising Encyclopedia* effectively relates the necessities to the possibilities, and in doing so will prove itself a valuable reference for serious cruising." *Sailing World* (USA)